The Akan People

Volume I
A Documentary History

D1732526

THE
Akan People

VOLUME 1
A Documentary History

Edited by
Kwasi Konadu

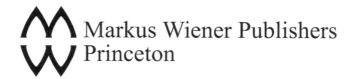
Markus Wiener Publishers
Princeton

Cover illustration: Ashanti yam ceremony, 1817. Reprinted from *Mission from Cape Coast Castle to Ashantee* (London, 1819; reprinted by Frank Cass, 1966), between pages 274 and 275.

For information, write to:
Markus Wiener Publishers
231 Nassau Street, Princeton, NJ 08542
www.markuswiener.com

Library of Congress Cataloging-in-Publication Data

The Akan people : a documentary history / edited by Kwasi Konadu.
    volumes cm
    A two-volume anthology.
    Includes bibliographical references and index.
    ISBN 978-1-55876-579-5 (hardcover : alk. paper)
    ISBN 978-1-55876-628-0 (paperback : alk. paper)
    1. Akan (African people)—History—Sources.
    I. Konadu, Kwasi, editor of compilation.
    DT510.43.A53A45 2014
    305.8963385—dc23
                    2013032467

Markus Wiener Publishers books are printed in the United States of America on acid-free paper and meet the guidelines for permanence and durability of the Committee on Production Guidelines for Book Longevity of the Council on Library Resources.

Dedication

For A. Adu Boahen (1932-2006),
Kwame Y. Daaku (1933-1974),
and J. Kofi Fynn (1935-2005)

Pioneer historians who paved the way for others

Contents (Emu Nsɛm)

Acknowledgments (Aseda)

Mpaeɛ. Onyankopɔn, Asase Yaa, abosompɛm, nananom nsamanfoɔ, m'abusuafoɔ, meda mo ase pii. Na monim sɛ meresua, momma menhu da biara. To Ronnie (Amma), Abena, Sunkwa, and Afia, *ɔdɔ yɛ dɛ te sɛ ahwedeɛ.* There are many people to whom I owe a debt of gratitude. Special thanks are due to Emmanuel Akyeampong, Kwabena Akurang-Parry, Jean Allman, James Anquandah, Kofi Baku, Stefano Boni, Owusu Brempong, Lynda Day, Harvey M. Feinberg, Adam Jones, Ole Justesen, Ray Kea, A. Norman Klein, Tom McCaskie, David Owusu-Ansah, James Sanders, Kenya Shujaa, Ray Silverman, Sam Spiers, Pierluigi Valsecchi, Ivor Wilks, and Selena Winsnes. Such thanks are also in order for the other contributors who are no longer with us: the late Sue Benson, A. Adu Boahen, Kwaku Effah-Gyamfi, and David Kiyaga-Mulindwa, among others.

I am also grateful to the following institutions and publishers for permission to reprint much of the materials found in this collection: The Institute of African Studies at the University of Ghana, the Ghana Academy of Arts and Sciences, the Historical Society of Ghana, Duke University Press, Cambridge University Press, Indiana University Press, Oxford University Press, Edinburgh University Press, the University of Wisconsin-Madison, University of Chicago Press, the Wenner-Gren Foundation, and the British Academy. Thanks also go to the editors of *History in Africa*, to Mary Dakubu and Akosua Ampofo of the Institute of African Studies, and to Kwesi Yankah, then Pro-Vice Chancellor of the University of Ghana.

Finally, I am profoundly grateful to the external readers of the manuscript, to the editors at the press, and for my conversations over the years with Kwasi Bempong, Nana Kwaku Sakyi, and Kofi Sarpong. Indebtedness aside, the standard disclaimer applies.

A Note on Style (Asɛm bi)

This two-volume anthology contains works from many different historical periods, authors, and perspectives. I have tried to keep my editing and abridgment to a minimum in the interest of preserving tone and reflecting the historical context in which each work was written. In doing the translations and transcriptions for this volume, I have attempted as much as possible to remain true to both the flavor and meaning of the original text. I have tried to choose English words that are as close as possible to the Twi (Akan) or European language counterparts. In instances where it seemed essential to provide some further explanation or clarification, I have used brief and unobtrusive brackets. A number of the selections were substantially abridged due to space considerations, and most of the parenthetical references and all the footnotes were removed. Interested readers can find at the end of each volume the full citations of the original articles or the sources used.

Those familiar with the changing history of Twi (Akan) orthography will notice variations in the spelling of commonly (and not-so-commonly) used words—among others, *okomfo* and *ɔkɔmfoɔ*, *oman* and *ɔman, kese* and *kɛseɛ*, Ashanti and Asante, and Brong and Bono. With respect to proper names and Twi (Akan) language orthography, I have made a practice of rendering these as they appeared in the original texts and in all the essays by the contributors. Some Twi terms have different spellings, but because the contributors, and the sources herein, did follow a prescribed or consistent orthography, I hope readers will bear with us.

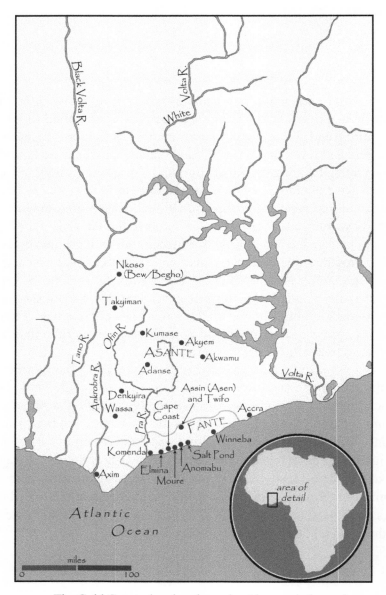

The Gold Coast, showing the major Akan societies and
settlements examined in this collection.
Map drawn by Rebecca Wrenn.

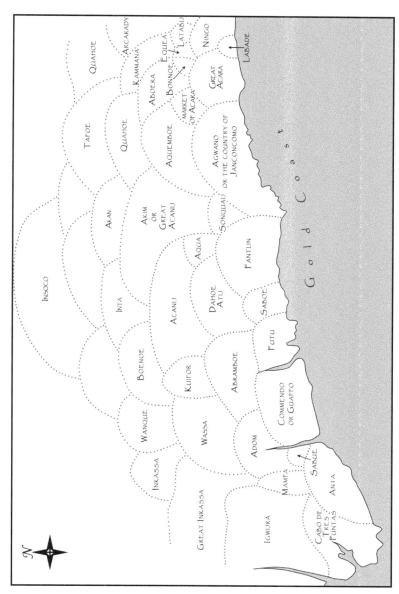

A 1629 map of the Gold Coast attributed to Dutch cartographer Hans Propheet. The map, according to Dutch understandings of local politics and polities, shows a range of Akan settlements and *aman* ("states"). Map redrawn and revised by Rebecca Wrenn.

Introduction (Nnianimu)

[I]t is most desirable that a history of the Gold Coast and its people should be written by one who has not only studied, but has had the privilege of initiation into, the history of its former inhabitants and writes with true native patriotism.

—*Carl Christian Reindorf,*
History of the Gold Coast and Asante

The Historiographical Setting (Abakɔsɛm)

In the 1860s, Carl Christian Reindorf embarked upon the most ambitious historical project of his time, creating the first "national" history of the Gold Coast by an African who wrote with the kind of "native patriotism" that also suited the tenor of intellectuals a century later. African political independence in the late 1950s and 1960s brought with it the corresponding attention of Africanist historians, who sought to enlighten the mind that Africa too possessed a history among histories of the world, and a history concomitant with the cultural and political needs of the emergent nation-states. Reindorf's *History of the Gold Coast and Asante* ended with the consolidation of British rule in the 1850s; in 1957, Ghana (the former Gold Coast) became the first African nation to become politically independent from British colonial rule. Both Reindorf and his successor historians of the mid-twentieth century viewed the same region as an important site for the reclamation of a "usable" past, grounded in a quest for empires, states, kings, and "big men" (*ɔbirɛmpɔn*). Essentially, from historians pursuing such a past, a political narrative constructed around the former empire of Asante (the most powerful polity in the eighteenth and nineteenth century), to the near exclusion of other Akan and non-Akan peoples,

1

emerged in the new Ghanaian republic. (The Akan were, since at least the fifteenth century, the most politically and culturally dominant group in what became Ghana, sharing a common language, agrarian ethos, calendrical system, sociopolitical organization, spirituality, and material culture.) These Africanist historians began to interrogate a confluence of archival and oral sources in several languages in their reconstructions and, in doing so, paved the way for many important studies of that era and beyond. Yet, many of their concerns revolved around political history and the political context of African people's lives, but not necessarily what propelled the culture and society of those same people through their own history.

This political narrative approach, though not without analysis, was largely devoid of a cultural context; and unbeknownst to its authors, such histories became their authors' own worst enemies: in appealing to a universalistic claim that Africans too had a history *like* others—operating on similar premises and sets of imperatives—those Africans were denied *their own* continuities and complexities in how their cultures and societies moved through their histories. Thus, historical narrative became political narrative, and such accounts and their supporting facts were deemed unproblematic, and even celebrated. The era of political independence became a midwife to the paradigm of political narrating, and, reciprocally, that paradigm underscored research and politics in the new republic. But this paradigm's gestation began in the mid- to late-nineteenth century amongst a Gold Coast intelligentsia of Westernized, Christianized, urbanized, and moderate-to-conservative individuals.

The paradigm of political narrating and its framing of history and culture was prominent in the 1950s and 1960s, but the importance of this paradigm among historians of the Gold Coast/Ghana was preceded by a century of uneven conflicts, ambitions, and intellectual production among the Gold Coast intelligentsia of the mid-nineteenth and early-twentieth centuries. Seduced by Westernization and Christianization, this intelligentsia had its roots in an insignificantly small, racially mixed community in major urban settings such as Cape Coast and Accra. As the twentieth century drew near, this group saw itself decisively as the purveyor of Christianity and "civilization."[1] Some members belonged to the Basel Mission, such as the pastor-historian Carl Christian Reindorf, while many were Wesleyan Methodist converts. Between the mid- to late-nineteenth century, even the most "creolized" and Western-educated in the Gold Coast colony displayed ambiguity toward indigenous culture in their quest to be buffers between the "native" and colonial orders—antecedents of mid-twentieth century political struggles between "chiefs" and "educated elites." Consequently, these Gold Coast "buffers" turned to "traditional" institutions and office holders to organize a challenge against colonial policies, but this protest sought inclusion since the colonial government incorporated so-called traditional leaders as part of British indirect rule. Thus, in their quest for partnership with British colonial authority and institutions, these elites sought the "traditional" in order to position themselves in the colonial regime as buffers, and toward that end, some even manipulated succession principles to be installed or did so through the *asafo* paramilitary organization (where membership is based on a patrilineal principle), since these traditional offices provided status and financial rewards in the colonial order.

That quest for partnership created factionalism among the "elites" and within their communities, and as the patriarchal nuclear family began, in the nineteenth century, to establish itself at the expense of kin networks, two divergent visions began to emerge on the Gold Coast. Those living inland, beyond the coastal enclaves, held onto their histories and culture with minimal British influence, while the coastal "elites," usually of African and European parentage, pursued "traditional culture" and things African as a proxy for their interests but held that culture in contempt and sought to simultaneously refashion it in their pursuits. In the nineteenth century, Akan communities were overwhelmingly non-Christian, though we begin to see a split later in the century between them and urbanized Christian converts along "class" lines. These urbanized "elites"

---

1. Roger Gocking, "Creole Society and the Revival of Traditional Culture in Cape Coast during the Colonial Period," *International Journal of African Historical Studies* 17, no. 4 (1984): 602.

developed a Christian distaste for but ambivalence toward indigenous spirituality and cultural institutions. This attitude, however,
was invariably confined to those on the coast and in greater proximity to British authority, values, and institutions.

The Gold Coast intelligentsia offered their "native" subjectivity
and their knowledge of the colonial language and institutions as the
strongest evidence for their roles as buffers between the colonial
and indigenous order. For example, John Mensah Sarbah was
trained as a barrister in British jurisprudence but had to be competent in Akan "customary" law as well in order to be an influential
buffer for the bevy of local court cases so commonplace under and
after colonial rule. In the early twentieth century, Nana Ofori Atta
of Akyem Abuakwa was granted the position of official representative for the "Twi (Akan) speaking" peoples in the legislative council of the colony, giving the very conservative Ofori Atta clear
political influence among the Akan in the Gold Coast colonial structure. His brother, J. B. Danquah, a barrister and author, was also influential in coastal politics; like him, he manifested the cultural
ambiguity that confounded men who sought to reform the colonial
from within for their benefit—rather than overthrowing it.

It is within the context of the above considerations related to
Gold Coast politics and the political role of the local intelligentsia
that we can examine their issues with British imperialist historiography and the ways in which they shaped an Akan historiography.[2]
Arguably, the first assault on British versions of Akan history was
by Basel Mission pastor and historian Carl Christian Reindorf.
Reindorf's self-published *History of the Gold Coast and Asante* in
1889 (with a revised English version in 1895) was the first general
history of the Akan and other Gold Coast peoples written independently by an African; in other words, he did so with minimal dependence on British source materials or on external funds to underwrite
the costs of publication. His book included a judicious selection of
published and oral sources (from "more than two hundred persons

---

2. On matters discussed here, see Richard Rathbone, "Law, Politics and Analogy in
Akan Historiography," *Journal of Imperial and Commonwealth History* 36, no. 3 (2008):
473–86.

of both sexes") and was supported by his own finances.[3] His protracted struggles to publish this work on his own terms and at his own expense have direct implications for contemporary African (historical) scholarship. In 1887 and in 1893, A. B. Ellis, a British army officer, had published *The Tshi-Speaking peoples of the Gold Coast of West Africa* and *A History of the Gold Coast of West Africa*, respectively. Reindorf's cultural material and his Gold Coast history, whatever its technical shortcomings, was far more comprehensive than Ellis's, and while Reindorf's general approach to history can be appreciated—though almost half of his material focused on Asante—Reindorf's *History* was not written for a general Gold Coast audience but rather for his contemporaries, the Gold Coast intelligentsia. And a number of key individuals who formed part of that intelligentsia made good use of Reindorf's *History*. John Mensah Sarbah, the barrister, who was also the author of *Fanti Customary Laws* (1904), viewed Reindorf's *History* as a valuable work and as a text that lent itself to early nationalist thought; Samuel R. B. Attoh-Ahuma, Methodist minister and author of *The Gold Coast Nation and National Consciousness* (1911), saw Reindorf's text as a key source for Gold Coast history and used it quite liberally in his own work, likely toward his own proto-nationalist ends.[4] J. B.

---

3. Carl Christian Reindorf, *History of the Gold Coast and Asante* (Basel: author, 1895), iv. In 1889, the original title for Reindorf's (English language) text was *Gold Coast and Asante: History Told by Oral and Written Narratives*; all the while he was revising his English and Gã versions before and after the publication of the *History of the Gold Coast and Asante*. On Reindorf and the significance of his work, see Heinz Hauser-Renner, ed. and trans., "A New Annotated Edition of Carl Christian Reindorf's History of the Gold Coast and Asante: Based on Traditions and Historical Facts Comprising a Period of More Than Three Centuries from about 1500 to 1860: With a Translation of His Unpublished Gã Manuscript (1891) Kept at the Basel Mission Archives" (Ph.D. diss.: University of Zürich, 2006); Idem, "Tradition meets Modernity: C. C. Reindorf and His History of the Gold Coast and Asante. A Late 19th Century Voice from Urban Accra," *Transactions of the Historical Society of Ghana* (New Series) no. 8 (2004): 227-255; Paul Jenkins, ed., *The Recovery of the West African Past: African Pastors and African History in the Nineteenth Century, C. C. Reindorf & Samuel Johnson* (Basel: Basler Afrika Bibliographien, 1998); Ray Jenkins, "Impeachable Source? On the Use of the Second Edition of Reindorf's 'History' as a Primary Source for the Study of Ghanaian History: I," *History in Africa* 4 (1977): 123-147.

4. Ray Jenkins, "Impeachable Source? On the Use of the Second Edition of Reindorf's 'History' as a Primary Source for the Study of Ghanaian History: II," *History in Africa* 5 (1978): 91.

Anaman, a Wesleyan minister who delivered services exclusively in the Fante language, shared Attoh-Ahuma's views, as did the aforementioned J. B. Danquah, an important scholar who not only sought to dismantle British imperialist historiography of the Gold Coast but also provided the name "Ghana" when the former Gold Coast became politically independent.

By the early twentieth century, the Gold Coast intelligentsia found value in Reindorf's *History* not only as an exemplar of the historian's craft but also as an early piece of nationalist literature written and self-published by an African. In essence, Reindorf's *History* was reduced to a political and politicized history suitable to the politics of the Gold Coast intelligentsia, and thus was put to political ends such as "native court" cases where Reindorf's material was used for claims of an ancestral nature, involving land tenure and other kinds of litigation. Sarbah's and Attoh-Ahuma's work showed a growing trend toward political narrating (linked to concerns of the Gold Coast intelligentsia) and reducing history to political narrative. Likewise, even the British writers who viewed Reindorf's *History* as invaluable or whose work relied upon his— such as William W. Claridge's *A History of the Gold Coast and Ashanti* (1915), Wesleyan missionary William T. Balmer's *A History of the Akan Peoples of the Gold Coast* (1925), and Robert S. Rattray's *Ashanti Law and Constitution* (1929)—did not differ from their Gold Coast counterparts but telescoped their concerns, like Reindorf, on Asante. The collected works of Robert S. Rattray constituted one of the key instances of the almost-exclusive focus on Asante in Akan historiography. Though Rattray was not a historian, his political narrative of Asante in *Ashanti Law and Constitution* provided a blueprint for British "indirect rule," which had experienced a crisis in the 1920s and prompted colonial officials to restore the Asante Confederacy along "native" lines in 1935. This "indirect" colonial rule also subverted indigenous bases and structures of authority, and, indeed, such subversion contributed greatly to the morass of succession disputes and cases of deposal for which barristers like Sarbah and Danquah gained greater notoriety and influence. As for Claridge's text, his work focused on Asante and the coast—the latter the locus of the Gold Coast intelligentsia—with a limited number of pages devoted to non-European activities on the Gold Coast, a theme shared by William E. Ward's *A History of Ghana* (1948). Upon the publication of Ward's *A History of Ghana*, Reindorf's *History* was no longer the "invaluable" or most comprehensive reference on Akan and non-Akan peoples, and soon Ward's work became the standard among Gold Coast students and in Gold Coast historiography.

Ward's *A History of Ghana*, as well as his previous history lessons and works through Achimota College, came under criticism in the 1930s and 1940s from Nnambi Azikiwe, J. B. Danquah, and Danquah's nephew, William Ofori Atta. The criticisms centered on Ward's competency to teach and write African history as part of a racist project, but, based on Danquah's relentless pursuit of Ward in the press and through private correspondence, we might suspect that his or perhaps their issue with Ward was not only his historical writing. The matter appeared to have been personal, for Danquah praised the work of other European writers, such as J. G. Christaller.[5] Ray Jenkins has suggested that it was Christaller's well-known dictionary of the Asante-Fante language that inspired Danquah to engage in historical-cultural research leading to Danquah's claim that the Akan were a part of ancient Ghana (Wagadu); hence, the name "Ghana" for the independent nation in 1957.[6] Danquah and others would continue to use studies of Akan history as part of a political paradigm wherein these histories would engender national and "race" pride.

Thus, during the era of decolonization, ancient Ghana was more than symbolic for the nationalist movement. History was a key political force. As a Gold Coast colony, its cocoa was the basis of its economy, and during the push for reform in the 1940s, mass urban and rural upheavals posed an economic threat. When the colonial state was unable to curtail or crush them, it offered accommoda-

---

5. Ray Jenkins, "William Ofori Atta, Nnambi Azikiwe, J. B. Danquah and the 'Grilling' of W.E.F. Ward of Achimota in 1935," *History in Africa* 21 (1994): 178.
   6. Jenkins, "Achimota in 1935," 180.

tions. The so-called chiefs, former instruments of indirect rule, provided little leadership; and because they could not facilitate the
goals of the various upheavals, the colonial state discarded them in
favor of the urbanized nationalists, who positioned themselves as
the solution to the crisis of the state. Indeed, "decolonization in the
late 1950s did not follow either from the failure of reform or from
loss of control. The nationalists were simply easier to persuade—
indeed did not need to be persuaded—that political independence
was the solution to the economic and social problems of colonial
society."[7]

In the decolonization processes of the 1950s and 1960s, several
key texts in Akan historiography marked the power of the political
narrating paradigm (with a focus on Asante or the coastal region)
and the absence of culture in historical works of the period. Some
of those texts include Madeline Manoukian's *Akan and Ga-Adan-
gme Peoples of the Gold Coast* (1951), a poorly researched text of
extracts and summaries; Kofi A. Busia's *The Position of the Chief
in the Modern Political System of Ashanti* (1951), originally his Oxford dissertation and with an exclusive focus on Asante political institutions; David Apter's *The Gold Coast in Transition* (1955),
which also focused on political institutions; J. D. Fage's *Ghana: An
Historical Interpretation* (1959), which was based on lectures given
shortly after Ghana's political independence; David Kimble's *A Political History of Ghana 1850–1928* (1963), which charted the development of early nationalist thought on the Gold Coast between
the 1850s and 1950s; Dennis Austin's *Politics in Ghana* (1964); and
Robert July's *The Origins of Modern African Thought* (1967),
which focused on the Gold Coast intelligentsia as important nationalists. These works were reflective of the times, and so the critique
here is not that they were inappropriate, but rather that they consistently and narrowly focused on political action or context, as if the
peoples they examined were solely political beings. During the first
half of twentieth century, the Gold Coast was punctuated by a series

---

7. Richard C. Crook, "Decolonization, the Colonial State, and Chieftaincy in the Gold
Coast," *African Affairs* 85, no. 338 (1986): 83.

of urban riots and protests by youth associations, farmers, producers, trade unions in the capital of Accra, and intellectual societies such as the Accra clubs that laid the groundwork for party politics and the political independence movement. World War I and II, trade union organizations, and the cross-fertilization effect of the pan-African movement in and outside of Africa, including the various Pan-African Congresses, all informed the mood of the proto-nationalist spirit that fought for African political independence. Yet these movements inherited, rather than created, that momentum. The struggles for reform at the local and international levels were also matched by cultural struggles over values, belief systems, and institutionalized colonial and embedded indigenous cultural practices in the Gold Coast colony. For example, the *abosommerafoɔ* or so-called "witch-catching cults" (e.g., the *ɔdomankama* movement in Asante) were extremely popular in local communities, and the grassroots cultural dimension of the nationalist movement was important to youth groups, rural and urban leaders, and women and men of various social rankings.[8] The Ghanaian philosopher W. E. Abraham in his *Mind of Africa* (1963) attempted to capture the very cultural dimensions of African decolonization—using the Akan—and their prospects for an independent Africa.

Popular revolts in the Gold Coast colony were the key to political independence, and Kwame Nkrumah became a key catalyst who transformed widespread discontent into a nationalist struggle. But since Nkrumah was the inheritor rather than the creator of that struggle, the role of J. B. Danquah, Nkrumah's former associate turned rival, shifted to the background of a Nkrumahist foreground that captured the times. The aspirations and euphoria that accompanied political independence in contemporary Ghana, and Nkrumah as its

---

8. Kwasi Konadu, *Indigenous Medicine and Knowledge in African Society* (New York: Routledge, 2007), 55–56; Ivor Wilks, *Asante in the Nineteenth Century* (New York: Cambridge University Press, 1975, repr. 1989), 519-21. See also William C. Olsen, *Healing, Personhood and Power: A History of Witch-Finding in Asante* (Ph.D. diss., Michigan State University, 1998); Natasha A. Gray, *The Legal History of Witchcraft in Colonial Ghana: Akyem Abuakwa, 1913–1943* (Ph.D. diss., Columbia University, 2000); and M. J. Field, *Search for Security: An Ethno-Psychiatric Study of Rural Ghana* (New York: W. W. Norton and Co., 1960).

first prime minister and president, were followed by the concentration of political power into a central authority, party politics, discontent within the armed forces, and military coups. The political landscape of Ghana during its first three decades of independence was punctuated by these coups in 1966, 1972, 1978, 1979, and 1981. The fracturing of civilian rule was reflected in falling cocoa prices as well as the country's spiral into economic decline, which saw a deteriorating financial system and devaluation of currency. In a decade in which four out of five coups took place, we saw, for instance, the publication of Kwame Daaku's *Trade and Politics on the Gold Coast* (1970); Francis Agbodeka's *African Politics and British Policy in the Gold Coast* (1971); J. K. Fynn's *Asante and Its Neighbors* (1971); Ivor Wilks's *Asante in the Nineteenth Century* (1975); John Vogt's *Portuguese Rule on the Gold Coast* (1979); and F. K. Buah's poorly researched and written *A History of Ghana* (1980). We should also include the excellent study by Ray A. Kea— that is, *Settlement, Trade and Politics in the Seventeenth-Century Gold Coast* (1982)—which focused on the transformation of socioeconomic structures as part of the "politics" of that period. During the ten years or so in which these works appeared, thousands of cocoa farmers became prosperous and created tremendous income gaps between themselves and the urban professionals on the one hand and subsistence farmers and underemployed migrant laborers on the other. In addition, there were profound social and cultural tensions as many farmers cultivated cocoa and challenged the sociocultural structure of Akan societies that provided security for its members. Declining cocoa prices helped facilitate an end to Nkrumah's administration, but stable prices contributed to the country's economy in the 1980s. Authoritarianism and socialist ideals had given way to structural adjustment and liberalization following unfailing devaluation of the currency—but the political narrating tradition continued.

Culture in History (Amammerɛ)

In recent years, African history in general and Akan history in particular have been subject to more nuanced studies that problematize "facts" and place politics and culture at the center of analysis, while seeking to interpret that center from the perspective of Africans themselves. Notable among these historians of the Akan are Emmanuel Akyeampong, Ivor Wilks, T. C. McCaskie, Larry Yarak, and a host of others. Yet many of these scholars focus their inquiries largely on Asante—and, to a lesser extent, the Ewe or Gã—with little or no real consideration of other Akan polities and peoples. Thus, their focus reinvigorates a trend of earlier Africanist historians and their preoccupation with the "state" of Asante. Ivor Wilks's *Forest of Gold: Essays on the Akan and the Kingdom of Asante* (1993) and *Asante in the Nineteenth Century* (1975) are characteristic of both the paradigm of political narrating and the exclusive focus on Asante society. With some notable exceptions, local and expatriate writers have also followed the paradigm of political narrating: Ernest Obeng's *Ancient Ashanti Chieftaincy* (1988), Joseph K. Adjaye's *Diplomacy and Diplomats in Nineteenth-Century Asante* (1984), and Adu Boahen's *The Ghanaian Sphinx: Reflections on the Contemporary History of Ghana* (1989) are but three of many examples, while Larry Yarak's *Asante and the Dutch* (1990) and Jean Allman's *Quills of the Porcupine: Asante Nationalism in an Emergent Ghana* (1993) followed in the footsteps of their former teacher and dissertation advisor, Ivor Wilks, up to the end of the twentieth century.[9] Indeed, a number of recent historical works on the Akan and Ghana—rather than gender, belief, and the like featuring specific individuals or communities in Ghana—have yet to move from political narrative and analysis and to instead embrace multidisciplinary perspectives that elucidate culture in history. For example, Roger Gocking's *The History of Ghana* (2005) is a polit-

---

9. The late Ghanaian historian A. Adu Boahen was also active in politics. He co-founded a political party in 1990 and even ran for office in the 1992 presidential elections; he was, however, unsuccessful in his bid.

ical history of the republic of Ghana from largely coastal and European perspectives and does little to explore concerns of culture, spirituality, or ecology, much less the structuration of so-called "precolonial" societies. Even when such concerns are addressed, they are often distilled through Asante and with a sense that knowledge of Asante society translates into a deed of epistemological ownership—the intellectual *abirɛmpɔn* or "big men" of Asante studies. As the cultural nationalism of the nineteenth and twentieth centuries failed to articulate an unambiguous embrace of African and European cultures, so too Akan historiography has yet to fully articulate a groundedness in culture and history as complements rather than as competing grounds according to the politics of the day.

There is an urgent need to examine the ways in which Akan societies moved through their histories, for it is not enough to list or state what people did, even on a detailed daily basis, without conveying the agency of their nuanced thinking and cultural transactions in their own historical setting—and then call this "Akan history." Yet the contextualization in culture of Akan history requires greater attention to a composite idea of culture—one beyond anthropological readings that covet "culture" as their own intellectual property. Captivated by the "graybeards" as significant data sources, Robert Rattray of the 1920s and Eva Meyerowitz of the 1950s and 1960s produced about ten books between them on Akan culture and history, though the colonial anthropologist Rattray was no historian and neither was Meyerowitz. The collected works of Rattray are often utilized as a baseline source for Asante and Akan studies, whereas Meyerowitz's works—*The Sacred State of the Akan, Akan Traditions of Origin, The Akan of Ghana: Their Ancient Beliefs*, and *The Early History of the Akan States of Ghana*—have been thoroughly discredited as highly flawed and driven more by passion than by the rigors of historical research. In both cases, the authors viewed culture in statically archived and parochial ways motivated by temperament rather than craft, and they hardly advance us toward a composite yet historicized concept of culture (though Rattray's "ethnographical" material remains a rich source for the study of Asante society in the early twentieth century). On the literature produced by Ghanaian writers relating to Akan culture and history, Kofi Antubam's *Ghana's Heritage of Culture* (1963) and Peter Sarpong's *Ghana in Retrospect: Some Aspects of Ghanaian Culture* (1974) provide us with additional, local perspectives—though with a Christian gloss—that should be read with Rattray and Reindorf. But Antubam and Sarpong, who collected much of Meyerowitz's material, were not historians and thus provided a catalog of cultural ideas, iconography, and information without historical context and adhered to a generalized definition of culture. This failure to arrive at a historically useful concept of culture may owe to the disciplinary conflicts between anthropology and history, since, in those disciplines, there are no unambiguous parameters as to what constitutes "culture" and its historical development among those studied.

These concerns about culture and history are not new, but they remain bound up in the ways Akan culture and history are framed in some of the best recent scholarship on and in organizations built around Akan (and Ghanaian) history. A combined scholastic and organizational example should suffice. The Akan Studies Council came into existence in 1988; devoted to history and as the publisher of a semiannual bulletin, the Council applied a transnational approach to the equally transnational Akan (as a cultural and linguistic category) among scholars working on "Akan studies" in the Ivory Coast, Ghana, Britain, Italy, France, and North America.[10] By the early 1990s, the transnational Akan Studies Council was transformed into a national body called the Ghana Studies Council (GSC). To many, this shift was characteristic of the transition from an "ethnic" to a "national" scholarly association, casting a wider net over the larger Ghanaian cultural landscape. Viewed another way, the name change was a "downsizing" in the transnational scope of Akan studies and signaled a sharp decline in scholarly production about and from Akan peoples, including its intellectuals. The Akan began to morph into "Ghana studies," and intellectuals of Akan cultural origin fixed their eyes on "broader" matters of

---

10. See *Journal of African History* 32, no. 1 (1991): 175, under "Shorter Notices."

gender and sexuality, development, ecology, political economy, and the exigencies of globalization, but without speaking to these matters from their own culture or writing about their culture in its interaction with such matters.

The irony of all this is that most of the human subjects in studies and organizations such as the GSC that take "the state of Ghana" as their axis of analysis are Akan language speakers and culture-bearers, and that, unlike Ghanaian historians of the 1960s and 1970s, the most nuanced and substantive accounts of Akan peoples and their culture have come from without rather than from the capable individuals within. The issue here is not that Akan or Ghanaian scholars *should* focus their inquiries only on their own culture(s), but that most of them do not, even though there is (and will always be) a need for their perspectives on matters for which they are well positioned—in terms of linguistic competency and access to local archives and peoples—to make substantial contributions. Imagine how much more enriched our intellectual lives and the parochial narratives about "ethnicity" and "history" in Ghana would be if *State and Society in Pre-colonial Asante* (1995) and *Asante Identities* (2001) by T. C. McCaskie, for instance, were also addressed by Emmanuel Akyeampong or any of the equally competent Akan scholars. In this universe of possibilities, the meanings of history and modernity could be distilled from integral perspectives and a deep cultural reading of a range of issues made more meaningful by Akan and Ghanaian scholars, for they would have greater effect on the course of scholarship and on the course of their own society. Take, for instance, Kwame Gyekye and Kwasi Wiredu, whose reflections on philosophical concepts in Akan culture have produced an impressive body of work linked to discourses on African culture and philosophy. This has rightly made them leading African philosophers of the twentieth century. In sum, we would have more intellectual projects that move us beyond the paradigm of political analysis or an Asante-centric preoccupation and toward nuanced and interdisciplinary readings of Akan societies that situate those studies in the history of themselves and the larger world.

Implications for African History (Dwene ho)

The study of Akan history, therefore, has three pragmatic implications for the study of African history. The first concern is that of sources. An African history of its cultures must confront the need for a useful composite approach to historical knowledge—one that marries culture and history (for people, ultimately, are nothing but their spiritual, ideational, and material culture) to articulate a comprehensive and complex African history. In writing African history—as one way to propagate that history—sources shape perspective, and here the problem that confronts and often confounds Africanist historians is that many of the "primary" sources come from Europeans or their literate agents, and these sources invariably proscribe African agency and culture. Often these written accounts, no matter how detailed, do not convey the emotional, physical, and physic dynamic of the historical situation observed. The approach commonly used by historians who digest these accounts is to look for consistency in the observations among as many independent observers as possible, in order to deduce the most probable scenario of what *actually* happened and why. However, such reports necessitate caution. Even if European observer accounts are independent and consistent, they are still constrained and are often impoverished in relating the thought, belief, and linguistic systems that underwrite the behaviors or actions of those observed. Consider most of the German sources for the seventeenth- and eighteenth-century Gold Coast, wherein the observers were Protestant: whether "religious men" or merchants, their accounts favored their Christian disposition and colored whatever they saw or thought they saw or heard. It is, therefore, critical to reread European sources, as well as the Islamic ones, with greater scrutiny in light of historians who have extolled the virtues of these sources and have relied sometimes too heavily upon them in the narration of their dissertations, articles, conference papers, and books.

The second concern is the perceived problematic use of oral historical sources. The undue but pervasive overreliance on scribal sources has predisposed the use of oral historical sources to be less than authentic, or not even historical. It makes one wonder whose "African history" these Africanist historians were writing if Africans themselves chose non-scribal modes for archiving, recalling, and transmitting their histories. In fact, it is only when oral accounts appear in print, like that of Reindorf, that they tend to become the authoritative versions vis-à-vis other unpublished or recently collected ones.[11] The main issue historians have with oral sources seems to be that they cannot be chronologized and thus conform to "accepted" standards of historical evidence, such as those aligned with the Julian, Georgian, or Islamic calendrical systems.[12] Yet, the critical evaluation and use of sources, whether scribal or spoken, must be read with the disclosed assumption that, as McCaskie has noted, African and European "historical explanations are [not] synonymous equivalences," and African, European, and Arabic sources must be "interpreted as authored constructs emanating from discrete historical situations and intellectual traditions."[13] A classic case of "discrete" intellectual traditions among the Akan involved the Golden Axe of Asante. In short, the axe was sent to British governor W. Brandford Griffith in 1881 as a sign of peace; the governor was unaware of its meaning, and so he inquired about it among the Fante, an Akan society whose members themselves did not understand the symbolism of the axe. The Fante's misinterpretations almost led to war, and this was largely because its particular intellectual and historical tradition was shaped by protracted Westernization.

Be that as it may, the fragility and lack of currency associated with oral traditions apply to written traditions as well. In fact, given the sophistication of certain indigenous knowledge archives in Akan society—such as drum and flute text—the oral method of preservation and transmission may be more reliable than written sources,

---

11. On this point, see Elizabeth Isichei, *A History of African Societies to 1870* (New York: Cambridge University Press, 1997), 9–10, 24–26.

12. See Kwasi Konadu, "The Calendrical Factor in Akan History," *International Journal of African Historical Studies* 45, no. 2 (2012): 217-246.

13. T. C. McCaskie, "Komfo Anokye of Asante: Meaning, History and Philosophy in an African Society," *Journal of African History* 27 (1986): 317-18.

which may themselves misinform, omit, or purport something other than the "facts." On this matter, Rattray wrote, "The custodians of the [societal] lore, each of whom has his or her understudy, have to be absolutely 'word perfect.' Their memory is constantly exercised in the numerous rites they attend at which they have to repeat correctly long lists of names and events in their proper order. . . . I was informed that in the old days two executioners (*abrafo*) would have been detailed to stand behind [the custodian], and that if they made a mistake they were 'taken away.'"[14] Orality was and is linked to a demonstrated propensity to store and recall volumes of information verbatim; through recurring and culturally mandated rituals, the ear and the tongue were trained to keep and speak what was heard rather than distort or interpret the archived oral texts. To distort or reinterpret such "texts" would have resulted in serious consequences in terms of one's physical health and life. This is how seriously the Akan took the issues of preservation and propagation, and this same ethic (of seriousness) has implications for African historical research.

The third and last concern involves the process of recording and making history, and this is a more immediate challenge for historians of the Akan and of Africa. No one records or writes history as it happens; all history is memory, and that memory is later transmitted through oral or print media based upon the recollection, disposition, sensibilities, and tools (e.g., other participants, observers, or recordings of the event) at the recorder's disposal. Historical writings present themselves largely through events, but human life as multilayered experiences do not unfold within the rubric of events or accounts of what happened. There is (human) reality and the attempt to capture that reality, and for historians, the latter, at best, is all they can attempt to do using the sources they have at their disposal. This is so because history, however one defines it, is based on the memory and diligence of others, neither of which can be presumed, including the writer's. Even in today's gadget-oriented

---

14. R. S. Rattray, *Ashanti* (Oxford: The Clarendon Press, 1923), 219. What Rattray and others call the "abrafo" are in fact the *adumfoɔ*, "executioners."

societies, not even the best video cameras can panoramically "capture" a place, time, or sequence of events from more than one angle
at a time; and even then, the motivations and intentions of the actors
remain unrevealed, their relationship (if any) to others undisclosed,
and their "doings" shrouded in questions, no matter how many
times the videotape or digital video disc is replayed. In my view, a
composite approach to culture and history is the panoramic device
to be used in accessing and assessing the spiritual, ideational, and
temporal actions and subjectivity of Akan peoples as their culture
continues to move through its histories.

In his *African Perspectives on Colonialism*, the late Adu Boahen
claimed, "In the cultural field, the colonial impact has already
proved to be superficial and ephemeral."[15] The strength or weakness
of such a claim in regard to culture can be gauged by the sheer and
alarming "lack of interest of Ghanaians in their own culture and tradition," as one writer who did several decades of fieldwork in
Ghana observed, and this intellectual apathy exists also "at the academic level. The number of historians, as well as social, cultural,
and linguistic scientists, who have produced significant work [in
Ghana] is minimal."[16] It would, thus, appear that the "native patriotism" of Reindorf has urgent and increasing value, for in his time
he advocated the study of Gold Coast (Ghana) history, arguing that
history provided strategies for the future, and that an investment in
one's own history was part and parcel of one's cultural heritage and
self-confidence. The current state of historical knowledge production and divestment in culture among Akan and Ghanaian scholars
would have troubled Reindorf the historian, rupturing his "desire
to produce a complete history of the Gold Coast."[17] Though a "complete history" of anywhere or any group of people is neither desirable nor possible—since histories are without closure—Reindorf

15. A. Adu Boahen, *African Perspectives on Colonialism* (Baltimore: The Johns Hopkins
University Press, 1987), 111. Boahen includes a brief but commonplace interpretation of
the psychological impact of colonialism, pp. 107–8.

16. Sjaak van der Geest, "Opanyin: The Ideal of Elder in the Akan Culture of Ghana,"
Canadian Journal of African Studies 32, no. 3 (1998): 490–91, n. 14.

17. Reindorf, *History*, v.

recognized the need to gather "every source within our reach" and ensure they were "carefully compared," so that "a subsequent edition [of whatever histories we compose] may be more complete."[18]

The Sources (Nimdeɛ bi fibea)

The sources in Volume fall into two parts: indigenous and exogenous sources. Part One begins with a prefatory essay that provides a context for reading and using *all* these sources, as well as an overview of Akan cultural history and thus of this collection at large. In that essay, "Akan Cultural History: An Overview," Kenya Shujaa's broad assessment of the current states of knowledge about the Akan past equips readers with some of the major research questions that have guided investigations into Akan prehistory, outlines some of the scholarly contributions to these dialogues, and offers prospects for their continued exploration. In particular, she focuses on the question of Akan origins, the processes of urbanism and state formation, the networks of interaction, and material and cultural exchange. Against Shujaa's broad assessment, Kwame Daaku's "History in the Oral Traditions of the Akan" offers a preface to the category of indigenous sources that follow his own contribution. Daaku evaluates the historical content in oral traditions and reflects upon his methods as a field historian who encountered a range of subjects (and subjectivities) in the chronicles he recorded. Much historical content was and is still present in these sources, as well as the historical attitudes of those who shared their orally archived knowledge.

The indigenous sources, which are recorded in often unpublished oral accounts, begin with an excerpt from Carl Christian Reindorf's *History of the Gold Coast and Asante* (1895). Like Daaku, Reindorf wrote about the histories of his "country" from European scribal sources and a large body of oral traditional sources—that is, according to Reindorf, narratives, proverbs, oaths, songs, drum language,

---

18. Ibid., iv–v.

and the like "from more than two hundred persons of both sexes
. . . carefully compared to arrive at the truth."[19] Reindorf had hoped
to amass a range of sources in his monumental text, and an analogous attempt has been made here to collect a representative sample
of oral historical sources across Akan societies. To that end, oral accounts in this text have been selected from the settlements and peoples of Nsoko (Begho/Bɛo), Takyiman, Wassa, Sefwi, Denkyira
Adanse, Ahafo, Asante, Assin (Asen), Twifo, and Fante, including
an excerpt from Asantehene Agyeman Prempeh I's early twentieth-
century account. Some may regard most of these oral sources as
"dated" and, indeed, when and from whom they were collected is
important, but not as important as what these sources disclose and
what insights into historical peoples, places, and processes they
might provide. Notwithstanding the limitations on the degree to
which these oral sources shed light on historical matters, the value
of such sources is often realized when they are in dialogue with external sources, usually those of European and, to a lesser extent, Islamic origin. In the best of research scenarios, scribal and spoken
sources—in addition to reading these against the available archaeological and linguistic data—should be probed in tandem, though
gaps in one cannot necessarily be filled by recourse to the other,
since both often derive from and speak to different explanations
about (even the same) human phenomena.

The exogenous sources, not unlike the indigenous oral sources,
also cover a wide temporal range, though they are written by individuals whose observations came from outside the Gold Coast and
with their own religious, cultural, and commercial biases. Included
in these written accounts, however, are a few by individuals such
as David Asante, who was a "native pastor" of the Basel Mission
and wrote in an indigenous language, as Reindorf did. Asante's report is found in the section on "exogenous sources," however, because it was a *written account* based on observation (and, at times,
propaganda), whereas Reindorf's work was largely grounded in oral
historical sources. Hence, we find Reindorf's excerpt included in

---

19. Reindorf, *History*, iv.

the section on indigenous sources. Nonetheless, like Asante's nine-teenth-century account, many of the exogenous sources were based on observation and came, ultimately, from individuals who spent varying degrees of time on the then Gold Coast. The first set of ex-ogenous sources readers will encounter are the Iberian sources, among which are select passages from Eustache de la Fosse's 1479–1480 voyage; Duarte Pacheco Pereira's *Esmeraldo de situ orbis* (1508); a Spanish account of the founding of what is now the Elmina (slave) fortress (1515); a letter from the Portuguese gover-nor at Mina (São Jorge da Mina/Elmina) to Queen Catarina of Portugal (1557); and an anonymous report on Mina (1572). Unfor-tunately, the historical record for the late fifteenth century and entire sixteenth century is rather thin on "ethnographic" and historical con-tent because the Portuguese, who maintained a commercial monop-oly during that period, were more concerned with their gold and slaving enterprise. We can also be certain that the destruction of archival records in the 1755 Lisbon earthquake has reduced the like-lihood that we may one day unearth content of this nature based on the account of Portuguese nationals who lived on the Gold Coast.

When, by the mid-seventeenth century, the Dutch ousted the Por-tuguese from the Gold Coast, a greater silence plagued the Por-tuguese sources, whereas the Dutch, unlike the Portuguese, left a more detailed set of records until they relinquished their Gold Coast holdings to Britain in 1872. Dutch sources form part of the second set of exogenous sources, in addition to one—but significant—French source. Admittedly, the French presence on the Gold Coast was at best tenuous, and the number of French (authored) sources reflects this. Be that as it may, Jean Barbot's late-seventeenth-cen-tury account—archived in an original journal in French dated to 1678—remains an important primary source, though Barbot's ob-servations were geographically and socially limited and often re-stricted to the coastal fringes; hence, much of his information came from residents, traders, officers, and European agents. Though I have made use of Barbot's account in English translation, students and scholars should consult his extant manuscripts and the anno-tated edition of Barbot's works under the title *Barbot on Guinea:*

The Writings of Jean Barbot on West Africa, 1678–1712. Barbot's writings and those of the seventeenth century, of course, can and should be read against the Dutch sources, including Pieter de Marees's account; the Hans Propheet map of 1629 and related descriptions of the settlements drawn in the map; and the accounts synthesized by Dutch compiler and possible physician Olfert Dapper, published in 1686 as *Naukeurige Beschryvinge der Afrikanensche Gewesten.*[20] Beyond Barbot, readers are treated to a range of sources from the archives of the Second Dutch West India Company (WIC), including *A New and Accurate Description of the Coast of Guinea* by company merchant Willem Bosman, as well as sources from the Archief van de Nederlandsche Bezittingen ter Kuste van Guinea (Archives of the Dutch Possessions on the Coast of Guinea [NBKG]). The Dutch sources end with two significant documents underscoring the nature of Dutch-Elmina relations, a "Counts of Indictment and Defense of the Negroes" (1740) and "Pen and Contract" (1755), followed by a number of key document excerpts from the early nineteenth century *Journal and Correspondences of H. W. Daendels* (1815–1817), the Governor-General of the Dutch possessions on the Gold Coast.

The corpus of Dutch sources reproduced herein is but a sample of a larger collection on the Gold Coast/Ghana—and the recent publication of *Sources for the Mutual History of Ghana and the Netherlands* (1593–1960) by Michel R. Doortmont and Jinna Smit will surely encourage further use of those sources. Readers will be quick to realize that their value lies not simply in their coverage or quantity but rather in what they yield when read against the contemporary German and Danish sources. It should be kept in mind, however, that nationals of each country and their respective trading

---

20. Interested scholars can consult the various early editions of Pieter de Marees's account. Cornille Claesson published de Marees's account in both Dutch and French in 1602 and 1605, respectively, and translations into German by Gotthardt Artus appeared in 1603 and into Latin the following year. Samuel Purchas's (shortened) English translation appeared in 1625; for the new English edition, see Adam Jones and Albert van Danztig, eds. and trans., *Description and Historical Account of the Gold Kingdom of Guinea* (New York: Oxford University Press, 1987).

companies were stationed on different parts of the Gold Coast; thus, specific Akan societies who established trade relations and interacted with officials from these companies received their relative share of attention in the official reports sent home to the Netherlands or Denmark. For the records concerning relations between representatives of Akan societies and the Danish Trading Companies (1657–1754), much of the Danish material sent back to Denmark is to be found in *Rigsarkivet* (the Danish National Archives) in Copenhagen, including the key treaties that underscored those relations.

In the third set of exogenous sources, the focus turns to the German and Danish sources. The German sources begin with the surgeon Samuel Brun's account while stationed at Fort Nassau in Moure/Mouri (1611–1620) and Lutheran pastor Wilhelm Johann Müller's account of Fetu (1662–1669). The Danish sources begin with an essay by Ole Justesen that contextualizes the significance and limitations of these sources and includes no fewer than thirty Danish sources in the body of the essay. The Akan societies that received the greatest attention in these thirty sources were Fetu, Akwamu, Akyem, and Asante, and we can be sure that matters of politics and profit rather than preference dictated the type and the sequential order of those societies recorded in the Danish sources. The remaining Danish sources include the accounts of merchants Erick Tilleman (1697), Ludewig F. Rømer (1760), and chief surgeon Paul Erdmann Isert (1788). The German sources continue with Christian George Oldendorp's account (1777) and close with David Asante's late nineteenth-century report (written originally in Twi and translated into German) and missionary Friedrich Ramseyer and Johannes Kühne's late-nineteenth-century account based supposedly on diaries kept during their captivity in Kumase (1875).[21]

The last sets of exogenous sources are the English and Islamic ones. For the English sources, one of the earliest collections with

---

21. On issues related to Ramseyer's (and Kühne's) account in manuscript and published form, see Adam Jones, "'Four Years in Asante': One Source or Several?" *History in Africa* 18 (1991): 173-203.

relevance to Gold Coast and Akan history is Richard Hakluyt's twelve-volume set, which included the mid-sixteenth-century voyages of William Towerson and William Rutter, among others; excerpts from both have been reproduced here. To students of the Akan (Twi) language, Towerson's account will be notable, for the London merchant recorded perhaps the earliest English sampling of the Akan lexicon, following, of course, the late-fifteenth-century Akan vocabulary collected by Eustashe de la Fosse in 1479–1480.

The next selection comes from ship surgeon John Atkins. Atkins's *A Voyage to Guinea, Brazil,* [and] *the West Indies* (1735) was published during the height of the international enslavement enterprise, in which Britain was the leading slaving nation, and in which the Gold Coast plays no small part—its 335 miles of coastline were punctuated by no fewer than 45 slaving fortresses representing the volume and an unmatched variety of European interests. Before the latter part of the seventeenth century, English sources are sparse; however, once the British acquired Cape Coast from the Dutch and made it their commercial headquarters, the British presence and the volume of its records increase from the late seventeenth century into the twentieth century, when the Gold Coast became a British colony by 1901 and a post-colony in 1957. Representing the eighteenth century are selections from a large body of Royal African Company (RAC) records, though students and scholars should consult the three-volume annotated collection of those records, which has been recently edited by Robin Law under the title *The English in West Africa* [*1681–1699*]: *The Local Correspondence of the Royal African Company of England.* The early- to late-nineteenth-century excerpted accounts by Henry Meredith (1812), John Leyden (1817), Thomas E. Bowdich (1819), William Hutton (1821), Brodie Cruickshank (1853), and Dennis Kemp (1898) follow the RAC records, and selections from the collected works of Robert S. Rattray on the subject of a Takyiman *adae*, the Asante *odwira*, funeral rites for an *ɔkɔmfoɔ* (spiritualist, healer), and *ɔkɔm-foɔ* Anokye close out the early twentieth century.

In lieu of a significant body of Islamic sources on Akan history, reflecting the limited effect Islam has historically had on the land-

scape of Akan life, readers will nonetheless find two important essays and a list of Arabic manuscripts housed at the Institute of
African Studies, University of Ghana at Legon. The first essay is a
bibliographic one authored by Raymond A. Silverman and David
Owusu-Ansah; in it, they survey the Arabic and European primary
source literature pertaining to the Muslim presence among the Akan
peoples of Ghana. The second essay, by the late Nehemia Levtzion,
focuses on the early-nineteenth-century Arabic manuscripts from
Kumase—that is, three bundles of Arabic manuscripts, containing
about 900 folios, at the Royal Library in Copenhagen—and an interpretation of these manuscripts. In the end, Levtzion found that
over 90 percent of the manuscripts were concerned with "magical
formulas" or prescriptions for preparing talismans. Little or no historical or "ethnographic" content was recovered from these manuscripts. The list of Arabic manuscripts kept at the University of
Ghana, many of which await translation, closes the first volume in
this collection and opens the door for the scholarly perspectives
grounded in many of these sources. Those perspectives will be en-
compassed in the next volume, *The Akan People: A Historical
Reader.*

PART ONE

(ɔfa a ɛdi kan)

Indigenous Sources

— 1 —

Akan Cultural History: An Overview

KENYA SHUJAA

The following contribution is an extraordinary state-of-the-field essay, erudite and masterful in its synthesis of Ghanaian archaeology, history, and linguistics. Kenya Shujaa's synthesis was written before and is thus best read in conjunction with Gerard Chouin and Christopher DeCorse's article, "New Perspectives on Southern Ghana's Pre-Atlantic History (800-1500)," published in the Journal of African History *in 2010. The forested region of southern Ghana was well settled by agricultural communities—of which the most prominent were earthworks sites—prior to the opening of transatlantic commerce in the late fifteenth century. Chouin and DeCorse evaluate previous archaeological data in light of current research, placing the history of the Akan in a much broader and deeper context.*

Introduction: Issues in Akan "Prehistory"

Until recently, scholarly knowledge of Akan cultural history could be described as grossly inadequate. Though historical and modern phases had become increasingly well-documented, chronological and spatial frameworks remained uneven, and there was a poor understanding of the formative processes of Akan cultural development. The last few decades, however, have witnessed a remarkable increase in Ghanaian archaeological research, contributing to a growing body of information regarding Akan prehistory. Although enormous gaps remain in the ethnomaterial record, researchers have begun to direct attention to increasingly complex questions regarding the nature and processes of Akan social, economic, and cultural organization and change.

This essay is intended to serve as a broad assessment of current states of knowledge regarding some of the central problems that have engaged scholars concerned with the Ghanaian-Akan past. I examine some of the major research questions that have guided investigations into Akan prehistory, outlining some of the scholarly contributions to these dialogues and offering prospects for their continued exploration. In particular, I focus on three ongoing themes in the ethnoarchaeological literature: (1) the question of Akan origins; (2) processes of urbanism and state formation; and (3) networks of interaction and material and cultural exchange. In order to achieve a more holistic perspective, I attempt to approach this study from a landscape perspective, employing multiple scales of analysis in my review.

The Natural and Cultural Landscape

Cultural Background

The Akan are one of several peoples occupying the central Guinean Coast in the area bordered to the west and east by the Komoé and Volta Rivers, respectively, and extending north to south from the upper limits of the Black Volta to the Atlantic Ocean. Although the Akan's ultimate origins remain obscure, archaeological investigations indicate that by the end of the first millennium CE, Akan settlements had been established both in the northern forest margins of Ghana and in the forest heartlands in the Pra-Ofin confluence area. Over the next few centuries, the Akan clans dispersed throughout the Guinean Coast, obtaining land through warfare or purchase, and mixing with or displacing the populations they encountered. By the sixteenth century, Akan peoples had come to inhabit and dominate the areas of what are now central and southern Ghana, western Togo, and eastern Côte d'Ivoire.

As a result of the dispersals and admixture with "indigenous" peoples, the Akan came to be separated into two major linguistic groups, East and West Akan, which are further divided into subpopulations. The Eastern subgroup includes the Asante, Kwahu, Bono (Brong), and others who interacted and mixed with the Guan in central, southern, and eastern Ghana, the Ewe in eastern Ghana and Togo, and the Gã-Adangme of southeastern Ghana. The western subgroup consists of the mixed Akan-Bia speakers of the lagoon region of western Ghana and southeast Côte d'Ivoire, including the Anyi-Baule, Aowin, and Nzema-Ahanta. Ethnolinguistic research has resulted in the identification of several "core" Akan cultural developments, including the exogamous matrilineal clan and dual male-female leadership systems, the practice of farming, the annual yam harvest festival, a socio-ritual calendar based on a month of forty-two named days, and the system of giving children two names, one for the day of birth, the other determined by the father's clan.

Physical Environment

Most of the southern portion of the Akan region (except for a small strip of coastal scrubland and thicket zones) is an area of approximately 31,760 square miles, and consists of closed, lowland tropical forest that was extremely dense before the twentieth century, covered with a wide variety of trees and other vegetation. The overall structure of the forest zone was mosaic in nature, with numerous clusters of trees and shrubs representing areas with varying degrees of regeneration. Generally, forest areas are composed of several strata. First, there is an open layer of "emergents," that is, irregularly spaced, mature trees ranging between 120 and 200 or more feet high. Below this is a layer of open "dominants," that is, primarily mature trees 60-120 feet high, but also including younger forms of the emergent type. Third, there is a lower canopy (30-60 feet high) of mostly immature trees and tall shrubs. There is also an "understory," a closed canopy of small trees, shrubs, and saplings; and lastly, there is the "herb layer"—ground flora in varying degrees of concentration, depending on the amount of sunlight reaching this level.

A small portion of the forest in the southwest (2,905 square miles) is recognized by ecologists as "true" rainforest, receiving approximately 70-120 inches of rainfall annually, with only a short (about one month) dry season. The annual temperature ranges from 69.6 to 86 degrees Fahrenheit. This area includes numerous freshwater swamps, and has generally not been heavily farmed. Over ninety percent of the region (25,610 square miles) contains moist, semi-deciduous forest, where rainfall averages 50.70 inches per year. The remainder of the forest region consists of an ecotone between the rain forest and semi-deciduous areas. In this heavily farmed area, four seasons are recognized: *ɔpɛ bere* (dry season), December to March; *Bampon suo* (big rainy season), April to July; *ofupɛ bere* (short dry period), August to mid-September; and *Kyikirikyi suo* (minor rains), mid-September to November. Although rainfall averages greater than four inches in rainy periods, even during the remaining dry months, total rainfall rarely, if ever, falls below one inch.

Approximately forty to fifty miles north of Kumase (7° 45' N), the forest begins to grade into "Guinea" savanna via an intermediate savanna–woodland zone. Additionally, a thin tongue of savanna along the Ghana–Côte d'Ivoire border extended nearly to the coast. Approximately 57,095 square miles consists of savanna and savanna–woodland zones. In these areas, although there are seven to eight rainy months, there is just one peak rainfall period, in August and September, and total rainfall averages only about forty-two inches per year. Although there are some short-branched trees (averaging fifty feet tall), these are widely scattered, and shrubs and tall grasses dominate the area. Because of the annual fires that sweep the area during the dry season (November to April), the most common trees are fire resistant, with extremely thick barks. One small area at the extreme northeast (755 square miles) consists of Sudan, or open savanna, with shorter grasses, even fewer trees, and a longer dry season. Overall, savanna soils are much poorer than those of the tropical forest; even in this century, population densities in the northern zones are much lower than those in the cleared areas of the forested region, and communities there are primarily situated near roads.

Chronological Framework

Overall, Ghanaian-Akan cultural history parallels the broad sequence—if not necessarily the chronology—of development documented at sites throughout West Africa. Evidence for ceramic production emerges in the Late Stone Age around the mid-third millennium BCE, followed by indications of sedentism and food cultivation in the early third and late second millennium. The development of iron metallurgy has been traced to the late first millennium BCE and early first millennium CE, with scholars delineating three broad phases: the Early Iron Age (500 BCE-500 CE); Middle Iron Age (500 CE-1500 CE); and Late Iron Age (1500-1900). The temporal focus of this essay spans the fifteen hundred years between the early first millennium CE and the mid-second millennium. Although preceding and later phases will also be mentioned, it is this period—which witnessed the appearance of the earliest definitive evidence for Akan settlements, as well as the emergence of iron technology, urbanism, and states—that is most relevant to the scope of this essay.

The Problem of Sources

Written Documents

The first written appearance of the term *Akan* dates to journals written in the late fifteenth century by Portuguese navigator Pacheco Perreira, who applied the title "Hacanys" to an as-yet-unidentified interior group whose merchants traded at the coastal markets. References to Begho/Bitu/Nsoko could also found in the accounts of Arab Muslim travelers and writers, though before the fifteenth century, few of these had any knowledge of the forest region, believing it to be uninhabited. Other fifteenth to seventeenth century European sources referred to "Arkanny," "Akan," "Accanny," "Acanes," "Heccanny," or "Arcania." A 1629 map distinguished between Bonoe (Bono), Insocco (Begho/Nsoko), Wankyi (Wenchi), Wassa, Fantijinn (Fante), Saboe (Asebu), Aquemboe (Akwamu), Quahoe (Kwahu), Akan, Arcarady, Akim/Greater Akanij, and Akanij. By the late fifteenth century, however, many of the groups mentioned in later accounts, such as the Brong or the Fante, had long been settled in their present areas. Although such names as Bonoe, Quahoe, and Wankyi are easily linked to known ethnolinguistic groups, attempts to infer modern connections for others have proven difficult. Kiyaga-Mulindwa argues that numerous changes have occurred in the use of the term "Akan" over time, and that before the sixteenth century, there was no overarching, explicitly "Akan" identity. Rather, the forebears of the peoples now known as Akan emerged from diverse origins, developing similar cultural traits and related dialects through centuries of contact and exchange.

Historical Linguistics

Language studies, when correlated with other sources, have proven enormously useful in the reconstruction of Akan cultural history. On a larger scale, comparative methods have allowed researchers to examine relationships between Akan and other Ghanaian and West African languages, and thus postulate a protolanguage and delimit possible areas of early cultural development. Using the method of mass comparison, Greenberg classified Akan within the Kwa branch within a larger West African Niger-Congo language family. Greenberg's work, in which the Kwa languages extend through the West African forest between Liberia and the lower Niger, has been used to trace Akan origins to as far east as the Chad-Benue region. Subsequent studies have resulted in the removal of many of the languages from the extreme west and east (such as Kru, spoken between the Bandama and Tabu Rivers, and many of the Nigerian languages) from the Kwa subfamily. Based on dialect distributions, many researchers now locate the Kwa languages in the central Guinean forest between the Bia River in modern Côte d'Ivoire and the Togo-Benin border. Within Kwa, researchers have isolated Guan, Akan-Bia, and Ono (spoken near the Ono lagoon in modern Côte d'Ivoire) in a Volta-Komoé group separate from the Gã-Adangme, Ewe, and Central Togo languages. A Tano subgroup comprising Akan and the Bia languages (Anyi-Baule, Chakosi-Ahanta -Nzema) is considered distinct from the Guan and Ono subgroups. Using glottochronotogical and archaeological analyses, Painter suggests that the Volta-Komóe languages separated from Ewe and Gã-Adangme as early as the mid-second millennium BCE, and that the split between Guan and Akan occurred in the early part of the first millennium BCE, a period associated with the end of the Kintampo Complex at many archaeological sites. Subsequent studies have indicated an earlier divergence for Volta-Komóe and Ewe-Gã-Adangme (ca. 3,000 BCE), yet they have largely supported the timetable for the Guan-Akan split, although Painter's dates coincide precisely with the period for which archaeologists have the least documentation. One observation used to support this model is the appearance of regional stylistic variation at late Kintampo sites, which is sometimes interpreted as an indication of increased ethnic or cultural differentiation; however, a number of researchers have warned against the potential fallacies inherent in making direct linkages between cultural and linguistic processes.

Within the Akan language, researchers have uncovered a number of intriguing features. Three major dialect groups—Brong, Asante-Akyem-Kwahu, and Fante-Agona-Akwapem—have been identified, although the geographical and temporal points and socio-cultural circumstances of their divergence continue to be debated. A major linguistic development is the identification of Brong as the most "archaic" or conservative of the Akan dialect groups (based on grammatical and vocabulary structures), and the classification of Asante and Fante as equidistant descendant branches; a notion which appears to be supported archaeologically by the concentration of the oldest known Akan sites in the Brong region as opposed to the central and southern Akan areas. Until recently, however, some scholars questioned whether the Brong speakers were actually even "Akan" at all. In his 1966 study, Boahen excluded the Brong from his list of Akan groups, and Rattray emphasized the absence of Asante/Fante clan names and totems among the "pure Brong," who (like many Guan speakers) based their matrilineal clans on the streets or quarters within the settlement, as well as the absence of a military wing organization in the northern polities. Yet linguistic research has firmly established Brong as an Akan dialect. Based on studies of Fante, among whom some segments maintain traditions of origin from Takyiman and have preserved elements of Brong socio-political vocabulary, it is argued that the *abusua* (pl. *mmusua*) and military wing structures are later socio-cultural developments, and not necessarily indicative of linguistic relationships. It may also be noted that while the southern Akan *mmusua* were not directly named after streets or quarters, there was indeed a close association between the two in central and southern Akan settlement layouts. Lastly, the archaeological record has demonstrated much closer similarities between aspects of Brong and southern Akan material cultures as opposed to non-Akan-speaking groups such as the Grusi-Mo or Mande-Dyula. The closer relationships between the central and southern dialects suggest later divergences between these (perhaps associated with the fourteenth- through eighteenth-century migrations), although similarities may also be attributable to the intensive and ongoing interactions between populations during the late Iron Age. In particular, politically or economically prominent groups such as Asante or Akwamu exerted considerable cultural and linguistic influences on both Akan and non-Akan speaking communities. Diachronic studies have traced the gradual Akanization of many Gã-Adangme, Guan, Senufo, and other non-Akan-speaking populations. Other investigations demonstrate the increasing linguistic divergence of Fante from Brong and the development of closer similarities with southern dialects such as Adanse and Asante or Assin between the seventeenth and twentieth centuries.

Oral Traditions

Oral histories are valuable both because they are so widespread and for the wealth of data they offer on socio-cultural activities and events. Yet, comprehensive surveys are lacking for many Akan groups, making both individual reconstruction and cross comparisons between population histories difficult. Additionally, the oral histories of many Akan groups only extend to the fifteenth through seventeenth centuries, limiting the levels of time depth that can be obtained, while others have been continually altered over the centuries to reflect social or political manipulations. Kiyaga-Mulindwa notes that the later Iron Age was a period of fluid cultural movements and changes among Akan speakers as well as other groups. New identities and histories were adopted by a number of populations, either through absorption into Akan polities, through migration away from a preexisting settlement, or in efforts to assert claims on land or prestige. Upon the formation of the Asante Confederacy, for example, at Osei Tutu's orders, its constituent members discarded their old histories and regalia, adopting the new "Asante" traditions established by Osei Tutu and Okomfo Anokye. Later, as other polities—both Akan and non-Akan—were incorporated into the Asante State, they too created new histories.

Fortunately, none of the above problems applies equally in each case. Interestingly, it appears that many of the histories lacking significant time depth are associated with groups claiming to have migrated into their present areas. On the other hand, the traditions of many groups claiming autochthonous status, such as the Brong of Wenchi, Bono Manso/Takyiman, and Begho/Hani, and the Asante at Asantemanso, may extend their origins to the Early Iron Age, and these have often been supported by archaeological data. In some cases, members of a single ethnolinguistic group may offer competing histories, with some segments claiming to have arrived at their locations through migration while others assert indigenous status. For example, though one Asante story claims origin from the sacred hole of Asantemanso, another asserts that this site was merely the location of their descent from a golden chain from the sky.

Oral histories have proven to be especially crucial in locating the remains of now-abandoned settlements, as well as the identification of prominent features within and beyond them. Sites such as Begho, Bono Manso, and Adansemanso were all located with the aid of local informants, who also pointed out the major streets and ethno-linguistic/occupational quarters within the towns, as well as prominent roads connecting them to local, regional, and international networks of interaction and exchange. This is especially significant given that many Akan towns remain impossible to identify by ordinary reconnaissance methods—whether worn down by erosion or obscured by tropical vegetation or later constructions of farms or settlements.

Archaeological Research

Archaeologists working in the Akan-occupied areas have long been concerned with two related issues: (1) tracing the ultimate origins of the Akan peoples, and (2) linking prehistoric regional units with historic and/or modern Akan cultural groups. Archaeological research in Ghana formally ensued in the early twentieth century, yet, until very recently, much of early Akan cultural history has remained obscured by a gross lack of archaeological data. It was not until well after independence that enough sites had been investigated to allow researchers to expand the scope of their analyses beyond the realm of artifact classification and the formulation of patchy linear chronologies, and begin making wider inferences regarding Akan cultural development. In the Akan areas, archaeological materials have been uncovered dating as far back as the Middle Pleistocene, although these have primarily consisted of isolated finds of stone tools along rivers, belonging to geographically widespread industries and unassociated with other cultural or human biological remains. The Late Stone Age, particularly the period of the Kintampo Complex, is among Ghana's best-documented periods, but efforts to connect Neolithic with modern populations remain controversial.

Until the late 1930s, archaeological research in Ghana was

largely carried out under the auspices of the Geological Survey Project, whose directors were primarily focused on conducting reconnaissance surveys, which were supplemented with a few test excavations at scattered archaeological sites. A few early researchers, such as R. P. Wild, also collected ethnographic information in the vicinity of some sites in an effort to ascertain the ethnolinguistic "identities" of their occupants. In the 1940s and 1950s, archaeologists such as Shaw and Nunoo began to expand the scope of archaeological research in Ghana, engaging in extensive ethnographic surveys as well as providing more detailed analyses of excavated data. Shaw is notable for his excavations of the Late Stone Age site of Bosumpra Cave (Kwahu region) and the Guan/Akwamu Iron Age town of Kyerepong Dawu. Nunoo's investigations include a Kintampo Complex site at the Kumasi University campus, several Iron Age sites in Fanteland (e.g., Befikrom, an iron production settlement, and the Asebu capital), as well as the Gã capital of Ayawaso (Great Accra). Despite such efforts, however, by the late 1950s, only a few geographically scattered sites had been excavated in Ghana, and of these, the material culture assemblages of only a small percentage could be linked to Akan-speaking populations.

In the decades since independence, Ghana has experienced a dramatic increase in both the quantity and the scope of archaeological research. In the 1950s and 1960s, Davies mapped over two thousand sites ranging from the Early Stone Age to the nineteenth century. Over forty of these were surveyed as part of the Volta Basin Research Project (VBRP), a salvage operation initiated prior to the flooding of the area due to the construction of the Aksombo Dam. Although much of the area represented in the VBRP is outside of that dominated by Akan speakers, the project resulted in some of the first radiocarbon dates for Ghanaian sites, allowing researchers to postulate dates for other pre-European cultural occupations. Davies also conducted surveys throughout the Asante area, and excavated or supervised the excavation of nearly forty archaeological sites, including Kintampo Complex occupations at Ntereso and Christian's Village, as well as the Akan Late Iron Age sites of Mampongten and Ahinsan in the central forest. During the same period, Ozanne embarked upon a detailed field study of sites in the Accra Plains and adjacent areas, surveying and excavating dozens of sites in an investigation of Iron Age urbanism and state development among the Gã and Adangme, as well as some Guan and Akan (e.g., Agona, Akwamu, Akwapem) speaking populations in the vicinity. Ozanne's work in the Accra area is especially significant because it was based on these excavations that he developed a chronological sequence for the Late Iron Age in the region based on the relative dates assigned to well-documented European imports and imported and locally made tobacco pipes. This tobacco pipe sequence comprises three broad styles or phases dating between 1640 and 1730; Ozanne noted a general pattern whereby imported round-based pipes were gradually replaced in the archaeological record by local imitations, which in turn eventually gave way to pipes with locally inspired forms and decorations. Subsequent pipe typologies at other Ghanaian sites have largely substantiated Ozanne's cultural sequence, although researchers have sharply criticized efforts to apply his chronology to inland sites, whose populations were exposed to European wares later than those near or on the coast. Overall, the work of Ozanne (and later Anquandah) has rendered the southeast Ghanaian coast and adjacent forest among the best-documented areas for the Iron Age.

The Brong-Ahafo region, located in Ghana's northern forest margins, is among the best-documented Akan-occupied areas. In the 1970s, the first major regionally based archaeological investigations were initiated in Ghana during the West African Trade Project, an interdisciplinary study aiming to elucidate the origins and dynamics of urbanism and exchange in the vicinity of Begho. Under director Merrick Posnansky, researchers investigated the languages, oral history, and archaeology of the Begho area, excavating twenty-seven sites and illuminating aspects of economic and cultural development in the region from the Kintampo Complex to the late Iron Age. Similar projects, albeit on a smaller scale, were initiated during the 1970s and 1980s in the Bono Manso and Wenchi areas, adding further to the body of ethnoarchaeological knowledge regarding Brong prehistory.

For a variety of reasons, archaeological investigations in the forest have been much sparser than in other ecological zones, primarily consisting of scattered surveys in which ceramic scatters are analyzed for form and functions, and site dates estimated based largely on the presence or lack of European artifacts. One reason for the dearth of excavations in the tropical forest is poor preservation; the humid climate and acidic soils rapidly deteriorate most organic biological and cultural remains, making it difficult both to identify sites and to obtain radiocarbon dates for those that are located. Other sites may be obscured by thick vegetation, requiring the aid of oral tradition to locate, and others may be overlain by more recent settlements or disturbed by farming activities. All of these problems are exacerbated by the tendency of many Akan communities to periodically relocate settlements, thus limiting levels of mound accumulation, and rendering sites more vulnerable to encroaching vegetation and erosion. Despite such difficulties, however, researchers have recently begun to devote more attention to the forest, locating sites with the aid of oral historians. In addition to early studies at Mampongten and Ahinsan, excavations have been undertaken in the vicinity of Akan political capitals in the Assin (Twifo Hemang), Agona, Akwamu (Nyanoase and vicinity), and Adanse areas, as well as at sites in the Akyem and Akwamu occupied areas in the Birim Valley. Yet, most projects have been site-oriented, rather than regionally based, and the publication of research results has largely been limited to brief descriptions of site chronologies and artifact forms, without the detailed reports and analyses need to make inferences about social or cultural development. In addition, the majority of these sites appear to date only to the Late Iron Age; a period already thoroughly documented by written and oral sources (Adansemanso and Asantemanso are conspicuous exceptions, although most of the results and interpretations associated with those excavations remain to be published). Other sites, based on the lack of European imports, appear to predate this period, yet disturbed stratigraphies and preservation problems have limited the analysts' ability to obtain radiocarbon dates. Lacking absolute dating methods, archaeologists have tried to establish local chronologies for major ecological zones, including the central and southern forest and coastal plains.

One major difficulty hindering the reconstruction of Akan cultural history is the dearth of detailed published reports and analyses of research results. While some scholars, such as Davies and Posnansky, have been relatively prolific, information regarding crucial projects such as the University of Calgary excavations in Adanse and Asante, Ozanne's work in southeastern Ghana, Davies and Calvocoressi's Ahinsan investigations, and Nunoo's endeavors at Asebu have remained limited to a few scattered articles, depriving scholars of the opportunity to make independent analyses of research findings. It is crucial that researchers make more efforts to complete and publish more detailed reports in order to help address some of the more complex questions regarding Akan socio-cultural development.

The Question of Akan Origins

Before the 1960s, the predominant scholarly view was that the Akan had migrated into Ghana from the north, either from ancient Ghana (whose capital has been traced to southern Mauritania), the Nile Valley, the Sahara, or even Mesopotamia. More recently, however, combined linguistic, archaeological, and physical anthropological evidence firmly place the Akan in the company of other populations considered "indigenous" to West Africa, where human settlement dates to at least the mid-to-late Pleistocene. Yet the question of a specific location for Akan cultural development remains unresolved, largely because of difficulties in establishing connections between present and past ethnolinguistic groups. Although a wide variety of sources are available for the reconstruction of later prehistoric and historic periods, as one extends further into the past, information becomes more scattered and tenuous. Written sources, for example, are invaluable to our understanding of later centuries but rare before the fifteenth century, while oral traditions, also prolific in historical and modern times, are similarly limited in temporal scope. While linguistic analyses often have somewhat greater time depth, in the absence of corroborating archaeological data and without the detailed reports and analyses needed for evidence, the resulting interpretations must remain merely speculative.

The Kintampo Complex

Documentation for the Kintampo Complex spans roughly 1,500 years, from ca. 2,500 BCE to about 750 BCE, although most dates cluster between the nineteenth and twelfth centuries BCE. Geographically, although many are concentrated in the savanna-forest ecotone, Kintampo sites are distributed in all of Ghana's major ecological zones, including the central and southern forest and coastal plains. The material culture of the Kintampo Complex includes polished greenstone axes (called *nyame akuma*, "God's axe" or thunderbolts, by Akan speakers), polished or flaked stone arrowheads, stone beads and jewelry, domestic pottery consisting of heavy rimmed, extensively decorated vessels, stylized animal and human figurines, and occasionally, terracotta spoons. This phase is also well-known for the wide distribution of scored, often well-worn stone or clay objects, sometimes called "cigars" or "rasps," for which the purpose remains debated. Although many Kintampo settlements were located in caves and rock shelters, archaeologists have uncovered house outlines and large fragments of daub or stone. Many Kintampo sites also contain quartz microliths, as well as the remains of both wild and domesticated animals and plants, including cattle and sheep, oil palm, and possibly cowpeas. Kintampo communities appear to have largely practiced a subsistence economy, remaining self-sufficient for most foods and other materials, yet there is considerable evidence that at least some items were produced on a larger scale and traded across relatively long distances.

Archaeologists have widely debated the place of the Kintampo culture in Akan and Ghanaian development. In the archeological record, many of the excavated sites appear as fully developed manifestations, with little evidence of either preceding or following occupations. Models of the origins of the Kintampo Complex have thus often emphasized themes of diffusion and population replace-

ment, with sources stressing stylistic and technological similarities
between Kintampo elements and those of earlier artifact complexes
in the Sahelian and Saharan zones. Yet, while others acknowledge
the presence of northern elements at Kintampo sites, they note that
the Kintampo Complex was also characterized by a number of exclusively local adaptations in agriculture and material culture. For
example, while elements such as cattle or sheep can be easily traced
to northern pastoralists, others, such as "guinea fowl," oil palm, and
yams are of local or forest origin. Differences between Kintampo
and Sahelian sites are even more pronounced in the tropical forest
regions, where the humid climate requires that agriculturalists employ tools and methods far different than those in drier zones. In
addition, as more Kintampo sites are excavated, it is becoming ap-
parent that at least in a few locations, this complex was in fact preceded by—and overlaps with—an earlier occupation, the Punpun
or Buobini Phase, characterized by intensive exploitation of wild
foods and associated with Ghana's earliest known pottery. While
some researchers have emphasized discontinuities between the two
periods, other excavations have revealed that at some sites, the Kintampo Complex appeared more as a transitional occupation than as
a sudden and simultaneous change in material culture and activities.
Rather, Stahl characterizes the Kintampo Complex as a period of
gradual intensification, during which local populations experienced
or initiated enormous changes in subsistence, technology, settlement
patterns, and social organization.

Continuities with the Kintampo Complex have also been observed for later periods. Research in several areas suggests that in
the period following the Kintampo Complex, not all caves and rock
shelters were completely abandoned, as previously believed. Rather,
many sites continued to be used for special purposes, such as temporary camps, food-processing locations, or large-scale production
centers for ceramics, stone tools, beads, and other manufactures. In
addition, a number of early first millennium CE villages were spatially associated with Kintampo sites. Yet, in order to more fully understand the nature of the connections between Late Stone Age and
later populations, more research is needed to bridge the chronology
gap separating the Kintampo Complex and the Early Iron Age.

The Early Iron Age and the Akan Emergence

The period from the first millennium BCE to the end of the first millennium CE remains among the most poorly documented in Akan and Ghanaian culture history. Only a few geographically scattered sites have been excavated from this time, and it has proven difficult to establish links between this and temporally adjacent phases in the archaeological record. Until recently, this period was assumed by archaeologists to represent a "hiatus" in Ghanaian cultural development; many Kintampo Complex sites appear to have been abruptly abandoned by their original occupants after the tenth century BCE, and later populations seem to have favored different locations for their settlements. Yet increasingly, evidence is surfacing to suggest that this perceived hiatus might be more a reflection of inadequate archaeological research than of inhibited cultural development, although notions of continuities between Kintampo and later sites have been hotly disputed. For example, although Boachie Ansah has observed stylistic links between ceramics at Kintampo sites and those at Bonoso (Wenchi), such as the use of square-tooth and walking-comb stamps, other researchers dismiss notions of a cultural connection between the Akan-speaking and Late Stone Age populations, noting dramatic differences in pottery fabrics, forms, and decorations between the two types. Kintampo pottery was characterized by its coarse fabrics, often including quartz grit, thick walls with overhanging rims, and elaborate ornamentation, while early Akan ceramics lack extensive decoration and possess thinner walls and finer-textured fabrics. A few scholars have also suggested that members of the Guan linguistic group, believed to be much older than the Akan, may have been responsible for these settlements, yet this claim also remains largely unsupported archaeologically. It is worth noting that Kintampo sites are distributed throughout Ghana, and have been discovered in every major ecological zone. While Kintampo Complex and earlier sites generally demonstrate large degrees of both stylistic and compositional homogeneity across space (although some interregional differentiation has been observed), by the mid-first millennium CE, the regional differentiation reflected in historic sources becomes increasingly evident. In addition, studies of the Volta-Komóe protolanguage correlate its center of dispersal with the areas delimited by the Kintampo Complex, although Painter's date of the mid first millennium BCE for the Akan divergence remains to be fully corroborated.

I would suggest that the archaeological record seems to support the broader linguistic pattern of an early "Volta-Komóe" population, which became increasingly diverse during the later Stone and Early Iron Ages, during which the process of ethnolinguistic fragmentation (resulting in present linguistic classifications) may have begun. Both the earliest iron production sites and the first identifiably Akan cultural elements seem to occur in the savanna-forest ecotone, particularly in the Begho, Bono Manso, and Wenchi areas. Ceramic analyses in these areas have revealed close parallels between pottery fabrics, forms, and decorations used locally by Early Iron Age and modern Akan populations. Although scholars generally locate the Early West African Iron Age between the 500 BCE and 500 CE, in Ghana, the earliest evidence of iron working does not appear until the early first millennium CE. The oldest known Ghanaian (and Akan) iron-working site is located at the site of Nami at Hani (Begho), where charcoal associated with iron slag and tuyere and furnace fragments yielded a radiocarbon date in the second century CE (180 ± 75 CE). In the Bono Manso area, iron production dates to the fourth century CE at the former iron industrial sector of Abam (320 ± 30 CE), and to the fifth century at the sites of Gyamma and the sacred ancestral hole at Amuowi I (440 ± 70 CE). While Gyamma is generally associated with a non-Akan group later absorbed into the Bono State, traditions name Amuowi as the ancestral hole of emergence for the ancestors of Bono's founders. In the Wenchi region, iron production appears to have ensued somewhat later, with radiocarbon dates ranging from the eighth to tenth centuries CE at the nuclear settlement of Bonoso.

Oral Tradition, Archaeology, and the Problem of Akan Origins

Effah-Gyamfi classifies Akan traditions of origin into three, although, in this case, such claims are often supported by broad categories: (1) traditions of migration, from archaeological research, in which the mechanism lies either within or outside of Ghana's borders; (2) traditions of descent, usually a gold or silver chain (*nkonsonkonson*) originating from the sky; and (3) traditions of origin from caves or a brass bowl (*ayaa*). Though most migration stories claim an origin within the borders of present-day Ghana, a few have also been recorded that suggest journeys from more distant places. Daaku, for example, recorded traditions from Adanse-Akrokerri claiming an ultimate origin in Egypt, while Meyerowitz collected stories from Takyiman contending that the founders of the Bono state had migrated from beyond the Mossi area, possibly in ancient Ghana. Yet, traditions of long-distance migration are now widely refuted by anthropologists. For one, many stories are somewhat vague on such details as the source of the migration and the routes taken. In addition, recent ethnographic research in the Takyiman area, as well as along the coast, has revealed severe inconsistencies in Meyerowitz's work. In Effah-Gyamfi's interviews with seventeen informants in the 1970s, only two—both Muslims—were found claiming ancient Ghana as the home of the Bono; the other fifteen, including several of Meyerowitz's original interviewees, all claimed local ancestry for the Brong of Takyiman/Bono Manso.

Conversely, many of the stories involving migration from within Ghana's borders have been substantiated with corroborating evidence from linguistics, archaeology, and oral and written histories. The Denkyira and several Fante towns (e.g., Edina [Elmina], Makessim, Efutu, Eguafo) claim to have migrated to their present locations from Takyiman, from which their founders had seceded after a series of political conflicts; the Fante claims have been supported by Takyiman oral traditions as well as ethnolinguistic analyses. Other groups claiming to have migrated from Northern Ghana are the Akwamu, who have a tradition of migration in various stages from the Mande-Dyula town of Kong, and the Akyem Bosome, who have mentioned Ejura (also in the savanna belt) as their ultimate source. Many of the forest states, however, such as Dwaben, Kokofu, Akyem Kotoku, and Assin Atandanso, tell of migrations from the Adanse area, where overpopulation and political conflicts forced the gradual dispersal of an early "core" forest Akan population. Based on historical information, the migrations from the savanna-forest fringes appear to have preceded those from the Adanse area by two to three centuries. The Fante, long settled by the late fifteenth century, are believed to have arrived at the coast during the fourteenth and fifteenth centuries based on dates assigned to local king lists, and the movement of Dwaben, Kokofu, and other forest states into their present areas has been widely documented as having occurred between the sixteenth and eighteenth centuries.

Traditions of origin from the sky have also been widely interpreted as indicating northern origin, although in this case, such claims are often supported by archaeological research. In these stories, the mechanism of descent is usually a gold or silver chain (*nkonsonkonson*) or a brass bowl (*ayaa*), and upon arrival the people are provided with necessary skills or technologies by the Creator (Onyame), or a chief or ancestress, who preceded them on their journey to Earth. Effah-Gyamfi notes that in the Twi language, the term *soro*, often used in these traditions, can be used to refer to the north as well as to the sky. Posnansky also points out that between the thirteenth and late fifteenth centuries, brass bowls were obtained largely from the trade between the Middle Niger area and Akan and other ethnolinguistic groups located along the savanna-forest fringes. In the Brong occupied areas, there are three large brass bowls explicitly associated with founders—one in the Begho area at Nsoko, one in Kagbrema in the Bono Manso area, and one from Bono Manso—that are all claimed to have descended from the sky on the same day. Although the bowl from Bono Manso is said to have been seized during the 1722-23 Asante invasion, the others have been identified as of North African manufacture, dating to around the fourteenth century. While such links are intriguing, as we have seen, the Brong presence in these areas dates at least to the first millennium CE, centuries before many Islamic or northern contacts are demonstrated archaeologically. Based on the dating of the bowls, I would suggest that it is possible that these stories refer more to the founding of towns or states, or the initiation of Islamic contact, than to Brong or Akan origins. It should be also noted that a number of southern Akan groups, such as the Bretuo clan of Mampong, also claim descent from the sky, yet no brass bowls associated with "founders" have been uncovered in these areas.

Traditions of the last type, those concerning origin from sacred holes or caves, have been widely interpreted as mythological. Emergence from the ground was perceived to symbolize an effort to claim status, thus establishing groups as the legitimate owners of the lands they occupied. Recent archaeological investigations, however, have suggested that such traditions may extend beyond mere symbolism, and that the locations mentioned are often among the oldest associated with a particular group. In the Brong-Ahafo region, the sacred hole of the founders of Bono, Amuowi I, was found to adjoin a large rock shelter, which when excavated, showed a former occupation dating to the fifth century CE. Elsewhere in the Bono Manso area, shelters with similar material culture assemblages have been associated with other Akan groups forming the nucleus of that state, and the sacred hole of the Gyamma people was found to contain tools representative of the Kintampo Complex. About thirty kilometers to the northwest of Bono, investigations at Bonoso, the sacred hole of the Wenchi State, produced radiocarbon dates in the eighth and tenth centuries CE. In the Begho region, the Brong of Hani and other nearby settlements claim to have emerged from a sacred hole at Nsesrekeseso, which was located near a manmade water cistern resembling Sudanic bilegas. The area surrounding the hole was pitted with numerous grinding hollows, associated in oral tradition with the grinding of millet or sorghum, and several Kintampo Complex sites were located in the vicinity. Lastly, and most surprising, recent work at Adansemanso and Asantemanso, sacred holes of emergence for the Asante and many other forest Akan groups, yielded radiocarbon dates suggesting occupation by Akan peoples as early as the ninth and tenth centuries CE. As I have mentioned, remarkable similarities have been reported between ceramics at these early sites and those produced by the historically known peoples with whom they are associated. It is also interesting to note that many of these sites of origin, such as Nsesrekeseso, Gyamma, and Bonoso, are spatially associated with Kintampo Complex materials, although efforts to establish cultural linkages between them have remained tentative.

Overall, the ethnoarchaeological record indicates two major clusters of sacred holes: (1) the Brong area in the northern forest margins and (2) the Adanse area in the central forest. The names given to two ancient Akan states, Bono, or "pioneer," and Adanse, "foundation," also suggest these areas as the earliest regions of Akan development. Effah-Gyamfi adds that these regions are the most prominent in migration stories as centers of origin for many Akan populations, and it is also notable that they comprise the areas with the oldest known sites with identifiably Akan material culture assemblages. The earliest known Akan sites in the Brong area predate those of the central forest by about seven hundred years, and as I have mentioned, linguistic analyses also demarcate Brong as the most archaic of the Akan dialects. Yet, more forest and coastal sites need to be excavated in order to determine if the Brong area is indeed the "ultimate" center of Akan development. More research is also needed throughout the Akan areas to examine the timing and circumstances of the divergence between the Brong and the southern Akan, as well as the nature of subsequent relations between the regions. Lastly, more efforts must be made to trace aspects of Akan development before the Early Iron Age. What, if any, links exist between the Akan and the producers of the Kintampo Complex assemblages? The differences between Akan and Kintampo pottery would seem to suggest that their makers came from distinct cultural traditions, yet the modern descendants of Kintampo populations remain to be identified. A number of researchers have observed similarities between Kintampo Complex assemblages and sites containing "earthworks ware," which either precedes or is present independently of Akan material culture at many sites, yet others dispute such linkages, and the producers of those wares also remain to be named.

Specialization, Urbanism, and the Development of the Akan State

Akan traditions and vocabulary explicitly differentiate between villages (*akuraa*) and towns (*nkuro*), not based only on size but also on function and political status. Villages were led by lineage leaders, the *abusua panyin* and *obaa panyin*, while towns were ruled by *ahene* ("chiefs") and *ahemaa* ("queen mothers"), or in the case of political capitals, by *amanhene* ("kings") and *ahemaa*. Villages also tended to have relatively homogenous populations, and performed one or a few specialized functions, such as agricultural or ceramic production, while towns were usually multifunctional and ethnically heterogeneous, and their residents occupied a wide variety of socio-economic positions. Towns were classified as either political or commercial centers, as well as according to their respective positions within a political unit.

Based on ethnohistorical and archaeological data, researchers propose a four-tier settlement hierarchy for most Akan states: *oman* (city-state or state); *ahenkuro*; *kuro/krom*; and *nkuraa*. Among most Akan groups, the basic political unit was the *oman*, whose capital city generally bore the name of the polity itself. Because of its large size and political prominence, the capital city was referred to as the *kuro kese*, "great city" or *ahenkuro*, "chief /king's town." In most Akan states, the *oman* and *kuro kese* were one and the same, although in "confederacies" such as Asante, Adanse, or Bono, the latter title was sometimes shared between the capital and other founding states. Located at the center of ritual, social, economic, and political activities, the capital was distinguished both by its larger size and by having the most streets. Bono Manso and Adansemanso were the only towns within their respective states to have 177 streets, while second-tier towns, such as Takyiman (Bono), had 77 streets, while on the other hand, Kumase, Asantemanso, and Abankesieso (Denkyira) were separated from lesser towns by their 77 streets. The *kuro kese*'s only permanent residents were the *omanhene* and *omanhemma*, the various chiefs or "stoolholders" who administered the government, and the unfree dependants of both. Non-royal elites maintained residences in the capital for use when summoned for important events, yet they also had permanent residences in their own states. Merchants, artisans, and other free non-officials also had homes in the state capitals but viewed their natal villages as their permanent residence.

The second tier, also composed of *nkuro kese*, was primarily occupied by provincial capitals, although this number also included commercial centers and the capitals of prominent subject states. Each of the provinces had a capital city of the same name that served as the seat of government for its *omanhene*, whose title echoed that of the *oman* itself (e.g., Dwabenhene, Takyimanhene). Additionally, each *oman* had its own "satellites," smaller villages which produced food or goods for the *oman*'s use. The next level in the Akan settlement hierarchy was occupied by the various *nkuro/nkrom*, or towns, that dotted the landscape. The *nkuro* were non-urbanized, noncommercial towns that had not been founded by an *omanhene*. Generally, sites occupying this tier consisted of specialized farming or craft production centers, many of which served as satellites for rulers of the first two tiers. Leadership in the *nkuro* rested in the hands of lesser chiefs and queen mothers, the *ahene* and *ahemaa*. The fourth tier consisted of *akuraa*, small agricultural villages, which were inhabited by several related *abusua* (matrilineages) and led by a village head, the *odekuro*, a senior lineage female, the *obaa panyin*, and council of elders (*abusua panin*). There were also a number of temporary settlements, such as *nnanso*, or hunters' camps and farming hamlets, which defied classification. These latter two were only occupied seasonally, although they often developed into permanent settlements if they were found to be on fertile land. In theory, even an *oman* could develop out of a hunter's camp.

Based on a variety of sources, it appears that the Akan settlement system was of considerable antiquity. Oral traditions identify the *oman* as among the earliest of Akan political features; all traditions of origin involve the leadership of an *ohemma* (and sometimes an *ohene*), and a four-tier settlement hierarchy is associated with the Bono State in both oral tradition and archaeological research. The pattern became more widespread between the fourteenth and seventeenth centuries, when urbanization seems to have intensified throughout the Lower Guinean Coast. Numerous sub-regional systems developed in all of the ecological zones, with towns and their surrounding villages increasingly bound by ties of politico-military, economic, and socio-cultural interdependence. The *nkuro kese* were located at the center of these interactions, shaping the organization and flow of trade, military activity, religious ceremony, judicial action, and even language use in the polity. The *oman* also controlled external relations, constructing and/or maintaining the major routes leading to its allies, rivals, and trading partners. Under the Asante, however, another layer was added, as once autonomous systems were drawn into a sphere of control previously unknown in the area, and Kumase became the center of vastly enlarged network. In many ways, the *aman* became microcosms of Asante itself, maintaining their internal structures even as they were drawn into the ambit of Kumase.

The Material Culture of Urbanism and State Development

The roots of urbanization in Ghana could arguably be said to extend to the Late Stone Age, during which the Kintampo Complex is distinguished by the "revolutionary" cultural changes accompanying it. It is during this period that archaeologists observe the first evidence of permanent settlements and houses, accompanied by dramatic increases in the accumulation of material culture, with evidence of near-industrial level production of food, ceramics, tools, ornamental jewelry, and decorative art. And it is in the period immediately following this one that researchers have uncovered evidence of the near-total abandonment of rock shelters and caves and the widespread establishment of permanent village settlements in areas near them. Kintampo Complex settlement sizes ranged from about 2,000 square meters (Mumute [Bono/Brong]) to 115,300 square meters (Boyase [Kumase]), and the evidence of local economic specialization is indicative of at least some levels of communication or organization for the purposes of food processing or the manufacture of ceramics, beads, or stone tools and ornaments.

Yet, while the material culture of the Kintampo Complex is well-known, archaeologists have little information regarding social organization during this period.

In the Akan archaeological record, evidence of urbanism and political centralization occurs in various forms. In the Brong region, the remains of towns are often clear, sizeable, spatially discrete arrays of large and small mounds and surface pottery. In the forest, however, thick vegetation or later activities such as farming and construction frequently obscure the sizes and forms of towns, although with the aid of oral historians, towns may still be distinguished from smaller settlements by their higher levels of associated midden accumulation and the distribution of nonperishable remains such as ceramics and iron slag. Evidence of occupational specialization is observable both within individual sites and by postulating economic relationships between them. At centers such as Begho, Bono Manso, and Dawu, excavations have revealed the remnants of mass-production sites for such goods as beads, ivory ornaments, pottery, iron, textiles, and brasswares. In the Adanse area, a possible factory site for the production of funerary terracotta portraits was excavated at Ahinsan. Towns with commercial functions may also be identifiable according to layout; at Begho, occupational and ethnolinguistic quarters appear as spatially discrete arrays of mounds and other artifacts, and the purported market area is clearly demarcated by an exposed outcrop of laterite. At Ahwene Koko and Nyanoase (Akwamu), residential quarters are visibly distinguished from market and assembly areas, and features such as middens or cemeteries are separated from the main village occupation. Interestingly, however, ethnic differentiation has sometimes been difficult to discern in the archaeological record. Stylistic attributes associated with ceramics and other trade goods often transcended political or cultural boundaries, although ethnohistoric sources have aided researchers in identifying such features as mortuary practices or ritual assemblages with particular groups.

When adequately preserved, Akan royal capitals are often clearly identifiable by the presence of objects associated with royal personages. Brong regalia included horses, stools, ivory side-blown trumpets and ornaments (ivory was a royal monopoly), and Arabic-inscribed brass vessels, as well as fine textiles, elaborate pottery, gold weights and jewelry, and precious beads. The Bono State was distinguished by the *sika puduo*, the Golden Stool brought from Amuowi I, while Ahwene Koko possessed the *ahwene dua*, a stool made of red beads. The regalia of the south have been widely documented since the late fifteenth century, including gold-plated umbrellas, sandals, swords and spears, as well as the talking drums, trumpets, and stools of the north. Researchers have observed close parallels between northern and southern regalia; oral traditions report that after the conquest of such polities as Bono, Wenchi, Denkyira, and Tafo, Asante relocated many of the states' ritual, craft, and technological specialists to the Kumase area, importing deities, priests, and skills as well as regal paraphernalia. Even the *sika dua*, the Asante Golden Stool, appears to have had a direct predecessor in regalia of the Bono State. Yet, after the sixteenth century, southern Akan royal burials were often distinguished by terracotta funerary portraits—stylized heads or figurines depicting deceased royalty as well as nobles, courtiers, and items of regalia such as trumpets, drums, sandals, or state swords. (Such sculptures are particularly valuable for their depictions of items not archaeologically preserved.) Other items, such as *abusua kuruwa* (ceramic clan pots) or *kuduo* (brass vessels used to store precious goods) are also elaborately decorated with figures or scenes of royal personages and paraphernalia.

Archaeologists, with the aid of oral histories and written sources, have also begun to trace the expansion of some Akan states. In some cases, evidence of political subordination is seen in shifts in material culture of a settlement, whereby ceramics or other items associated with Akan populations are either gradually or suddenly introduced in the archaeological record. In the southeast region, for example, archaeologists have documented the "sudden" appearance of funerary terracottas at mid-seventeenth-century levels at several Guan-speaking towns, including Larteh Amanfo, Kyerepong Dawu, and Abiriw (all in the Akwapem Hills), as well as in Adangme and Gã settlements such as Ayawaso and Adwuku. After the destruction (by

Akwamu) and subsequent relocation of such towns during the late seventeenth and early eighteenth centuries, these items disappear from the archaeological record of these areas, and there is no evidence for their use in nineteenth or twentieth century ethnographic contexts in other areas, such as the Birim Valley earthworks sites, demographic expansion may be observable in the sudden or gradual displacement of "earthworks wares" by ceramics identified stylistically as Akan. Unlike the Akwapem and Accra-area towns, however, these populations appear to have been eliminated or absorbed by the incoming Atwea (Akyem) peoples; such sites do not demonstrate any indication of continuous occupation by their previous inhabitants, and ethnographic inquiries have not aided in the identification of the earlier ware's producers. The founding and expansion of the Asante State has been similarly documented by the dating of a mass of sixteenth- and seventeenth-century town sites that appear in the area of the original *amantoo* (the founding states of the Asante Confederacy), and its eighteenth-century wars of expansion are associated with the destruction and/or abandonment of a host of contemporary sites. After the mid-eighteenth century, archaeologists note a shift in the artifact assemblages of many areas reportedly defeated by the Asante, whereby overall local and regional ceramic heterogeneity decreases, and many items associated with Akan-Asante regalia appear in the ethnoarchaeological records of non-Akan polities. Such shifts may be related to the centralization of crafts and technologies by the Asante State, who relocated many centers to the Kumase area and imposed a wide range of social restrictions to limit variations in vessels used for particular purposes. After 1750, Tafo (once an Inta market, later defeated by and absorbed into Kumase) became the main pottery producer and exporter for Asante, exporting wares as far south as Sekondi and Accra. The villages of Ahwiia and Bonwhere became centers of woodcarving and weaving, respectively.

Urbanization and Centralization in the Savanna-Forest Ecotone

As in the case of farming and metal production, the ethnoarchaeo-logical record appears to indicate that the Brong area was a pioneer-ing one for Akan state building and urbanism. By the end of the first millennium CE, village occupations had become prolific in the re-gion, and smaller communities had begun to cluster around the emerging larger settlements. Many Middle Iron Age towns were surrounded by settlements of varying sizes, some of which date to the Early Iron Age and, upon survey or excavation, have demon-strated strong evidence of continuities with historic and modern Akan-speaking (as well as non-Akan-speaking) groups. By the eleventh and twelfth centuries, these settlement clusters had devel-oped into intricately linked systems, in which members were bound by socio-cultural, political, and economic ties. As these networks expanded, they became increasingly diverse, incorporating a wide variety of settlement sizes and functions, as well as an increasing number of ethnolinguistic groups. Long settled populations of Brong- or Guan-speakers were joined by later immigrants such as the Grusi-Mo, Kulango-Nkoran, Senufo-Nafaana/Pantera, or the Mande-Dyula, Ligby, Hwela, and Numu, who were attracted by both the growing opportunities for trade in the region and the secu-rity afforded by a well-established, defended community. While in some cases immigrants founded their own settlements, in other cases, they appear to have been largely absorbed into local commu-nities, although they often occupied separate residential sections. Residential segregation was a significant feature of many Akan set-tlements, and town and village layouts were largely determined ac-cording to clan or ethnolinguistic affiliation. Commercial centers such as Kramokrom (Bono) and Begho housed several ethnic groups, and their surrounding areas appear to have been inhabited and dominated by a variety of linguistic and cultural elements. Po-litical capitals such as Ahwene Koko and Bono Manso, on the other hand, were apparently less diverse, and Muslims and other "for-eigners" seem to have been restricted to separate areas or settle-ments. Members of non-Akan-speaking groups often performed specialized functions within the systems in which they were incorporated; Islamic Mande speakers often functioned as spiritual advisors or educators as well as merchants, the Numu (non-Islamic Mande-speakers) served as blacksmiths at Begho, Bono Manso, and Ahwene Koko, and the Mo potters were full-time suppliers to Begho, and exported their wares throughout the Brong region.

Begho

Begho, known by the Akan as Nsoko, was famed for its position along the Mande trade routes, yet oral traditions at the successor state of Hani associate its founding with the ancestress Efua Nyarko. Excavations and oral histories have revealed that before the thirteenth century, the area was primarily occupied by Brong- and Guan-speaking communities. Although the Mande trade, traced to the late fourteenth and early fifteenth centuries, may have facilitated wealth accumulation by the Brong landlords, Begho's economic foundations are usually attributed to an expanding agrarian economy supplemented with other local industries and early regional trade with other groups in the Ghana-Côte d'Ivoire area. Oral traditions at Hani and Nsawkaw trace Begho's ultimate foundations to the nuclear settlement of Nseserekeseo, established by the *ohene* Kutu and his mother *ohemma* Bene, who are said to have governed with the aid of stoolholders and other officials. The earliest archaeological evidence associated with the city was uncovered at the proto-urban settlement of Nyarko, dating to 1045 ± 80 CE, centuries before any indication of the long-distance trade ties with the Islamic world appeared. The area was reported to be dense with pottery of diverse forms and decorations and house mounds dispersed across an occupation area of about one square kilometer. The Nyarko quarter yielded dense concentrations of both local and imported ceramics, as well as artifacts associated with the local production of iron, textiles (spindle whorls), and ivory goods, and its inhabitants appear to have practiced a subsistence economy based on hunting, farming, and pastoralism. By the fourteenth through the sixteenth centuries, Begho had developed into a prosperous urban trading settlement, with over five hundred house mounds of varying sizes and a population of about five thousand spread over five territorially distinct quarters built around the Nyarko nuclear settlement, with that of the Brong ruling family, at over a half kilometer across, being the largest.

In addition to the Nyarko quarter (which housed non-royal Brongs as well as Senufo-Pantera and Guan speakers) and the rulers' residence, the town consisted of the Kramo (Muslim), Dwinfour (artisans), and Gyetundi/Dwabraim (market) areas, as well as Dapaa, the iron smelting area located on the town's outskirts. Dozens of satellite villages of varying sizes were located within a twenty-five-kilometer radius: their Brong-, Dumpo-, Pantera-, Mo-, or Mande-speaking residents provided Begho with the foodstuffs and equipment required to sustain its residents and some of the luxury goods consumed by merchants and nobility. There were also several multiethnic, non-Akan dominated market centers in the vicinity, such as Old Bima (Guan-Dumpo), which had expanded contemporaneously with Begho.

Evidence of Begho's increasing participation in the Islamic trade is attributed by the presence of numerous imported raw materials and manufactures, such as fragments of Chinese porcelain and Venetian and Dutch glass beads, as well as evidence for new or expanding local industries, including woven textile production and brass smithing and casting. The Dwinfour quarter yielded an abundance of remains associated with the specialist production of brass and copper, beads, textiles, ivory, and ceramics, including numerous spindle whorls, fragments of glass, stone, and shell beads, over five hundred brass crucibles, brass-casting molds, gold weights, and carved ivory bracelets, combs, and side-blown trumpets. The Dapaa quarter consisted of nearly sixty slag mounds, the largest of which was about two meters high and fifty meters across, covering an area of about two hectares and containing large quantities of iron slag, tuyere, and furnace fragments, as well as finished objects such as knives and agricultural tools. The use of horses by the ruling Brong are attested by several excavated horse bones, as well as by the uncovered outlines of several "horse paths" used by parading royalty.

Burial excavations support the notion of Begho's ethnic heterogeneity; a wide variety of burial positions and associated goods have been found associated with the different residential quarters, indicating the practice of several distinctive ritual systems.

During Begho's seventeenth-century "peak," its quarters grew closer together, with a population estimated at seven to ten thousand occupying up to fifteen hundred house mounds within an area of approximately eight by five kilometers. The outer boundaries of the metropolitan area were well-marked by an expanse of farmland, which stretched much farther afield, and roads linked the city to production and trading centers throughout West Africa, and beyond through the Sahara to the Mediterranean markets. Begho's "decline" is associated with both internal and external factors: Within the township, increasing tensions within the Dyula community, and between the Dyula and ruling Brong, are said to have rendered the area increasingly vulnerable to Asante incursions from the north during the early eighteenth century. The Brong eventually relocated to the nearby villages of Hani and Nsawkaw, while the Dyula communities, also unwilling to submit to Asante control, dispersed to Mande-dominated savanna centers such as Kong, Bondoukou, or Bobo-Dioulasso.

Bono Manso

Although Begho is well-known as the earliest Akan trading center, it is Bono Manso that is identified as the earliest Akan state capital. The earliest evidence of Akan settlements in the Bono Manso area occurs at the site of Amuowi I, dating to the fifth century CE. Ceramics found at the site exhibit close stylistic similarities with those of the early settlers of Bono Manso. Effah-Gyamfi also discovered five other ancient sites with features corresponding with Amuowi, all of which were located in or near hills containing rock shelters or caves with streams, and contained ceramics virtually identical to those of the Amuowi I and earliest Bono Manso wares. Ethnohistorians trace the growth of statehood to the late early and mid-second millennium CE, when several chiefdoms are said to have begun the process of amalgamation into a single regional unit, with Bono designated as the central and ruling town. Although the histories of communities such as Gyamma or Badu (Kulango origins) suggest that the original founders of the state were multiethnic, other groups appear to have been largely absorbed into the sociocultural system of the Brong-speaking rulers.

Effah-Gyamfi denotes three major phases of urban development for Bono Manso. The foundations of the city were traced to small area dating to between the thirteenth and fifteenth centuries CE. Excavations and surface reconnaissance revealed a small, dispersed early population, with wattle and daub structures and slipped and painted pottery distributed over an area of about 2.3 square kilometers. Based on artifactual distributions, the population for the early part of this phase has been estimated at about four thousand persons, and artifactual, botanical, and faunal data indicate that Bono Manso's early residents subsisted on an economy based on agriculture and a vigorous regional trade with other growing towns such as Begho, Ahwene Koko, Ntereso, and New Buipe. The earliest ceramics associated with this period are simple and unburnished, with coarser fabrics and limited grooved or incised decorations, yet burnishing and more elaborate decorations are present by the fourteenth and fifteenth century levels. By the sixteenth and seventeenth centuries, the town appears to have become "truly" urban with an estimated population of about eight to ten thousand, larger house mounds made with mud-brick, and evidence of expanding inter-regional trade and local production and manufacturing industries such as gold, ivory, pottery, copper and brass wares, iron smelting and smithing, and textiles. Bono Manso appears to have been less ethnolinguistically and functionally diverse than Begho; there was no designated quarter for Muslims or other foreigners, and besides the ruling residence, the only major quarter identified was that of Abam, the iron industrial sector, which was apparently occupied largely by the Numu blacksmiths. Unlike at Begho, burial excavations indicate the presence of only a single, Akan-speaking population, and interestingly, unlike many other Akan towns, the remains of any large markets have not been recovered. Rather, oral traditions suggest

that merchants resided and traded in separate settlements, such as
Kramokrom (located four kilometers to the west), Besedan (a trad-
ing settlement used by Brong, Guan, and other local merchants), or
Ameyawkrom, located short distances from the capital.

Like Begho, Bono Manso was surrounded by specialist farming
and craft/technological villages inhabited by diverse ethnolinguistic
groups—such as Gyamma, a farming village, or Longoro Nkwanta,
a Mo settlement, or the Krobo (Dangme) potting settlement—as
well as several commercial centers and seven identified provincial
capitals, each of which had its own satellites. Unlike at Begho, however, the centralized leadership controlled most economic activities
in the area, and most of the other settlements were politically subordinate to the capital. In addition, as noted, the Gyamma and other
originally non-Akan-speaking groups were linguistically and socially absorbed into the Bono system. The Gyamma were the designated caretakers of Bono's *sika puduo*, the state stools, and the
Gyamma people, as well as the Numu blacksmiths at Takyiman, are
now Brong-speakers, although both groups have traditions and rituals that maintain their cultural distinctiveness. Ceramic and other
material evidence suggests that this phase saw the continued intensification of regional contacts, as well as increased participation of
the state in long-distance trade activities with the Islamicized groups
of the Sahel or Western Sudan. During the sixteenth and seventeenth
centuries, Bona's increasing prosperity also contributed to the
founding of other nearby states, such as the mixed Brong-Guan
polity of Dromankese, or Nkoransa, which was ruled by migrants
from the Adanse region. Effah-Gyamfi's excavations at the capital,
supported by oral and written testimonies, indicate that roads and
trails existed to link Bono Manso with both subject and foreign political and trading centers. Excavations, with the aid of oral traditions, also uncovered several of the *aponkokwan* or horse paths used
by parading royalty, which radiated from the center of the town.

The last urban phase (late seventeenth and early eighteenth centuries) is marked by larger, more spatially concentrated house
mounds, abundant pottery in diverse local and regional styles, and
a greater increase in both luxury material goods and population den-

sity (although the population had apparently shrunk to about eight thousand persons, these were confined to an area of about half that of Phase I), all of which support reports by oral historians of increased political centralization during this period. Although the decline of Bono Manso is associated with increasing internal disputes, these culminated with an invasion by Asante in 1722-23, and by the late eighteenth century, the town had been abandoned and the seat of the state relocated to Takyiman. The governorship of the Bono area was assigned by the Asante to the state of Nkoransa, a powerful polity once politically subordinate to Bono Manso.

Wenchi (Wankyi)

As mentioned, according to oral traditions, the seven clans of the Brong of Wenchi first emerged from a sacred hole at Bonoso, where they settled for "some time" before establishing their capital at Ahwene Koko ("red beads"). Archaeological research at Bonoso has resulted in two radiocarbon dates at that site: 710 ± 90 CE and 980 ± 85 CE. Although dates for Ahwene Koko are much later (mid- to late sixteenth century), oral and written histories suggest that the town's foundations date to before the fifteenth century, and close resemblances in pottery fabrics, forms, and decorative styles support traditional claims of cultural continuity between the two settlements. Decorations at both sites—consisting primarily of grooving or incision—also seem to conform closely to those at other contemporary Akan sites, such as Bono Manso and Twifo Heman, versus those at non-Akan sites such as Yendi and New Buipe. Boachie-Ansah also tentatively suggests continuities between the wares of Bonoso and those of the Kintampo Complex based on the use of similar comb stamp decorations, although the nature of any such relationship remains to be specified or corroborated with information from other sources.

While Bonoso is generally not viewed as an urban settlement, Ahwene Koko has been identified as a large town, about a mile wide and extending in patches along a stretch of about nine miles. Ethnoarchaeological sources indicate the presence of a central palace area, inhabited by Wenchi's rulers, as well as open areas demarcating an assembly place and market. Excavations support ethnohistorical accounts of the state's participation in regional and long-distance trade and several specialist industries, including potting, iron smithing, copper and brass casting (including two brass gongs or bells, a rare archaeological find), and textile production (spindle whorls and dye holes). Like Bono Manso, although the town also functioned as a center for production and commercial activities, Ahwene Koko served primarily as political capital, a centralized location from which to administer the Wenchi State, and appears to have lacked the ethnic heterogeneity of Begho. Less is known about the overall settlement system of Wenchi; due to limited funding, most research in the area was limited to the capital, at which only two small test excavations were performed. Ethnohistoric accounts and reconnaissance surveys, however, have indicated that like other towns, Ahwene Koko was surrounded by satellite settlements of varying sizes, functions, and ethnic compositions, which were linked to the capital by a network of roads. The destruction of the town is documented as having occurred in the early eighteenth century (1711-12) at the hands of Asante.

Urbanism and State Formation
in the Central Forest and Coast

General patterns of settlement throughout the forest have long seemed to support the claims of oral historians that Akan migrations into the region did not commence until somewhere between the fifteenth and seventeenth centuries. Although a number of pre-fifteenth-century occupations have been discovered, they have frequently contained pottery whose coarse fabrics, wide variety of shapes, red-slipping, and ornate decorations are considered quite distinct from the plainer, finer-textured, less ornately decorated wares generally associated with earlier Akan-speaking populations. These wares are distributed throughout both the Accra Plains and Southern Ghana and Asante forests, including the Western Densu

Valley, the Birim Valley, the Western Pra Basin, and the southern Kwahu Mountains. Sites containing such pottery have most frequently been located on hilltops or enclosed within constructed earthworks (from which the wares have received their name). "Earthworks ware" is often found associated with implements considered typical of the Kintampo Complex, such as *nyame akuma*, stone beads and microliths, but artifact assemblages also frequently include iron slag and tuyere fragments. Between the sixteenth and eighteenth centuries (earlier at Asantemanso), many of these sites and/or regions show evidence of a sudden or gradual displacement of earthworks wares with cultural features associated with Akan-speaking groups, including plain, unslipped pottery, terracotta figurines, and *mmukyia* (hearth pots). In other areas, the ethnoarchaeological record indicates that processes of depopulation preceded Akan settlement. Although, in some cases, earlier populations appear to have been absorbed into Akan socio-political units, others, such as those of the Birim Valley, seem to have been eliminated through warfare or slave raids, the pace of which increased dramatically with the expansion of the Atlantic slave trade. Both of these processes have served to largely obscure the cultural "identities" of these peoples, yet researchers note that in areas throughout the forest, including the Adanse-Akan and Brong "heartlands," both Akan and Guan oral traditions have emphasized the latter as the original inhabitants.

Ethnoarchaeological investigations also suggest the occurrence of other shifts in the demographic and settlement patterns of the forest after the late fifteenth century. Dramatic population increases and extensive land clearances are indicated by the proliferation of densely occupied village settlements and increased agricultural activities associated with post-fifteenth-century sites, and the emergence of large nucleated settlements in the midst of smaller villages and hamlets attests to the spread of urbanism. There also appears to have been shifts in settlement order or organization, whereby localized production of ceramics or iron was evidently replaced by increasing levels of economic interdependence, and craft and technological specialization became concentrated in or near the dominant towns. These localized and regional processes seem to be inextricably linked to two external factors: the arrival of European merchants on the coast and by the expansion of the Western Sudan traders into central and southern forests, both of which significantly increased the participation of southern communities in the international trade networks.

State building among the Southern Akan has been traced to about the fourteenth or fifteenth century, when Fante contingents from Takyiman began establishing towns and small states along the western coast. Fifteenth and sixteenth century Portuguese sources include Ahanta and the Fante polities of Asebu, Eguafo, and Fetu among other coastal states, describing aspects of economic activities such as gold mining and slave capture and sale, as well as members and functions of court members and regalia such as swords, stools, trumpets, drums, and military paraphernalia. In the forest, oral histories and excavations in Adanse indicate that while a number of political and commercial centers developed in the region during the early to mid-second millennium CE, these consisted of small chiefdoms, united only under temporary military leaders, whose members were bound by trade and kinship or agnatic ties rather than an allegiance towards any centralized rulers. Early leadership was based primarily on ritual, rather than politico-military functions: Family heads served both as priests and chiefs, kings or queenmothers, and disputes were mediated by the deities, of which each clan or community had its own patrons, as opposed to the national deities that united the later state.

Moves towards centralization have been traced to the late sixteenth to early seventeenth centuries, when a number of city-states—Adanse, Fomena, Dompoase, Akrokyere, and Ayaase, each representing a different clan (although both Adansemanso and Dompoase claimed the Asenee clan)—joined to form the Adanse Confederacy. Oral traditions identify their leader as Awurade Basa, king of Adansemanso, who reportedly caused the *afenakwa*, Adanse's state sword, to appear from heaven. Although Adanse was ruled by a central government, leadership—symbolized by custody of the sword—was said to have rotated among the founding clans, each of which maintained its own deities and provincial networks. During the sixteenth and seventeenth centuries, a number of family groups began to migrate away from the Adansemanso and Asante-manso areas, dispersing throughout the forest and establishing their own principalities and states. Some of these went north and east, to what are now the Kumase-Mampong area, founding political/market centers such as Tafo, Ekaase, or Suntreso, while others moved to the southern forest (Kwahu, Akwamu, Akwapem) or near the coast (Wassa, Twifo, Igwira). By the end of the sixteenth century, state building had become prolific in the Akan areas, and during the seventeenth century, numerous polities competed for political primacy. The foundations of a number of excavated forest centers, such as Nyanoase (Akwamu) or Twifo Hemang (Assin), date to this period, and a 1629 Dutch map depicts approximately thirty-eight political units in the southern "Gold Coast," of which over a dozen have been identified as "Akan." Oral traditions also trace the development of many of the more secularized or militarized aspects of Akan rule to this period. Although Akan rulers continued to serve ritual functions, by the mid-seventeenth century, leadership had become more secularly based, with power residing in military strength, control over natural commodities, such as gold or salt, and dominance over regional and international trade routes. Even before the proliferation of firearms (in the late seventeenth century), polities such as Akwamu and Denkyira had initiated radical changes in military tactics and organization, shifting from reliance on close quarter to missile fighting, and instituting a wing system to structure political and army leadership. In the mid-seventeenth century, city-states representing the Asante Oyoko and Bretuo clans formed and led a confederacy with several other small autonomous forest polities in order to overthrow the state of Denkyira, which had dominated the southwest Adanse zone throughout the 1600s. After the defeat of Denkyira around 1701, the Asante began to consolidate their power and expand their territory, an activity that culminated during the early nineteenth century, when Asante's territory spanned an area roughly equal to that of present-day Ghana and southeastern Côte d'Ivoire. Numerous surrounding groups, Akan and non-Akan, were conquered and incorporated into the state apparatus, with only the segmented Fante polities along the coast, closely allied with the British, escaping Asante rule.

The Pra-Ofin Basin: Adansemanso and Asantemanso

Research at Adansemanso and Asantemanso has indicated that the Akan presence at those "nuclear" settlements long predates that of other dated southern sites. Although radiocarbon dates at Asantemanso suggest a continuous occupation of the site from the tenth century BCE to modern times, there are indications of a pre-Asante occupation by earthworks ware producers, and oral traditions in the area identify the Guan as Akan predecessors. Akan ceramic styles abruptly begin to dominate at Asantemanso in the tenth century CE, and evidence of iron production dates to the early eleventh century, suggesting the early development of local industries. Little has been published regarding the settlement's size and layout, yet oral traditions suggest that Asantemanso grew into a large town with "seventy-seven streets," a feature that is paralleled at Kumase. Although the archaeological record has revealed little direct information regarding local subsistence, Shinnie postulates that the town's residents were largely sustained by a mixture of small-scale agriculture and hunting and gathering of wild foods. This notion is supported by the recovery of large quantities of animal bones, iron, and stone agricultural implements as well as by Asante oral traditions, which emphasize the importance of the hunter in early communities. Detailed descriptions of ceramics and other artifacts remain unpublished, yet the capital's participation in networks of production and distribution is suggested by excavations of several potting centers in the area (including Anyinam), and by the wide variety of forms and decorations at Asantemanso, which may suggest that this was primarily a localized industry. The concentration of slag in residential areas indicates that iron metallurgy was also, as in many forest regions, a village-based technology. Extra-regional contacts are hinted by the recovery of at least one clamshell, and clearly indicated by the presence of European imports in the seventeenth and eighteenth centuries. Surveys in the vicinity indicate that the town was surrounded by other settlements of varying sizes, including the historically important sites of Bekwae, Kokofu, Anyinam, and Esiase. Based on ceramic and house mound quantities, Shinnie estimates an earlier population of several thousand people, whose numbers gradually increased until about the fifteenth century, when oral traditions suggest that the settlement began to become over-populated. After the fifteenth century, the population steadily declined as family groups began to migrate to other areas, such as Dwaben, Kokofu, and Kwaman (Kumase) in search of arable land and greater access to long-distance trade. Today Asantemanso is only the size of a small hamlet, consisting of a few houses and a shrine to the Tano deity, despite its prominence in Asante religious and political ideology. Although the remains of ancient pathways have been located, Asantemanso is now inaccessible to major roads; the hamlet is adjacent to a sacred forest, the entrance to which is marked by seven clay bowls, said to represent the original Akan *abusua*. Archaeological research also associates Asantemanso with a ritual area of as-yet-undetermined function (now abandoned), consisting of several hundred pots distributed over an 800-by-700-centimeter area located two kilometers northwest of the earliest part of the town.

Unlike Asantemanso, Adansemanso, located twenty kilometers to the south, apparently shows little evidence of a pre-Akan population. Radiocarbon dates place its foundations to the ninth century, and by the thirteenth century CE (1210-70), it had developed into a sizeable semi-urban settlement, with traces of habitation covering an area over a kilometer long, numerous pottery scatters, house mounds up to one hundred meters long, and a wide distribution of iron slag and artifacts. Oral traditions attribute 177 streets to Adansemanso, and Shinnie argues that based on artifactual density and distribution, Adansemanso was considerably larger than Asantemanso. As it expanded, the town came to be surrounded by dozens of villages and towns of varying sizes, including the capitals of the confederacy's other founding states, such as Fomena and Akrokyere, as well as later centers such as Ahinsan and Obuase.

Manse oral traditions identify several towns that specialized in gold mining or iron production for the state, such as Kenyaase, Dompoase, Akrofrom, and Akrokyere, although these claims have yet to be investigated by archaeologists. Adansemanso is also associated with the oldest documented *asensie* (a funerary site where terracotta portraits [*mma*], *abusua kuruwa*, and other ritual objects are placed), located to the west of the town on a prominent hill. Although the *asensie* apparently yielded no radiocarbon dates, stylistic features of its fourteen terracotta figurines (such as their disc-like shapes, use of red-slip, and "crude" decorations, which demonstrate broad parallels with fifteenth and sixteenth century examples from Kwahu and Beifikrom) and ceramic vessels suggest a pre-seventeenth century date. Oral traditions date the abandonment of Adansemanso to about 1640, when its rulers relocated to the nearby towns of Dompoase and Ahinsan amidst conflicts with the rapidly expanding southwestern state of Denkyira. This claim is supported by the last radiocarbon date for the site, between the late sixteenth and early seventeenth centuries, as well as the presence of only one smoking pipe and the absence of any European imports. Excavations of the late-sixteenth- or early-seventeenth-century mausoleum at Ahinsan suggest continuities with Adanse's leaders; the site's over one hundred and fifty terracotta sculptures depict Adanse royalty, courtiers, and regalia, and are associated with abundant smoke-glazed pottery whose forms and decorations nonetheless retain stylistic links with those at Adansemanso.

Fanteland

Ethnohistoric accounts describe Fanteland as consisting of several loosely allied states—including Eguafo/Komenda, Edina, Asebu, Efutu, and Cormantin—extending along the western and central Ghanaian coast. Archaeological research has included the identification and excavation of several capital sites, such as Asebu and Edina (Elmina), as well as other settlements of varying sizes associated with Fante polities. Most of these investigations have involved only test excavations, or have focused on Fante interactions with nearby European towns and forts; this author is unaware of any regionally based studies of prehistoric Fanteland.

In the 1950s, Nunoo performed a test excavation at Beifikrom, a settlement located in the suburbs of Mankessim, the Borbor Fante capital (since the seventeenth century), uncovering evidence of intensive iron manufacture (including slag, tuyere fragments, knives, and bracelets), large quantities of pottery, and several terracotta figurines. Although no radiocarbon dates were obtained for the site, stylistic features of its terracotta figurines, as well as local pot typologies and the absence of smoking pipes or European imports support the fifteenth-to-sixteenth century date offered by oral historians. A number of other early Fante sites have been excavated in the Cape Coast area; these also produced dates beginning in the fifteenth or sixteenth century according to local pot typologies and oral histories. A number of these settlements appear to have been engaged in intensive iron and ceramic manufacture; excavations yielded large quantities of slag and tuyere fragments, iron knives and ornaments, and high quality ceramics made from local clays. At a number of Fante sites, specialist pottery production is associated primarily with sixteenth-to-eighteenth-century levels; older sherds are plainer and coarser than the finely crafted, more abundant, variably decorated vessels overlaying them. This increase in potting is accompanied by the indications of decreased localized iron production, a trend often attributed to the introduction of scrap iron by European merchants, which dramatically undermined the more labor-intensive local industries. Many groups shifted to or intensified other activities, such as slave raiding or salt, fish, pottery, or gold production. Participation in long distance networks is indicated by excavations at sites such as Asebu (sixteenth to eighteenth centuries) and Elmina (fourteenth to nineteenth centuries), which uncovered the remains of thousands of stone houses and several large market areas, as well as numerous mollusk shells, imported European and local pipe and porcelain fragments, and Venetian and Dutch glass beads.

Akwamu

By the end of the seventeenth century, the Akan state of Akwamu had become, along with Denkyira and Akyem, a dominant force in Southern Ghana, ruling an area over two hundred miles along the coast and extending over one hundred miles into the forests between Agona and Whydah. The process of Akwamu expansion has been widely documented in the ethnohistoric literature, which describes a series of wars between the state and nearby forest and coastal polities, and the destruction and/or abandonment of numerous towns and villages during the late seventeenth and early eighteenth centuries. Archaeological research has corroborated these sources by tracing the material evidence of Akwamu state development with surveys and excavations in the vicinity of its capital, Nyanoase, as well as in conquered areas within the Agona, Kwahu, Shai-La, Gã, and Guan territories.

Although European writers describe the Akwamu capital as extending along seven miles, it is archaeologically known as a series of mound concentrations along about three miles. Surveys and excavations at Nyanoase have uncovered the remains of a centrally located royal palace area (Amanfoso), a marketplace, an assembly area (denoted by open spaces adjacent to the mounds), and several large middens. Radiocarbon dates, along with ethnohistoric accounts and artifact typologies, date the main period of occupation between the late sixteenth and early eighteenth centuries, and written sources date the town's destruction to 1730, when a coalition of armies from the north and northwest invaded the region.

Nyanoase was reported to have been an important market center, located on the major trade routes between the eastern coast and the central and northern forests. Local merchants exchanged produce and iron tools for gold (Akwamu territory was poor in this resource), coastal fish, salt, pottery, and European imports, as well as livestock obtained from Whydah or Ardra. Excavations at the site yielded numerous tobacco pipe fragments and Akan black-burnished pottery sherds—including an Arab-inspired oil lamp and other luxury items, such as a *kuduo* lid and European porcelain and glass beads. European sources identify the capital with nearly two dozen surrounding towns of varying sizes, as well as numerous satellite villages and plantations, whose largely unfree residents supplied Nyanoase and other centers with produce and equipment. Reconnaissance surveys in the region have identified several outlying settlements whose ceramic forms, fabrics, and decorations suggest a cultural or economic relationship with the capital.

Outside the Nyanoase area, extensive ethnoarchaeological investigations conducted in the Accra plains (Gã and Obutu/Awutu [Guan]), Agana, Shai Hills, and Akwapem Hills (Guan and Akwapem) areas have elucidated many aspects of the Akwamu expansion process. Archaeologically obtained estimates for the destruction dates of such traditionally Guan towns as Larteh-Amanfro, Ayawaso, Kyerepong-Dawu, and Abiriw all correspond closely with the late-seventeenth- and early-eighteenth-century dates assigned by oral and written histories. Connections between Akwamu and Guan, Shai-La, and Gã populations are suggested from the mid-seventeenth century by the wide distribution of terracotta figurines and ceramic vessel and pipe styles throughout Akwamu, the Akwapem Hills, the Accra Plains, and the Shai Hills.

Ethnohistoric accounts from the late seventeenth and early eighteenth centuries emphasize Akwamu slave raiding and control over trade routes as major factors in the accumulation and maintenance of the state's power and wealth. Archaeological research in the Birim Valley corroborates the abandonment of sites inhabited by earthworks ware producers with the arrival of the Atweafo/Akyem and Akwamu polities, whose slave raids and wars led to instability and mass depopulation in the region. Yet, Ozanne has suggested that the capital's population may have initially been formed of "indigenous" Akan and Guan-speakers as well as the immigrant Akwamu. European writers assert that before the late seventeenth century, Akwamu had largely engaged in more diplomatic interactions with neighboring states, and they describe early Nyanoase primarily as a market site, strategically located to exploit the forest-coastal trade. In the early years of its development, it was necessary for Nyanoase to form economic and political allegiances with neighboring states in order to maintain access to the international trade routes, which, in the dearth of natural commodities such as gold, formed the basis of Akwamu's wealth. Yet such alliances did not merely enhance the flow of trade, they also involved exchanges of population and cultural ideas. At sites throughout Akwamu and neighboring regions, ceramic analyses indicate that while sixteenth-century populations may have relied more on village or site-based production, by the mid-seventeenth century, Agona pottery was present at Nyanoase, and a regional trade had emerged in Shai wares. It is also notable that the appearance of funerary terracotta dates to the same period in these areas, where they continued to be used for decades before the eventual defeat of the neighboring polities. During the early to mid-seventeenth century, the Akwamu had established enclaves in at least two capitals: Agona and Gã-Ayawaso, and Nyanoase itself had an Agona quarter. Lastly, ethnographic as well as archaeological studies have documented the growth of Akan cultural influence among the Gã, Shai-La, and the Guan of Akwapem Hills, Asante, and Kwahu areas, demonstrating linguistic borrowings or shifts, and the dissemination of Akan regalia, festivals, socio-political organization, and ceremonies. While some have attributed such patterns largely to Akwamu political dominance, others suggest that these links were at least partially due to the earlier exchange networks, in which ideas as well as materials transcended ethnic or local boundaries.

Trade and Exchange in Akan Cultural History

A major factor in the development of Akan urbanism and statehood was the networks of interaction and exchange that bound members of regional socio-political units to those both within and outside their borders. In the Akan areas, the origins of local and regional exchange extend at least to the Kintampo period. Evidence of small population movements or contacts with the Sahel or Sahara are observable in the remains of exotic domesticates such as cattle, sheep, and goats, as well as in close parallels between Sahelian, Saharan, and Kintampo fishing technology (e.g., bone harpoons and fish-hooks) and ceramic decorative motifs such as walking-comb stamping. There are also indications of contacts between ecological zones: Marine mollusk shells have been recovered from Kintampo Complex sites as far north as Ntereso, and mineralogical analyses of mica inclusions in K-6 pottery estimate the nearest location as seventy kilometers to the west. Other items, such as greenstone axes and stone rasps are distributed up to hundreds of kilometers throughout the Kintampo sites. Researchers have uncovered the remains of numerous special-purpose sites associated with this period, including locations devoted to large-scale food processing (grain milling) and the intensive manufacture of grindstones, ceramic vessels, terracotta and stone rasps, greenstone axes, stone beads and ornaments, and quartz microliths. While the majority of such goods were likely intended for local use—ceramic pastes, for example, were usually locally based, the wide distribution of many items suggests the occurrence of at least occasional contacts or exchanges between communities and regions. Broad regional similarities in pottery decorations and forms are also frequently interpreted as the result of communication and/or the development of shared or similar cultural traditions. Overall, however, most exotic good occur only in small quantities, and Kintampo Complex communities appear to have been largely self-sufficient.

During the Iron Age, localized and regional contacts appear to have both expanded and intensified as populations began to coalesce into ever-larger and more cohesive socio-political units. While Early Iron Age populations appear to have largely focused on localized food and ceramic production, distribution seems to have expanded for such commodities as mollusks and stone tools and ornaments. By the end of the first millennium CE, many communities had begun to engage in more regular exchanges, in which trade links extended beyond regional, political and ethnic distinctions. Evidence of intensive, localized, specialist food, ceramic, and iron production dates to between the fifth and tenth centuries at sites in the Bono Manso, Wenchi, Begho, and Adanse areas. Between the ninth and thirteenth centuries, indications of an ongoing regional ceramic trade emerges between settlements in the Brong region and savannah communities in the Daboya, Banda, and Gonja areas. There is also evidence of contacts with the south, with such items as gold, kola nuts, ivory, and salt being imported by the northern forest populations. These interactions appear to have intensified during the Middle and Late Iron Ages; after the initiation of the Mande, Hausa and Atlantic trades, the ethnoarchaeological record indicates a substantial increase in contacts between the Brong towns and the southern Akan communities, who were the major suppliers of the gold, salt, ivory, kola nuts, and slaves so urgently demanded by Islamic merchants. The Brong and other northern groups served as mediators between the forest and coastal peoples and the Islamic and European worlds, trading locally produced brasswares, ivory ornaments, and textiles along with northern imported goods for southern (and later European and American) commodities. At the local or sub-regional northern forest centers such as Bono Manso, Begho, and Ahwene Koko were located at the centers of multiethnic networks involving specialized production and exchange. Ethnoarchaeological studies demonstrate that the Brong economic systems included Mo and Krobo potters, Mande-speaking merchants, clerics, blacksmiths, dyers, and potters (spindle whorls and utility wares), Pantera weavers, as well as local Brong-, Guan-, and Senufo-speaking miners, traders, artisans, and farmers. Such networks have been demonstrated in the archaeological record of the Brong areas in the form of local sites for the mass manufacture of metal wares, pottery, spindle whorls and textiles, beads, and ivory, and by the wide distributions of pottery and smoking pipe forms and decorations both within and outside of the areas in which they originated. In addition, from the sixteenth to seventeenth centuries, evidence of intensifying cultural and/or economic relations with forest and coastal communities is attested both in the ethnohistoric record and in the distribution of copper and brass casting technology (evidenced by brass casting crucibles), European glass beads, gold weights, and ceramic styles in the Brong-Ahafo region and at southern sites such as Mampongten, Ahinsan, Asebu, Twifo Hemang, Dawu, and Ayawaso. Oral traditions report that exchanges between neighboring and distant communities were generally conducted by individual retailers and distributors, who traveled along footpaths to nearby production centers to obtain their goods.

In the southern Akan areas, the ethnoarchaeological record suggests that while early-second-millennium communities largely engaged in localized or village-based production activities, between the thirteenth and sixteenth centuries both Akan- and non-Akan-speaking groups appear to have become increasingly interdependent for foodstuffs, equipment, and luxury goods. Oral traditions in Adanse identify several settlements that specialized in iron smelting and smithing for the state, as well as a number of gold mining villages. In Fanteland, ethnohistoric and archaeological research indicates that towns such as Amanwa, Beifikrom, and Yabiew engaged in iron, and later, ceramic manufacture for nearby settlements. Oral traditions emphasize the early importance attached to the salt, fishing, and gold mining industries. Salt and fish are documented as having been exported by Eguafo, Komenda, and Efutu (among others), who supplied both the other Fante states and inland Akan or Guan groups in the Wassa, Adanse, and Brong regions. Other coastal communities specialized in such crafts as bead making (Edina) and canoe building (Komenda). Between the fifteenth and seventeenth centuries, archaeological and ethnohistorical accounts depict ongoing trade relations between neighboring forest and coastal communities, which, as in the north, transcended ethnolinguistic as well as geographical boundaries. Coastal and plains populations such as the Shai-La, Gã, Ewe, Fante, and Agona exported their goods for the stone tools, vegetable goods, ivory, gold, and brasswares produced at forest settlements, as well as the luxury wares obtained via the Brong through the Islamic trade. In the southeast, the Shai and La exported cattle, cotton cloths, pottery, salt, fish, and mollusks (often used as lime for whitewash in Akanland) to neighboring forest and coastal settlements in the Accra Plains and Akuapem Hills. In the Akuapem Hills, researchers have located and investigated several Guan towns, including Kyerepong-Dawu, Abiriw, and Larteh-Amanfo (all overshadowed by Akwamu or Akuapem after the mid-seventeenth century) that engaged in specialist production and trade with nearby regions. The Dawu midden mound excavations yielded over a half million pottery sherds (many with characteristic Shai decorations), brass crucibles, casting moulds and ornaments, ivory carved bracelets and combs, numerous spindle whorls, smoking pipes, beads of glass, bone, and shell, several gold weights, a gold ornament, and fifteen terracotta figurines.

After the sixteenth century, the archaeological record of the forest and coast demonstrates a major shift in patterns of ceramic manufacture and distribution, whereby the previously coarse-pasted, simply formed and decorated vessels whose fabrics and styles varied locally were replaced by elaborately shaped and decorated wares whose styles were largely homogenous over wide geographical or cultural areas. Shai pottery, previously confined to the Shai Hills, is distributed at post-sixteenth-century sites throughout the Accra Plains, Agona, and the adjacent forested Akwapem Hills and Akwamu regions. In the southwest, many Fante towns appear to have shifted from iron to ceramic specialization, although the precise distribution of their wares remains to be fully explored. In the forest, several Akan regions, most notably Wassa, Kwahu, Tafo, Ekaase (Adanse), and Akyem became widely known as gold mining centers, while others focused on iron smelting and smithing, ivory collection and carving, bead manufacture, brass casting, farming, hunting, and gathering.

In addition to the above, many forest and coastal communities also participated in an interregional east-west network, which linked production and market centers along the coast between modern Côte d'Ivoire and Nigeria, or what was known to Europeans as the Ivory and Slave Coasts, respectively. The Akan and other southern groups exchanged gold, ivory, cotton, and ivory for textiles woven in Côte d'Ivoire, Benin, Whydah (Dahomey), Ardra (Togo), and beads, leopard skins, and slaves from Benin. This network was documented by the Portuguese, who quickly established themselves as middlemen, expanding the flow of goods as far as Cape Verde. Subsequent writers frequently referred to the coastal trade, particularly the enormous demand for such luxury items as fine textiles and Benin's slaves and akorri beads. Little evidence for this trade is doc-

umented in the archaeological record, however; most of the commodities consisted of perishable items, and researchers suggest that
like copper and brasswares, gold, akorri, and other precious beads
are unlikely to have been buried or abandoned.

Regional Units, Trade, Ethnicity, and Material Culture

A critical issue in the study of Akan exchange networks is the impact of cross-cultural contacts and interactions on the material
record. On a larger scale, a number of researchers have explored
the influence of the Sudanic trade on Akan cultural development,
drawing attention to the links between Malian and Akan arts and
technologies. Archaeologists such as McIntosh and Posnansky have
observed parallels between the mud-brick, flat-roofed architecture
predominant in the Brong region and the building methods and
forms of the Western Sudan, and several of the items included
among Akan regalia are also believed to derive from the Mali area.
Ceramic discs from centers such as Begho and Dawu have been
found to conform within a few tenths of a gram to the mitkal and
wakia gold weight systems popularly used at Timbuktu and Jenne.
Ivory side-blown trumpets—found in sixteenth-century contexts at
Begho and on the Mozambique coast (Sofala)—are mentioned in
fourteenth-century Arabic references to Malian and Somalian
courts, and date to the seventeenth century at Benin. Islamic brass
vessels were also incorporated into Akan regalia; they are distributed among over more than a dozen sites in the Brong and Asante
areas, where they are venerated as sacred objects. Although they
appear to have entered central Asante after the conquest of the
northern states, most of the Brong settlements with which they are
associated maintain strong traditions of involvement in the Islamic
trade, and analyses of Arabic inscriptions on the vessels have revealed that all are of Syrio-Egyptian (Mamluk) manufacture, and
date between the fourteenth and mid-fifteenth centuries. Researchers speculate that Muslim traders, who used them for performing ritual ablutions, first brought such vessels into the area, and
that the Brong, having observed their ritualized function, incorpo-

rated them into their own spiritual systems. Some researchers have observed stylistic affinities between the Mamluk and later Malian cire perdue cast vessels and those of the Akan; the Syrio-Egyptian bowls, boxes and basins are postulated as prototypes for the early *kuduo* forms, and Malian features such as an emphasis on abstract geometric motifs, including segments of concentric lines, bells and cowries, or twisted cords, are often reproduced in the early Akan brass vessels. Perhaps even more intriguing are the similarities observed between the forms and motifs of Malian brassware and those of Late Iron Age pottery found at sites associated with both Akan- and non-Akan-speaking groups. The shift at many sites from the earlier, free flowing, sparsely but variably decorated wares to the later burnished, ornately decorated pottery with angular, pedestalled, and ring-based forms has been correlated with the southerly advance of Mande traders, which is believed to have inspired local attempts to copy the shapes of brass vessels from the Islamic world. In northern sites in the Gonja, Brong, and Banda areas, this shift occurs during the fifteenth and sixteenth centuries, while in the south, they are not found until late-sixteenth- to early-seventeenth-century levels, and even later at sites isolated from major road systems. Despite such parallels, however, the later Akan brass and ceramic wares possessed a number of distinguishing features, such as the use of pictographic proverbs as opposed to Arabic script, and even more significantly, the use of figurative art, including masks, goldweights, and applied polymorphic figures.

Although scholars have long been fascinated with the cultural effects of the Islamic trade, results obtained from recent archaeological investigations suggest that local or intraregional exchanges were equally significant forces in Akan development. It has already been noted that Akan populations did not occupy homogenous areas, but rather participated in a diverse cultural landscape. In the north, the Brong interacted with the Dangme-Krobo-, Guan-, Senufo-, and Mo- as well as Mande-speaking peoples, while the southern Akan mingled with Shai-La- (Adangme), Gã-, Guan-, Ewe-, and Bia-speaking peoples, among others. While in some cases, other populations were eliminated through slave raids or warfare, the

Akan polities also absorbed and borrowed from neighboring cultures. Ethnographic studies link features associated with the Akan ritual system, such as the calendar, with that still used by many Guan-speaking communities, and Guan, Gã, Adangme, and Ewe peoples adopted aspects of Akan regalia, religion, vocabulary, and music, sometimes adding their own meanings, but maintaining traditions of their imported nature. In areas such as the Akwapem Hills, the shift from Guan to Akan dialects has been traced at several towns, such as Akropong, formerly known as Kyerepong. While the "Akanization" of many communities is attributed largely to Akan—particularly Akwamu and Asante—conquests, the ethnoarchaeological record also indicates that Akan and other "local" groups engaged in mutual cultural exchanges. Items associated with Akan regalia, such as terracotta portraits and ivory ornaments, are widely and diversely distributed in the archaeological record, yet so too are products originating among the Shai, Krobo, and Mo potters, Akan and Guan sculptors and carvers, and Pantera and Akan weavers. In many cases, trade networks have masked the direction of cultural influences in the archaeological record, and unlike northern Muslim-dominated areas such as New Buipe, the ethnic diversity of Akan-occupied communities and regions is often obscured by relatively homogenous artifact assemblages. Yet, despite such overlaps, it remains possible for archaeologists to identify some stylistic boundaries, particularly in ceramic forms and decorations. Ethnoarchaeological investigations suggest that while red-glazed vessels predominate at communities or sites associated with largely Grusi-Mo-, Shai-La- or Guan-speaking populations, Akan and Gã pottery is generally black-burnished, if at all. Ethnographic studies of Mo potters demonstrate that they often catered to local preferences, rarely sending red-slipped, maize-stamped wares into the Brong markets. One issue that has not been adequately addressed is the links between such distinctions and cultural beliefs and practices of the peoples with whom they are associated. Ethnographic investigations, however, have often explored the ritual connotations associated with red in Akan cultures, in which the color is linked to notions regarding gender, sexuality, death, and birth. It is notable that at many Akan archaeological sites, *mmukyia* (sg. *bukyia*), or hearth pots, are among the only vessels containing red-slip or remnants of red-slipping. Such apparently minor stylistic variations may be related to more profound cultural and material distinctions, the understanding of which may yet aid researchers in identifying continuities in the archaeological record.

Roads and Patterns of Akan Interaction and Exchange

A final topic related to the study of Akan exchange networks concerns the role of roads (*nkwan*) in the development of patterns of interaction and material and cultural exchange. Roads, paths, and tracks have played a critical role in Akan cultural history. Akan oral traditions emphasize the role of paths and tracks in linking neighboring communities, as well as the significance of pathways and "streets" in structuring early clan and community relations both within and between settlements. Bono Manso and Adansemanso were both reputed to have 177 major streets, and Abankesieso and Kumase were famed for their 77 streets. At Bono Manso, Effah-Gyamfi uncovered the outlines of a number of streets (including the horse paths used by parading royalty), as well as the beginnings of several major routes leading from the capital. Within Akan settlements, paths served to organize lineage ties and delineate social statuses. Outside the settlement, roads, trails, and paths delineated relations between humans and both the natural and social worlds. Forest trails and paths provided access to a vast array of economic and cultural resources, such as streams, rivers, wild crops, and game. Bush tracks linked settlements to sources of water and farms, and on a larger scale, even formal routes often incorporated, rather than avoided, natural features. Roads and paths were also conduits to the supernatural realm, aligning with cemeteries, shrines, and sacred trees, streams, and caves, and serving to structure ceremonial interactions and ritual practices. A number of Akan towns and villages had names associated with roads, including Kwantonpenmu (Kintampo), Nkwantanan Abodum (Birim Valley), and Longoro Nkwanta (Bono Manso area), and there were also proverbs and

suman (symbolic representations of natural forces [*abosom*] associated with roads or road features). One of these was the *nkwantanan*, "the place of the four crossroads," which marked the ultimate
boundary of a settlement and the beginnings of the major footpaths
or roads that led out of it. The *nkwantanan* was among the most important features of both villages and towns; it was believed to be a
site of great spiritual power, dedicated towards the repulsion of both
supernatural and human invaders.

Within Akan settlement systems, networks of routes linked communities, production and commercial centers, and political capitals,
facilitating the flow of goods and information. While minor footpaths were associated with both villages and towns, major arterial
routes emanated from the dominant political and commercial centers, from which they often radiated to sites hundreds of kilometers
away. Oral traditions assert that roads extended throughout the West
African forest, and ethnohistoric accounts are replete with descriptions of the routes linking the Akan region to the international markets. Major roads used in the Islamic trade have been documented
since the early to mid-fifteenth century. One led northeast from
Begho through Gonja and the Mole-Dagbane markets/states to
Hausaland, while another branched northwest from Begho through
the Dyula towns of Kong and Bobo-Dioulasso en route to the
Mande markets of the Upper Niger, and beyond through the Sahelian and Saharan zones, finally terminating at the North African
ports. These routes, and the connections they represented, are
demonstrated in the ethnoarchaeological record in the distribution
of northern goods and technologies throughout the forest and
coastal areas of Ghana and other "Guinean" regions. They are also
reflected linguistically, in the proliferation of Mande loan elements
from Bono Manso to Elmina, and in the line of Mande-derived languages extending south from the Middle Niger to the Brong-Ahafo
region between Wenchi and Banda.

By the late fifteenth century, foreign travelers had also discovered
a number of southern routes, which linked the Brong towns with
the markets and states of the central forest and coast. One such
"path" was directed from Begho through Ahafo and Twifo

(Denkyira), terminating at the Fante markets in the Edina/Elmina area, while another western route passed through Begho and Wenchi, Tafo, Adanse, and Assin territory, from which it branched to the Cape Coast and nearby beaches. Later, during the sixteenth and seventeenth centuries, merchants also described an easterly route to the Ayawaso/Accra area. Other, less widely documented routes appear to have extended to the east and west, linking forest and coastal producers, markets, and courts between Côte d'Ivoire and Benin. Written and cartographic records from the late fifteenth to the eighteenth centuries portray routes crisscrossing the Lower Guinean Coast, often extending only a few kilometers, but at times linking sites through multiple ecological zones. Access to or control over these routes appears to have been a central factor in the development and maintenance of economic and political power. Centers such as Begho, Bono Manso, and Adansemanso were all located along preexisting trade routes, and oral traditions note that the locations of many prominent towns (e.g., Tafo, Nyanoase, Abankesieso, and Kumase) were chosen for their proximity to the northern and West African networks. Groups such as the Akwamu and the Asante were able to flourish based on the control exerted over trade routes in occupied territories. The Asante developed a road network encompassing its entire territory, both incorporating the ancient systems and adding new branches in order to link the state as a unit to the markets and courts of the outside world.

Previous research on pre-colonial Akan road use has primarily been limited to issues related to its political and economic roles, namely in the expansion and administration of hegemony and the facilitation of trade with foreign agents. While such studies are informative, in order to obtain a fuller understanding it is necessary to expand this perspective to include more information on their wider socio-cultural significance. Among the Akan societies, roads were neither used for nor conceived of in purely functional terms. Roads did not merely facilitate political and economic interactions; they also served to mediate and manifest socio-cultural and supernatural relationships. A few researchers have traced the spread of cultural influences along roads, particularly the dissemination of

Mande cultural and linguistic elements, which is observable along the routes between the Middle Niger, Brong-Ahafo, and Tafo-Kumase region. On a smaller scale, in the southeast, Ozanne has noted correlations between the distribution of terracotta figurines and smoking pipe and pottery styles along trade routes incorporating Akan-, Gã-, Dangme-, and Guan-speaking populations between the coast and the forest. Towns such as Dawu, Nyanoase, Agona, and Ladoku occupied key positions along the roads, serving as centers for the spread of cultural materials and ideas as well as wealth accumulation. Ethnoarchaeological studies of other regional trade distribution patterns provide hints of similar networks in other Akan-occupied areas, yet few scholars have examined the effect of such relationships in the material record.

Conclusion: Prospects for Future Research

After over a century of anthropological research, scholars have made significant contributions to the expanding body of knowledge regarding the Akan past. Ethnolinguistic studies have traced aspects of earlier language and cultural development, as well as later patterns of ethnolinguistic change. Archaeologists have examined the material record representing Akan history, elucidating features and conditions related to the emergence of farming and village life, the expansion of urbanism and states, and Akan participation in regional and long-distance trade networks. Yet chronological and temporal frameworks remain incomplete, and while some populations and time periods have been thoroughly documented, our knowledge of others remains hazy and obscure, patchily reconstructed from a foundation of largely speculative rather than material evidence.

Most of the problems limiting our perspective of the Akan past are related to issues of scale. A multiscalar landscape approach is crucial to the achievement of a more holistic view of Akan cultural history. For one, researchers must increase efforts to document relatively obscure temporal phases, such as the period between 500 BCE and 500 CE, as well as under-examined ecological or cultural zones, such as the central "Akan" forests. The period between the end of the Kintampo Complex and the Early Iron Age was a critical juncture in Akan development, representing the transformation of Volta-Komóe peoples from apparently broadly homogenous cultural groupings to more regionally distinctive ethnolinguistic formations. The lack of information regarding this time period seriously hinders any attempts to reconstruct Akan "origins" and early social organization. The earliest Akan sites appear as fully developed manifestations, relatively easily linked to later cultural groups, yet providing little basis on which to gain an understanding of the nature and causes of the socio-cultural processes that are reflected in their emergence in the material record during the first millennium CE. Establishing links between the Kintampo Complex and the Early Iron Age in the archaeological record is an important step in documenting this transition, thus providing a material basis to evaluate linguistic theories regarding Akan origins and early patterns of ethnolinguistic fragmentation.

The central forest, particularly the Adanse area, one of the core regions of Akan cultural development, is another neglected area of investigation. Archaeological research has long been hindered by the humid climate and dense vegetation, yet studies such those in Asante and Adanse and at Twifo Hemang indicate that, with the aid of ethnographic surveys, it may be possible to locate and examine many more sites than previously attempted. Other areas, such as the Begho area and the Fante coast and plains, have been more widely documented; however, scholars have often tended to focus on changes associated with long distance trade activities, particularly the Trans-Saharan and Atlantic networks, rather than on local or regionally based patterns of development.

On the other end of the scale, portrayals of many aspects Akan prehistory have been limited by the site-based nature of many investigations. Archaeologists have often concentrated on internal developments at scattered locations, usually major market or political centers, rather than on the temporal, economic, or socio-cultural connections that bound most communities. Yet, as we have seen, Akan communities did not exist in isolation; most were a part of larger regional units united by bonds of socio-cultural and economic interdependence. It is important to engage in more regionally based studies of Akan history and development, expanding the scope of analysis beyond single urban centers to examine broader Akan patterns of interaction, continuity, and change. Such an endeavor would involve both more detailed analyses of "internal," exclusively "Akan" developments, as well as more attempts to trace the nature and effects of Akan encounters with other ethnolinguistic groups. It is necessary to devote more attention to the exploration of temporal and cultural connections between Akan settlements or populations and those of groups such as the Guan, who appear to have preceded and/or coexisted in small but consistently dispersed numbers throughout both the northern and southern Akan areas. In ethnographic surveys, Guan-speaking populations have been identified as Akan predecessors in areas such as Asante/Adanse, Bono, Akyem, Akwapem, and Kwahu, encouraging some scholars to associate this more "indigenous" group with the makers of earthworks ware as well as some Kintampo Complex assemblages. The Brong system of clan and street names has been linked to Guan practices, as have the office of *okyeame* ("linguist, diplomat") and key features of the Akan calendar. While a few linguists have attempted to trace the origins and dispersals of the Guan, archaeologists have yet to engage in any detailed, regionally based examination of the Guan material record. Thus, current reconstructions have generally been based primarily on ethnographic information, with little supporting evidence presented from the material record. Yet, the archaeological record has clearly demonstrated that incoming Akan populations did often encounter or succeed other linguistic and cultural groups, and that, in many cases, earlier inhabitants, including the Guan, were not simply displaced or destroyed, but rather were absorbed into the socio-political fabric of the Akan societies. Some, such as the Dumpo near Begho or the Kyerepong of Dawu and Awukugua, managed to maintain their own languages, while others shifted to Akan dialects, thus helping to obscure their origins, yet nonetheless exerting profound influences on Akan economic and cultural development.

Lastly, another topic underemphasized in Akan cultural history is the use of roads in providing linkages between Akan communities, polities, and regions. While a number of historians have explored the political and economic advantages of roads, most archaeologists have devoted little attention to trade routes, and even less to the broader socio-cultural meanings of roads. Yet, as Ozanne has demonstrated, a more detailed examination of Akan routes might prove enormously beneficial in constructing culture-historical scenarios regarding issues such as migration, conquest, and material and culture exchange, providing tangible evidence of socio-cultural as well as political relationships across time and space. Roads connect certain points or features on the landscape in ways demonstrating aspects of organization on the political, social, ritual, economic, and individual levels. Even as Akan towns existed as centers for the dissemination of goods and ideas, roads served as conduits for these interactions, a physical manifestation of both past and present connections that linked individuals, communities, centers, and regions. Roads also embodied ritual connotations, establishing and representing avenues of access to—as well as protection from—the material and spiritual realms. By incorporating archaeological research on roads with the available written, cartographic, and ethnographic sources, scholars may be able to achieve more detailed reconstructions of both ancient and later patterns of activity and movement in the landscapes occupied by Akan-speaking peoples.

Archaeology is becoming a crucial tool in the reconstruction of Akan cultural history. Yet, previous investigations have often been limited in scope, usually isolating single populations or cultural groups from broader Akan cultural contexts, and frequently examining stages rather than processes of Akan development. A landscape approach could prove enormously valuable in reconstructing patterns manifested in the archaeological record of both individual sites and regional units, helping scholars elucidate broader Akan patterns of socio-cultural organization and activity as well as postulate more detailed connections and distinctions between various geographic and/or ethnolinguistic groupings. In order to achieve a more holistic portrait of Akan cultural history, we must examine not single scales of time, space or culture, but multiple levels of conception, activity, agency, and expression.

— 2 —

History in the Oral Traditions of the Akan

KWAME DAAKU

Focusing on the theme of historical content within oral traditions, the late Kwame Daaku offers an account of his approach as a field historian to the writing of Akan histories through oral "traditional" sources. He reveals to the reader the devices the Akan (have) use(d) to record and recall their histories.

An area of nearly a mile in circumference was crowded with magnificence and novelty. The king, his tributaries and captains were resplendent in the distance surrounded by attendants of every description fronted by a mass of warriors. . . . The sun was reflected with a glare scarcely more supportable than the heat from the massy gold ornaments which glistened in every direction.

More than a hundred bands burst out at once on our arrival with the peculiar airs of their several chiefs. The horns flourished their defiance and the beating of the innumerable drums and metal instruments and then yielding for a while to the soft breathings of their long flutes, which were truly harmonious, and a pleasing instrument like the bagpipe without the drone was happily blended. At least a hundred large umbrellas or canopies which could shelter thirty persons were sprung up and down by

bearers with brilliant effect, being made of scarlet, yellow
and most showy cloths and silks, and crowned on the top
with crescents, pelicans, elephants, barrels, arms and
swords of gold.

The above description [by British envoy Thomas E. Bowdich] may
apply to a durbar of chiefs, especially Akan chiefs, in any part of
modern Ghana. The umbrella tops, the drums, horns, gold-plated
linguist staffs and all that Bowdich saw in 1817 were telling stories
and eloquently depicting the heroic deeds of the departed ancestors.
Before him a visiting Dutch delegation under Huydecoper had also
been accorded a similar impressive welcome. Nor was this only a
feature of Asante court. In the earlier centuries European delega-
tions to African rulers had also been fittingly welcomed. John
Konny of Ahanta received a Dutch delegation in the 1710s with
several soldiers forming a guard of honor, and amidst drumming
and dancing. The kings of Akwamu and Denkyira had also been
known to have fittingly welcomed their guests. On the coast, one
of the occasions that the Europeans looked forward to was the annual dance festival of the Fetu, to which they were usually invited.
And as far back as 1482, the ruler of Elmina had treated the Portuguese governor, Diego de Azambuja, to a similar welcome when
he arrived to negotiate for land on which to build their castle.

During such orderly and impressive ceremonies or durbars, history is literally and figuratively outdoored. At such times E. H.
Carr's definition of history as "that undying dialogue between the
present and the past" truly finds expression among the Akans. This
periodic reliving or reenactment of the past enables people to learn
the general outlines of the history of the whole state. It must, however, be pointed out that such festivals are not only a feature of the
Akan states; many African peoples such as the Yoruba, the Bakuba,
the Baganda, to mention but a few, hold festivals in one form or the
other in which the past is vividly brought into the minds of the living. The Masai and the Embu of East Africa also have elaborate ceremonies in initiating age sets and generation groups. From all
accounts these periodic festivals have had a long history going back

to the very foundations of the states. For the past to be scrupulously reenacted, these societies have devised many methods to aid them in the transmission of their traditions. In all the preliterate African societies these traditions were handed down by word of mouth with a number of mnemonic devices. Let me define what I mean by oral tradition. By this I mean any stories designed to teach the history of a people, which are passed on by word of mouth. Oral traditions have been the main method of teaching the history of many African peoples, and it is by studying them that the Africans' view of themselves and their relations with their neighbors may be understood and appreciated.

It must be admitted that in the past two decades African history has traveled an appreciably long way. It has progressed from the period when one eminent British historian could describe Africa as sleeping for several centuries "forgotten of the world and by the world forgotten." Since 1964, when Professor Trevor Roper expressed surprise that undergraduates should ask to be taught African history, which to him is nothing but "darkness" or, at best, "the unrewarding gyrations of barbarous tribes in picturesque but irrelevant corners of the globe," research in African history has been advanced in several areas. What is surprising about Trevor Roper's "surprise" is not the fact that the eminent professor was ignorant of African history as such but his dangerous assumption that there could ever be any group of people anywhere in the world without any sense of their history. It is not unlikely that Trevor Roper's dismay over students' demands to be taught African history stems from his uncomfortable realization that his pet idea, held by many of his kind, that history is "primarily a concern with the tracing and development of Western Civilization," is no longer tenable.

It is the object of this paper to show how the Akan of Ghana preserved and still preserve their history. Although the Akan model cannot be directly applied to other African groups, a knowledge of the devices they have adopted to record and to recall their past can help to determine where to look for the history of other preliterate groups. The Akan form about half of the total population of modern Ghana. They are essentially matrilineal. The basic social organization is the family. They are organized in eight principal exogamous clans. Politically they are monarchical, each town or village having its own chief. The various chiefs owe allegiance to a superior chief who is the head of the *Oman,* or state. This is the *Omanhene* or Paramount chief. The most important symbol of authority of the Akan is the stool, and certainly the best known of these stools and the most revered is the Golden stool of Asante.

Most, if not all, of the Akan states have a tradition of having developed their institutions of chieftaincy and their culture in Adanse. In Akan mythology it is where God started creation. This fact is well enshrined in their drum music. Thus on festive days the talking drums of the chiefs beat the refrain: Noble Ruler, you hail from Adanse where the creator created things.

Among the several devices adopted to preserve their history and tradition may be mentioned the pouring of libations, the music of the drums and horns, the creation of special linguist staffs, oaths, songs, proverbs, and funeral dirges. To a people who settle most disputes by having recourse to history it is of supreme importance that members of the various families and clans tell their stories to their young for, as they aptly put it, "Tete ka asom ene Kakyere," that is, ancient things remain in the ears, which means traditions survive only by telling them. Again their respect for history is made explicit in the frequent assertion that "Tete are ne nne," i.e., the very same ancient things are today, or history repeats itself.

One of the devices for preserving traditions, especially those of rulers, is by making stools for departed chiefs. On the death of a chief his favorite stool is blackened and kept in a special stool room. The room is usually under the charge of a court official, the *Nkondwasoafohene,* head of the stool bearers. He is expected to know the chronological order in which the stools are arranged in the room. On each fortieth Sunday, the *Akwasidae,* libation is poured by the chief and his elders on the stools. On such occasions the names of all the ancestor chiefs who died in office are mentioned with their special attributes and bynames. This among other things enables the chief to remember all the departed ancestors. It is from these stools that one can have an accurate list of kings who had reigned previously. It is interesting to note that libation is poured on all-important occasions when the chief and his councilors feel the need to invoke the guidance and blessings of the ancestors. Stools are also created for all the important councilors of state and heads of clans. When pouring libations, chiefs attempt to summarize the history of the people. Not only the departed ancestors, but also all the principal tutelary deities are also called upon and the beliefs and norms of the people reiterated and reaffirmed. A chief may call upon his ancestors and gods [i.e., *abosom*] in the following manner:

> Lord God omnipotent, drink,
> Mother Earth, whose day of rest is Thursday, drink,
> Great Deity Bonsam, drink,
> Nana Agya Ananse Obooman (destroyer of towns)
> Nana Yeboa Asuama, etc., drink.

From such a short libation one will be able to learn much. Let us take the name Agya Ananse Obooman. Agya Ananse was the most famous of the captains of the king of Denkyira. Because of his many successful wars he earned for himself the appellation Obooman, destroyer of towns. From the words of a libation the historian may have a good start with his informants. Explanations of phrases used always lead to the unfolding of the history of the town or state. Libations tend to underline the important landmarks in the traditional history. Names and events that people want to hide from the researcher are freely mentioned on such occasions.

Another important and certainly one of the most sacrosanct devices in recording history and aiding memory is through the institution and the use of oaths. Oaths are normally instituted to commemorate calamities or national disasters, events such as defeats in war, sudden and unexpected deaths, epidemics and other events. Oaths may, therefore, be defined as the public repetition of such disasters. It is believed that unless the spirits of the ancestors are properly atoned, the dead would take revenge when such disasters are mentioned. One may therefore invoke a public oath only to show the seriousness of a cause. This is often done when people are disputing over something. The complainant may invoke a chief's oath and on the strength of it will force their dispute to be heard in public. All important chiefs have their own oath in addition to state or national oaths. When citizens do not get satisfaction from a lower court they may invoke the oath of a higher chief and thereby remove their case to a superior court. From the historian's point of view the importance of the oaths lies in the fact that the people know precisely the events which these oaths commemorate and how and when they came about. Some of the popular oaths are the *Ntam Kese Mmiensa* and the *Koromante Memenada* of Asante. The former commemorates the deaths of Opoku Ware's father and his two brothers while the latter was instituted when Osei Tutu, the founder of Asante, was killed on a Saturday in the Asante War against Akyem in 1717. The Denkyira have the oath *Benada ne Denkyira*—Tuesday and Denkyira—which commemorates the day they were defeated by the Asantes.

Closely related with the oaths may be mentioned the music of the short horns and drums. Both usually are played to sound the motto of a chief. In most cases these mottoes are adopted either after victory or defeat in wars. Examples from Assin may well illustrate the importance of these mottoes. The early settlers in Assin are known as the Eti. In the course of the sixteenth and eighteenth centuries, the Etis were overrun by the Fanti who later were followed by some Asante immigrants. The Eti are now subjects of the Fanti and Asante immigrants who are presently known as the Assins. Although the immigrants and the aborigines are now mixed, and speak the same Twi dialect, they still observe different festivals and try to show their political, social, and economic differences in various ways, as is exemplified in the following messages. The horns and short drums of the Eti usually sound the flourish:

> *Firi tete, firi tete; yenka nkyere mo! Borebore Fanti betoo*
>   *Eti, Eti koronkoron.*
> 'Tis of old, 'tis of old, let it be known Bobore Fanti came
>   to meet the Eti, the true and holy Eti.

And one will not have to seek far for the truth of this, to which the political and social organization bears eloquent testimony. The Assins in particular still look back nostalgically on the gold-rich land from which they were ousted by the Asantes. Their feeling still runs through the short message of the *Omamhene* of Assin Attandansu when these words are sounded *Assin gyamenanpon Ahia yen, ahia henyinaa,* "*Assin gyamenampon,* we are reduced to utter poverty," or *Dee oyee me, dee oyee me, dabi meye no bi,* "He who brought this on me must know I shall take my revenge one day." With this music of short drum and horn pieces it is easier for the historian to ask fruitful questions to learn the causes of migrations, and the political set-up in such a society. For although the Assin wield the political power, economically many of them depend on their Eti subjects who own most of the land. Perhaps no written document could well illustrate this plight better than the beautifully made gold-plated linguist staff of one of the important Assin chiefs, Assin Nyankomasi, which depicts the spider that has taken refuge on a ceiling. According to the chief this symbol shows how the once powerful and wise king now owns nothing but lives on the charity of others. It is interesting to note that the traditions of Adanse, the former home of the Assins, bear testimony to the latter's former glory. In Denkyira the short drum of the paramount chiefs beats the motto "Kotoko Som Amponsem," that is, the Porcupine (Asante) is subject to Boa Amponsem, the King of Denkyira, to show that Asante was once a tributary to Denkyira.

In addition to all these devices must be mentioned the all too important drum, the Talking Drum. In the Akan set-up the one who plays the drum is among the most privileged, and is certainly the most knowledgeable person with regard to the traditional history. Popularly known as the *Odomankoma Kyerema,* the Divine or Creator's drummer, the drummer was believed to be one of the earliest functionaries at the court of the king, and this he himself proclaims on his drum in this way.

Odomankoma boo adee,
Borebore boo adee,

Oboo deeben?
Oboo Esen,
Oboo Kyerema,
Oboo Kwawuo,
Oboo Kwabrafo titire.

When the creator created things,
When the manifold creator created things,
What did he create?
He created the court crier,
He created the Drummer,
He created the Principal State Executioner.

The court crier maintains order and is sent on several errands, and in addition he also recites praise poems at court to show the power and reputation of the king. The drummer of the Talking Drums is expected to be able to call on the names of all the ancestor chiefs in their chronological order, calling on their bynames, telling of the noble deeds and of the places of origin. In addition he must know the appellations of the elders of the chiefs, and be able to call their proper names and use the appropriate words which go with them whenever thay take the floor to dance on important occasions. In short, the principal drummer may be very well described as the chief historian of the state. Among other things the drummer of Denkyira may give messages such as these on any *Akwasidae* festival. Very early in the morning he calls the names of the first drummer of the state to bid good morning to the chief and the people in the following words:

Amponsa Saamoa se oma wo akye, aku,
    oma wo akye abraw amu.
Amponsa Saamoa bids all of you good morning.

After going through the bynames of the chief, the drummer may recite the attributes and the symbolisms of the state, to show the power of the ruler and his position in the whole state. Here I will give only a few examples:

Moma yenkom a Odikoro, akye,
Moma yenkom a Obirempon akye,
Odikoro mawo adwa a tena so
Obirempon ma wo adwa a tena so
Na Obirempon na oman wo no koronkoron, koronkoron.

Let's go say good morning to the chief,
When the noble one gives you a seat take it,
For it is to the noble one that the state belongs.

A second example:

Adawu, Adawu Denkyira menesono,
Yesore a yefre menesono,
Yekoto a yefre menesono,
Obi ntutu mmirika nkohwe Denkyira Meneson,
Menesono da ye a, Wanyane, Wanyane koronkoron.

Let everyone hasten to cast a glimpse on mighty Denkyira,
Denkyira which swallows up whole elephants.
When we kneel down it is to the mighty Denkyira,
When we rise up we look up to Denkyira,
If Denkyira went to sleep it is now awake,
The Swallower of elephants is truly awake.

In these words the drummer brings to mind the once all-important Akan state, which was brought to its knees in 1701 by the rising Asante. In spite of the defeat, the drummer still calls on these by-names and symbolisms to show and honor the state. Interestingly it is not only the drummer of the states who gives these attributes to Denkyira; in some of the songs of the hunter's association the name of Denkyira as an all-powerful and all-conquering state is frequently mentioned. Today, as of old, it is not uncommon for a successful

elephant hunter after he has shot an elephant in his moments of ela-
tion to burst out into the following strain:

> Duedu Akwa, Father Duedu Duben, Oben and Denkyira,
>   trier-of-Death
> The Hunter has done well!
> The Hunter deserves to be congratulated.

In killing the elephant, then, one can well compare himself to the
once powerful Denkyira.

It will be a mistake to assume that all historical traditions of the
Akans are court-centered. Admittedly the chief as the principal political agent who is also at the very center of the social organization
is expected to know and to preserve all the important traditions of
the state. At the same time it is expected of every citizen to be able
to recount the history of his clan and family. Whoever is unable to
quote history and traditions to support his claim to particular property, especially to land, may soon see his patrimony taken away by
one who can make a better historical claim. And in social situations
such as funeral celebrations, history is also constantly invoked. It
is in the funeral dirges of the Akan that every citizen's knowledge
of history is very much put to the test. A good mourner must know
of the dead ancestors of the departed friend or relation and, like the
drummer at court, be able to tell from where one first originated,
and what he was able to achieve in life. Dirges, then, may be defined
as "traditional expressions stored up in the minds of individuals and
recreated by them in appropriate contexts."

Among the Akans each clan has its own dirge forms which are
sung in times of death, and these invariably trace the deeds of the
dead person to those of the founding ancestor. On the death of a
member of the Bretuo clan, especially a royal of the Bretuo of Gya-
mase in Asante, the dirges usually end with the following words:

> Noble Adu Gyamfi said,
> He was going to vanquish the thousand and the mighty
> The results of his exploits would be

Displayed in the capital (Kumasi) during the *Akwasidae*
Noble Adu Gyamfi, who made Kumasi wear gold nuggets
Adu Gyamfi's grandchild hails from Wonoo.

This dirge sums up the exploits of Adu Gyamfi, who played a
significant role in the conquest of the gold-rich state of Bono-Taky-
iman in the 1720s. For a member of the Dwamuana lineage, the
following dirge may be heard at his funeral.

Grandchild of Minta that hails from Dunkesease.
Grandchild of Obeeko Asamoa that hails from Bonkaben.
Grandchild of Obiyaa that hails from Aborodesu,
Grandchild of Otu that drinks water trickling down the rock
Grandchild of Yeboa Oko, the offspring of a Tia man . . .
Grandchild of Ohene Kwabena that hails from the cave in
    the rock
If he is going back to the cave, we should not prevent him
for it is his place of origin.

The above dirge not only mentions the last habitat of the deceased, but takes it to the cave where his ancestors were supposed
to have lived. In 1701 Denkyira was defeated at Feyiase by Osei
Tutu of Asante. This defeat led to the dispersal of the members of
the Agona to many parts of Ghana. Feyiase then marked a new era
for the Agona. It marked the nadir of their political fortunes, and is
therefore an event always remembered with sorrow. The following
dirge sums up what Denkyira was like, when and where it fell [:]

Ntim Gyakari, the wealthy noble
Who led his Nation to its doom at Feyiase,
Ntim Gyakari's grandchild hails from
Feyiase the field of battle.

In this short dirge, the mourner not only mourns the departed relative but also the tragic ending of the once powerful state of his ancestors, and compares the tragedy which befell Denkyira at Feyiase

where Ntim Gyakari lost his life with the death of the friend, viewed as a similar event for the family of the deceased.

In spite of all these devices, it must be pointed out that the Akan historian is always faced with a number of problems. The most obvious is one of dating. Although the stools and king list may tell of the number of kings, the Akan, like other African peoples, is primarily interested in events. His concept of time, like that of the Bakuba, is not mathematical but based on ecological facts or structural recurrences, such as droughts, periods of epidemics, wars, and reigns. Also the traditions tend to attribute events to a few successful rulers. Warrior kings are always said to have fought all kinds of wars, whilst all laws may emanate from a particular ruler. The Asante attributes most events to Osei Tutu and Opoku Ware, Denkyira to Boa Amponsem and Kwadwo Otibo, and Akwamu to Ansa Sasraku. Although the Akans have an interesting device to record events and count weeks, this is not accurate enough to make any absolute dating possible. In several Akan areas, the priests of the traditional deities perform the work of timekeepers. At Gomua Manso, for instance, there is a state timekeeper who records weeks and months by the use of raffia threads. On every Friday a piece of raffia is tied to the priest's wrist, and the old one removed and hung up in a special room. The Sunday of every sixth week is the *Akwasidae,* when libations are poured to the departed ancestors. These pieces are tied up in groups of six. Eight such bundles make the Akan year. By such means the priest is able to determine the proper time for sowing and harvesting and when annual festivals may be celebrated. It must be admitted that such a device can only show relative but not absolute time. An equally interesting method of counting the length of reign is found in Takyiman.

To supplement these methods of dating and try to arrive at some time near any absolute the traditional historian tries where possible to correlate his recordings with accounts of European traders who had been on the coast since the fifteenth century. When available, Arabic records may be used. And where possible, attempts are made to relate the stories to some well-known events, like the battle of Feyiase, Mankattasa (Macarthy War), Sagranti War, and Sir Garnet

Wolsey's War, locally remembered as *Too too,* the strange sound of the Snider rifle. People also remember such occurrences as epidemics, earthquakes and eclipses, which enable the historian to fix an exact time. It is also in the field of dating that the works of other related disciplines such as linguistics, botany, and archaeology come in handy.

Although oral traditions are strong in reconstructing political and social histories, they are not altogether unhelpful in economic history. Depending on the type of questions the researcher asks, and the type of people he approaches, one is always able to reconstruct any aspect of a traditional history. There are still people who know something about the organization of trade in the precolonial times, what items and currencies were involved and how these were obtained. Indeed some of the proverbs and witty sayings of the people and their popular songs are full of references to social, economic, and political events. There are popular songs about firearms, gunpowder, beads, and blankets of all types, showing where they were made and what values were placed on them. There are also traditions of associations and craftsmen. All these together enable the social and economic historian to attempt a reconstruction of the traditional economic patterns. But like documentary evidence, oral traditions must be treated with care, since they are mainly political and legal testimonies to present what data the narrators want their listeners to hear.

Despite shortcomings, the Akan oral traditions, like similar traditions of other African people, are the best evidence the historian of Africa can employ to understand the Africans and their history. They enable us to understand their ideas and relations with other people. How for instance did the Akan view his relations with the European traders? For an answer one may look into Akan proverbs about foreigners. The Akan realized that the white man was not there for his love of Africans or for any altruistic reasons other than to improve his fortunes. Hence the assertion, "Se ohia nni Abrokyire a anka oburoni ammeketa ne ntoma wo Abihirem" (Had there been no poverty in Europe the white man would not have come to spread his clothes in Africa.) There are several such sayings that may help the historian to understand the people he deals with. In work and at play, means were devised to disseminate knowledge of history. The Akan used methods not very dissimilar from the Bakuba of the Congo who make the study of history a joy for the young. History is passed on through play and songs and thus unconsciously children learn what the society considers must be known by all. Bakuba children "sitting in circles usually around one or more adults, play games enlivened by songs. The children reel off the names of ten animals, birds, plants, chiefs and national heroes of the region." Whenever one is able to give the correct names the people sing a chorus in approval. The slightest misquotation sends one out of the game. Here the most humiliating penalty for one who cannot recite his group's traditions faultlessly is to be made the laughing-stock of the members of the community.

It can be seen that history plays an essential role in the lives of African peoples. Among the Akans it is brought up vividly on special occasions for the citizens to be inspired by the glorious past of their ancestors. On typical festive occasions people rededicate themselves to the ideals of their founding fathers when songs and objects depicting the various phases of their history are shown in public. The umbrella tops tell stories of bravery in wars, the horns defiantly flourish the mottoes of chiefs, and the music of the drums that Bosman described in the seventeenth century as "the most charming Asses Musick that can be imagined" contains phrases which bring the past to the consciousness of the present to serve as inspiration for the future. To the Akan and to many Africans, history must be scrupulously relived in festivals and on many social occasions. . . . To understand the history of the people the historian must be versed in the oral traditions which in many places still remain the vehicle for the transmission of history and all that Africans hold dear.

History of the Gold Coast and Asante

CARL CHRISTIAN REINDORF

*Basel Mission pastor and historian Carl Christian Rein-
dorf produced the first general history of the Gold Coast
peoples written by an African, using a judicious selection
of published and oral sources from "more than two hundred persons of both sexes." Excerpts below, beginning
with a preface aimed at his compatriots, are taken from
his* History of the Gold Coast and Asante *published in
1889 (with a revised English version published in 1895).*

To the Educated Community in the Cold Coast Colony
Dear Friends,

The sole object of this publication is to call the attention of all
you my friends and countrymen to the study and collection of our
history, and to create a basis for a future more complete history of
the Gold Coast. A history is the methodical narration of events in
the order in which they successively occurred, exhibiting the origin
and progress, the causes and effects, and the auxiliaries and tenden-
cies of that which has occurred in connection with a nation. It is, as
it were, the speculum and measur[ing]-tape of that nation, showing
its true shape and stature. Hence a nation not possessing a history
has no true representation of all the stages of its development,
whether it is in a state of progress or in a state of retrogression. In
the place of a written history, tradition, which from antiquity was a

natural source of history, was kept and transmitted regularly by our ancestors to their children in their days. It was not, of course, in uniform theory, but existed and exercised its influence in the physical and mental powers of our people. This important custom of a nation—which our forefathers felt obliged to preserve and transmit from one generation to another, so as to enable us to compare our times with theirs—has, since the dawn of education, been gradually neglected and forgotten. Since then it has been the good fortune of the Gold Coast to possess educated men of powerful mind, who I am sure were well qualified to collect the traditions of their forefathers as a basis for a future history of the Gold Coast. But unfortunately such collections have not been preserved by their successors, but have been left to the memories of the uneducated community. Such a work as writing a history of the Gold Coast would not have been difficult for such of our brethren as the late lamented Rev. William Hansen, and Charles Bannerman, and some others in Fante; they possessed the mental powers which would have enabled them to do it successfully. Unfortunately, however, these lights on the Gold Coast were earned away by death in the prime of life.

A history of the Gold Coast written by a foreigner would most probably not be correct in its statements, he not having the means of acquiring the different traditions in the country and of comparing them with those which he may have gathered from a single individual. Unless a foreigner writes what he witnesses personally, his statements will be comparatively worthless, as it is the case with several accounts of the Gold Coast already published. Hence it is most desirable that a history of the Gold Coast and its people should be written by one who has not only studied, but has had the privilege of initiation into the history of its former inhabitants and writes with true native patriotism.

It is no egotism when I say I have had the privilege of being initiated into, and also possessing a love for, the history of my country. My ancestors on the father's and mother's side belonged to the families of national officiating high priests in Akra [Nkran/Accra] and Christiansborg. And I should have become a priest either of Nai at Akra or Klote at Christiansborg, if I had not been born a mulatto and become a Christian. My worthy grandmother Okako Asase, as in duty bound to her children and grandchildren, used to relate the traditions of the country to her people when they sat around her in the evenings. My education and calling separated me from home, and prevented me from completing the series of these lessons in native tradition. However, in 1860 I felt a craving to spend some days with her, so as to complete it; but she died whilst I was absent from home in Krobo as a catechist. Four years later Rev. Fr. Aldinger asked me to collect traditions for him; but the old lady was dead, and the old people, though possessing a vast store of tradition, refrained from imparting it; so I obtained very little for him. This treatment of the then old people stirred up a greater desire in me to use all available means in my power to collect traditions. From more than two hundred persons of both sexes I obtained what knowledge of the subject I now possess. These traditions I have carefully compared in order to arrive at the truth. The result I now humbly present to the public, to whom I have to suggest a few remarks. If a nation's history is the nation's speculum and measur[ing]-tape, then it brings the past of that nation to its own view, so that the past may be compared with the present to see whether progress or retrogression is in operation; and also as a means of judging our nation by others, so that we may gather instruction for our future guidance. When such is not the case with a nation, no hope can be entertained for better prospects. Keeping this in mind, we shall more clearly understand the necessity of collecting materials for a complete history of the Gold Coast from every source within our reach.

The title chosen for this publication, "History of the Gold Coast and Asante," may be deemed to promise more than I was actually able to give. For, from want of reliable information, the principal and important portion of the Gold Coast, Fante, the land of history, the land of poetry and enlightenment and semi-civilization, could not be treated from its origin. Still I venture to have the book so named in the hope that our brethren and friends on the Gold Coast, both native and European, may possess better sources of information for a history of the Gold Coast, and may, laying aside all prejudice, be induced to unite to bring the history of the Gold Coast to perfection; I deem it impossible for one man unaided to carry out such an important work to perfection. Having described the principal object I have in view in writing this work as a desire to produce a complete history of the Gold Coast, I trust, my friends in Fante, or elsewhere, will cooperate with me in revising, if need be, what I have written, and in assisting me by furnishing additional information, in order that a subsequent edition may be more complete.

Another important subject, besides that of Fante, &c., which ought to be more fully investigated before the work would be complete, is the different conditions and concerns of various European nations on the Gold Coast and their connections with the people there since their establishment in this country. I may also state briefly my object in connecting the history of Asante with that of the Gold Coast. There must be a starting point in writing a history of a nation. If the kingdom of Akra, which appears to have been the first established on the Gold Coast, could have continued and absorbed that of Fante, or been absorbed by the latter, I might have easily obtained the starting point. But both kingdoms having failed and the kingdom of Asante having become the leading and ruling power, a Gold Coast history would not be complete without the history of Asante, as the histories of both countries are so interwoven. Thus my present work carries us from the origin of the different [groups] to the year 1856, i.e. the rebuilding of the town of Osu or Christiansborg, a period of at least three centuries. If, in conjunction with the united efforts of all the educated community of the country and those foreigners who take a special interest in us, we could collect materials of those dark days to complete this pioneer work, that from 1857 up to the present time, some thirty years only, could be easily obtained, as there is sufficient matter already in store for us.

Regarding dates and historical facts, I have made references to such works as I could lay hand upon. The records of the Colonial Government would have furnished me with correct dates and substantial informations, but I was unable to obtain access to them. I am, however, highly thankful to the Rev. P. Steiner for the translation of some pages from the following work into German, viz.: W. J. Muller, Danish chaplain in Frederiksborg (now Fort Victoria) near

Cape Coast Castle from 1662-1670, published in Hamburg, 1673, and in Nürnberg, 1675; Fr. Romer, a Danish merchant in Christiansborg from 1735-43, published at Copenhagen, 1769; Dr. P. E. Isert, Copenhagen, 1788; H. C. Monrad, a Danish Chaplain in Christiansborg from 1805 to 1809, Weimar, 1824; Dr. O. Dapper's *Africa*. The short history of the Bremen Mission was kindly given me by the Rev. G. Binetsch, of the North German or Bremen Mission on the Slave Coast.

Besides those, I have got the following works in English: William Bosman, *A new and accurate Description of the Coast of Guinea, [divided] into the Gold, the Slave, and the Ivory Coasts*, 1705; Bowdich, *Mission to Ashantee*; Cruickshank, *Eighteen Years on the Gold Coast*; Sir [John] Dal[rymple] Hay, *Ashanti and the Gold Coast*; *The British Battles*; *A brief history of the Wesleyan Missions on the Western Coasts of Africa* by William Fox, 1851; the *Report of the Basel Mission for 1879, or a Retrospect on fifty years Mission Work*; and the *Gold Coast Almanack* for 1842 and 1843, with some few manuscripts of the late Old James Bannerman and Charles Bannerman, which were kindly communicated to me by Edmund Bannerman and from which I obtained some information about Sir Charles McCarthy's war with Asante. And lastly, I am thankful to the Rev. A. W. Parker and the Rev. John H. Davies M.A., the Colonial Chaplain, for their information. . . .

And in conclusion I must beg you, my native friends, not to despise this work coming from one of your own brethren, but let it rather encourage you to assist me by your kind information and co-operation, so as to get our own history complete. To interest you chiefly I collected so many names of our forefathers, who defended our country from the yoke of Asante, trusting that every one of you will be pleased to find his grandfather's name in the lists. May our dear Lord bless this poor means I now offer to the public for the improvement of ourselves as well as our country. . . .

[Chapter Four]

All the different Tshi [Twi groups], as already mentioned in the preceding chapter, seem to have been driven by the Moors from Central
Africa, and settled first between the Kong (Kpong) mountains and
the River Pra.

Enumerating those [groups] or districts, we shall in the first place
take Amanse. Amanse means the origin or foundation of the people,
where they seem to have emigrated to, and then dispersed over the
country. It was a district between Kumase and Adanse. A large portion of them separated and settled at Adanse ([Dutch merchant
Willem] Bosman calls this district "Ananse"), which also means the
foundation of the buildings, i.e., the building of the Tshi nation. The
next district was Asen, i.e. *wanseri*, which means, numerically sur-
passing the site they then occupied on the right bank of the Pra.
North of Amanse was the Ofeso [Ofinso] district and that of Takiman [Takyiman]. Kwabire and Osekyere districts lie N.E. of
Amanse, and Mponoa and Nsunoa districts on their S[outh],
Odomara and Atshuma districts on the N.W. of Amanse, Dampong
(i.e. the big building) or Asante Akem [Akyem] on the East, having
Okwawu on its N. The district of Dankera [Denkyira] (i.e. *dan
kyekyerewa* = small, wretched building) and Tshuforo [Twifo
groups] crossed the River Ofe and settled in the S.W. The districts
of Safwi [Sefwi] on the W., and Parama (Wasa), Dwabo, Maraso,
and Tannofo, all not proper Tshi [groups], N. of Dankera. The Akem
[group] crossed the Pra and settled in Akem.

Adanse was the first seat of the Akan nation, as they say by tradition: there God first commenced with the creation of the world.
They were the enlightened [group] among the Tshi nation, from
whom the rest acquired wisdom and knowledge; there the first Tshi
ruler or king by the name Awirade Basa began to establish his power
over the other emigrants. His powerful linguist was Okwawe
Nfrafo, through whose means he exercised his power, hence the
proverb, *Yekasa Nfrafo, nso yene Awirade*, i.e., "We complain
against Nfrafo, we mean, however, the king himself." It appears,
when Awirade was establishing his power over the people to form

the kingdom, his subjects complained against his treatment. Fearing to mention his name, all was said against the linguist. We do not know his successors, but there was one Abu, who seems to have been one of the kings of Adanse, who instituted the order of family among the Tshis; hence lineage is designated *abusia*, i.e., imitating Abu. As the power of the Adanse kings was acquired by enlightenment and also by the fame of their [ɔbosom] Bona at Akrokyere, but not by war, it did not last long, neither was it very glorious, till they were conquered by the Dankeras. All the principal districts or [groups] mentioned above were independent and had their respective chiefs over them.

Dankera was the district of which Bosman says, "This country, formerly restrained to a small compass of land and containing but an inconsiderable number of inhabitants, is, by their valor, so improved in power, that they are respected and honored by all the neighboring nations, all of which they have taught to fear them, except Asiante and Akim." Their tributary countries then were Wasa, Enkase, and Tshuforo. By trade and plunder they grew very rich and powerful. They became so arrogant that they looked upon all other nations with contempt, esteeming them no more than slaves, and on that account they were disliked.

Nothing particular is known about the first king of Dankera, Bomoreti, and his successor, Okarawani Apaw. The third sovereign was Owusu Bore, who grew very rich and powerful, and made shields of gold and gold-hilted swords. Obenpong Akrofi, the king of Tshuforo Atoam, died during his days, and after the funeral custom was over, Owusu claimed from the estate two twin brothers with their 300 retainers as his share. Asiedu Apenteng, the successor of Akrofi, refused to comply, and consequently war broke out. Floats were made by the Dankera army to cross the Pra. During the heat of action, the Tshuforos removed these floats, and being disappointed when falling back, the Dankeras were defeated, and the original ivory stool (throne) was drowned and lost. Owusu became so uneasy for the loss, that he slept on palm-branches, hence their oath "Dankera berewso," Dankera palm-leaves. Asiedu Apenteng, having been slain in the war, was succeeded by Ofosuhene Apenteng. He was obliged to remove from Tshuforo Atoam to Ahuren, a place near Kokofu and Dadease. This [group] continued wandering to different places, owing to the incessant invasions of the Asantes, till they finally settled in the Akem country, with the name Akem Kotoku, as we shall find hereafter.

The warlike Owusu Bore again declared war against Ansa Sasraku of Tshuforo proper, who seemed unwilling to submit to him. Ansa was defeated and compelled to flee for shelter to Asamankese, which afterwards became the capital of the Akwamu kings. As a sign of his unwillingness to serve him, Ansa gave orders to beat a certain drum *perempe*, i.e., "I wouldn't serve one like you." As Owusu was bent upon war, he found fault with Oburum Ankama I, king of Safwi, for not having assisted him against Ansa. He thereupon invaded his country, defeated him, and carried off large amounts of gold in barrels and palm-leaf baskets to Dankera. Abrimoro, the king of Parama, also fell a prey to Owusu, which caused him to flee through Safwi forest and settle in Wasa.

The fourth king of Dankera was Akafo, whose surname is Obiaka, which means "there is one more yet." The royal family did not expect there would be a powerful king after the demise of the last [three] sovereigns. He instituted the *kwadwom*, a song expressive of sorrow or heroism of the ancients, delivered in a dramatic manner by a number of virgins trained for the purpose. Dankera Kyei was the fifth king. He instituted the harem for kings, brought in all his wives there, and set eunuchs and guards about them. He also increased the number of the fan- and horsetail-bearers, who used to fan him and drive away flies from him when sitting in public. Amoako Ata I succeeded him. He also made several symbols of gold, all amounted to 1000: some on state umbrellas, on swords &c. He made 2 gold stools and 12 gold-headed state-canes for linguists; even on his drums and tympanum was gold.

After the death of Amoako Ata I, Asare or Boa Pomsem ascended the stool of Dankera. His mother's name was Aberewa Kukusi, so called for wearing too many jewels. Akoabena Bensua was her daughter. It was this Asare Pomsem who invented playing on the tambourine, i.e., a skin stretched over the upper opening of a large calabash, which sounds in beating, *pomsem*, *pomsem*, hence his name.

Having come so far with the kingdom of Dankera, we turn now to another district which also had in the meanwhile acquired power. It was that district of Amanse, of which Bosman says, "all the neighboring nations had been taught to fear Dankera, except Asiante and Akim." The district of Amanse comprised these principal towns, viz., Asumenya Santemanso, Dwabenma, Booman, Adwampong, Bekwae, Amoafo Pompong, Adumai, Asaneso, Danyaase, Adankranya, Amoagja and Ahuren. The first king of this district, Kwabia Ahwanifi, resided at Asumenja Santemanso. All we know of him is that in his days gold was not known, the currency was pieces of iron. After his death Oti Akenteug ascended the stool. He made war with the king of Kwadane at the place where Kumase was afterwards built, and captured Dareboo. At that time the Amanse people had the opportunity of seeing that place, and desired to remove there; but they were told that it belonged to Kwaku Dompo, the king of Tafo. Oti Akenteng was intending to remove there, when he was overtaken by death, and was succeeded by Obiri Yeboa Manwu. He removed first to Kokofu, and, after staying there awhile, negotiated with King Kwaku Dompo, and obtaining his consent, he and his chiefs emigrated there. As King Obiri Yeboa had emigrated back towards the north into the district of Kwabire and settled between Makom, Tafo and Udomara, he was obliged to enter into friendly communications with the kings there. He sent compliments to Akosa of Makom and Kusi of Odomara; after this the boundaries between these three kings were shown to him, and then he prepared a site for his town. Under a tree known as Okum near Odenkyemmanaso or Crocodile-pool, close to the town of Akosa, he founded the capital, and named it Okum-ase, i.e., under the okum-tree. The capital having been founded, the headmen of the Oyokos, chiefly, the Akoonas, a family to which the king belonged, viz., Duabodee of Kanyarase, Kagya Panyin of Mamponten, Kwaw Panyin of Faobaware, Antwi of Sawua, and Nyama of Saman, built their towns around the capital. Ankra was the chief of this Oyoko family; but Gyamin and Afriyie were left in charge of Kokofu.

Now the confederate kings or chiefs of Amanse were obliged to emigrate to where the capital had been founded. Adakwa Yiadom of Dwabenma removed and settled near Boama Kokoboate, the king of Pianyirase, and founded Dwaben. The other king of that district was Ntiamoa Mankuo of Abooso. Tweneboa Kotia of Komawu, an ally of the Amanse king, said where he was. Agyin of Boman founded Nsuta (by the chief of Beposo?). Maniampon I of Pompon founded Mampon, but Egu Ayeboafo of Bekwai stayed where he was. It appears that lie was left there on purpose to protect the frontier against any invasion of the Dankeras. Thus the confederate Amanse chiefs fortified their kingdom, which afterwards became the universally famed and dreaded Asante kingdom.

When Obiri Yeboa was at Kokofu, his sister Manu was married to chief Owusu Panyin of Aberenkese, having no issue. After a long time, the fame of the [ɔbosom] Otutu in Berekuso reached them. Messengers were dispatched to Ansa Sasraku, the king of Akwamu, to assist that some medicine might be obtained from that [ɔbosom] to administer to the only sister of Yeboa. Their request was granted, Manu conceived and a boy was born, to whom the name of the [ɔbosom] "Tutu or Otutu" was given. Others have the opinion that Manu came there in person and was married to Kwadwo Wusu, nephew of Ansa Sasraku. If she came to Berekuso at all, her husband Owusu Panyin may have accompanied her, and when she had conceived, they returned home. This prince became the illustrious Osei Tutu of Asante. When his uncle Obiri Yeboa removed from Kokofu, his son Afriyie was left there. The connection between Dankera and Asante is traceable from this fact, that Osei Tutu, the nephew of king Obiri Yeboa, was employed as a shield-bearer of Boa Pomsem. This shows that the connection was somewhat tributary, as the custom with the Tshis is that all tributary kings have their nephews in the king's service, as horsetail-, fan- and shield-bearers. At all events, this is certain that the Dankera king was superior to the Asante king, superior in power as well as in glory, and Osei Tutu may have been sent there to study the politics of the Dankeras.

Tradition says that Akoabena Bensua, the only sister of Boa Pomsem, had no issue, and Okomfo Anokye, the far-famed [indigenous] priest of Awukugua in Akuapem, who was full of magic powers, was invited to Dankera by the king, to try his best that his sister might be fruitful. Anokye predicted that he could manage that a single son could be born, but that this prince would be the ruin of the Dankera kingdom. The reply to this was, that the Dankera army amounted to 300,000 men; if the prince squandered the whole property of the kinodom, and if one third of this army were lost, with the two thirds he could hold on; he must do his best to get a male child born. This case strengthens what the Asantes say about Ntim, as being the son of prince Osei Tutu. For Tshi princesses are known generally as loose characters, especially as Akoabena Bensua and her brother were very anxious of obtaining a nephew as his successor.

Prince Osei Tutu privately administered the [ɔbosom] Ekumasua to Akoabena, that she must never be known any longer to her husband but himself. This being so, she was found to be in the family way, and there and then she advised Tutu to effect his escape from Dankera as speedily as possible, because the husband was urging confession from her. He escaped with two servants and was pursued by armed men. The river Ofe being so over flown that they could not cross it, one of his men hanged himself on seeing the pursuers; but Tutu and the other concealed themselves in a hole of an armadillo. The pursuers, finding the river too swollen for anyone to cross, and not discovering the fugitives, returned home. The Ofe subsiding the following day, both Tutu and his servant crossed and safely reached Kumase. In memory of this escape in the hole of an armadillo, Osei Tutu named one of his sons: Para (armadillo). His uncle Obiri Yeboa advised him to seek refuge in Akwamu; this fact proves the superiority of the Dankeras over the Asantes at that time. Ansa hearing of the arrival of a good looking Asante prince in one of his towns, invited him to his house. His bold and majestic appearance as well as his personal beauty attracted Ansa's love, that he there and then took him to be his male-consort. It is fashionable with the Tshi kings that any woman, to whom they take a fancy, becomes a wife of the king. With a male person in a similar case a connection is formed of tender love, estimation and protection. On account of this love shown to the Asante prince, all the monarchs of Akwamu considered the kings of Asante as their male-consorts. Prince Osei Tutu had the opportunity of acquiring the politics of the two principal powers then existing, Dankera and Akwamu. Meanwhile Akoabena Bensua was delivered of a male child who was named Ntim. While Tutu was staying at Akwamu, his uncle Obiri Yeboa was busily engaged in acquiring power over the numerous [groups] among whom he had established his capital. Disputes with Kusi, king of Odomara, about the boundary of the land, brought on a war in which Obiri Yeboa was slain, although the Asantes pretend that he got sick in camp and died.

This sudden death of the king obliged the Asante nobles to recall their fugitive prince. Ansa, to protect his male-consort, appointed Anum Asamoa, the chief of the Anum people, then residing at Nsawam, with 700 armed men to escort him home. These Anum people became the Adums in Kumase; because they did not return back to Akwamu. A piece of the skin from the elbow of an elephant presented to him by a hunter, as well as the head of a king-fisher similarly obtained, Osei Tutu worked into a crown on his way to Kumase. Tradition says that he obtained a large amount of ammunition from the Danish Government on credit, which he secured by giving some of his people, whom he redeemed afterwards, on account of which he was surnamed Yeboa Afriyie. At the head of the 700 armed Anums and with that curious crown, he appeared in Kumase, and was proclaimed king of Asante. With his advent a new era began in the history of the Asantes. For the royal stool of the kingdom was constructed at this time by Okomfo Anokye, who seems to have removed from Dankera to Kumase, having become acquainted with prince Osei Tutu during his stay in Dankera. That the monarchs of Asante trace their lineage from Etwum and Antwi, whom they consider as their ancestors, comes from the tender care those two chiefs of Kokofu bestowed on their grandson Tutu when a child, but not that they were kings of Asante.

Osei Tutu, having prepared to revenge his late uncle's death, declared war against Odomara Kusi, whom he completely conquered. The refugees escaped to Awosu, where the king of the place asked them the cause of their flight and the circumstances connected with it. They told him, but as they were not willing to return to Odomara, the king gave the name "Gyaoman," "you have deserted your country," to those refugees. Those not willing to leave their country staid and built Abesem, Berekum, Odomase &c. and became tributary to Asante. Kyereme Sikafoo was appointed by Osei Tutu as the king over them, and became his Busumru. The kingdom of Gyaman was established by the contrivance of those Odomara refugees on the territory of the Mohammedans [i.e., Muslims] from Kong. They built Bontuku as its capital. The next king against whom Osei Tutu declared war was Makom Akosa. He was defeated and slain, and his nephew Aduamensa was appointed his successor by Osei Tutu. He formed an intimate friendship with Aduamensa, to whom he gave his sister Nyako Kusiamoa in marriage, and Opoku Ware was born. But Bafo, the brother of the late Akosa, left the country quietly and emigrated to Takiman, and sought an asylum with the great king Amo Yaw. Bafo was ordered by the king to stay in a village where only three old men were residing, which became afterwards the town and district of Nkoransa, i.e., *nkwakora mmiensa*, three old men.

Upon witnessing all these troubles brought on the aboriginal race of that district by mere foreigners, Osafo Akotong, the king of Tafo, gave orders to blow a horn "Osei Tutu, sore ho-o twa!" which means: "Get away from the place, you Osei Tutu!" Because they were taking undue advantage of the land as well as the fish in the Nsuben, which are strictly forbidden to be eaten. Irritated by this horn, Osei Tutu declared war against Osafo, whom he utterly defeated and captured his big drums, tympanum, gold guitar &c. as well as a whole district of 100 towns. After this conquest the king fell sick and was dying, when he was advised by Okomfo Anokye to propitiate Osafo for the injury done to him. The latter agreed on condition that the king should promise upon an oath that he would never kill any of his family. The oath was administered to his sister Nyako Kusiamoa, by virtue of which no one of the town of Akyenakurom has ever since been subjected to the executioner's knife of Asante. This being done, the king got well again, and henceforth the fish in Nsuben were strictly forbidden to be eaten, but were rather fed with the bodies of executed criminals. The fourth war was declared against King Wiafe Akenteng of Ofeso. He was beaten and conquered. Thus the whole district formerly belonging to the Odomaras, Atshumas and Kwabiris &c. became the property of Osei Tutu.

The policy then adopted by the king, which became the national law, strictly observed by all his successors on pain of death, was the naturalization of the conquered provinces with all due rights as citizens. Whoever dares tell his son: these people were from such and such a place, conquered and trans-located to this or that town, was sure to pay for it with his life. Neither were such people themselves allowed to say where they had been transported from. Considering these captives as real citizens, any rank or honor was conferred freely on them according to merit, but not otherwise. This made the people of the kingdom so united and therefore very powerful, that, what Bosman says, "except Asiante and Akim, who are yet stronger than Dankera at the time of Ntim," can be understood.

Ntim Gyakari, the youthful son of Osei Tutu, ascended the stool of Dankera after the demise of his uncle Asare Pomsem. One of Ntim's wives was Berebere, who having been married over three years without issue, enquired the cause of it from her [ɔbosom] Bona at Akrokyere in Adanse. The oracle obtained was "she must come in person and would conceive." This being the oracle, Ntim granted permission and appointed Obeng Antwi, the chamberlain, nephew of Bonsra, to escort her with 300 armed men to the place. For her personal expense she got 3 *peredwans* and 30 sheep. Forty days were spent at Akrokyere to undergo all the ceremonies required; but Berebere expressed a desire to visit Bonsra. As she stayed there another 40 days, the king became uneasy and ordered his nephew and Berebere to return home. But to his great surprise, she was in the family way from his nephew. Her words were a thunderclap to the old king. "Alas, my nephew, he said, thou hast ruined us!" He forthwith called for two of his chiefs, Kwaku Dwamara of Fomana and Apeanin Kwafaramoa Woyiawonyin of Abuakwa Atshumamanso, and told them the sad story. Three messengers were then and there dispatched to Dankera to inform Ntim through the linguist Safe and the Queen mother Bensua, what folly Antwi had wrought in Adanse. Safe was immediately ordered to proceed to Adanse with the messengers, with the injunction to bring back the unfortunate Berebere alive, but the criminal Antwi and his relations must be done away with. Thirty-two persons were slaughtered that day at Ayewase, among who were Obeng Antwi and his parents. Queen Abuwa, on hearing what the bystanders said against Antwi for having brought calamity into the country, replied "Berebere amma a, amane mma," i.e., Had Berebere not come, no trouble would have come. The bystanders then echoed "Enye obi na okum Antwi," Nobody is to blame, but Antwi who killed himself. King Bonsra and his chiefs are said to have emigrated to Akem on account of this case. Of 32 towns only few were left in Adanse. Berebere was brought to Dankera and was put on a block, and Ntim being satisfied with the conduct of the Adanses who stayed, ordered Safe to thank them, saying: *Se wo reso susurape na ohiahini to mu a, wuyi no kyene, na wowe wo susurape*, "When you catch flying-ants and the large black ant (emitting a bad smell) falls among them, you put the latter aside and eat the flying ants."

Ntim may have been either told of the past event, or was so jealous of the rapid growth of the power of Osei Tutu or the influence he had gained over the Adanses, that he dispatched three

ambassadors, a shield-bearer, sword-bearer, and a court-crier, with a large brass-pan to Kumase, saying, "The king of Asante and his chiefs must fill up the brass-pan with pure gold, and must send each the favorite among his wives and their mothers to Dankera to become his wives; besides, their wives must supply his wives with *mposae*, dry fibers of the plantain tree to use during their monthly courses." Osei Tutu summoned all his great chiefs to appear in the capital, and a grand meeting was held at Apebooso. There were present Adakwa Yiadom, Nsuta Agyin, Tweneboa Kotia, Mani-ampong, Amankwatia Panyin, general of the Koronti force, Asafo Awere, general of the Akwamu force, with the captains of his body-guard. The Dankera ambassadors repeated their message in the audience of the assembly, and the reply to it was blows given first by

Yiadom and then the other chiefs. Instead of gold, they filled up the brass-pan with stones, and sent the ambassadors bleeding home without the brass-pan. It is kept as a trophy in Kumase. This foolish demand of Ntim could hardly be believed; but when Bosman says, "Dinkira, elevated by its great riches and power, became so arrogant, that it looked on all other negroes with contempt, esteeming them no more than its slaves," no one will doubt the veracity of this statement. It took Ntim three months to prepare against the Asantes. He formed an alliance with the Dutch Government, by whom he was supplied with arms and ammunition, two cannon and some grenades and iron mails [i.e., armor]. He also succeeded in persuading Ofori Korobong, the king of Dampong, another powerful sovereign, who had hitherto been jealous of the prosperity of Dankera, to join him against Osei Tutu. The Dampong royal family were of the same stock of the Agona family group with the Dankeras. Dampong, the capital of this [group], is said to have been so large, that no large bird could fly through it without falling to the ground.

The generals commanding his overwhelming army were Kwame Tebi over the van [vanguard?]; Kwadwo Wiafe, the right wing; Kwaku Butuakwa, the left wing; Kwasi Pipira, the rear, and Asiama Tia, the body-guard. But Boa Kropa, the most powerful chief of Ntim is said to have refrained from joining them, on account of a quarrel which took place between them. The chief was demanding satisfaction from the king for an illegal connection with one of his wives. Ntim replied, "I discharge my stool into your gun!" His allies were of Wasa, Safwi Bekwai, Safwi Ahweaso, Tshuforo, &c. A large bundle of a certain plant was placed on the path the warriors had to march, which being cut asunder by the tread of their feet, Ntim was satisfied with the number of warriors, and then commanded the rest to return home.

Since the three ambassadors had been beaten and shamefully sent back to Dankera, Osei Tutu with his chiefs were busily engaged in preparing against Ntim's invasion, as they knew very well what would be the consequence. The king sent to the coast to buy arms and ammunition in great quantities. Bosman says, "The Dinkiras being foolish enough to assist him themselves, suffered his subjects to pass with it uninterrupted through their country, notwithstanding they knew very well, it was only designed for their destruction." Okomfo Anokye also was actively engaged in offering sacrifices and preparing war medicines against his old enemies, who ill-treated him when residing there. Tradition says, that one of the princes, Anim Kokobo, and the king himself, then orders to search for a special medicine plant growing only in Dwaben, where the Asantes were fortunate enough to find it. From this plant sacred water was prepared for the chiefs to wash with, and some to drink. The one who drank the last medicine was to be a victim in the impending war to ensure success. After his fall, Ntim would be slain and his kingdom destroyed. None of the great chiefs dared to accept the medicine, till Tweneboa Kotia willingly took and drank it, offering his life for the good of his country, on condition, however, that none of his offspring should ever be subjected to the executioner's knife, whatever his crime might be, when once the Asante empire was established. . . .

The overwhelming army of Ntim reached Adunku and gave battle to the Asantes, who kept him at bay for three days before they were forced to fall back. Some believe that the war lasted two

years; but the bloody battles were fought at Abooten, Putuagya, and Feyiase. Ntim's van [vanguard?] of 1,000 picked men in iron mails, with the drummer of the Kwantempong (a small drum placed in the armpit in beating) at its head, did much harm to the Asantes in every engagement. The chiefs asked Anokye, how is it? But he requested them to hold on till he could have him by magic. He had prophesied that Ntim was to fall at Feyiase, where, after three days engagement, Tweneboa Kotia fell, which was the predicted signal of victory, when Asiama Tia and Safe surrendered to the Asantes. Asiama Tia was fighting most gallantly, when one asked him, "Why do you trouble yourself so much for one like Ntim, who has just this moment beheaded your nephew, his aid-de-camp, and our wife, who once absconded, is among his wives in the harem?" The cause of the nephew's beheading was, that once, when the Dankeras were victorious, the king painted his right arm with white clay. The aid-de-camp, sharing his joy, painted his arm, as the king did, hence his death! Asiama hastened to the camp and found the report to be true. On account of the desertion of these principal men, the Dankeras were defeated and completely conquered.

Ntim being found sitting leisurely with one of his wives at a certain game, amusing themselves, having shackled their feet in golden fetters, Adakwa Yiadom came upon him suddenly and gave him a stroke with his sword, which he received on the valuable gold bracelet he had on his wrist, which was taken by Akosa of Edwampon and given to Adakwa. The stroke was repeated; the king was killed and his head cut off. It is chiefly through this bracelet captured by Yiadom that the Dwabens obtained the prerogative of placing a king on the stool of Kumase, on which occasion the king of Dwaben is required to place that sign of power three times on the wrist of the new sovereign. The estimate of the killed was said to be about 100,000 besides the loss of 30,000 Akems who came to their assistance. Their king Ofori Korobon was lost with all his body-guard. The Asantes were 15 days in plundering Dankera, and took thousands of prisoners and a large amount of gold. The one who placed the king on the stool was the chief of Wono, now called Gyamaase.

Among the slain on the Asante side was Obiri Yeboa's son Osaben Odiawuo, Tweneboa Kotia and Nsuase Poku. Safe was favored to succeed the latter, while Asiama Tia was disgracefully killed. They had sworn not to kill him, yet a public hole was dug, in which he was placed, his arms pinioned behind him, and people were ordered to go to privy upon him, which has given rise to a conventional expression in Kumase, "Mekoma Asiama akye," I am going to say good morning to Asiama. The cannon captured are now a trophy in Kumase. Other advantages accrued from this conquest, one of which was the monthly pay-note of the Dutch Government to the [Asante] king for Elmina Castle, which became a perquisite of the victor till the year 1872, when St. George d'Elmina with the Dutch possessions were transferred to the English Government. Dankera having become a tributary state after the conquest, Ohuagyewa, a lame princess, was placed on the stool by the victor. (Others believe that prince Boadu Akafo succeeded Ntim.) The debt contracted by

Ntim with the Dutch in making war is said to have been paid by Osei Tutu, an amount of 1,000 *peredwans*.

Okomfo Anokye was richly rewarded by the chiefs for his good services. The king gave him 300 slaves, 100 *peredwans*, and a large gold ring for the arm; he made him a principal chief with seven horns, one big drum, a state umbrella and four hilted gold swords, and appointed him to a command in the van [vanguard?] of the army. He received 100 slaves and 30 *peredwans* from Maniampon; Okyere Brafo, the successor of Tweneboa Kotia, gave 100 slaves and 20 *peredwans*; Oduro Panyin 100 slaves and 20 *peredwans*, and Nsantefu the same. But Adakwa Yiadom is said to have refused giving him anything; hence a curse was pronounced against him, that no glory should ever attend any undertaking of his, when acting independently of Kumase, whilst conjunctly with them, he should be more glorious. Out of this number of slaves, the priest formed the Agona district in Asante.

We insert the following as different opinions or statements about the war. Some say, what led to the war and consequently the overthrow of the power of Dankera by the Asantes was, that Akoabena Bensua, the mother of Ntim, was once very sick. There was a certain [group] called the Bontwumafo, now Atwomafo, i.e., red clay people, originally slaves, doomed by the law of the country to the most barbarous slaughter when any royal personage died. At such times the unfortunate Atwoma people were sacrificed by hundreds and their blood used as the red clay in painting some parts of the body of the deceased as well as persons of the royal family, and some of their dead bodies placed in the grave on which the coffin was laid. Ntim had a wife from this [group], who informed her people concerning the state of Bensua's health. They prepared to quit the country, as soon as they should hear of her death. She was there on a visit to her relations, when that sad intelligence reached them. The whole [group] now led for protection to the Asantes. The king sent for his wife and subjects, but they refused to go back, which of course broke the peace between Dankera and her tributary state . . .

— 4 —

Oral Historical Case Studies

Oral Traditions of Adanse

KWAME DAAKU

In 1969, Kwame Daaku and his team at the University of Ghana at Legon completed their compilation of Adanse oral tradition recordings and transcriptions in Twi (Akan) and in English translation. A synopsis of their findings, under the direction and authorship of Daaku, appears below.

Adanse, a small traditional state in southern Asante with a population of about 94,000 [in 1960], has a rich and varied history. Lying south of Bekwai, with the Pra to the south, Banka and Asante Akyem to the east, and Denkyira to the west, Adanse was once the home of most of the Akan clans. Indeed it is traditionally known in Akan cosmogony as the place where God started the creation of the world. In the area bounded by the Pra, [Ofin] and Oda rivers, the Akan first developed virtually all their political and social institutions. It was here that the Akan ideas of kingship, personified in the activities of Awurade Basa, first took shape. In traditional history Adanse was the first of the five principal Akan states, "the Akanman Piesie Anum," [and] the rest were Akyem Abuakwa, Assen, Denkyira, and Asante, in order of seniority, although not of power and resources.

Most of the ruling clans of the Akan forest states trace their origins to Adanse. Beyond Adanse all stories of migrations and modes of travel tend to be ill-supported, hazy and, more often than not, unintelligible. Akyem Abuakwa, Edweso and Offinso or the Asona clan, trace their origins to Kokobiante, near Sodua, a small village on the Akorokyere-Dompoase road. The Assen, both the Asenee of Attandasu (Fante Nyankomase), the Asona of Apemanim, the Afutuakwa of Fosu and the Aboabo of Assin Nyankomase traces their original homes to that stretch of territory between the Pra river and the Kwisa range. Their most renowned former sites being Nimiaso and Apagya for the Attandasu and Ansa for the Apemanim. The Denkyira people or the Agona clan were once known to have occupied the land stretching from Asokwa westward to the neighborhood of Obuase and Akrofo to the confluence of trhe Oda and Offin Rivers. Whilst most of the Bretuo of Mampong and Kwahu trace their home to Ayaase and Ahensan; Abadweem and Edubiase are known to be the early homes of the Oyoko clan. Adanse then could be said to have nurtured most of the important Akan clans. The Asakyire of Akrokeri and Odumase, however, trace their home to places in the north, while the Asenee of Dompoase trace their origins to the neighborhood of their present town. The Ekona of Fomena also claims to have originated from Adanse.

There appears to have been two main reasons why most of the people moved from the Adanse area. Whereas in the early days scarcity of land resulting from over-population caused many people to move out in search of land, at a later date, especially from the middle of the seventeenth century it was the rise of the empire states of Denkyira and Asante which forced out many people to emigrate to avoid being brought under the rule of members of different clans.

A significant and much more interesting factor in the raise of Adanse is the rule of its traditional deity, Bona. Unlike the successor states of Denkyira and Asante that became important on account of their striking force that enabled them to bring different clans under their control, in Adanse it was the deity sited in the neighborhood of Patakoro which wielded much power and influence. At the height of its power and prestige in the pre-Denkyira period, Adanse was merely a loose confederation of clans or city-states that only came together under one leader to defend themselves in times of war.

There never developed anything near the Denkyira and Asante systems in which one stool managed to impose itself on the others and got itself accepted as the paramount ruler. The degree of autonomy that prevailed is epitomized in the popular Adanse saying, "Adanse nkotowa nkotowa obiara da ne ben!" Freely rendered, it means the various towns were like little crabs each of which controlled its hole, thus showing that each clan was completely autonomous and could do as it pleased in its sphere of influence. In spite of the tendency to remain independent some time in the 16th century, Awurade Basa, the most renowned of the leaders of Adansemanso, attempted to unite all the clans under his leadership. This was done by creating a mystical sword known as the Afenakwa. Although it was generally accepted that whoever had custody of the sword should lead the Adanse in time of war, in peace time the leader was never accorded any special privileges.

Unlike the Sasatia of Denkyira which enhanced the power and prestige of the Agona clan, or the Golden stool of Asante the custody of which was permanently vested in the Oyoko clan of Kumase, the Afenakwa used to be passed on from father to son. It therefore never remained with one clan for a long time. First associated with Awurade Basa of the Asenee clan, the Afenakwa was inherited by his son, Apeanim Kwafromoa of the Bretuo clan in Ayaase. After Apeanim it went to Akora Foripa of Asenee clan in Dompoaso, and from there Bonsra Afriyie of the Ekona clan in Fomena, was given the sword sometime at the beginning of the eighteenth century.

It was Bonsra Afriyie, who wisely kept the Afenekwa at Fomena with the Ekona clan. This was partly because he did not marry from another royal clan outside Fomena itself, and principally on account of the fact that the Ekona were blessed with a long line of brave and active loaders who never became too old on the stool to be forced to hand over the Afenakwa to their sons in times of national crisis. In spite of the leadership that had been offered by the Ekona since the beginning of the eighteenth century, the tendency for the other rulers to harp on their autonomy still continued. It was the introduction of British rule in Asante at the beginning of the twentieth

century that crystallized Fomena's political leadership by raising it
to the status of paramount stool over and above the other stools.
From that period the Fomena chief was accorded the title of Adansehene.

On the other hand, from very early times people came to accept
the power of Adanse Bona (Adanse Kunturapaa), the tutelary deity
over all the state. At times referred to in the oral traditions as the
creator, not much is known about the origins of Bona. Sited somewhere in a cave in the grove between Akakyere and Patakoro, it was
the only regular connecting link between the various rulers.
Patakoro, where the Priest of Bonsam (the [divine] spokesman of
Bona) stays, has been the scene of regular resort of people of all
walks of life wanting to consult the deity on all sorts of things. At
the annual yam festival for Bona which falls at the end of August
or the beginning of September, not only the Bonsam priest and the
Bonahene, but also people from all parts of the state come to take
part of it. In every December a much grander festival known as the
annual dance is also celebrated. It is during this time that the priest,
the keeper of the national annual calendar sends Bonasuo (water
from the Bona cave) to all the stool occupants to be used in the general purification of the state. And in times of danger or national
calamity there is the "carrying of the Deity" or the divination ceremony for the whole state. It is during this ceremony that the sub-
servience of the chiefs to the Bona deity is clearly seen. The Deity
has allotted specific functions to be performed by each chief. The
Akokyerehene is the Akradwarefohene (Chief soul washer), the
Adansehene head of the hammock bearers, Ayaasehene, the chief
executioner, Akrofuomhene the Treasurer, Edubiasehene the
spokesman, and Dompoasehene the Gyaasehene. As a tutelar Deity,
not only is Bona expected to purify the state every year with the
Bonasuo, but also each town is given a Bonsamboɔ (Bonsam stone),
on which sacrifices are made to appease the God when people go
against his injunctions in the town. Thus people are spared the necessity of having to travel all the way to Patakoro when the deity is
offended. It is interesting to note that virtually in front of the palaces
of all the principal Akan chiefs who trace their original homes to

Adanse, are to be found Bonsamboɔ, which in all instances is considered sacred—visible relic of their Adanse origins.

Within easy reach of the European trading centers at the coast and not far from the sources of kola from eastern and western Asante, and the area itself rich in gold deposits, Adanse stood to gain from the long distance trade to the north and to the coast. Adanse traders were known to have traveled to both the northern land coastal markets to seek their fortune. In Adanse itself there developed an important market center at Edubiase, where people from far and near came to trade. Athwart the important trade route between Kumase and Cape Coast, the people benefited from the constant flow of traders moving up and down. Even those who could not go to the centers of trade profited from it by issuing their local foodstuff and by providing accommodation to strangers. The desire to derive maximum benefits from trade accounts for the fact that most of the townships moved their settlements as and when the trade route was diverted.

It was its favorable economic position that always drew her into the power struggles of the later states. From about 1696 when their refusal to help Asante against Denkyira forced them to cross the Pra to seek refuge in Akyem, parts or all the Adanses have suffered from constant emigrations across the Pra to the south. Whereas most of them had always returned to their former homes after such flights, the beginning of the [nineteenth] century saw a large part of Asante, the Apemanim, Afutuakwa, Aboabo, Attendansu, all now known as Assen, moving to settle permanently south of the Pra. The last wave of migration took place in the later part of the [nineteenth] century, when the Bekwai-Adanse war forced them once again to move across the Pra.

Oral Traditions of Ahafo

KWAME ARHIN

*In 1965, Kwame Arhin of the Institute of African Studies
at the University of Ghana published a short report based
on his oral history research on Asante and its relations
with Ahafo. That report, which focuses on oral historical
method as well as challenges, appears below.*

I [Kwame Arhin] paid a brief visit to Ahafo to start [a]n enquiry
into the historical relations of the peoples of Ahafo with Ashanti
[Asante], and the way in which Ahafo fits into the rise, growth and
development of historic Ashanti. I was not prepared for the high
level of historical self-consciousness of the chiefs and the "court"
chroniclers that I met. It is certainly the practice of Akan courts,
like those of many other centralized kingdoms in Africa, to have
their edited traditions recited during festive assemblies (to remind
the people of the glories and tribulations of their ancestors with implicit lessons for the present and future). And Court habitués did
hear versions of village, town or state histories during land and stool
cases at the chiefs' courts. Even so I did not expect to be greeted
with notebooks of recorded traditions, of files bulging with typed
notes of the same, and state secretaries fully conversant with the
traditions of their respective states.

It occurred to me on reflection that this probably meant that the
fever of historical research which allegedly assails a newly independent and, *ipso facto*, an acutely self-conscious state such as
Ghana, usually extends beyond her intellectuals and politicians; that
the "well-established point that every age and people is conscious
of, and is influenced by the social functions of history and seeks to
reconstruct the past in a large measure to explain the present," had
a wider application, at any rate, in Ghana than the National Assembly and Ghana's Universities. District and local history may be revised to conform to new notions of dignity and requirements of the
political system. Certainly the chiefs and Court Chroniclers of

Ahafo were more than aware of the social functions of history.

Perhaps it may help at this stage to state, briefly, the background to my own enquiry in Ahafo. It is well known that the Ahafo district which, like the Brong district, formed part of Ashanti, has recently been joined with Brong to form a new administrative unit, (the Brong-Ahafo Region), with a Regional Commissioner and her share of the new crop of District Commissioners. Before the Ahafo District was separated from Ashanti, many Kumase chiefs claimed parts of the Ahafo lands as their own: generally, their ancestors had been rewarded with these lands for their services in the Abiri-Moro War; i.e., the Ashanti war in the reign of Opoku Ware (1720-1750) against Abiri, the King of Aowin, and his son, Miro, who had sacked Kumase while Opoku was at war with the Akims. The Nkawiahene, Hiawuhene, and Barekumahhene, among others, had, under the Asantehene, received tolls and other services from the people inhabiting those lands. Other parts of Ahafo also owed feudal service to certain Kumase clan or wing chiefs, who provided powder and shot, and the local chiefs saw that their hunters furnished the Asantehene and the chiefs with venison. There were some towns which were free from these obligations. These facts were the basis of some Ashanti popular notions of Ahafo: in short, that Ahafo as a whole was a hunting settlement for the Asantehene and some of his Kumase chiefs, and, that the area was generally settled with captives of war; that Ahafo, therefore, was "bush" inhabited by "bush" people.

Ahafo resentment of Ashanti was a response to these notions and to what they considered to be the Kumase chiefs' conception of Ahafo as an area for exploitation. These notions form the background for Ahafo revision and recitation of their oral traditions.

Thus it emerges from the traditions I have collected so far that the district of Ahafo was not so called because the first settlers were sent there to hunt. The name, the leading chief was at pains to emphasize, originated from the general fertility of the land, and the abundance of the common necessities of life with which visitors were impressed. People kept on saying *eha ye fo*, "life here is cheap." The settlements in Ahafo were not the creations of Kumase chiefs at all but of individuals who, merely as Ashantis, obtained permission from their own chiefs in Kumasi, who often acted as their hosts when the original settlers arrived from earlier homes to form new settlements. For the founders of the early settlements were not captives of war but emigrants from Akwamu or Adansi, belonging in certain cases to the royal stocks of their places of origin. In any case, many of the founders themselves played leading parts, especially as scouts, during the Abiri-Moro War. It was in war, during the search for the probable routes of the Aowins, that they discovered the sites of the early settlements. Lastly, the sum of the traditions was that elaborate stories by Ashanti chiefs of the audacious exploits of their ancestors in the Abiri-Moro War were often merely manufactured during the establishment of the Ashanti confederacy in 1935 in order to validate claims to portions of Ahafo lands.

The recitation of oral traditions in Ahafo, however, is not always shadow boxing with Ashanti chiefs. There is a very practical side to it. There is at the moment only one Omanhene in the Ahafo district and many of the Chiefs wish to attain that status. Some have petitioned the government to that effect, and others are contemplating doing the same. I have never seen a petition to the government for recognition as an Omanhene, but I suppose such a petition states the size, population, resources and history of the proposed "traditional area." It does emerge from conversations with aspirant Omanhenes, however, that for them it is not enough that they be made Amanhene for services to Ghana: their claims must be supported by the part that their ancestors allegedly played in the evolution of Ghana. Thus many chiefs have written down traditions which establish the antiquity of their principal towns and villages before others, perhaps more politically elevated, with improbable dates of their foundations and also recounting the alleged heroic exploits of the stool ancestors.

This worry about the support of history for claims is probably shared in many parts of Ghana where chiefs are concerned about their political status. It has advantages and disadvantages for the collector of oral traditions. First, provided the student preserves a "correct attitude" towards the state or town chronicler, he can be certain of their cooperation. Few chiefs do refuse nowadays to recite their traditions, although the embargo is still laid, at any rate in Ashanti, on "revealing others' origins" and mentioning untoward events such chief so-and-so was killed and beheaded in this or that war by this or that people. I was often asked in Ahafo not to record what were regarded as improper slips and some of my informants were reprimanded for such slips. By the "correct attitude," I mean not expressing doubts or disbelief about certain accounts. All questions must appear to be ones in search of clarification or further illumination of a certain point. This is especially important in cases where recorded versions of tradition have obviously intruded into the local tradition. Views and doubts or disbelief about this should be reserved to oneself. Furthermore, the varied versions of traditions readily produced should facilitate checks and cross checks. The disadvantage that comes to mind is that the search for historical validation accentuates the characteristic shortcoming of oral traditions: bias. I am not sure whether the advantages outweigh the disadvantages. The situation is, undoubtedly, stimulating for the student. Perhaps interested bodies will one day organize a panel of chroniclers to discuss specific points on which the books and the chroniclers cannot agree.

Asante Stool Histories

Recorded by Joseph Agyeman-Duah and compiled by K. Ampom Darkwa and B. C. Obaka, the two-volume Asante Stool Histories *contain historical data on the political offices developed within the Asante state from its beginnings in the late seventeenth century to the early twentieth century. Though the structure and reliability of these stool histories need revisiting, they do, nonetheless, contain a wealth of information on the structure of the Asante political system, as well as on the social history of the Asante people. Copies of each volume are held at the Manhyia Archives in Kumase and at the Institute of African Studies, University of Ghana at Legon. The following excerpts come from Volume One.*

Ankobia Stool History, ca. 1963
Informants: Nana Kwaku Asumani, Ankobeahene; Okyeame
  Kwaku Baah, Ankobeahene's Linguist; Kwame Boakye,
  Senior Servant of Ankobeahene

The Ankobiahene is the Head Clan Chief of the Ankobia Clan. He swears to the Asantehene with the Mpomponsuo Sword. It is a stool of patrilineal descent. It is a stool for the grandsons of the Asantehene. The king can also appoint ordinary persons to the stool if he so wishes, when the stool becomes vacant. Traditionally, the Ankobia is the bodyguard of Asantehene. The Ankobia Clan always follows the king when he is going to war—the backbone and bodyguard of the king.

This stool was created by Nana Osei Kwadwo, the great fighting king who fought in the broad daylight. He was traditionally known as "Oko Awiah." The first chief of the Ankobia was called Kra Patapaafu from Oduropim, a village near Daaban and Sukoban about four miles from Eineasi. Kra Patapaafu, it is said, went to Banda with Nana Osei Kwadwo where the chief of Banda, Worosa, was decapitated and his head sent to Kumasi. He was succeeded to the stool by Busumoru Dwanini, a brother of Kra Patapaafu during the reign of Nana Osei Kwame—Asantehene.

It is said it was during this period that the Atipin Stool was created by Nana Osei Kwame under the Ankobia Clan. Nana Dwanini, a brother of Kra Patapaafu, was succeeded on the stool by Nana Amondwuah during the reign of Nana Poku Fofie. He was succeeded on the stool by Nana Nkansah during the reign of Nana Bonsu Panyin. It is said he went to the Gyaaman war with the king. It is further said that it was during that time that the king Nana Bonsu created the Anaminako Stool to come under the Ankobia Clan. Nkansah, it is said, was a royal of the Stool. He reigned up to

Nana Agyeman's time. He was succeeded on the stool by Nana Kwaku Tawiah during the reign of this same king, Nana Agyeman, that is, Nana Kwaku Dua I. It is said that this chief was a man of opulence. He was a chief of means and substance. He was a relative of Nkansa. He was succeeded by Atta Gyamfi during the reign of Nana Kofi Karikari. He was destooled for mal-administration. He was succeeded by Prince Owusu Yaw Kuma (a son of Nana Bonsu Panyin). He died on the stool during the reign of Nana Mensah Bonsu.

He was succeeded on the stool by Yaw Kyem, a grandson of the Golden Stool. He was destooled for mal-administration. He was en-stooled during Nkoranza war, that is, before King Prempeh I was taken away to Seychelles Island. He was succeeded to the stool by a grandson of the Golden Stool, Nana Kwame Kusi. He was en-stooled before King Prempeh was taken to Seychelles. He was on the stool during Yaa Asantewah campaign. Otumfuo returned from Seychelles to meet him on the stool.

He was succeeded on the stool by Nana Osei Kojo, grandson of the stool, during this present king. He was destooled for rebelling against the present king. Mr. O. S. Agyeman, a native of Nsuta and popular citizen of Kumasi, was the ring leader of this conspiracy. He was exiled along with others.

He was succeeded by Dwanini, a grandson of the Stool. He died on the stool. He spent 13 years on the stool. He was succeeded on the stool by Nana Kwaku Asumani, the present Ankobiahene of Kumasi, who is about 80 years old. He has been about 13 years on the stool....

History of the Asantehene's Talking Drum—Atumpan, ca. 1962
Informant: Kyerema Kwaku Pong (alias Kyerefufuo),
    Asantehene's Atunpamhene

It is said that in the old days the Asantehene did not have talking drums for ceremonial occasions. It so happened that after the fall of Denkyera Kingdom or the capture of Ntim Gyakari at Fehyiase by the Ashantis, the then Toasehene, Yim Awere, who was no doubt one of the war captives, called at the King's Palace to pay homage to him, or to exchange greetings with him. The King, it is said, having discovered that the Toasehene possessed some very kingly drums, became amazed at the manipulation of them.

It is said that the Asantehene, King Osei Tutu, became greatly amazed at the playing of these drums, especially when played by one Kyerema Pong. The King, it is said, ordered the seizure of these drums, and forbid them to be handed back to the Toasehene.

The Asantehene, it is said, further directed that the Toasehene, who came from Denkyera, should in future call at his palace to salute him or pay homage to him through the Bantamahene.

It is said that in a year's time the Asantehene had a change of mind with regard to the sequence of exchanging customary greetings, and further directed that the subjects from Toase who were connected with the beating of the drums should pay homage to him or call at his palace to serve him through his Chief Stool Carrier, instead of through the Bantamanhene. It is said that at a later date Otumfuo removed them from the Chief Stool Carrier to Akrampa Gyase, where they have remained until this day. At present Opanin Kyere Fufuo is the occupant of the Kyerema Pong Stool. The Stool of Kyerema Pong, it is said, came from Denkyera. It is probable that the Kyerema Pong was a sub-chief of the Toasehene. He was responsible for the manipulation of the talking drums when he called the following drummers of different categories to serve under the Chief of the Talking Drums:

1. Mpebi and Nkawerehene
2. Fasafo Kokohene
3. Nkyehumahene
4. Donnonkuruwahene
5. The Chief of the Prempeh Drum.

The History of Lake Bosumtwi, ca. 1962
Informants: Nana Akwasi Bugyei III, Asamanhene; Panyin
   Akyampong, Abontendomhene of Asaman; Panyin Asare
   Bediako, Ankobiahene of Asaman

Lake Bosumtwi is about 29 miles south-east of Kumasi on the Kokofu-Asamang Road. It is the spiritual center of the local people and is associated with many taboos. It is said that the lake was discovered by a certain hunter, in the person of Akora (old man) Bompe. It is said that during one of his hunting expeditions in that area he shot at an antelope which made off and was later found in a large pool. While trying to capture the animal, old Bompe saw a large shoal of fish of extraordinary brightness and color. He thereupon concluded that the antelope must be a god [i.e., *ɔbosom*] because it had been responsible for his finding the rich collection of luscious fish. The lake was thus named "Bosumtwi," meaning "god-antelope."

It is further said that old Bompe gave some of the fish to his dog to find out whether it was suitable for consumption. The animal devoured it with unaccustomed relish and without ill effects. It is said that the dog grew more lively and robust. Old Bompe then tried the fish himself and found it was beyond anything he had ever tasted. It is said he scooped out some of the fish and proudly brought them to his master, Akora Gyima, who unhesitatingly declared them excellent. The next time old Bompe went to the lake, he was shocked to meet two strange hunters—one from Kuntenase and the other from Manso. There arose a squabble amongst the three who had discovered the lake. They informed their respective Chiefs.

As a result of this there arose a series of wars in which the Manso people, after having vanquished Kuntenase, declared war on Asamangs. The Manse army was routed and its Chief, Bosompem Ntow was beheaded by the Asamangs. After these "Wars of the Fish" Nana Akora Clime became the undisputed owner of the lake and in his bounty bestowed various fishing rights along the periphery of the lake to friendly neighboring states. As a result 26 villages grew up on the shores. Now, however, there are only 24. One village was so badly stricken with leprosy that the inhabitants decided on mass suicide.

Notes on Some Taboos of the Lake

1. No boats are permitted on the lake. Only specially designed logs of the "Odwima" tree are to be used.
2. Hooks and snares are forbidden.
3. Crabs are not to be taken out of the lake.
4. Brass pans, bottles, and anything made of steel are not allowed to touch the holy water.
5. Women are forbidden to go near the lake at certain periods.

Infringement of any of these taboos involves elaborate and expensive rites, and taxes are levied on the offender's village.

The Asamanghene is the custodian of the lake for the Asantehene.

History of Ejisu—Origins and How It First Became a Member
of the Asante Confederacy, ca. 1963
Informants: Omanhene of Ejisu; M.Y. Nkansah, Secretary,
    Traditional Council of Ejisu

From time immemorial the Ejisus have belonged to the royal Asona [group]. Tradition has it that it was an elephant that brought the Asona from the ground into the world at a place called Adaboye, which is commonly known as Abuakwa. The elephant emerged with a woman called Asoh Boade, who begat Ofori Panin, Nyarko-Brei, and Dokuwah. Ofori Panin was the King of the Asona at Abuakwa. Asoh Boade died and was succeeded by her daughter, Dokuwah, as the Queen-Mother of the Asona. Ofori Panin died and left many stool properties, which were contested amongst the Asona royals, with the result that civil war broke out on a Wednesday. During this time the Asona was independent and was also not subservient to anyone. As a result of this civil war the various members of the Asona [group] scattered into various localities, namely into Buabinso, Kibi, Mpraeso, Ejisu and Beposo. The senior men's Stool of the Asona was that of Buabinso. That of Eibi was the senior women's Stool of the Asonas. The Asona Queen-Mother, Dokuwah, emigrated from Abuakwa Adaboye to a place called Kokobianter, and from thence to Akim Abuakwa (Kibi). Nyarko-Brei also emigrated to Manse Akrofuom. She begat Amponsah Ahenasa and Gyawah. Gyawah also begat Ejisuhene Abuagye Agyei who contested for the Stool of his uncle, Amponsah Ahenasa, after his death. Abuagye Agyei did not succeed and therefore emigrated to Amansie Patabu where he died and was buried in the Royal Mausoleum. The villages of Asona Apinkra and Nuaso were asked to watch the body.

Asuna Gyima succeeded Abuagye Agyei and brought the Ejisus from Patabu to their present settlement. On arrival they bought the land from the Akyiawkromhene, Nana Obui Asamoah, for 80 Pereguans. A certain chief called Kwakyi Depoa was an Obrempong of note in the neighborhood and harassed the surrounding villages. The Ejisus fought and beheaded him for the sake of peace.

Asuna Gyima died and Duko Pim succeeded him. . . .

During this time the King of Denkyira, called Ntim Gyakari, was the overlord of all the Ashanti chiefs. This Denkyirahene harassed those subject states under his rule, with the result that they resented his tyrannous rule, and ultimately formed a plot for his overthrow. The celebrated Komfo Anokye assured these malcontents that they could conquer Ntim Gyakari if they would all amalgamate and put up a united front in battle against their overlord.

Accordingly these several states became one compact body and the Ejisuhene, Duko Pim, was made by Komfuor [Komfo] Anokye to take his place among the "Nifa" chiefs in the right wing of the army. He had one thousand guns under him in the field. In order to ensure the success of the campaign, the celebrated Komfuor Anokye requested the sacrifice of a "Nifa" chief in the right wing of the army. If such a chief would fall in battle, that would be a good token for the success of the campaign. The Ejisuhene, Duko Pim, accordingly sacrificed himself and fell on the field of battle on one Sunday (Kwasiada). Hence that day was consecrated to the Ejisu Oath to perpetuate the memory of Ejisuhene Duko Pim at the battle of Feyiase.

Before Ejisuhene Duko Pim sacrificed himself and went to the field of battle, he made arrangements with the Kumaseihene that he

would never inflict capital punishment by execution on any member
of the Asona [clan] after his death. This arrangement was accordingly made between the two Chiefs before going to Feyiase.

The following are also some of the Asona villages: Asotwe, Bonwire, Tano-Dumase, Abrakaso, Anyinasu, and Busore. These people
were all living in their present settlements and were subordinate to
the Ejisuhene emigrated from Patabu. . . .

Gyase Stool History, ca. 1962
Informant: Nana Poku Mensah II, Gyasehene

Gyasehene: One responsible for the upkeep of the office of the
king's household.

Gyase Stool: The Gyase Stool was created by Nana Opoku Frefre, who is traditionally known as Okatakyei.

Position of Gyasehene: He is supposed to be the most senior chief
of the Gyase Division of Asantehene. He is apparently the recognized Head Clan Chief.

Functions at the King's Palace: The first duty of the Gyasehene
is to wake the Asantehene early from bed. He sees to it that the Asantehene takes his bath at the proper time. He gives money to buy
food to the household servants. So far as tradition is concerned the
Gyasehene is the only person who knows the financial position of
the king. He is more or less the Financial Secretary, or Chancellor
of the Exchequer of the king.

Although the Asantehene has a Sanahene who is the traditional
Treasurer of the king, he takes his instructions from the Gyasehene
so far as the activities of the household are concerned. All those
concerned: the king's household comes under the category of the
Gyasehene. . . .

The Gyase stool is one of patrilineal descent, Mma Dwa. The
king cannot use his prerogative in the appointment of a candidate
for this stool. It is no hereditary royal stool. The stool belongs to
the descendants of Nana Opoku Frefre, and is so confirmed by the
Asantehene.

The first chief was Adusei Atwenewa. He is supposed to be the chief for whom the stool was created by King Opoku Ware. He was succeeded by Opoku Frefre, who was enstooled during the reign of Nana Opoku Ware. Buabasa was a title conferred on Opoku Frefre by the king. Buabasa means the breaker of hands or shoulders of war captives. He died on the stool.

He was succeeded on the stool by Nana Kwaku Boahene, a brother of Opoku Frefre. He went to no war. He died on the stool and was succeeded by Adu Bofuo during the reign of Nana Karikari. He was the son of Opoku Frefre. He went to war in Togoland (the Hwem war which lasted for three years). He died on the stool. He was succeeded by his son Kofi Poku, who was enstooled during the reign of the same king, Kofi Karikari. He died on the stool. He was succeeded on the stool by Poku Mensah, a son of Adu Bofuo. He went to the Yaa Asantewa war. He was on the stool before King Prempeh I was taken to Seychelles Island by the British imperialists. He died on the stool. He died when the Yaa Asantewa war was in progress. He died a natural death at Kumasi. He was succeeded on the stool by Manwere Opoku, who spent about four months on the stool. He was killed during the Yea Asantewa campaign in 1900. He was shot by the British at Jachie.

He was succeeded on the stool by Kwame Tuah, who was not in any way connected with the stool, but was appointed by the British Government after the Yaa Asantewa campaign in 1900. He was later destooled for mal-administration. He was succeeded on the stool by Asubonteng, a son of Adu Bofuo. He went to no war. . . . He was also destooled for a charge of desecration of the Golden Stool. He was deported or exiled after the case had been tried by Asanteman.

He was succeeded on the stool by Nana Kojo Poku. He was also destooled for mal-administration during Mr. O. S. Agyeman's conspiracy against the present Asantehene. He conspired against the present Asantehene. He was enstooled during the office of this same king and destooled by him.

He was succeeded on the stool by Kofi Poku, a son of Adu Bofuo. He was also destooled, after spending about four years on the stool. He was destooled for selling stool property.

He was succeeded by Adu Nantwi, a son of the stool. He was

also destooled by the present Asantehene for mal-administration. He was succeeded on the stool by Akwasi Adu Bofuo, a son of the stool. He was destooled by this present Asantehene for an act of conspiracy. He was succeeded on the stool by the present chief Poku Mensah II, a descendant of Adu Bofuo. He has reigned for almost five years on the stool.

The History of Ashanti Kings and the Whole Country Itself
AGYEMAN PREMPEH I

Agyeman Prempeh I wrote The History of Ashanti Kings and the Whole Country Itself *at the beginning of the twentieth century, and his account of the origins of the ruling (Oyoko) dynasty of Asante is the earliest we have. In the following excerpts from Prempeh's work, we find the story of Ankyewa Nyame, founding ancestress of the royal Oyoko in what became Asante. Therein, her arrival from the sky and the emergence of her people from holes in the ground, in effect, register the claim that the Asante are an autochthonous people, that is, none are immigrants from north, south, east, or west.*

[*The Arrival of Ankyewa Nyame at Asantemanso*]

After the beginning of the world at an Ashanti town called Akim Asiakwa there was a hunter. [Then the thing to do is hunting.] Once he said he was going to the forest and then he saw a Bear in a hole, but this hunter [knows all] had recognized the speaking of every creature, and this Bear told him that after a certain Ashanti feast, the son of God will come on earth. And a week after the feast the hunter went to the forest and hid himself in some [bush and] place. Then a great thunder burst 3 times and then a long gold chain descend from heaven to the earth and Essen came down carrying a bell & a stool called *Dufua* [early form of a stool consisting of solid block of wood with a handle] and wearing a fur [hunter] hat made of animal skin and then an immense copper dish ornamented by statues of beasts and inside a [*man sitting on*] woman carrying a stool and then another woman called Anchōyami [Ankyewa Nyame] [*came*] by the chain and sat on the stool and the former gave her the stool and sit behind her and this woman saw the hunter and called out for him with her hand because she was [*something . . . *] Ohemah and that woman made a press gesture with his hands and sat (?) in a little circle and then pointed his hand to his mouth but that man (?) was unable to understand it. And in a minute after the woman and the copper dish together flew and came right to in the [middle] midst of the city and all the citizens gather near [him] her and did the same press gestures as before and the people killed a hen and made a soup for [him] her when she had tasted it then she was able to speak. The only [thing] word she said was "I only mistakenly come here. Here is not the place I mean to come."

So saying she disappeared and went to a district called Asumyia Santimansū [Asantemanso]. And there certain [people?] from the ground appeared near her and the 10 family Royal [all] also appeared from the ground in different parts. The first came, and she was nearly bear a child and at that time people can go to heaven, and return afterwards. When that woman enter (?) he said: I am the son of God and my mother is called [Afua (?)] Insua and there it was sent to him from God 2 Sūman ["any protecting power, including the *abosom*"] one called Kwābināh & the other [one Kotuo (?)] Kūntror and a medicine called damtua [came] with (?) together. That's why when any Ashanti woman is nearly to bear her son, they put (cloth?), but Kwabinah is only worn by all the royal persons.

[Ankyewa Nyame and the Gathering of the Clans (mmusua)]

When Anchioyami came upon a place called Asumyia Ashantimansu a family called Oyuku sprang from the ground and sat at her right hand. Then another family called Dākū sprang from the ground and sat on her left hand. Then another family called Oyuku sprang and sat on her right hand. Then seven other different families came altogether but, they were not her families.—(Marginalia: from a place called Adansi Ahinsan [Adansimansu]. When they heard of Anchoyami they flocked to her).

Biletuo [Bretuo]
Atnah (?)
Agonah [Agona] [or] and Assokole
Jume [or] and Assunnāh [Asona]
Ekuonah [Ekɔna]
Assachily [Asakyiri]
Adduanah [Aduana] [or] and Achua

But there are some more Ayuku which are not families of Anchi-ayami. At that time when Anchiayami came to Assumi Asantimanso but it has been further explained that Yuku were the first people to come to her. There are three kinds of Oyuku. When these Yukun came near to her she asked one "Who are you?" and they said we are [part] member of your Yukun: and she told them "if you are Yukus, then I am Yuku-Kor-Kor-Kon, i.e., I am more Yuku than you." She also asked them what was the name of their Yukus and they said "we are Oyuku Abohen." To the second Yukun she asked them what was the name of their Yuku; they said "we are Yuku Atu-tuō." To the third she asked the name of their Yuku and they said [that] "we are Yuku [Bléman] Blaémam." There are three kinds of Oyukun Abohen

1st are called Asarman (The [*chief*] head of all Yuku)
2nd are called Kenassie.
3rd are called Manpontin.
There are three kinds of Atutuo
1st are called Adenchimansu
2nd are called [*Papasu*] Panpasoo
3rd are called Ayuomu

Oral Traditions of Denkyira: Two Views

In 1970, Kwame Daaku, through a UNESCO Research Project on Oral Traditions, compiled a dense set of oral traditions for Denkyira. The collection contained "raw data" of interviews transcribed in Twi (Akan) and English, and Daaku's synopsis of its findings represent, for our purposes, one view. Another view was compiled in the 1980s by C. E. Aidoo, who wrote, "These historical notes were compiled by kind permission of Nana Owusu Bori II, Denkyirahene." Aidoo's typeset nine-page document is available at the Africana Library at Northwestern University and at the Institute of African Studies, University of Ghana at Legon. Both Daaku's synopsis and excerpts from Aidoo's "historical notes" appear below.

Oral Traditions of Denkyira, ca. 1970

Adawu, Adawu Denkyira, that devours elephants,
Whenever we kneel down, we call on the name of Denkyira,
Whenever we rise up we look to Denkyira,
The Mighty one
Let one hasten to look at Denkyira,
The great one,
That swallows elephants,
If Denkyira went to sleep
It is now arisen, it is arisen indeed!
The Porcupine [i.e., Asante] is subject to Amponsem
Boa Amponsem, who uses only the freshly mined gold.

These and several other praises [were] always called out on festive occasions by the creator's drummer (Odomankoma Kyerema) of Denkyira to tell the story of the heroic past of the state which, between 1650 and 1700, was without doubt, the most powerful and certainly the most wealthy all [of] the Akan forest states of modern Ghana. Now divided into Upper and Lower Denkyira, which are separated by Twifo, it was once a vast empire stretching as far west to the Tano.

The people were formerly known as the Adawufo, but during their very long stav at Nkyiraa in the Brong Ahafo region they became known as the Denkyiras. Before the 1650s, Denkyira formed part of a loose confederation of states known as Akani, which were found in the area washed by the Oda, Ofin and Pra rivers. Throughout the first half of the 17th century the most important of these states was Adanse, which was being centralized by Ewurade Basa of the Asenee clan. Although all the states of the confederacy were grouped around their clan leaders, they had a common bond of unity in their worship of their traditional deity—Bona.

By the beginning of the seventeenth century, however, the long trading contacts with the north and with the coastal states were creating many difficulties and problems which could not be easily solved by the traditional consultation of Tutelary Deities. This was because trading, especially the coastal trading with the Europeans, brought in prosperity with its attendant problems such as population growth and new economic demands.

When in 1482, the Portuguese erected their castle at Elmina, they brought the sources of supply of foreign manufactured goods closer to the states of the Akani Confederation. The problem of population growth is evidenced by the frequent reports of wars in the interior. But it was the period after 1650 which was to intensify the struggle to assert one's power over one's neighbors. Several factors made possible the increased rivalry in the inland states. Firstly, there was the rush for footholds by virtually the whole of the Western and Northern European nations. The defeat of the Portuguese by the Dutch in 1637, and their eventual expulsion in 1642, was the beginning of a long period of keen and bitter European rivalry on the coast of Ghana. Between 1650 and 1701, the Brandenburgers, Danes, Dutch, English, French, and Swedes, established the[ir] forts and castles along the coast. The period of European concentration witnessed a great proliferation of firearms on the Gold Coast

(Southern Ghana). These firearms helped in intensifying the inter-ethnic wars, which produced countless slaves for the trans-Atlantic trade. It is interesting to note that it was not the coastal states which first came into possession of firearms which led in the building of Empire states on the Gold Coast. This was primarily due to the dependence of these states on the European trading nations, which overtly and covertly interfered in local politics for their own benefit.

The rise of Denkyira in 1659 is closely associated with the spread of firearms. Lying farther away from the area of direct interference of the Europeans, Denkyira was able to concentrate its efforts in subjugating all the neighboring states. By the end of the 1680s when it directed its attention to the southern and southwestern states, it had already laid a good foundation of the state. By the end of the 17th century Denkyira had subjugated Adanse, Asante, Assin, Sefwi, Wassa and Aowin. To the east, Denkyira had entered into an alliance with Akyem Abuakwa, one of the important Akan forest states.

Like Asante after it, Denkyira had a common bond of unity in the sacred objects which its rulers succeeded in introducing to the state. The most celebrated of these are the *Abankamdwa* (made of beads), the *Sasatia* and the Executioners Sword. These objects are said to have come together during the reign of the founding ancestress Adekra Adebo. The foundations of a politically strong state were said to have been laid by the fourth ruler, Wirempe Ampim, who in 1659, rid Denkyira of Adanse rule. A strong ruler, Wirempe Ampim, was perhaps the most fearful of the Denkyira rulers. In his drive towards national unity he caused the court and all the institutions of kingship to be well regarded. Those who disregarded his instructions were severely punished, hence the saying "Wirempe Ampim a owo ntam nso yenka," i.e., Wirempe Ampim whose oath is not to be sworn.

It was, however, Boa Amponsem I, whose name is closely associated with the stool. In spite of the fact that he was the fifth king, the Denkyira Stool is known as "Amponsem Stool"—A testimony to his enlightened leadership. Coming to the stool in about 1662, at the tender age of eight, he ruled until 1692. In his eventful reign, he extended the borders of his empire to reach the Tano in the west and the Birim in the east. It was he who brought virtually all the gold mining areas under Denkyira rule. Gold from the tributary states poured into the coffers of Denkyira at Abankeseso, hence the popular epithet, "Boa Amponsem a odi sika atomprada," i.e., "Boa Amponsem who uses only the freshly mined Gold."

At the height of its power, Denkyira, under Boa Amponsem, controlled not only the sources of gold, but [also] all the trade paths that led to the European establishments dotted between Half Assine and Anomabo. All the European companies endeavored to attract traders from Denkyira to transact business with them to the exclusion of their rivals. It was with this in view that between 1680 and 1694, Abankeseso, the Denkyira capital, became the resort of messengers from the European companies. Nor did the King remain an inactive participant in the trade. To safeguard his interests and those of his nationals, he appointed his trade consul to the coast. Tributary states [that] disrupted the free flow of trade were sure to incur the displeasure of Denkyira. In 1697, for instance, Assin was punished for interfering with the coastal trade.

Between 1670 and 1700, it was Denkyira which dictated the terms of trade because of its control over the sources of supply. Since Denkyira was the most powerful Akan State on the Gold Coast, it was to be expected that the Dutch, which was also the most powerful European trading nation in the area, would seek understanding and friendship with it. It is not certain when Dutch-Denkyira relations were first forged. But it is most uncertain that the Elmina Note, which formed the basis of the relationship between the two did not come into Denkyira possession by a mere accident of war. It is believed that at a certain point in its history, Denkyira took the "Note" from Eguafo to whom the ground rent of the Elmina Castle was being paid. The evidence in support of this contention is hard to come by. It is true that the Dutch were on friendly terms with Denkyira, and that Denkyira might have received some payments from the Dutch. But the origin of the agreement is more likely to have been a commercial agreement to induce the Denkyira traders to come to the Elmina Castle to trade with the Dutch. The haste with which the Dutch dispatched an emissary to Kumasi after the Asante defeat of Denkyira, to induce the Asante traders to come down to their forts confirm one in this belief.

By 1670, Denkyira had evolved an administrative machinery to suit its ever advancing empire. The whole state was divided into three fighting forces—The Akumatire (Right Wings), the Kyeremfem (Left Wing) and the Agona Adontendom (Advance guard). [E]ach of these divisions was under an Osafohene or war leader who exercised political control over his division in time of peace. Under the Osafohene were some chiefs and village heads. Under some of these major divisions were such officials as the Gyasehene, Tumantuhene, Dwanetoafohene, Kronkohene etc. These divisions were later to be perfected by the Asante, who introduced such titles as Kronti and Akwamu, etc. With its wealth, fame and strong government, the court of Denkyira was filled with royal hostages from the various tributary states whose continuous safety depended on the good behavior of their states. Here the young royals were educated in the intricacies of the Akan system of government. One of the most renowned of such hostages was Osei Tutu, who served his royal apprenticeship under the famous Boa Amponsem. This event, above above all else, may have given rise to the popular saying "Kotoko som Amponsem," i.e., The Porcupine (Asante) is subject to Amponsem (Denkyira).

Power and wealth seem to have blinded Denkyria to the plight of its subject states. Bosman and other contemporary observers described Denkyira as "haughty and overbearing." It did not hesitate to punish tributary states which defaulted in the payments of their yearly tributes. Tradition has it that it was because of such excessive demands that the Asante under Osei Tutu rebelled and fought its successful war of independence between 1699 and 1701. His policy of extortion did not endear Denkyira to its tributary states, which patiently awaited an opportunity to rebel against their overlord. Contrary to the popular assertion that it was the over-confidence and thoughtlessness of Ntim Gyakari which brought about the defeat, the evidence seems to suggest that it was the desertion of the [tributary] states which played a decisive [role] in the defeat of

Denkyira. Of all the many states it was only its ally, Akyem Abuakwa, which was known to have fought for Denkyira at this crucial moment. This fact explains the presence of the Abuakwa-hene of Denkyira who is now the Nifahene of the Denkyira State.

The defeat of [the] Denkyira state was one of the most significant, and certainly, the most remembered event in the traditions of the Akan people. This event is well-remembered by the famous dirge, which shows when and where the Denkyira nation fell; it runs:

Ntim Gyakari,	Ntim Gyakari,
Obrempon honyani a,	The wealthy noble
Osoa ne man kobaa no Feyiase,	Who led its nation to its doom at Feyiase,
Ntim Gyakari Nana firi Feyiase akoem	Grandchild of Ntim Gyakari hails from Feyiase, the field of battle

That Denkyira was the wealthiest nation at the end of the [seventeenth] century is borne out by the fact that it took Asante over ten days to gather together the spoils of war. For several years after the war the gold trade was at a standstill. Until the Asante had healed their wounds of battle there was no state strong enough to provide gold, ivory and slaves to satisfy the European demand on the coast. Although Ntim Gyakari is perhaps the best known of the Denkyira Kings because of the disaster [that] was suffered during his reign, his very name is anathema at the court of Denkyira. It is against Denkyira custom to name any of the succeeding Kings after him.

Between 1700 and 1820, Denkyira was under the rule of Asante. Characteristic of Akan government, as long as tributary states paid their annual tributes and provided the necessary contingent in time of war, they were left to rule themselves. As a result of this policy which was adopted by the Asante, Denkyira was able to regain its strength in [the] course of time. [It...] was during this period that one of the rulers Owusu earned the appellation Bore, or creator, on account of his inventiveness. He is said to have improved and added much to the material possessions of the King. Until 1820, however, the evidence seems to suggest that Denkyira reluctantly submitted itself to Asante rule. It was during the reign of Kwadwo Otibo that there developed a [rupture] in the Asante-Denkyira relationship, which lead to the eventual migration of the latter to Jukwa in Fanteland.

Tradition has it that during the Gyaman war [and] the Adinkra war, the Denkyirahene so distinguish himself by his bravery that he excited the envy of the Asantehene. In welcoming the troops back at a durbar at Kumase, the Asantehene was said to have greeted the Denkyirahene in the following words, "Kwadwo mo, wokoma po ni ne wokofa," (Well done Kwadwo, if this is how you fight for an ally, how would you fight your own war?). This innuendo was quickly retorted by one of the Denkyira executioners, who praised the Denkyirahene by saying that when he again bestirred one day, the white lion would turn black. This according to Denkyira tradition led to the flight of the Denkyiras from across the Pra. It is significant to note that it was the same king, Kwadwo Otibo, [who] was a signatory of the Bond of 1844. In Denkyira history, therefore, he is perhaps the most revered ruler next to Boa Amponsem I.

From about 1834, some of the Denkyiras began a gradual movement of people across the Pra into the ancestral homes. This led to the division of the state into upper and lower Denkyira, as we have it to this day. By the end of the first century after its flight, Upper Denkyira had become much more important, economically, than the settlements around Jukwa in Lower Denkyira. Indeed a return to their ancestral homes was being advocated by a large number of the people. That the stool is still at Jukwa and not at Dunkwa is due to the inordinate fear and abhorrence the Denkyiras entertain towards Asante. This abhorrence was so great that for some time after their migration, whenever the flowered plantain pointed towards Asante, it had to be felled. In 1945, however, under the rule of Owusu Bore II, the economic and administrative capital was moved to Dunkwa. But it is at Jukwa that all stools are kept and important rituals performed.

History of the Denkyiras, ca. 1980s

The Denkyiras, like other Akan [groups], had their original home somewhere in the area between the Volta and the Niger. They migrated southwards for reasons which have not definitely been established, but probably because of wars and famine. Nor can we give dates to the migration, but it was probably during the 16th century. The Moses of the Denkyiras, who led them southwards, was their great queen Ayɛkra Adebo. They had to fight continually, and suffered great hardships. They tried to settle by the Volta but because of the war with Atede Frempong, King of the Brong people, crossed the Volta and continued southwards till they reached the area of Techiman. They did not stay long in Techiman and in further treks lived for a while with the Nkyiraa section of the Brong. They adopted some of the customs of the Nkyiraa people and so got their name "Denkyirafoo," that is, naturalized Nkyiraa.

The migration continued till the Denkyiras reached a place in the present Adansi state called Ntutummɛ, two miles from Akrokyere. The Adansis had preceded the Denkyiras in the journey from the north, and had already settled at Akrokyere, Dompoase, Ayaase, Adubiase and Akurofurom. From Ntutummɛ, the Denkyiras moved to the western border of the Adansis, and found their famous capital Abankɛseɛso by the Ofe River near the present village of Abuakwa.

Queen Ayɛkra Adebo had three male and one female [child] by her husband, Yao Awere. Their names were Anin Kokobo, Ahi, Aha and Afunwaa. Anin Kokobo succeeded his mother and became the first king of the Denkyiraas at Abankɛseɛso. He was a prominent chief but died young, and was succeed by his brothers Ahi and Aha. It is not known whether these two princes shared the government or whether one succeeded the other. However, they must have been able rulers as under them the Denkyiras grew strong and expanded, and it is stated that in the time of the next king the capital Abankɛseɛso was a large city with seventy-seven streets and watered by seven streams.

Ahi and Aha started a divisional system of rule. They divided their people into three sections, Akumantine, Kyeremfem and

Agona Adontendom. These names are still retained, but the three divisions are now better known as Benkum, Nifa and Adontene, respectively. Agona-Adontene comprises the main body of the army, and was composed of Twafo, Adontene and Kronko sections. In addition, there were the Gyase and Kyidom sections which formed the bodyguard and rear-guard of the king.

It was at this time, according to tradition, that the Denkyiras received their "Abankam-dwa" (stool made of shining stone) together with a sword and the "Sasatia" ([ɔbosom or suman] of the executioner), which all descended from heaven. These greatly revered articles are still in existence.

After Ahi and Aha came Mumunumfi, of whom practically nothing is known. He was followed by Werempe-Ampem—*Werempe-Ampem a ɔwɔ din a yemmɔ* (Werempe-Ampem who has a name which is not pronounced). He earned this name because he inspired so much terror. Frivolously swearing an oath in the king's name brought immediate death penalty. He had a long reign and on his death was succeeded by Boadu Akafe Brempong.

Boadu Akafo Brempong fought the first of the great wars which made Denkyira into an empire, against the Aowins. This was about the middle of the seventeenth century, when the Denkyiras were already amongst the strongest of the Akan people. The Aowins then lived southeast of Sehwi [Sefwi], in the area now inhabited by the Wassaw Amanfis. Under the king Oti Akenten they had grown very rich, and Boadu Akafe Brempong heard with envy tales of the magnificence of Oti's palace. He therefore determined to subdue the Aowins. The war which followed dragged on for years and during it Oti Akenten died. His successor Abiri Mmuro carried on the war, but received a crushing defeat by the Denkyiras, and the Aowin power was completely destroyed. The victors captured large quantities of gold.

Boadu Akafo Brempong died a few days after his great victory over the Aowins, before the arrangements had been completed for the triumphant entry into Abankɛseso, the capital. The chiefs therefore met on the battlefield and having decided that a new king must be elected before the army returned to Abankɛseɛso, sent a messenger home for a prince to be sent [to] them.

There then existed in Denkyira the position of heir-apparent, and the heir at this time was one Boadi Akyem. (He had been brought up among the Akyems). The people, however, refused to accept Boadi's candidature and he failed in his efforts to obtain the stool. He refused to accept the people's descision and resorted to force but was defeated, and though owing to the intercession of some of the chiefs he was not executed. . . . [He] lost his position of heir-apparent, a post thereupon abolished forever in Denkyira.

To succeed Akafo Berempong, a son of Bensua, sister of [the] late king, was chosen. This was the great Boa Ampunsem. He was only 8 years old when he was sent to the army to lead them in the triumphant entry into Akankɛseɛso.

Boa Ampunsem had a very long and prosperous reign, and under him the Denkyiras reached the height of their power and prosperity, having dominion over all surrounding [groups], including the Ashantis. Boa Ampunsem encouraged and developed the gold industry and it was he who first introduced a gold currency amongst the Akan peoples. A thousand men were detailed to be the king's farmers, and they were the ancestors of the Akuapems (Thousand Farmers). The Denkyiras traded with the Europeans on the coast. Claridge describes them as being now the richest and most powerful of the inland [groups]. Boa Ampunsem organized a treasury system, the first treasurer (fotosanfoɔhene), being Kwaku Pran. . . .

Boa Ampunsem was succeeded by Ntim Gyakari, son of Ako Abenaa Bensua, the late king's sister, and reputed to be the son of Osei Tutu, Asantehene. Osei Tutu, the only nephew of his predecessor Obiri Yeboa, was in his youth a sword bearer and hostage at the Abankɛseɛso court. While there he made love to Abenaa Bensua, who when he found herself pregnant by him advised him to flee. This Osei Tutu wisely did, and took refuge in Akwamu. It was while he was in Akwamu that his uncle Obiri Yeboa died and he was summoned home to be the new king.

After his popular predecessor, Ntim Gyakari soon earned the dislike of his people. He treated them harshly, and under his tyrannical rule the subject [groups] became restive. Chief of these restive [groups] was the Ashantis, who under Osei Tutu were on the threshold of their greatness. The story of their rebellion against Denkyira is bound up with the history of that famous of all West African [spiritualist], Okomfo Ankoye. . . .

[The Asante defeat of Denkyira thus] ended the paramountcy of Denkyira over the Akans. Ashantis now became dominant in the forest country and remained so till British power was established.... Ntim Gyakari was succeeded by Owusu Bori I who is said to have started his wars 40 days after installation. Unable to push northward, he sought to establish Denkyira power in the area between the offin [Ofin River] and the sea, and he is said to have brought the Fanti [group] under his sway. . . . Owusu Bori's successors were mainly peaceful kings, who on the whole were loyal to the Ashanti dominion, though there was an occasional revolt against the Ashanti. Their reigns take up the middle and latter half of the eighteenth century. Little is remembered or recorded about them. The Denkyiras still lived on both sides of the Offin, subjects to the Ashanti north of the river but in the south still powerful. . . .

Subsequent history of the Denkyiras up till the beginning of the twentieth century is a tale of peaceful expansion, interspersed with participation in the frequent campaigns against the Ashantis when the treaty of 1867 between the English and Dutch was signed under which the sweet river was made the boundary between the spheres of influence, all to the west being Dutch, the Denkyiras objected strongly to be placed under Dutch protection, and took the leading part in the formation of the Fanti Confederation and the subsequent blockade by the Confederation of Elmina. In 1873 during the Fifth Ashanti war, a battle was fought at Abuminam on the oukskirts of Jukwa, where the Ashantis were again victorious.

In the subsequent Ashanti campaigns the Denkyiras played their part along with the other colony [groups], but they were now too weak to be of great assistance to the British. They were at a great disadvantage in being divided into two sections, one at Jukwa and along the Offin at about 50 miles apart. [W]ith the coming of a lasting peace in the Gold Coast they shared in the general improvement in material conditions, though they shared in the prevalent political chaos due to the impact of European ideas and practices on a primitive and non-progressive form of native government. In recent years, however, there has been a great improvement.

Nana Owusu Bori II, the ex-Denkyirahene, decided in 1943 to move his headquarters from Jukwa to Dunkwa, easily the largest town in this state, by the Offin in Upper Denkyira where the mass of this people live and where the land has belonged to his stool from the time of Boadu Akafo Berempon. There in 1945 came a very great step forward when a treasury system was adopted. The first president of the finance committee was Nana Kofi Adu, the Kurontihene, who had the example of the *fotosanfoɔhene* Kwaku Pran of Boa Ampunsem's reign to inspire him. Later in 1945 the neighboring states of Twifo and Hemang decided to federate with Denkyira, Nana Owusu Bori II being the first president of this confederacy, which links up the two halves of his state and extends for more than 100 miles from [the] Upper part of the Offin River almost to the sea.

Oral Traditions of Assin (Asen) and Twifo
KWAME DAAKU

Among his pioneering role as oral historian, Kwame Daaku also collected oral traditions among the peoples of Assin (Asen) and Twifo in 1967 and 1969. The first selection is a synoptic essay on the peopling of Assin, while the second is excerpted from a longer interview conducted in Assin-Nyankumasi.

[*The Etsi and Assin (Asen)*]

By the first half of the seventeenth century the Etis (Etsis) were established throughout the central portion of the forest and coastal areas of Ghana as far north as the Pra and Offin rivers. Political power was invested in small independent village chiefs. According to Fanti tradition there were seventy-seven Eti (Etsi) state umbrellas. Nevertheless the evidence would seem to suggest that the Eti population was very thin. Their language was a precursor of modem Fanti. Owing to population movement and state formation to the north of the Etis (Etsis), groups of Fantis began to move across the Pra to settle with the Etis (Etsis). Most of these Fanti migrants moved to the coast to found the Fanti states (Anomabu etc.)

In spite of occasional struggles with the Fantis, the Eti maintained their independence. During this period, because of European commercial activity and the influence of the Fanti on the coast a number of Eti (Etsi) states were formed, the most powerful of whioh were Abramboe, Asebu, and Sunkwa. The relationship between these states and the Fantis remains obscure and must be left to further studies in Fanti history. Nevertheless we can safely say that the Eti (Etsis) and Fantis lived side by side in the area throughout the seventeenth century.

With the rise of Denkyira in the latter part of the seventeenth century, the independence of the Eti (Etsi) was threatened. North of the Etis (Etsis)—across the Pra [River]—lay the Akanni Confederacy, the westernmost part of which was Denkyira. Contacts with the coast led to formation of a strong and expending Denkyira state which soon absorbed the remaining members of the confederacy, i.e., Adansi, Assin (then north of the Pra) and the nucleus of the Ashanti state.

The relationship between the Etis (Etsis) and the Denkyira is not clear, but it appears that by the 1690s Adansi and Assin had been conquered by the Denkyira state. Small sections of the Assins may have fled across the Pra to establish themselves in the area immediately south of the river. The Denkyira empire did not last long. By 1702, it had fallen into obscurity due to the rise of Ashanti which took over most of its conquests. In the confusion subsequent to the fall of Denkyira, several small trading states seem to have existed in the Pra valley under the loose control of Ashanti. The most outstanding of these was Koshea whose leader Agyeinsem is mentioned by the Dutch Governor General Sevenhuissen in 1702 in the instructions to his sub factor Nyendaal. Koshea was one of the most important crossing points on route to Denkyira and Ashanti. It had resisted Denkyira in 1697 and had been defeated. With the fall of Denkyira, Koshea became a natural ally of Ashanti and for half a century reaped the benefits of its position. Southwest of Prasu, another group, the Akotis, had probably formed by this time.

The position of the Etis (Etsis) at the turn of the century became particularly difficult as a result of the large-scale migration of the Borbor Fantis through their land to the coast. After conquering the coastal Fanti states they began to expand northward. Soon the chief of Abura exercised a loose authority ever most of the Eti (Etsi) states in the Ochi Valley. Further north the Etis (Etsis) probably fell under the influence of the Assins. In the second decade of the eighteenth century the Ashanti began to raid from Adansi and Assin into the lands of the Etis (Etsis) and Fantis. Assin Attandaso tradition records six expeditions across the Pra. This probably reconciled the southern Etis (Etsis) to a shaky alliance with the Ashantis. The uneasy alliances of Assin and Ashanti, Eti (Etsi) and Fanti lasted through the first half of the century. But soon the strains caused by the great growth of the Fanti and Ashanti powers produced a shift in the policies of their buffer states, Eti (Etsi) and Assin.

Shortly after the middle of the century the Fantis attacked Asebu which was soon supported by the rest of the Etis (Etis). The slave raiding and other exactions of the Fantis had, finally disrupted any link there might have been in defense against the Ashantis. Asebu fell and most of the Etis (Etsis) fled to Assin, north of the Pra, some of whose people had already settled south of the river. Here developed the relationship between the Eti (Etsis) and the Assins which was to last until this day. The Assins, north of the Pra, were divided into several independent groups—some of whom fought in the Adonten (vanguard) of the Ashanti army. One group, whose ruling family probably lived in the Amakom near Kumasi controlled the area around Apagya in Adansi. Another group lived at Ansa just to the north of this. The Eits (Etsis) fled to Adansi [and] it was these rulers with whom they took refuge.

The break in the Assin-Ashanti accord was the result of long Assin cooperation with Ashanti aims without adequate reward. The Assins had taken part in all of the Ashanti wars, given the lives of many men and were always charged a crippling war tax. Trade, however, had brought prosperity, a population increase and perhaps arrogance. This the Ashantis could not tolerate. Together Eti (Etsi) refugees and Assin of Apara moved south of the Pra to escape then. Led by Otsibo Korobanda, they founded what is now Assin Attandaso, called after their first seat in the Konkan forest.

Despite the war between the Etis (Etsis) and the Fantis, the Fanti King of Abura still claimed jurisdiction over the southernmost Eis and it was with the acquiescence of Abura that the Attandaso controlled the southern Etis. Towards the end of the eighteenth century the Attandaso followed their Etsi subjects to the more attractive land about Bosumadwe. Although the Attandaso owned the land in the Konkan forest, here they were the tenants.

Sometime after the Attandaso settled at Fanti Nyankumasi, the people of Ansa accompanied by their share of the Eti (Etsi) refugees moved south across the Pra. But unlike the Attandaso, they found no empty land and were granted use of the land by the Etis (Etsis) of Andoe. Because the only land they owned was north of the Pra, the Ansas, now called Appimenim, were much more dependent upon their Etsi landlords. They eventually settled at Manso, which soon became a busy slave-trading center.

In 1807 full-scale war broke out between Assins and the Ashantis. The Assins were said to have interfered with Ashanti trade and poisoned their merchants. This war probably consolidated the leadership of the Attandaso and Appimenirn *Amanhene* over any group of Etis (Etsis) and Akotis which may have previously been independent. The two strongest chiefs of Attandaso were the *ɔmanhene* at Fanti Nyankuinasi and the chief of Assin Nyankumasi. Among the Appimenin, the *ɔmanhene* at Manso and his Eti landlord, the chief of Andoe, were most important.

In the years after 1807 several small groups arrived in Assin from the north, fleeing the Ashantis. They were generally granted land by the Eti (Etsis) with the acquiescence of the *ɔmanhene*. However, it was after 1874 that the last large population movement occurred. Once again people in Adansi turned against the Ashanti. Because of their experiences in wars, a number of them came south of the Pra to serve as scouts for [the British commander] Garnet Wolseley. After the war, relations with Ashanti and Adansi worsened and in 1886 full-scale war between the Ashanti and Adansi drove thousands of the latter south of the Pra. In many villages of Assin the majority of the people are descendants of this latest Adansi movement.

Oral Traditions of Assin-Twifo, ca. 1969

[Opening ritual with libation (*mpaeε*) . . .]

Q: You see Nana, in the old days, the Dutch called the Assins not Assins but Akanni or Akan. They wrote that the Assins were Akans? How true is this?

A: That's quite true. In the olden days all those who spoke Asante that is all these people were called Akans.

Q: Does it mean therefore that there was no state called Akan?

A: No. You see Northerners are not called Akans nor are those people beyond the Volta called Akans. In the old days an Akan meant an Ashanti. . . .

Q: Where did the Assins come from to settle here?

A: We came from Adansi but those who are ignorant of the facts will say they came from Ashanti, which is completely fallacious . . . .

Q: Who led the people on their migration here?

A: Kwaku Aputae and Tsibu. They used to go hunting with the Asantehene Osei Tutu.

Q: In 1701 before Osei Tutu fought the Denkyiras, the Ashantis had fought against the Assins three years previously. The Assins were supposed to have been under their chief Agyensem whose name is not clear but who was believed to have probably been a king of Kushia. Does Nana know of any chief in your tradition whose name was Abinsan or Akyinsan, or something of the sort?

A: Was it a town?

Q: No, it was the name of a chief. Reindolf claims a chief of Kushia was the Agyensem. Was there a Kushia chief called that?

A: The Denkyirahene who fought against the Assins was called Owusu Bore. He was drowned in the River Pra.

Q: Why is the Assin state called Assin? What is the meaning of the name Assin?

A: The meaning of the name is that Osei Tutu came with 40,000 warriors to fight us but he could not defeat us. So he complained that he had conducted things in half measures with us, and thus had made the situation serious (Assin). . . .

Q: Why is that although there are many other clans in this town in addition to the Oyoko clan, it is the Ayoko who reign and not for instance Bretuo or Asakyiri?

A: These are the clans we met here. You see there were already different clans of people staying in their town and so if our clan came to meet them then it did not mean that they should all belong to one clan.

Q: But suppose the incoming clan was superior in arms to the already established one and so if they fought and the old clan was vanquished then . . . ?

A: If they fought and the new overcome the old then the order of the new became law. . . .

Q: Nana, can you tell us some more of the history of the Assins. For instance you said that the Edubiase and Kwamiatta people moved here from Edubiase in Adansi. Can you tell us where the other Assins moved from in Adansi?

A: The Kwamiattas moved from what is now New Edubiase in Adansi. . . . The Nyankumasi people came from Aboabo [in Adanse]. . . .

Q: How did it come about that some Assins are called Apemanim whilst others are called Attandansus?

A: That is because each of them has his own state. Nana Nkyi's was Apemanim and he came from Ansa [in Adanse]. When he arrived he had a thousand guns (warriors?) that hence Apemanim. It was Kofi Ntodwa who came with the thousand guns. . . .

Q: Nana, can you tell us something also about the Attandansus especially their origins?

A: The Attandansus had a river called Ntandanna which later on became corrupted to Ntandannansuo.

Q: You see many people believe that because this town is called Assin-Nyakumasi it is Assin, while Fante-Nyakumasi is thought to be Fante in origin?

A: No, that is not so; they are all Assin. . . .

Q: We understand that Bosomadwe and Akrampa are Etsi; who are the Etsi?

A: Those we met here when we first came.

Q: Did you meet the Bosomadwes and Akrompas?

A: Yes. Thus they are called Etsi. . . .

Q: Another thing of great importance to us is to determine how long it has been since people migrated here. A way to do this is to get a list of all chiefs who have been on the stool. Can Nana give us such a list starting from the first chief to yourself?

A: That is the reason why we pour them libation. On an Akwasi-dae or Awukuade we pour libation to them and call upon such or such a chief to come and drink some wine. If they are then, we call upon all of them but if a chief did not die on the stool, then no libation is poured to him.

Q: So, if one did not die on the stool then no black stool is made for him?

A: No, no rites are performed for you. . . . [After a list 6 names is given] These are the ones who died on the stool. Those who were destooled or who abdicated have not been included. If you did not die on the stool, then you lost all association with the stool. You had no name. . . .

A: [After a resounding defeat at the hands of the Asante some time in early the eighteenth (?) century] we then ran to Cape Coast where the Asantehene took his sword of state and swore that he had fought across the sea and so had completed his fight. Many families with their families then left for hiding places in the forest. The Dutch had come then and seeing us requested us to send our people on board their ship to be taken overseas to serve their King. There were wise ones amongst us so we refused and instead sought hiding places in Sefwiland, Nzimaland, and other places of safety. We asked the Dutch to help us and they supplied us with rifles on the agreement that we would let them stay with us for 99 years. . . . When the Ashantis were driven off we came to settle here.

Oral Traditions of Bono-Takyiman

DENNIS M. WARREN AND K. OWUSU BREMPONG

In 1971, Dennis M. Warren and K. Owusu Brempong published one of several oral histories resulting from their collaborative research on the Techiman (Takyiman) Traditional State. This collection, unlike Daaku's, appeared only in English translation. The topical excerpts below cover a range of subjects, allowing the reader a fuller picture—deduced from a fairly large body of oral accounts—of Bono society and history as recalled by some of its key elders and indigenous political officials.

[*Interview with Nana Kwame Nyame, 1969-1970*]

1. The Early Chiefs and Nyame

It is not true that in the early days Techiman [(Takyiman)] was ruled by women (queenmothers), or that women led the soldiers in time of war. From time immemorial, Techiman has had chiefs; men have always ruled. Nor is it true that in the early days Techiman served Nyame [(the Creator)] which was the moon, a female [ɔbosom]. It is also not true that the men rebelled against the women, therefore the women chose one of the men to be a chief (Krontihene) to run the affairs of the state while the queenmother's council still worked. Techiman has never been ruled by women. The person who told this history did not learn history from his father; it is a fabrication of his own mind. When an Omanhene dies, the Krontihene is the next chief in power to rule the state. Nana Kwame Nyame does not understand the reason why [the London-based researcher Eva] Meyerowltz wrote that Nyankopon was *owia* ("the sun") and Nyame was *bosome* ("the moon"). He does not know where Meyerowitz got these materials. Nyankopon, Nyame and Odomankoma are the same, [Creator].

2. Who Are the Fanti?

It is not true that the Fanti brought the [*abosom*] Taa Kora and Taa Mensah from the *sarem* [(savanna)]. All these [*abosom*] were picked in Techiman. Nana Takyi Firi [, the founder of Takyiman,] was not a Fanti from the *sarem*. The Fanti migrated from Techiman. If the Fanti claim that they migrated from the *sarem* then it can be said that Techiman people came from *sarem* but their origin is Techiman not the *sarem*. It was war that sent the Fanti away [to the coast in the fifteenth or sixteenth century].

3. Yam Festivals

It is not true that when chiefs celebrate yam festivals it means their soul is dead and they want to revive it. Nor is it true that when [the] *ɔbosomfo* celebrate yam festivals it means the [*abosom*] are dead and they want to revive them. The yam festival is a tradition; every state celebrates one. It is like the Christmas celebrated by Europeans. During yam festivals they first give food to the [*ɔbosom*] Taa Mensah because the soul of the state is in the hands of this [*ɔbosom*]. After the yam is given to the [*ɔbosom*], the elders (the chiefs) also celebrate their yam festivals one by one.

4. Diala and the Sahara

It is not true that Techiman people came from a place called Diala. Nana Kwame Nyame was not there when this history was told [to Eva Meyerowitz]. Techiman people came from a hole at Amowi [in the adjacent district of Nkoransa]. It is not true that the ancestors of the Akan were white people living at the *sarem*. There were no white people living at the *sarem*.

5. Nana Brempong Katakyera

He was a very old chief. His nephew was Kwakye Ameyaw, a handsome young man. All the young men and the chief's servants loved him very much. Nana Katakyera was very old and would not die to leave the stool vacant for Kwakye Ameyaw. The servants always loved debating. One evening they sat beside an open fire in the courtyard of the palace. They began to debate the topic "Who can face hunger for thirty days." Some servants declared that some people could do it, while others said that no one could do it. Nana Katakyera was there. He was moved by the topic and told them that, although he was old, he could face hunger for thirty days. This was the time when the Techiman capital was at Maaso. Maaso means that town which is big. . . .

All the sub-chiefs lived in their villages and only the chief and his servants lived at the Maaso palace. The sub-chiefs had elected some of their elders to take care of their Maaso wards in their absence. These elders did not go to the chief's palace, but stayed within their wards. They went to their farms everyday and stayed in their houses. The chiefs came from their villages and went to the palace only when there was trouble, or during Monokuo when they wait to celebrate the Adae. After the Adae they went back to their villages leaving the elders behind to take care of their wards. Nana Katakyera Brempong promised to face hunger the next day. He would stay in a room without any food or drink for thirty days. He did not know that it was a trick that Kwakye Ameyaw and the servants were playing to kill him. He was not forced to do it, but it was a trap into which he fell. He began the fast. Every morning talking drums were beaten to call him to make sure that he was not dead. They beat the drums, "Brempong Katakyera Wobetumi ne kom adi abemerese?" "Brempong Katakyera, can you face hunger?" The chief answered "Maadi maawie" "I have already faced it." This went on for twenty-nine days. On the twenty ninth day, the chief's voice became very small and dry. He could not answer the call of the talking drums properly. On the last day, the thirtieth, no answer was given to the call of the drums. Nana Katakyera had died and the stool was vacant for Nana Kwakye Ameyaw.

The death of the chief brought silence in the palace. The other chiefs were in their villages and the servants kept it hidden from the elders in charge of the Maaso wards. Later, they informed some of the linguists secretly. The announcement of the chief's death brought disorder to the capital. The Krontihene was informed in his town. Men began to ride about on horses. Killings began simultaneously in all directions. The riders used their big cutlasses on the head of every person they met. They went to the palace at Maaso to see the dead chief. All the chief's servants, about three thousand, were killed in the presence of the Krontihene. Nana Kwakye Ameyaw succeeded. The spirit of his predecessor was not satisfied with him; it was during Kwakye Ameyaw's time that Techiman was destroyed [during the 1722-1723 Bono-Asante war]. . . .

[Interview with Nana Akumfi Ameyaw, ex-Techimanhene, 1970]

1. Bono Culture and Traditions

It is not true when people say that Techiman had no culture or tradition of its own. Techiman taught the Asante how to wear cloth. Techiman people used to wear ornaments made of gold. The Asante used pieces of iron from the blacksmith's shop and they called it gold. Techiman Queenmother Dwamenawaa taught the Asante what gold was. Techiman knew pure gold and it was only pure gold that they used. . . . The culture of Asante came from Techiman. Ohene Ameyaw was a great king. His treasury was different from that of Asante. Techiman had a gold treasury but Asante had pieces of iron. Asante had no gold. How could they make gold ornaments? The Asante did not know anything like gold state swords. Everything they had was made of iron, the same as is used for making hoes, but they called it gold. Kente weaving came from Techiman. Even the ancestors of the present Bonwire Chief came from Techiman. When the Asante conquered Techiman, they picked some of the people who knew handiwork and took them to Asante. They selected goldsmiths and men who knew other crafts.

The beating of the talking drums came from Techiman. It is the responsibility of every chief to know the first words of the talking drums. The words go like this: "Odomankoma boa adee ɔbɔɔ Bono ansa na abɔɔ adee biara." This means: "When [the Creator] created things, he created Bono before any other thing." There are many people who do not understand these words. The Asante had similar sayings [but in] their [own] words. Instead of "Odomankoma boo adee ɔbɔɔ Bono," they play "Odomankoma boo adee Boreofo boo ada." They do not want to play "ɔbɔɔ Bono," "it created Bono." The Bono are proud to say that they are the first born people, the first people to come to this land. Techiman has a golden stool still on Techiman land. The Asante took another of the Techiman golden stools away to Asanteland. [For instance,] the Buoyam Stool is pure gold. No one is allowed to see it. It is not in the village, and no one knows where it is kept. People are afraid that if the golden stool were shown to the public it would be stolen.

2. The Importance of the Yam Festival

The yam festival is celebrated every year. During yam festivals the chiefs remember their ancestors. They prepare mashed yam, sometimes mixed with palm oil, call the ancestors, and give the food to them. That particular day is a meeting day. The entire family congregates to pay homage to its chiefs. The most important thing about the yam festival is the family reunion. They meet the members who are sick. They ask what has happened to those who could not come. They pray to the ancestors to help them and guide them through another year.

3. Kra Dwadee ("Washing the Soul—Purification of the Kra [(Soul)]")

Kra dwadee is the purification of the *sunsum*, "spirit." The elders say that a man's life and his capacity for hard work depend on his *sunsum*. During the *kra* purification, they call on their *sunsum* to give them long life. They include the names of Onyankopon and the earth [Asase], Yaa. It is a blessing and they beg to meet another year. When they pour a libation, they first call Onyankopon [Creator], followed by Asase Yaa and the ancestors, asking them to come and drink wine. The new year has emerged. They beg for long life, for success and for children. They also beg for the protection of the farmer against cutlass wounds, protection of hunters against gun wounds, and the protection of travelers. They beg for children for women who are not productive and beg that women regain those of their children who died after birth. They also ask help for the building of the family. Finally, they promise to give Onyankopon, Asase Yaa and the ancestors another sheep next year if they still have life. Libation is prayer. The chiefs' yam festivals and the *musuo yi* ["removal of misfortune"] are the same as those of the *abosomfo*.

4. The Fante at Tano Anafo

The grandparents of the Fanti migrated from Techiman to the coast about seven hundred years ago. Fanti Abakrampa people are called Aborafou meaning Bonofɔ, Bono people. Brobro Fanti means Bono Bono Fanti. Bono Bono has been changed to Brobro. The Abakrampa asked that Nana Akumfi Ameyaw stay with them when he was young. He stayed with them for some years before he became a chief. He was a chief when the Anomabohene died. He buried the Anomabohene. As Techiman's chief, he used to go to Abakrampa, Mankesim and other Fanti towns on occasions such as funerals. He encouraged most of those people to come to Techiman. Later, some of them came and Nana sent them to Tano Anafo via Nsuta. They settled there and started cocoa farms. Nana knew this would encourage other Fanti to come back to Techiman, their place of origin. During Nana's reign, the Fanti at Tano Anafo used to come to greet him every year during festivals. They sent him gifts of wine and money. They know they are part of Techiman.

Oral Traditions of the Fante:
Komenda and Kwamankese
JOHN KOFI FYNN

In the mid-1970s, the late John Kofi Fynn published the results of his oral history research among the Fante polities of coastal Ghana. In the volumes which constituted "Oral Traditions of the Fante States," Fynn utilized both oral and documentary evidence found in the national archives of Ghana and elsewhere concerning, in his own words, "the origins, state organization and customs of the Fante states." These focal points follow closely the template developed by Kwame Daaku, who pioneered the same kind of oral historical research among Akan societies of southern Ghana as well as among non-Akan groups, such as the Gonja in northern Ghana. The synoptic histories of two Fante polities—Komenda and Kwamankese—appear below.

Komenda, ca. 1974

The Komenda state is bounded on the west by Shama; on the east by Elmina, on the north by Wassa; and on the northeast by Eguafo and Abrem. The capital of the state is Akatakyi known in European records as Little Commando, Aitaco, Akitakij, or Ekke Tokki. Apart from Akatakyi, the state of Komenda consists of Aboransa, Antardo, Bisease, Dominase, Dompoase, Kissi, Kwarhinkrom, Kyiasi, Kokwaado, Kafodzidzi and a number of villages. The population of these towns in the 1970 census was 16,590.

According to their traditional accounts, the founder of the Komenda state was one Kɔme who migrated with his people from Takyiman in the present day Brong-Ahafo Region of Ghana. It is said that, in the remote past, the Takyiman area was constantly in great turmoil; there were wars and rumors of war. In this general state of insecurity, it became necessary for a number of families to leave their homeland in search of peace and security. It was in a moment of such crisis that Nana Kɔme, a warlord, and his sub-chiefs and people left Takyiman and began the long march south-ward to the coast. They fought on their way until they reached Mankesim where they stayed for some time. From Mankesim they moved to Kromantse, Yamoransa, Eguafo and finally to Akatakyi. It was here that the peoples dispersed to found settlements which later on constituted the Komenda state.

Eguafo tradition, however, states that the Komenda people orig-inally part of the Eguafo kingdom and that, in the olden days, Eguafo stretched from the Benya River in the east to the mouth the river Pra in the west. They add that Akatakyi itself was formerly a small fishing village peopled by immigrants from the Nkusukum area.

Some twenty years ago, Nana Kofi Asefua, chief of Kankan (Dutch-Komenda), and his elders told Mrs. Eva L.R. Meyerowitz that Akatakyi was founded by Akyene Takyi, a grandson of the first Eguafo king, and that it was referred to in the early European records as "Little Eguafo." The Komenda people admit that the lands they now occupy formerly belonged to the Eguafo but they insist that the founder of their state was Kɔme and that they had never been subjects of Eguafo kings. Their story is that when Kɔme and his people arrived in Eguafo, they appealed to Abo Takyi, the king of Eguafo, to give them a place to settle. Abo Takyi told the Nkusukum immigrants that all his lands had been taken up and set-tled except the area between Kankan and the estuary of the river Pra which was inhabited by a man-eating monster. The Eguafo king further told Kɔme and his follower that if they could capture and kill the monster, he would give the land to them as a present. Kɔme, being an old warrior, accepted the challenge. He attacked, captured and killed the monster which he found to be half-human and half-animal. After completing this assignment, Abo Takyi and Kɔme "drank [ɔbosom]" to be friends. The king of Eguafo not only hon-ored his promise by giving the land between the Benya and the Pra rivers to Kɔme and his people but also he brought a young girl who had just reached her puberty age to be sacrificed to the gods [i.e., *abosom*] to mark the occasion.

There is documentary evidence, however, to show that up to the early years of the eighteenth century, the kings of Eguafo controlled the land area now occupied by the Komenda people. A "Dutch Map of the Gold Coast of Guinea" drawn at Moure in 1629 shows that (a) the Eguafo kingdom stretched from the east bank of the Benya River to the Pra River and (b) that Akatakyi was a small fishing and salt making village on that coast. Secondly, in 1687, the English reported that the French were attempting to settle at Komenda with the assistance of the king of Eguafo. The following year, Amoasi Esilfi, king of Eguafo, on behalf of himself, his chiefs, and their descendants, signed a treaty with N. Sweerts, the Dutch Director-General at Elmina, which, among other things, ceded the beach "beginning from the river of Shama (Bosompra) as far as to the river of del Mina named Banja (Benya) on which beach are situated the small villages Cottebre, Obriebie, Akitakij or Commany and Ampenyi." The chief of Eguafo also agreed not to permit any foreign nation to settle on the said beach except the English who should be allowed to keep their lodge at "Akitakij or small Commany." And in the early 1690s, king Abo Takyi of Eguafo invited the English at Cape Coast to build a fort at Akatakyi.

In 1695 it was reported that the Dutch were angry that the Eguafo had invited the English to settle in their country so they solicited the help of the Twifo and the people [of] Cabes Terra to fight the Eguafo. The English added that they assisted the Eguafo in raising a large army which defeated the Dutch and their allies.

Nevertheless, by the middle of 1696, the English had not completed the building of their fort and they had no goods to sell. In January of that year, the Council at Cape Coast Castle noted that "Aguaffo is dissatisfied that Commeda is neglected which cannot be done without supplies . . ." Since the Eguafo people wanted trade badly, especially guns and gun powder, king Abo Takyi signed a humiliating treaty with the Dutch in October, 1696. Among the clauses was one which stipulated that nobody should be allowed to build a fort or lodge "between river Banja and Bosompra."

Finally, in 1700, Takyi Adico, who had become king of Eguafo with the support of the English, exempted the latter from paying ground rent whenever there was not enough trade at the English fort at Akatakyi. It is clear from these accounts that by the second decade the eighteenth century at least the people of Komenda formed an integral part of the Eguafo kingdom. The political growth of Akatakyi from a dependent market center into an autonomous city-state was largely the outcome of the perpetual tension between rival European trading companies which competed among themselves for commercial supremacy on the Eguafo coast. The servants of the European trading houses wanted to ensure that the reigning king in Eguafo was in their respective company's interests. Thus, from the second half of the seventeenth century, the European traders actively interfered in the politics of Eguafo. During this period, kings of Eguafo were enstooled and destooled in rapid succession, largely as a result of troubles formented by the Dutch and the English. In 1698, for instance, Nicholas Buckeridge, the English Governor, lured king Abo Takyi into Cape Coast Castle and murdered him. Buckeridge, who believed the king of Eguafo was too independent to be trusted, had helped to replace him with Takyi Ankan, the king's younger brother who had been for long in English pay. Also, between 1714 [and] 1716, the Dutch were known to have enlisted the support of the Fante to reinstate Takyi Kuma who had been deposed at the instance of the English.

Thus, in Eguafo, as in neighboring Efutu, one of the results of European contact was the subversion of the traditional power structure. Akatakyi in which stood the English fort became a fast growing town and the town's prosperity and wealth from the increased volume of trade enabled the Akatakyi chiefs to rival the Eguafo kings in importance and power. It seems to me therefore that the political instability in Eguafo during the second half of the seventeenth and the early years of the eighteenth century largely as a result of the European contact partly explains the emergence of Akatakyi as a new center of political power.

The Komenda state was organized like any other Akan state. The Omanhin was the political, judicial, military and religious head of the state. But he was not an autocrat. His principal advisers were the divisional chiefs who also commanded the divisional armies in times of war. Hence they were called the Nyimfahin, Benkumhin, Dontsihin, and the Kyidomhin. But it appears that, unlike a number of Fante states, the Asafo companies were, and still are, the most powerful elements in the Komenda state. Very little of an official nature could be done without their approval or participation. In fact, they are responsible for the enstoolment and destoolment of the kings of Komenda. At the moment the Asafo Companies are five: Ankobea, Enyampa, Akyem, Wombir and Anfer. The head of all the Asafo groups is the Tufuhin who is also the chief of Dominase. My information is that the Asafo Companies wielded such immense powers because it was they who fought and won the lands in the state, and that the divisional chiefs were originally warlords (Asahin) who led the Asafo groups.

Komenda has three major festivals: Eguadoɔto, Adwedi and Nyeyi. Aguadoɔto is the time when the chiefs give food and drinks to their dead ancestors symbolized by the stool which they had occupied. During this period, the chief pray to their ancestors to guide their conduct and to help them rule wisely and improve the conditions of their peoples. Adwedi (the eating of new yams) marks the harvest of new yams and other crops. It is a festive occasion when there is feasting and merry making throughout the land. Nyeyi is a much more serious affair. It is a festival instituted to remember the dead ancestors. It is a sad occasion marked by weeping and wailing by the womenfolk. The festival lasts for a week and during this period, the various family heads pour libation on the family shrine to the ancestors and pray to them for an increase in the size of the family. It is also celebration of this festival that disputes in the town or state are settled and decisions are taken concerning the general improvement of the state. It is considered such an important festival that, in the olden days, all members of the state were expected to be present for the celebrations.

The Akatakyi people are farmers, fishermen and salt boilers. Their agricultural products include such crops as maize or guinea corn, plantains, cassava, bananas, yams, cocoyam and vegetables. These crops are grown mainly by the people living in the interior.

In ancient times, these inland peoples sent some of their farm products to the coastal towns and villages and exchanged them for fish
and salt.

The coastal peoples concentrate on fishing and the boiling of salt
which they sent into the interior for sale. I was informed that salt
was carried far into the inland places such as Wassa, Kumase, Bonduku and "Sarem" (i.e., the north[ern region of Ghana]) for sale. In
return, these traders known collective as Abatafo bought back slaves
and types of cotton cloth woven in the savanna lands. The Komenda
people also traded extensively with the Europeans when the latter
arrived on their coast. In exchange for gold and slaves the Europeans gave them guns and gun powder, cloth, knives, mirrors, brassware and other exotic goods.

Kwamankese, ca. 1976

Kwamankese state shares borders with Assen Attandanso in the
north, Abeadze in the east, and Abora in the south and west. Apart
from Ayeldo, the capital, the Kwamankese state consists of Kwaman, ɔbosome, ɔsekyerew, Tekyiman, Nyamebekyere, Brenyi,
ɔdɔmpɔ, Katakyiase and a number of villages. Kwamankese literally means "Great Kwaman" and derives its name from Kwaman,
the ancient settlement of the Bɔrbɔr Fante. The people of Kwamankese claim that they did not join the other Bɔrbɔr Fante who
settled at Mankessim and that their chief, Idan I, organized the state
out of the remnants of the Akans who stayed behind at Kwaman.
Hence Kwaman was traditionally called "Akan nkaase," "remnant
Akans."

The earliest mention of Kwaman known to the writer is contained
in a Dutch report of 1653. In that year, Louys Dammaert noted
in his *Journal* that as a result of civil war in "Fantyn" (i.e.,
Mankessim), the Braffo of Fante "with the most part of the Ca-
boseros (chiefs)" had departed to *Quaman* (Kwaman) and that
Adonnie (Adonu), the leader of the fraction opposed to the Braffo,
had fled with his followers who were too few to Anianj (Eyan).
Some versions of Bɔrbɔr Fante tradition assert that the Kwaman

formerly formed part of the Abora traditional area and that the chief of Kwaman was the ɔbaatan or mother of the Aboras.

The Kwaman people, however, say that their state had always been independent and that it was the Aborahin Samuel Gardiner (Otu V) who made unsuccessful attempts to incorporate Kwamankese within the Abora state. They admit that in the olden days they closely cooperated with all the Bɔrbɔr Fante, including the Aboras for the defense of Fanteland against the incursion of their common enemy—the Asante. But they deny that they had ever been subordinate to Abora. The Abora-Kwamankese dispute was the subject of a judicial enquiry by a Commission appointed by the British Colonial administration in the early years of this century. In spite of the evidence of the Amanhin of Mankessim and Anomabu, or J. B. Brown and of John Mensah Sarbah to the effect that Kwaman had always formed part of the Abora division of the Bɔrbɔr Fante, C. H. Harper, chief Assistant Colonial Secretary ruled that:

1. Kwaman and Dominase are not subordinate in their ordinary jurisdiction to Omanhene Oto Ababio of Abra.
2. Omanhene Otu Ababio of Abra has no control over Dominase and Kwaman lands.
3. On ceremonial occasions, the Omanhene of Abra takes precedence of the chiefs of Kwaman and Dominase and the tie between Abra, Kwaman and Dominase is [a] sentimental and ceremonial one in that they have at different times been in alliance in time[s] of war and have consulted together in times of peace, but that the Omahene of Abra has claim of right to the assistance in war and in council the chiefs of Kwaman and Dominase. As a result of this, the British colonial government recognized both Abeadze and Kwamankese as independent states and their chiefs Amanhin.

It seems to me, however, that it was the policies pursued Otu V, Aborahin, which brought about dissensions in the Abora division of the Bɔrbɔr Fante, which eventually led to the break up of the division. Samuel Gardiner was enstooled Aborahin in 1900 but was deposed four years later. The available evidence indicates that the chiefs who engineered his deposition included Ewusi Tsenase, chief of Dominase, Idan I, chief of Kwaman, Kwesi Abawa, chief of Mpeseduadze and Adontsihin of Abora, and Kwaa Yeboa, chief of Odonase and Tufohin of Abora. For instance, Ewusi Tsenase played a major role in the enstoolment of Kwame Tawia of Bondze as successor to Gardiner. In a letter dated 10 November 1906, Ewusi Tsenase informed the Provisional Comissioner, Central Province, that "I have completed the installation of Kwamin Tawia as the Omanhene of Abra pending a reasonable explanation which I shall give at the next proposed meeting on hearing from you after the agricultural show; as the people do not think fit that the district should remain without one who owns the head on account of those who refuse to join it."

Kwame Tawia or Otu VI, however, abdicated in 1906 and Samuel Gardiner was brought back to the stool as Otu VI Ababio. Samuel Gardiner, of course, could not have as his principal advisers those who had been the cause of this removal from office in 1904 and so he initiated moves to punish the chiefs whom he regarded as ringleaders. It was against this background of uncertainty and confusion that some of the chiefs decided upon non-cooperation with the Aborahin. As Kwesi Abowa, the Adontsihin of Abora told Commissioner Atterbury, "It is a fact that Abura, Abiadzi and Kwaman were united together. One is not above the other but we should be strong in order to fight against the Ashantis. If the three chiefs meet together they call each other brother. I heard from ancestors that they make one up to Kwesi Brebo's (Otu IV's) time. The Omanhene called Gardiner has brought a dispute amongst the division. He stopped the supply of gunpowder being given to Abeadze and Kwaman unless the applications are sent through him. This brought the dispute." He noted further that Gardiner laid claims to Abeadze lands and requested that if anything was to be done in Abeadze and Kwaman he should be informed. He added that Gardiner was "fond of litigation so everybody must be independent of him."

Oral Traditions of Nsoko (Bɛo/Begho)
Postscript: Pottery from the Begho-B2 Site

*In the spirit of Kwame Daaku and John K. Fynn, E.S.K.
Owusu collected a set of oral traditions in Badu, Seikwa,
Nsoko, and Nkorankwaga in 1976. The following excerpt
comes from an interview conducted in the important
commercial town of Nsoko, where Owusu noted, "On my
arrival at Nsoko I found out that there was a stool [i.e.,
political] dispute. As a result two candidates are bitterly
contesting the vacant stool [symbol of authority and
leadership]. The Krontihene and Gyasehene are spon-
soring each of the contestants. Thus, the Nsoko Traditional Area has been split between these two candidates."
This was the context in which the interview occurred. At
the end, a postscript concerning archaeological findings
in Nsoko/Begho has been appended, the source of which
is L. B. Crossland's* Pottery from the Begho-B2 Site (*Calgary: University of Calgary Press, 1989*).

[Informants: Krontihene Nana Kofi Twumasei (b. 1919); Okyeame
Yaw Nsowah (b. 1917); Kwaku Aduo; Kwasi Mainoo; and Yaw
Burongo, 19 September 1975]

Q: Where did you come from to settle in this area?
A: Beo (Begho) near Hani.
Q: Who was the leader?
A: Kutsu-ne-Bente.
Q: Do you know anything about Ntɔn?
A: Yes. My ntɔn is Aduana. That of Nsokohene is Asona.
Q: How did you come to settle here?
A: Aduana and Asona clans came first. In due course of time
many other groups came to join us.
Q: What language did you speak when you arrived here?
A: Bono. . . .

Q: Do you think your language has changed?

A: No.

Q: Who was the founder of your state?

A: Asunkunu.

Q: Was he the first chief?

A: No. The first was Kutsu-ne-Bente. We migrated from Hani to Nsoko and our first ruler at Nsoko was Asunkunu.

Q: What clan did the first chief belong to?

A: Asona.

Q: Is his clan still the royal family?

A: Yes. . . .

Q: What are the rules of succession in your state?

A: Whenever the stool is vacant it is the responsibility of the Queen to find a suitable candidate. The candidate could be her own son. If selected he is presented to the Krontihene and the elders before his installation. A day is appointed where the chief-designee comes to swear allegiance to his elders and they too do likewise.

Q: Who takes precedence in succession to the stool; the chief's material brothers or nephews?

A: Much depends on the reigning chief for he could at times bypass the brother and ask a nephew to supplant him. . . .

Q: Were your ancestors Christians, Muslims or ancestral worshippers?

A: We worshipped [the *abosom*].

Q: What are some [of] your state [*abosom*]?

A: Bosom Hene, Taa Kwasi, Tua Amoa, and Ahra Bosom.

Q: Of all the [*abosom*], which was the most prominent?

A: Taa Kwasi. . . . In the past we had to consult it before we went to war. It would tell us our chances in the war. If there were an outbreak of disease, drought or famine it would tell us what to do. The other three gods give us blessings when we pray to them.

Q: How did you come by these [*abosom*]?

A: Nana Nsokohene brought them from the place we came from—Beo (Begho). They help him in the administration of the state. . . .

Q: Are there any ancient sites, relics, cemeteries, etc., in your state?

A: Yes. We have one called *Nana-Asuom*. No one is allowed to go there. We visit there yearly to perform some rituals. Secondly where Nsoko chiefs are buried is out of bounds. The bush is neither cleared nor a twig of branch cut. It is called *Banem*. . . .

Q: Is there any meaning attached to your town—Nsoko?

A: Yes. . . . When we emerged out of the hole we first settled at Beo (Begho). Somebody (a self-styled creator) came with the mother to our settlement. The mother was called Asɔ. She died afterwards. When the "Creator" was told of this mother's death he exclaimed "Asɔ kɔ," literally Asɔ has gone (to her death). Asɔ kɔ subsequently became Nsokɔ, a name we have borne to this day.

Postscript: Pottery from the Begho-B2 Site

Much has been written about the importance of Mande [Muslim] traders at Begho. [Ivor] Wilks (1961) and [Jack] Goody (1965) [have written much about] their contribution to the prosperity of the settlement, and it was expected that their presence would be traced in the ceramic from the Kramo ["Muslim"] quarter. Too many variables are involved in the effects of contact or conquest on arts and crafts to allow simple generalizations in the case of Begho. So far, the ceramic evidence at Begho indicates no appreciable influences by the Mande on local ceramic traditions. It is doubtful whether the alien element dominated the local population in large numbers. If that was the case, they were probably men who traveled the long distance, settled and married local women, and this movement need not have resulted in changes in vessel forms.

The question of whether red slipping was a northern trait remains unsolved. At the Begho-B2 site, red slipped sherds were present throughout all the layers in proportions varying from 29.2–35.5 percent of the total number of sherds analyzed. They were common in sites around Begho and New Buipe and the problem can only be solved when sites exhibiting a transition between the Kintampo "neolithic" and those of Begho times can be found and correlations made with periods of predominance in the Sudanic belt. It is quite possible that pottery forms such as pedestals, potstands, and certain forms of carinated wares still identified in the Begho area today as "kramo kola" by the Mo, which does not form part of the indigenous ceramic traditions of the Begho area, may have been introduced. Another indirect effect on potting traditions was probably the influences of brass bowls on shapes of earthenware. Some of the brass bowls in the Nsawkaw [Nsoko] collections and those collected by [James] Anquandah from graves at Techiman [Takyiman] exhibit to Begho-B2. The speculations regarding the use of the ground potsherds as gold weights provide other evidence of the economic activities of the Begho quarters. The pottery weights were found in small numbers in all the quarters and indicate that [three] sections of the population were probably engaged in the gold trade.

PART TWO

(*ɔfa a etɔ so mmienu*)

Exogenous Sources

— 5 —

Iberian Sources

The Voyage of Eustache de la Fosse, 1479–1480
EUSTACHE DE LA FOSSE

The West African voyage of Flemish merchant Eustache de la Fosse included the former Gold Coast, precisely the area that is now Elmina. In the "Mina" (Elmina) part of his account, he offers the earliest known written sampling of the Twi (Akan) language—dating to the late fifteenth century—as well as the early commerce in captive Africans.

And after we had for long frequented the aforesaid coast, we [two vessels] made towards the Mine of Gold and arrived on [Friday] 17 December 1479, the Saturday following being Christmas Day, and we left the other caravel at the Malagueta Coast [present-day Liberia] since they wanted to obtain more pepper and some slaves to bring to the Mine [i.e., São Jorge da Mina/Elmina] to sell there. And before departing one behind the other we drew lots for which of us should go further forward six leagues, because there are two harbors at this Mine of Gold, the first of which has the name Shama and the other, which is six leagues further on, Village of Two Parts, so called because there are two villages a bowshot apart, and it fell to my lot to go the six leagues further on. And for this reason I left the day after I arrived at the aforesaid Mine in order to go to my agreed locality, this being the Sunday before Christmas, and then we put ourselves under the protection of the *manse* and the *care-manse*, who are the king and the viceroy, and the next day which was Monday we set about to begin our sales, but we did little the first four or five days until the merchants in this country were alerted to our arrival, and then we saw the Berrenbucs who made their way down from the hills and came to buy our goods. In this land "merchants" are called *berenbues*, "gold" *chocqua*; "water" *enchou*; for "you are welcome" you say *berre bene*, and for "love-play" *chocque chocque*; *barbero* means "a child," *baa*, "white," *barbero baa*, "a white child;" "cloth" is *fouffe*, *concque roncq* means "a chicken," *concque ronconcq agnio* "eggs," *bora* a ring to wear on the arm made of brass, *dede* "good," *fanionna* "bad," etc.

And on [the] Twelfth Night, which was a Wednesday, early in the morning when there was a heavy drizzle/thick mist, there appeared four Portuguese ships which fired their guns at me in such a way that they overcame us and we were left at their mercy. And the previous day they had taken the other ship that came with us, and on their way by sea they met another one which they brought back with them to the Mine, and we were all pillaged. And then since we leading men were prisoners they handed over one of our caravels to the sailors and poor members of our company, with water, biscuit, a sail, and an anchor, and sent them off [to take their chance], and thus they returned to Spain, and the Portuguese kept back us, the leading men, in order to take us to the king and daily we helped to sell our own goods which they had seized from us, but those of us who were kept there were divided among several ships, four to one and six to another. I was placed with a fine knight called Fernand de les Vaux who treated me very honorably, but since he was charged to go 200 leagues further, I asked to be placed in one of the ships remaining at the Mine and this was granted, and I was placed in the ship of a man called Diogo Can [Cão], who was a thoroughly awkward creature, and I was no longer as well treated as I had been before, which I had to put up with. This Diogo Can bought my caravel out of the booty and, as said earlier, I daily helped to sell my goods and daily accounted for them.

And once as I was going through the streets and carrying two basins to sell I was called into one of their houses hoping that I would sell my basins, and when I went in I saw there several women, standing up and talking together, some five or six of them nattering together while I held my basins in each hand. I cannot explain how these women so bewitched me that I left my basins behind and went out of that house. And when I was two or three houses away in the street it came to my mind what I had done with my basins, and I instantly returned to that house and went in and found no one there, and there was a young lass who came to attend on me by asking if I wanted *chocque chocque*, and she began to take off my breeches, thinking that I wanted to dally with her, which I had no will for, being vexed by the loss of my basins, which remained lost.

And so we stayed there, selling until Shrove Tuesday itself, and just as we were ready to depart, there then arrived the two caravels which had gone 200 leagues further on to the River of Slaves, bringing back a large number of slaves, a good 200 each, and they sold most of them at the Mine of Gold, but despite this we left in the evening of Shrove Tuesday in order to return to Portugal and I was placed back in my own caravel which Diogo Can had bought as booty and it was named *La Mondadine* . . .

Esmeraldo de situ orbis, 1508
DUARTE PACHECO PEREIRA

Duarte Pacheco Pereira was a Portuguese navigator and later governor of the São Jorge da Mina fortress on the early-sixteenth-century Gold Coast. This account has been dated to about 1508, though events he described could have occurred as early as the late fifteenth century.

[*Book 2, chapter 4*]

The islet of Anda lies NE/5W from St. John River, eight leagues [further] along the route, a very small and narrow river, at high tide only a fathom and a half at its mouth and this mouth can only be seen when very near it. Here is a place called Sama [Shama], with 500 households, the first place in this land where trading in gold was done, and at that time it was called the Mine [i.e., São Jorge da Mina fortress]. This trading place and its commerce were discovered, on the orders of King Afonso V, by João de Santarem and Pedro d'Escobar, his knights and servants, on a certain day in January 1471. These two captains carried as pilots Alvaro Esteves, citizen of Lagos, and Martin Esteves, citizen of Lisbon, the former being the most competent man of his trade in Spain [i.e., Iberia] at that time. . . . From Sama Bay to the village of the Crooked Man is three leagues . . . and from there to the Castle of St George of the Mine is three leagues.

[*Book 2, chapter 5*]

Since in the penultimate paragraph of this second book we have previously spoken of how the excellent prince, King Afonso V of Portugal, had the Mine discovered, and of the captains and pilots who for this purpose were sent, it is now fitting that we should tell how his son, the most serene prince, King João of Portugal, after the death of his father, ordered the first work in founding the castle of St George of the Mine to be made. On the command of this magnanimous prince it was built by Diogo de Azambuja, knight of his household and *comendador* of Alter Pedroso in the Order of St. Benedict, [beginning] on the first day of January 1482, having taken out and being accompanied on nine caravels by as many other captains: most honorable men, Diogo de Azambuja being commander. Also he took out two *urcas*, ships of 400 tons each, with lime, worked stone, and enough other material to construct this fort. And although there was much disagreement between the blacks of this land and our people about the building of this fort, for they did not wish to agree to it, finally it was done despite them, so that, with great service and diligence, there was completed what was then necessary for the lodging and defense of all our men, and afterwards, as time moved on, the same King João II accepted as necessary that it was appropriate to construct much more. We know that in all Ethiopian Guinea, this was the first solid building to be constructed in this region since the creation of the world . . .

Spanish Account of the Founding of the "Mina" Fortress, 1515

ANDRÉS BERNÁLDEZ

Andrés Bernáldez was chaplain of Don Deigo de Deza, archbishop of Seville, Spain. Bernáldez's Memorias de los Reyes Católicos *is concerned with the historical events surrounding the reign of Ferdinand and Isabella (1479-1516), including a discussion of the reign of Enrique IV and numerous copies of official letters. The excerpt below comes from a section entitled, "De la mina de oro que descubrieron los portugueses" (the gold mine that the Portuguese discovered).*

In the year 1471 the fleet of King D. Afonso discovered the mine of gold which today the kings of Portugal possess, which is on the coast of the oceanic sea towards the south of us, past the coasts of the Jolof blacks and their limits, and much further on, being concealed a little less to the north than they are, with the roundness of the earth. At the time they discovered it and in the first voyages there the majority of the sailors fell sick and died without a remedy, but afterwards, when they continued their voyages, the journey became easier and they kept well and no longer died.

From that mine of gold very great riches and honor have benefited the kings of Portugal, and daily much profit comes to all their kingdom. This is so, not because they are lords of the harvesting of the gold or lords of the land where it is collected, but only on account of the trade, at a fortress which they possess there on the sea, built recently, to which the blacks from all the neighboring districts, willingly and for gain, bring the gold, to sell and exchange for goods taken there from here—copper, brass and pewter goods, cloths, and many other showy things not of much account and value—and seashells from the Canaries which the blacks esteem and value greatly.

Letter of Mina Governor to the Queen, 18 April 1557

AFONSO GONÇALVES BOTAFOGO

The selections below come from a letter sent by Afonso Gonçalves Botafogo, then governor of the São Jorge da Mina fortress, to Queen Caterina (Catherine) of Portugal.

[*Defining the "Gold Coast"*]

The whole coast from one end to the other . . . namely one part from Axim to this port, and the other from here to Cara [Nkran /Accra]....

[*Portuguese Relations with Rulers of Nkran/Accra and "Great" and "Small" Akani*]

It seemed good to Cristovão d'Oliveira, before leaving for Portugal, to send Pero da Costa to Cara with gifts for the king and his brothers, gifts which, at his request, I gave the latter from this trading post. With him he sent his ship's master, and I sent the pilot of the *caravellão*, and the master mason who was here, to investigate and observe where it will be best to build the fortress, and in what way the coast can be approached, and whatever else they can find out. . . . The gifts which the King our Lord sent from Portugal for this King of Cara it did not seem right to give at present, since the fortress is not built. I sent other gifts, as I now inform Your Highness, and the former ones will be kept until the King our Lord and Your Highness order what is to be done with them.

I wrote to Your Highness by the previous fleet about how I had to [send] a man to the kings of *Acanes Grandes* and the *Acanes Pequenos* to get them to mend relations and open up their roads to this fortress. This man spent more than eight months there and reconciled these kings and made them friends, and he opened roads that had been blocked for many years. As a sign of reconciliation and friendship he brought to this fortress a son of each of the kings. The son of the King of the *Acanes Grandes* is his oldest son and heir, and is called António de Brito, the António de Brito who used to be captain here having once visited him. These hostages I received at this fortress very warmly, and I ordered them to be given their customary food.

After these roads had been opened up and all was completed, there happened to come here a brother of the King of the *Acanes Pequenos*, and over a black whom he killed in this town a great fight broke out. I and some men hurried there, but the black came out of it dead, without my being able to intervene. To have this set right also cost me afterwards a great deal of trouble, and in bringing the matter to a peaceful conclusion some expense. Dom João [ruler of Fetu] also helped in this, and now I have everything settled and all runs well.

After these ships came to port, the wife of António de Brito came here to be with him. I warmly welcomed her and soon made her a Christian, and she took the name Dona Catarina, in recollection of Your Highness, and I and Cristovão d'Oliveira were her godparents. Opening up these roads, like opening the others I have cleared from restrictions, has cost me a great deal of trouble and I have spent on this activity some of the property of this establishment and also some of my own salary. Since all is for the service of the King Our Lord and of Your Highness, it must be counted well-spent.

[*Trade between Africans and Europeans*]

So that the King our Lord and Your Highness may not blame me for not making approaches to the kings of the surrounding districts, to persuade them not to trade [with the enemy], as I did last year, [let me explain]. I was very ill when the pirates [i.e., competing European nations] began to arrive, despite which I did not fail to approach the kings, through men I sent to the kings of Afuto [Fetu] and Comane [Komenda], for these are the leading kings in terms of wealth and power, and if they withdrew from trade what was left would be little. I ordered the men to offer them gifts and other things if the kings desired them, just as was done successfully by me the previous year. Notwithstanding all this, I was quite unable to bring the kings to agree to renounce trading. Dom João, in which I most trusted, gave as an excuse that it was only because his people were compelling him to [permit] this against his own wishes. If last year they had not traded it was because they were bribed and given more than 500 *pesos*, but now he did not dare to quarrel with them. Nevertheless neither he nor his son-in-law was trading. But all this was mere words, an evasive reply from blacks who do not recognize or keep to the truth, especially when self-interest is involved. I have found out through spies that Dom João and his son-in-law, and the people of the king of Comane, traded more than 30,000 *pesos*. Whenever pirates come they will do this and will not forbid trading, because self-interest and the profit they gain count for more than whatever this fortress can give them in bribes.

An Anonymous Portuguese Report on Mina, 29 September 1572

[*The "Alandes," a Probable Akan Group of the Western Gold Coast*]

The Alandes, who inhabit the area from near Cabo das Palmas to close to Axim, do not have cloth nor do they have gold, but they have much ivory which they exchange for bracelets, porcelain beads, cornelian, and I think leather goods. I am reliably informed that this [trade] could be very important, because there is so much ivory, which is very cheap. Moreover it could be bought with the goods I have mentioned, and what is necessary to enter the rivers found in that district could be carried on a small ship. The people there are our friends and the countryside is peaceful. They are in the habit [of] coming to Axim, where I have seen them, to sell their ivory and other goods, such as crocodile skins and *vandas*, which are strips of cotton cloth a palm or two wide, these being bought by the natives and whites, the natives to cover themselves, and the whites to sell when the opportunity arises. The blacks put the skins on the handles of their daggers and on that part of their spears by which they hold them when throwing them. They also bring slaves to sell and these are usually very good ones. . . .

[*Christian Teaching*]

I rejoice that they [the *padres*] have put into effect the saying of mass at a certain hour, and have taught the blacks the stations of the cross; and I believe that eventually there will be a roll-call, as is done in many parts, including Spain, which seems to me very necessary because the blacks are an indolent and careless people; and also so that they can hear their Christian names repeated, because I understand that all the other [converts] after leaving the company of Christians and returning to their village, call themselves by heathen names, [for instance,] the man named Joanne being known as Tabo and the woman Maria as Adua [Adwoa]. . . .

[*Foods and Domestic Animals*]

The blacks sow *milho grande* [large *milho* = ? maize] which they call *Bruy* [*aburo*, "corn"] and which in Castile is called "Indies corn," and *milho meudo* [small *milho*] which I think is the same as the small *milho* there [in Castile]. They sow yams, which in this land provide a very good staple good, and another sort which they call *cocos* [cocoyams], which is really *rumilho* [?], food for pigs in Castile, but the blacks, especially those at Axim, eat a large quantity of them. They also plant bananas, which in the Spanish Indies they call *platanos* [plantains]. . . . Very good cotton is produced in this land, and a great deal of profit could be made from it.

The only domestic animals I know about are goats, sheep and cows. The goats are very small. The sheep are the size of those there [in Castile]. . . . The cows are very small and the same color as those over there. The pigs, which are brought here, adapt well in this place but badly at Axim, where the governor's horses and an ass also died. Dogs are found in this land, and the Alandes bring them here to sell. . . .

[*Gold Mining and Gold in the Interior*]

They do not open mines or seek gold anywhere that is at all far from the water [required] to wash the earth from which they remove the gold. Even if they find gold elsewhere they do not dig for it, because of the difficulty in carrying the earth to where there is water. . . . There has now come here a black, a son of the King of the *Asaees Grandes* as they say, who was baptized in the time of António de Brito, then a Captain here, and took his name. He is a respected black, of good bearing, and he brought with him a son, a youth of about twenty years of age. When asked about that land, in the presence of the Vicar and in his own house, he [the son] replied—for he speaks Portuguese reasonably well through having been here with his father—that it was very rich, but that the gold which came from there was not extracted from the lands of this grandfather, who is still alive, but from further on, in another kingdom, which he says he has visited, by making a five days' journey. The kingdom or lands where the mines are to be found is called Taafó [an area north of Asante]. He stated that he saw the mines, and also lumps of gold, just taken from the earth, some as big as his head or his fist, some large and some small, but even when only the size of hazelnuts, still worth a lot. As far as I could judge from his manner, it seemed to me that the black was telling the truth. He also told me that when a black man or woman went to extract gold, normally twelve *pesos* would be extracted in one day. I asked him if the ground where the gold was found was loose earth or rock; and he replied that the land had all types of ground, but that I would only be able to collect gold from ground which was like *arzilla* [sticky clay], and fairly compact, some lumps emerging from it almost like stones, and he added that these lumps were white.

— 6 —

French and Dutch Sources

A Description of the Coasts of North and South-Guinea, 1678-1688

JEAN BARBOT

The selections to follow come from French merchant and slaver Jean Barbot (1655-1712). His account, A Description of the Coasts of North and South-Guinea, *was published in 1732. The best (annotated) work on Barbot remains P.E.H. Hair, Adam Jones, and Robin Law, eds.,* Barbot on Guinea: The Writings of Jean Barbot on West Africa, 1678-1712 *(2 vols.: London: Hakluyt Society, 1992). Barbot's original journal in French is dated to 1678 and his published French account to 1688. Jean Barbot made two voyages on French slaving vessels to Guinea (West Africa). The ships on which Barbot traveled spent between four and five months on each voyage (1678-1679 and 1681-1682), making their way from Senegal to the Gold Coast to the Principe Islands. Barbot's observations are geographically and socially limited and restricted to the coastal fringes. He collected his information from residents, traders, officers, and European agents as well as from acquaintances.*

[*Of the Inland Polities on the Gold Coast*]

Having, from my first entering upon this work, resolved to give a complete description of *North* and *South Guinea*, as far as it is

known to us; I now, in pursuance thereof, design to give some short
account of the inland countries lying farther up above those of the
Gold Coast already described; tho[ugh] in treating of the maritime
countries, something has been occasionally said of the others, as
matters offered themselves; and in the map of the *Gold Coast*, I
have given the position of the most noted inland countries.

I desire the reader will accept of what I offer in good part, and
put the best construction upon it, if anything should seem to him
extravagant or preposterous, none of the Europeans dwelling along
the coast, having ever ventured far up the land, that I could hear of;
so that what account can be given of it, is taken from the most intelligent Blacks, particularly as to the remotest countries, it being
extraordinary difficult and dangerous, if not altogether impossible,
for Europeans to venture so far into such wild savage countries,
where the roads are, for the most part, narrow and hard to find,
being in most parts hid with woods, and overgrown with shrubs;
besides, being everywhere pestered with robbers, in many places
quite desert, without any dwellings or subsistence to be found, or
any carriage of horses, carts, or the like; all which, together with
the treacherous disposition of the inhabitants, and the excessive heat
of the days in the summer-season, being the [proper] time for travelling, and the continual heavy rains in the winter, is in my opinion
sufficient, adding the danger of ravenous wild beasts, which swarm
in those countries, to deter the boldest and most resolute man from
undertaking such journeys, especially considering they are to be
performed a-foot.

To proceed methodically in this description, I must return to the
beginning of the *Gold Coast*, as far as *Awine*, which I take to be
near *Adom*, the first on the *Gold Coast*. The Blacks of that country
usually return large quantities of fine gold to *Isseny* [Assinie] and
other parts along the coast. They are very civil, and the fairest dealer
of all the Blacks, so [it . . .] is a pleasure to trade with them.

The Kingdom of Igwira

Borders southward on that of *Atzym* or *Axim*, and *Little Incassan*; northward, on *Great Incassan*; and eastward, on *Mompa*. It is accounted extraordinary rich in gold, and that of the purest sort, commonly dug out of the ground, or taken from the bottom of rivers, most whereof come down in small streams or torrents from the vast high hills, separating *Incassan* and *Igwira*, which streams are formed by the excessive rains of the wet season, washing the ground, and carrying down what gold lies near the surface of the earth; and the rivers of *Igwira* being all cloaked with rocks and falls, bearing away the mould with great swiftness, the rich metal which is among it, by its natural weight sinks to the bottom, and for the most part among the aforesaid rocks and falls; where the Blacks commonly dive for it, because there, in [the] process of time, it gathers into little heaps.

Most of this fine *Igwira* gold is conveyed to *Axim*, or to *Isseny*, as occasion offers, for which reason, those two maritime places have generally the finest gold of all the coast, either because it passes through few hands before it comes thither, *Igwira* confining on those territories; or, for that the Blacks in general are more honest, and less covetous than at many other trading places on the coast, where the mystery of adulterating gold, is known to perfection.

Two Blacks of *Commendo* [Komenda] went some years ago into *Igwira*, with European goods, to trade, and made a very good hand of them, as they reported; but the roads between *Commendo* and that country, being very seldom free from robbers, and the distance great, and several nations being in the way; which always guard the passes through their liberties, and extort heavy duties for the liberty of trading: these things, I say, considered, there are few who care to venture frequently between *Commendo* and *Igwira*.

I observed, in the description of the river Cobra [Ankobra] near *Axim*, that the Portuguese, in former times, made a considerable advantage of their trade in this *Igwira* country. How the Dutch factory at Axim, having driven the Portuguese from thence, manages that affair now, is a secret to all the world besides themselves; but it is beyond all doubt, that they, who are such cunning traders, must find a very considerable return there.

The Kingdom of Great Incassan

[It has] for its boundary, on the south, that of *Igwira*; on the east, those of *Wassahs* [Wassa] and *Vanqui* [Wankyi] and unknown countries on the west. The natives of it, are almost unknown on the Gold Coast; only a few of them now and then coming down through the country of *Adom*, to trade at *Little Commendo* or *Isseny*; and [often] to the Latter, as being much nearer to them than the other.

The Kingdom of Incassia Iggina

On the south, reaches to that of *Great Incassan*; on the east, to those of *Wassahs* and *Vanqui*; but to what parts it extends north and west, I could not learn. The natives have no manner of correspondence with the Europeans on the coast; and therefore it is quite unknown beyond the next neighboring nations.

The Little Territory of Tabeu

[It has] *Anta* [Ahanta] on the south; *Adom* on the west and north; and *Commendo* or *Guaffo* [Eguafo] on the east, being separated there from it by a little river. The Blacks of *Tabeu* drive their trade with the Dutch at *Sama* [Shama], carrying thither corn, poultry, fruit, planes, and other things or the product of their country. *The Portuguese of Mina* used formerly to draw the subsistence of their garrison from thence, as well as from the country of *Axim*.

The Kingdom of Adom

[It has] *Tabeu* on the west, *Guaffo* on the south, Wassahs on the north, and Abramboe [Abrem] on the [east]. The Blacks of this country generally turn their trade to Little Commendo, when the passes are not open, and the rocks clear from robbers between them and the coast, either to Axim or Boutroe [Boutri], whither they otherwise resort.

The Country of Mompa

[It is] utterly unknown, but said to extend westward to Igwira; northward to Great Incassan, Wassahs and Adom; and eastward to Anta.

That of Wassahs

[It has] Vanqui on the north; Qui-Foro [Twifo] and Abramboe on the east; Great Incassan on the west, and Incassia-Iggina on the north-wet. It is famous for the great quantity of gold brought out of it, tho[ugh] it has but few rivers; and therefore some say the natives bring that metal from other remoter parts. The land is generally barren, and produces nothing considerable, which is the reason that most of the inhabitants make it their chief business to gather gold, to purchase European goods, and so drive a trade with their neighbors.

The Territory of Vanqui

[It is] bounded on the west by Incassia-Iggina; on the south by Wassahs; on the north by Bonoe. The natives have the art of weaving fine fluffs with gold, which they fell to the people of Accany, who again sell them to the Arabs, inhabiting about the famous river Niger, as also to the people of Gago and Akam, north of them.

The Kingdom of Aquamboe

[It e]xtends to Adom and Wassahs on the west; to Guaffo on the south; to Accany [Akani] on the north; to Atty [Eti] on the east, and to Fetu on the south-west. 'Tis a very populous country, and of great commerce; great numbers of the natives constantly resorting to Mouree [Mouri/Mori] to exchange their gold for linen and iron; and some of them keep their families there altogether, acting themselves as brokers for many of their countrymen, who are considerable dealers.

These Aquamboes [Akwamu] are naturally brave, resolute and warlike, and for the most part at variance with the Accanese, by whom they for many years past had been much infested; they having made several inroads into Aquamboe; destroying all with fire and sword. They are now at peace, which 'tis likely will not last long, there being such a natural aversion to each other.

The Land of Quy-Foro

[It t]ouches Wassahs westward; Abramboe southward, Bonoe [Bono/Brong] northward; and Accany eastward. 'Tis a very barren country, and the people generally of a small capacity and simple, having no trade on the coast.

That of Bonoe

[It r]eaches westward to Vanqui; southward to Quy-Foro; eastward to Accany and Inta. The natives never go down to the coast any more than those of Mompa.

The Territory of Atti

[It has] Abramboe on the west, Fetu, Sabou [Asebu] and Fantin [Fante], on the south, and Dahoe on the north. These people had formerly a great trade with the Dutch; but being empoverished, and almost exhausted by their long wars against Sabou, their main employment now is tillage, the country being naturally very fertile. They have some sort of dependence on Accany, whose inhabitants can hinder them from trading on the coast, when they think it for their advantage, and they are a people sufficiently inclined to engross all the traffic of those countries. To this effect, they have settled a great market at Accany, on certain appointed days in the year, whither a multitude from the neighboring countries usually resorts to buy iron, which the Accanese bring from the coast.

The Kingdom of Accany

[It is] commonly distinguished by the names of Accany-Grande, or the Great, and Accany-Pequeno or the Little. Accany-Pequeno, or the Little, is said to extend on the west of Quy-Foro and Bonoe; on the south to Deboe, Atti, and Abramboe; on the north to Inta; and on the east to the kingdom of Akim [Akyem], or Atchim. The great town of Daboe is near the frontiers, next to Atti. These Accanese are famous for the trade they drive not only on the coast, but up the inland. These Blacks, in company with those of Cabestierra, a country between them and Saboe, used to bring down the gold of Assiante and Akim, together with some of their own, to trade upon the coast, and that which they sold there, was so pure and fine, that to this day the best gold is by the Blacks from Commendo to Wiamba [Winneba], called Accany Chica [Akani *sika*, "Akani gold"], or Accany gold; because it was never any way mixed, like that of Dinkiara [Denkyira].

These people are naturally of a turbulent temper, haughty and warlike, which makes them either much feared or loved, by their neighbors round about, and every where entertained cost-free by them, when they travel through their countries. Their usual weapons are an Assagaya, or javelin, a buckler and a scymiter [i.e., a curved saber]. The language is much the same as that of Fetu, Atti, Sabae, Abramboe and Fantin, only somewhat softer and more agreeable to the ear. The Accanese merchants carry all the goods they buy at the coast by land, on their slaves' backs, to the markets at Atti, Saboe, and other places up the country, paying the duties at the passes, to the respective governors of those countries and territories, through which they travel. Many of them call still speak some few words of Portuguese, and the Lingua Franca they learnt of their fore-fathers, when the Portuguese had the whole commerce on that coast. This Lingua Franca is a corruption of Italian, Latin, French, and Portuguese.

[Denkyira]

The country of Dinkira or Dunkira lies above ten days journey by land from Axim, and five from Mina, due north, having Cabesterra on the east, Adom on the west, and Accany on the north. The roads to it from Axim and Mina are very bad and winding, which makes it double the distance in travelling thither, that it would be, were they good and [straight]: whether the Blacks will not or cannot remedy that inconveniency is uncertain. It was formerly a country of a small compass, and not very populous; but the natural valor of the natives has enlarged its borders, and raised its power so high, that its people are feared and honored by all the nations round about, except those of Assiante and Akim, who are still more potent than they. The inhabitants of Dinkira are vastly rich in gold, as well brought from other parts as what their own mines afford; the first sort whereof they get, either by plunder, or by trade, wherein they are infinitely more expert than any other Blacks. When the roads to the coast are free and open, the Dinkira merchants come together, with the Accanese, as I said before, either to Sama, Commendo, Mina, or cape Corso castle [Cape Coast Castle], according to the distance of the places where they live at home. If the passes happen to be stopped in the inland country, they go farther up the coast; by which means, those upper factories have a brisk trade in their town and plenty of gold, when it falls short at the middle forts of the coast.

The Dinkira gold is commonly very fine, but too often mixed with *Fetishe* gold, which is a sort of composition of several ingredients, in some very odd shapes, as I shall particularly describe hereafter.

[Asante]

The territory of Inta [Gonja, north of Asante] or Assiante [Asante], which a modern author supposes to be one and the same, is limited on the west by Mandinga; on the north by unknown regions; on the east by Akim and Acham; and on the south by Accany. Nothing can be said of this country, which is utterly unknown, for want of correspondence, but that it is very rich in gold, some parcels whereof are brought down to the Gold Coast, in peaceable times, by the Accanese who trade thither, when the roads are open. It lies well for the trade of Isseny and Axim, as being feared towards the head of the river of Suiero da Costa [Tano River]. Akam, Akim, or Ahim, or Accany-Grande, the Great Accany, borders westward on Accany-Pequeno, or Lietle Accany; on Aqua, and Sonqua southward; on Inta and Achara northward; and on Abramboe and Quakoe [Kwawu] eastward. . . .

Most of the gold of this country is generally conveyed to Acra, and thence to the western roads and forts of the coast, very fine and pure, without any mixture or corruption. The Black of Akim are very proud and haughty, and as rich again in gold and slaves, as the Little Accanese for which reason they pretend to some superiority over them. The natives drive most of their commerce towards the countries lying along the Niger, being those of Gago [Gao?] and Meczara on the north of them. Gago is a large kingdom, abounding in gold, a great quantity whereof is rent to the kingdom of Morocco, with caravans, by the way of Tombut [Timbuktu]. The Accanese trade also with their other neighbor nations, as Assiante and Akam, this latter lying north, the other north-west from them, where they sell abundance of their short cloths and other goods for gold. They also sometimes repair to the markets at Abonee, near Acra, and there, as well as at Little Accany buy European goods those Blacks carry from the coast.

Insoko [Nsoko/Begho]

According to the account the Accanese give of it, [it] is a country distant five days journey from the coast; its southern borders little known, because [it is] scarce[ly] frequented, by reason the roads generally swarm with thieves and robbers. The natives of it are notable weavers, making curious stuffs and short cloths, which yield a good profit, sold to the neighboring nations; who purchase them for plate and pieces of eight, as also for Haerlem cloth. The Accanese say, that those Blacks know not what copper or gold are, having never seen those two metals in their country.

All the above mentioned kingdoms and territories in general, are not so woody, as the country about Cormentin, and the others higher on the gold coast, nor so fruitful. By what I have said of them, it may well be concluded, that they are for the most part extraordinary rich in gold; but particularly Inta, or Assiante, Awine, Iguira, Dinkira, Akam, and Accany afford vast quantities; most of the gold traded for along the whole coast coming from those parts, where there are many rich mines of that metal, besides what the natives draw from their neighbors, by way of trade, which is a very considerable quantity. Mandinga, Gago, and Tafoe, furnish them with very much in exchange by goods, or by way of plunder; and these again, besides what their own land produces, receive it from many unknown countries northward, on both sides of the Niger. Those places, according to the accounts of all authors and travelers, producing an immense store of gold. . . .

Names

As soon as the Confoe [ɔkɔmfoɔ], or priest, has blessed the child, if we may so call it, or sung about it those preservatives above-mentioned, the next thing is to give it a name. If the family be above the common rank, the infant has three names given it; the first is the name of the day of the week on which it is born; the next, if a son, is the grand-father's name; and if a girl, the grand-mother's; others give their own name, or that of fame of their relations.

At Acra [Accra], the parents having called together all their friends, take the names of all the company, and give the child that which is born by most in the company. The names for boys are commonly Adom, Quaqou [Kwaku], Quaw [Kwao], Corbei, Coffi [Kofi], &c. and for girls, Canow, Jama, Aquouba, Hiro, Accasiaffa, and many more. Betides these names of their own for boys, they frequently add our Christian names, as John, Antony, Peter, Jacob, Abraham, &c. being proud of those European names; but that is practiced only by those that live under the protection of the forts on the coast. . . .

Circumcision

[It is] used at no place on the whole coast, but only at Acra; where infants are circumcised by the priest, at the same time that they receive their names; and the ceremony is performed in the presence of all the relations of both sexes, and ends with dancing and feasting.

Language

[Though] the Gold Coast be but of a small extent, as has been shown, yet have they seven or eight languages, so different from one another that three or four of them are unintelligible to any but the respective natives. The people of the country called Junmore, twelve leagues west of Axim, cannot understand the language of Egwira, Ancober, Abocroe, and Axim; and those between Cormentyn, and Acra have also four several dialects, tho[ugh] there are but twenty leagues distance from the former to the Inner.

The Axim idiom has a disagreeable brutish sound [while] that of Anta is sweeter and more pleasing, tho[ugh] not very beautiful neither. But that of Acra is the worst of all, and the most shocking, and nothing like any of the rest.

The language of the inland Blacks of Dinkira, Akim, Adom, and Accany is much pleasanter, and more agreeable as any person of but indifferent judgment may soon discern, and not only better sounding, but more intelligible, and might be learned very well in a few years: whereas those on the coast can scarce be attained in ten years, to any perfection; the sound of some words being so strange, that it is extremely difficult to express them by European letters, any more particularly by the English alphabet: the pronunciation of letters being in English of another sound, than they are in all other nations of Europe. And since the Blacks can neither write nor read, and have no use of any characters, it is consequently impossible to express their faults, and as difficult to learn their language in two or three years, of constant practice amongst them; for many have lived there ten years, and yet could not understand and speak it to perfection, nor scarce hit the pronunciation.

The Fetu language being most generally understood at the Gold Coast amongst the Blacks, as I have said before; I have made a collection of some familiar words and phrases, which shall be found in the supplement: and if the letters and vowels are pronounced as in French, I doubt not but a Black will understand it, when so sounded and expressed. Had I lived any considerable time among them, I had collected a much greater number of phrases and words to help sea-fearing men in their commerce with the natives of the Gold Coast; besides the other languages, in which we can talk to them: for many of the coast Blacks speak a little English or Dutch, and for the most part speak to us in a sort of Lingua Franca; or broken Portuguese and French.

Description and Historical Account of the Gold Kingdom of Guinea, 1602

PIETER DE MAREES

Pieter de Marees was a Dutch merchant whose account, originally published in 1602, remains one of the earliest detailed European descriptions of West African societies, focusing largely on the Gold Coast. The excerpts below cover two areas this merchant came to know adequately enough while on the Gold Coast.

[Markets and Trade]

They also keep fixed Market-days, on which one finds more for sale there than on other days. If one Town has its great Market-day on one day, another Town has its Market on another day: thus they keep their Market-days on separate days. If their Market-day falls in the week, they may also have a Market on two consecutive days. They also have certain Market days in the week on which the principal

Peasants or Traders from the Interior come to do their trading with the Ships. They have a Sunday too, and on that day they do not trade.

Very early in the morning, at day-break, the Peasants come to the Market, carrying on their heads two or three bundles of Sugar-cane, like Faggots. They untie the bundles of Sugar-cane and spread them out on the Market-place. Then the Inhabitants of the place come and buy Sugar-cane from the Peasants there, one buying two Canes, another three, according to their needs. Thus these Peasants quickly dispose of their Sugar-cane, for people are accustomed to eat a great deal of it.

By the time these Peasants have sold their Sugar-cane, the Peasant Women are beginning to come to Market with their goods, one bringing a Basket of Oranges or Limes, another Bananas and Bachovens, [sweet] Potatoes and Yams, a third *Millie,* Maize, Rice, *Manigette,* a fourth Chickens, Eggs, bread and such necessaries as people in the Coastal towns need to buy. These articles are sold to the Inhabitants themselves as well as to the Dutch who come from the Ships to buy them. The Inhabitants of the Coastal towns also come to Market with the Goods which they have bought or bartered from the Dutch, one bringing Linen or Cloth, another Knives, polished Beads, Mirrors, Pins, bangles, as well as fish which their Husbands have caught in the Sea. These women and Peasants' wives very often buy fish and carry it to towns in other Countries [in the interior], in order to make some profit: thus the Fish caught in the Sea is carried well over 100 or 200 miles into the Interior, where it is considered of great value. . . .

[A]fter devoting six days of the week to work and other things connected with their handiwork, they reserve the seventh day of the week for not working and keep it as a rest-day or Sabbath, calling it *Dio Fetissos*. In our language this would mean Sunday; yet they do not observe it on our Sunday or on the Sabbath of the Jews, but on Tuesday, the second working-day of the week. What principles or reasons lie behind this I cannot find out from them. They consider Tuesday as their Sunday and on that day Fishermen are not to go to sea to fish. The Women or Peasant women are not to come to Market with their fruits either, but stay at home with their merchandize. The Peasants do not bring their Wine to Market: instead they deliver their Wine (which they nevertheless do tap from the Trees) to the King, who offers it in the evening to his Noblemen for them to drink and enjoy. People abstain from doing any manual work on that day or engaging in any trade with each other; but the Inhabitants of the Coastal towns do not on that account refrain from going to the Ships and buying merchandize from the Dutch.

In their Market-place they have a square stand, about 4 foot square, with four Pillars rising 2 Cubits above the ground; it has a flat top made of reeds. All around it they hang straw wisps or *Fetissos*. They put *Millie* with palm oil or water on it and give this to their God as food and drink, to sustain him lest he die of hunger or thirst; for they think that he eats and drinks it and lives on it, whereas in fact it is the Birds of the sky which eat the grain and drink the water. When it is finished they smear the little Altar with Oil and replenish it with food and drink, thinking that in this way they do their God a great service and sacrifice.

They also have a man whom they keep as a Vicar [a "preacher" (*osɔfoɔ*) rather than a spiritualist (*ɔkɔmfoɔ*)], or in their language *Fetissero,* which means as much as a Servant of their God. On their Sabbath this person comes and sits on a Stool in the middle of the Market, opposite the little Altar or scaffold where they make sacrifices to their *Fetisso.* The people—Men, Women and children—come and sit around and he delivers an admonition, to which they all listen. . . .

[The Gold Coast and Its Settlements]

[T]he Dutch consider the Gold Coast to extend from Cape de Trespunctas to Rio de Volta. This Cape de Trespunctas lies at a latitude of 41/2 degrees. It was given this name, which in our language means "the cape of three points," because it juts out into the sea at three points or capes. As the Portuguese have a castle there, called Aziem [Axim], the Negroes are not allowed to barter with the Dutch. Ships therefore do not come there to trade; but since it is a recognizable Landmark, they always make their first landfall there in order to proceed along the coast.

Five miles further to the Leeward lies a place called Anta [Ahanta] and it is here that Ships usually Anchor first, for the Negroes buy much iron and are very good at making weapons. . . .

A mile below is the River called Rio de St. George [Pra River] and a place called Iabbe, and Cama, where the Portuguese have another house. Since this area or district is very fertile, about three or four Portuguese, who receive the Toll on the Fish caught here by the Negroes, live here and also buy other food and provisions, which they send every day to the other Castles, such as Aziem and d'Mina [Elmina], for their upkeep. In the sea at the mouth of this river there runs a great reef, so that one cannot enter it with Ships, but only with large Canoes or Sloops.

Just over a mile below lies the village called Agitaki [Akatakyi] by the Negroes, Aldea de Torto by the Portuguese and Comando [Komenda] by the Flamenchos [Flemings]. Although we call it Comando, that is not its name, for Comando lies on the Mountain where the King lives; but because it is the easiest to pronounce, it is called so by us. The Village, together with a small Thicket and a Rivulet running into the Interior, lies NNW of you if you lie at Anchor here, a quarter of a mile from shore, the great quantity of Gold that is brought there from Foetu [Fetu], Abrenbou [Abrem], Mandinga and other States, which lie over 200 miles inland.

The Traders do not come here in large multitudes but only in small numbers. When they come, however, they bring much money and buy many trade-goods, including a large amount of Linen and a reasonable assortment of Basins and Cauldrons. The King of Foetu is sovereign here and has his Toll-Keeper here to receive the revenue of these places. The Village lies on a hillock, in front of which is a huge Rock, on which the sea breaks so loudly that one can hear it from far away. The people here [at Cape Coast] are bad, for they are in daily communication with the Portuguese and most of them are Negroes and Blacks who have lived in the Castle. This place has a beautiful square Market, superior to those of other coastal towns.

A mile further down lies the principal trading town of the whole Coast, called Mourre [Mori]. If you are a mile offshore and it lies NNW of you, then Cabo Corsso [Cape Coast] lies WNW and Kormentin NE by E of you. This was the first place to show hostility towards the people of the Castle and they were the first to prove friendly towards the Dutch, letting them go ashore. Seeing this, the Portuguese one night came and broke all their Canoes into pieces. They [the people of Mori] have never shown any enmity or killed any Dutchmen, except for one; and that was their own fault. . . .

This place is also known as the Dutch Churchyard, because many of our people are buried there. It is the most famous place on the whole Coast: more trade and business are done and more Ships anchor here than anywhere else. And when the Ships want to leave this coast, they come here to take ballast, fetch water and cut wood; and from here they set out for Capo Lopo Gonsalves. The Village lies on a hillock. The place is not beautiful or convenient, and [consists] mainly of an untidy Market-place. Much Palm wine is brought here, as well as other Fruits, to meet the needs of the Dutch. The King of Sabou [Asebu] has jurisdiction here and receives his Toll also here. Traders from Cane [Akani] and other great States of the Interior come to this place in large numbers and bring much Gold, fresh from the Mines and in the same state as it comes out of the ground. They buy much Linen and many Basins, Knives, Mirrors, medium-size Cauldrons etc. It did not use to be a famous place, and no great traders used to come down there, but since the Ships began mostly to anchor there, the Traders have gradually grown accustomed to coming to trade there and thus it has become the most famous trading place.

Hans Propheet Map of the Gold Coast, 1629

KWAME DAAKU AND ALBERT VAN DANTZIG

In 1966, Kwame Daaku and Albert van Dantzig published their translation of the text accompanying a 1629 Dutch map (and manuscript) in the journal Ghana Notes and Queries. *The map was drawn by Dutch cartographer Hans Propheet, and it remains a significant one on account of its detailed descriptions of early Gold Coast polities.*

Atchin [Axim] – the place where the Portuguese have a little castle with three villages nearby. They are great fishers.

Little Incassa – these people are farmers, but they also fish, mostly for oyster shells from a river, of which they burn great heaps for lime and bring that for sale at Atchyn [Axim], to whom they are devoted and from whom they have learnt how to burn lime, but most lime is burnt at Atchyn itself for the maintenance of both her (Portugal's) castles at Atchyn and El Myna [Elmina].

Igwyra – rich in gold. Here the Portuguese use to have a little stronghold, where they traded, and brought their trade goods up the little river in canoes but now that our (Dutch) nation has so strongly started to trade along that coast and the blacks could get the goods more cheaply than from them, (they) have abandoned it, and have brought their force together on the beach. I am informed, and (I) believe it also to be true that the gold that comes from Atchyn and Abeny, 15 miles west of Cape Three Points, is all from Iqwyra. Down at Little Commendo [Komenda] there live on the coast two citizens who both have been with a few trade goods in this country—they returned rich, but there is some danger of highwaymen on the way. Little more is said about great Inkassa than that (they sometimes come), occasionally passing through Adom, to sell some gold to us at Little Commendo, principally when there is on the Gold Coast, say Quaqua Coast, no ship before Assinie or Abeny.

Incassa Iggwyra – little (is known?).

Anta [Ahanta] – ruled like a republic, and has no King. They are almost always at war with those of Adom who attack them on the beach, being fishers, and inland they are farmers. They (bring) also some gold that those of Igwyra deliver and Mompa can bring them some, but (being) at war this hinders much. At Aioba the Portuguese have a small redoubt and they receive there the fish-toll as also at Saconde [Sekondi]. Then their neighbors have called them to their help some years ago against the other Ahantas by whom they were much plagued. Taccorary [Takoradi] is the main village of the Ahantas on the coast.

Jabeu – a little country with a town on its own, coming down the river. Men, women and children trade with the Portuguese in Cama [Shama] in fowls, millet and other goods, which they send to Myna [Elmina].

Adom – this people come often with their neighbors to the coast (bringing) gold, in order to spend it amongst us at Comendo, as the road through Anta is now not free because of the war.

Mampa – these trade amongst those of Adom and Anta inland.

Wassa – has the fame amongst the blacks of being extraordinarily rich in gold, such that the inhabitants nearly always work therein and farm little but are well fed by their neighbors. They say also that the country is not so very fertile; those of Adom mainly come with the gold of their people to the coast.

Wanquie [Wankyi/Wenchi] – has beautiful cloths, also gold, [they] trade inland with the Acanists [Akani].

Guaffo [Eguafo] – or great Comendo has another language than those of Anta; they are also a free people. In the old days Comendo, Futu [Fetu] and Saboe [Asebu] use to be under one king and let themselves be called, as still now amongst the foreigners Adesyners, like those of Fantyn [Fante], Fantyners. But they are now divided into those three, who live on the coast. They are courageous fishers, they farm inland, have a great town, which they call after their country Guafo, where their king lives. There are many people and they bring many victuals to Myna for fish and gold; sometimes the road is closed because of a quarrel. Their main village on the coast is Aijtaquie [Akatakyi]. They are our great friends, generally one of our ships lies there and trades with them; [they] have several times been burnt by those of Elmina who came to visit them over water in canoes, as they would otherwise be surrounded by those of Guaffo. Those of Abremboe have once warred against this country at which battle they killed their king.

Futu [Fetu] – a kingdom separated from Comendo. They hold themselves neutral between us and Elmina, but are friends of the Portuguese. Their main village on the coast is Cabo Cors [Cape Coast]; they are fishers; the Futus come to buy their fish in exchange for victuals and gold; they feed Elmina still more than those of Comendo, but are also much submitted to Abramboe.

Myna [Mina/Elmina] – the greatest Portuguese castle, called St. Jorge da Myna; the village [named Edina] which lies there is big and very populous. In the old days one half use to be under great Comendo, the other under Futu [Fetu], who came there to collect their contribution, but that subjection has been annulled a few years ago by some Portuguese Governor, so that they live now as a republic on their own and are mostly governed by the Portuguese Governor. Not only are there several chiefs of blacks as Mayors, the village is also divided into three, each part has its captain. They are brave fishermen, greatly outnumbering all their neighbors both in canoes and people. They engage in polishing beads which the Portuguese bring there, and which they sell back. They are "alschaek" Christians and marry some to the Portuguese.

Moure [Mori] – here lies our fort Nassau and a rather good village where the inhabitants are still submitted to those of Saboe (to whom they pay some contribution), but fight with all our subjects against those of Elmina and her allies. They are mostly fishermen but they dare not go deep into the sea because of the power of Elmina. Those of Saboe come to feed them, in exchange for fish. They even sow and reap and they also have their own captain and caboceers. Many work in order to serve as brokers for those who come to buy some goods from us, with which they make good profits; because of our trade the coast now has intercourse of foreign peoples from inland so that apparently (provided that the trade continues here) this place will much increase its population.

Saboe [Asebu] – a small kingdom but they consider themselves brave warriors, which they are indeed because those of Aty [Etsi] have come to visit them thrice with many thousands, and they have withstood them bravely, and chopped off the heads of several hundreds which they (as our principal countrymen) came to show us at our factory at Moure [Mori]. And those sixty or seventy muskets which they borrowed from us have much helped, as some of them know very well how to use them, and also two small [cannons?] which have been lent for their assistance. The country around here is very fertile for victuals. So as it happens to be the king and the inhabitants here are very devoted to us.

Abremboe [Abrem] – by itself populous; they busy themselves with agriculture, but come every week to Moure to sell some gold in exchange for draperies and linen, but principally iron. Some live also at Moure, who help the newly arrived trader in negotiating with us. They are good warriors. They are not good friends of the Akanists, as they have warred with them ten or eleven years ago; many of them have been defeated, and most of their villages have been burnt. After this they have agreed so that they are friends now . . .

Description de l'Afrique, 1686
OLFERT DAPPER

Olfert Dapper, Dutch compiler and possibly a physician, never left Holland but instead synthesized published accounts about Africa. The Gold Coast excerpts below (in English translation) come from the 1686 French edition of Description de l'Afrique, *rather than the original Dutch edition of Dapper's work.*

[*The Forest Polities of the Gold Coast*]

The kingdom of Igwira borders on the north the coastal kingdoms of Atzin [Axim] and Little Inkassa, on the south Great Inkassa and on the east Mompa. It is said to be a land very rich in gold. The Blacks say that the gold that is brought to Assinie and Albine fifteen miles west of Cape Three Points is all Igwira gold. A few years ago two citizens lived on the coast at Little Comendo went to this country with a few trade goods and returned richly laden. There are, however, many highwaymen who make the roads extremely dangerous. The Portuguese formerly maintained a fort there in which they traded. They carried their trade goods in barges or lighters on the river that flows through Igwira to the sea. When the Dutch began to trade heavily on the coast and the Blacks could buy goods from them more cheaply than from the Portuguese, they abandoned the place.

The kingdom of Great Inkassia or Inkassan touches the kingdom of Igwira on the south and the kingdoms of Wassa and Wanki [Wankyi] in the east. The Dutch know little of these people through trade; occasionally they bring a little gold through the kingdom of Adom to Little Kommendo especially when there is no ship at anchor in Assine or Albine.

The Kingdom of Inkassa Aggina touches Great Inkassia on the south and Wassa and Wanki on the east. The Whites have very little to do with the inhabitants.

The Territory of Tabeu is a small country touching the coastal kingdom of Anten [Axim] on the south, Adom on the west and north, and Guaffo [Eguafo] on the east from which a small river separates it. Not only the men but also the women and children trade with hens, grain and other goods at Sama [Shama] where the Dutch have a fort. Formerly the Portuguese bought everything and sent it to the castle of the Mine (Elmina).

The Kingdom of Adom touches Tabeu and Guaffo in the east, Wassa in the north and Abremboe in the east-northeast. The inhabitants and their neighbors sometimes bring gold to the Dutch at little Komendo, especially when the route to Ante [Ahanta] is unsafe because of wars.

The Kingdom of Mompa touches Iqwira on the west, Great Inkassia, Wassa and Adom on the north, and the coastal kingdom of Anten on the east.

The Kingdom of Wassa touches Wanki on the north, Abremboe and Kuiforo [Twifo] on the east, Great Inkassia on the west and Inkassia Iggina on the northwest. It is said to be a land rich in gold; the inhabitants spend all their time mining and sow no grain hence they are supplied by their neighbors. It is said that their fields are not very fruitful. They get their food from their neighbors. They bring nearly all of this gold together with that of Adom to the coast and sell it to the Whites in exchange for European goods.

The Kingdom of Wanki touches Inkassia Iggina on the west, Wassa to the south and Bonoe to the north. It has gold and beautiful cloth that the inhabitants make very artistically and sell to the Akanisten [Akani merchants] in the country.

The Kingdom of Abremboe touches Adom and Wassa on the west, Guaffa or Great Kommendo on the south, Kuiforo on the north, Akani on the northeast, Atti [Etsi] on the east and the coastal kingdom of Fetu on the southeast. It is a very populous country. Most of the inhabitants maintain themselves with agriculture. Many of them also go weekly to the sea village of Mouree [Mori] to sell their gold to the Whites for linen, cloth and particularly iron. Some live permanently at Mouree and help newly arrived traders in their dealings with the Dutch. They are good soldiers and are not great friends of the Akanisten because many years ago the Akanisten attacked them and killed many people and burnt most of their villages and fields. After that they came to an understanding.

The Kingdom of Kuiforo touches Wassa on the west, Abramboe on the south, Bonoe on the north and Akani on the east. One finds no bushes there at all and the population is very simple or uncouth and bad. The Dutch trade with them very little.

The Kingdom of Bonoe is a different country from the Bonoe mentioned below. It touches Wanki on the west, Kuiforo on the south and Akani and Inta on the east. There is little trade in this area.

The Territory of Atti touches Abramboe on the west, on the coastal kingdoms of Fetu, Sabou [Asebu] and Fantin [Fante] on the south, and Dahoe on the north. The inhabitants mainly occupy themselves nowadays by agriculture. Before the war they used to trade with the Dutch, as did the people of Saboe, but the Akanisten, who nearly subdued them, took the trade from them. In Atti is a very large market to which many people from far off places go, especially the Akanisten who bring to the market iron and other goods which they obtain from the Dutch.

The Kingdom of Akanien, whose inhabitants are usually called Akanisten or Akanier, touches Kuiforo and Bonoe on the west, Dahoe, Atti and Abramboe on the south, Inta on the north, and Ahim [Akyem] or Great Akani in the east. The Akanier, who have become very famous because of the trade which they conduct between the Dutch and other Whites and the Blacks of the interior, are people with whom one can get on very well but are also very warlike and can use their shields, lances and swords to good effect. Their language is the same as that of Fetu, Atti, Sabou, Kommendo and Abramboe, and also of Fantin, but is somewhat nicer. Those who trade on the coast with the Dutch almost all speak a broken Portuguese. They are rich in slaves and gold and are great traders as well but are somewhat haughty. They bring two-thirds of the gold that the Whites buy on the gold coast each year. Normally they come to little Kommendo, Kormantin and especially to Mouree to trade. Many of them live with their wives and children at Moure and help new traders who come to the coast and have to pay customs duties on their goods. They are deceitful and cunning in trade. Their slaves carry the goods that they buy to various markets in the interior. They are able to travel everywhere with great freedom, through Atti, Sabou and other surrounding territories, enjoy great freedom and are welcomed by everyone. On the Atti border is a village or place called Dahoe.

The territory of Inta touches Akani in the south, in the west and north borders on an unknown land, and in the west touches Ahim and Akam. This country is very little known to the Dutch through trade. Ahim, which the Dutch call great Akani, touches Akani on the west, Aqua and Sonquay on the south, Inta, Akam and Kuahoe [Kwahu] on the north and Aquemboe [Akwamu] in the east. The inhabitants are very arrogant and are debauched in their eating and drinking, rich in slaves, and far surpass those of Little Akani over whom they almost want to impose hegemony. These people rarely come to the coast to trade with the Whites but conduct their trade in gold, cloth and other wares with their neighbors to the north. They mainly go to Abonoe near Akara [Accra/Nkrañ] because they exchange most of their gold for European goods. They also trade a lot with their neighbors the Akaniers.

The Territory of Akam touches Inta in the west, Ahim in the south, an unknown land in the north, and Kuahoe and Tafoe in the east. The Dutch have little knowledge of it through trade.

The Territory of Aqua or Aka touches Atti and Dahoe in the west, the coastal territory of Fantin [Fante] in the south, and Ahim in the north. It is not of great importance and belongs to the chiefdoms of Fantin.

The Territory of Sanquay touches Fantin on the south, Ahim in the north, and Agwana in the east. The people of Sanquay buy a great deal of fish . . . which they carry inland. The territory mainly comes under the kingdom of Agwana.

The Territory of Aquemboe [Akwamu] touches Ahim in the west, Kuahoe in the north, Agwana in the south and Abonoe and Aboera in the east. It is very unimportant from the point of view of trade.

The Territory of Abonoe is a small country touching Aquemboe in the west, Agwana in the south, Aboera in the north and Great Akara and part of Aboera in the east. There is a large market here called the market of Great Akara about two hours behind Akara. Great crowds of people come there from many lands.

The Territory of Kuahoe touches Akam on the west, Aquemboe and Ahim on the south, Tafoe on the north and Aboera and Kammanah on the east. The inhabitants make "bad noise" and are thought to be deceptive by their neighbors.

The Territory of Tafoe touches Akam on the west, Quahoe on the south, Kammanah and Quahoe in the east. It is said that the territory is excessively rich in gold and that most of this gold is brought to Abonoe. Some is occasionally brought to the seaside village of Mouree.

The Territory of Aboera touches Aquemboe in the west, Quahoe and Kammanah in the north, Abonoe and Great Akara in the south and Bonoe in the east. Very much gold is found here which the inhabitants bring to the market at Abonoe.

The Territory of Quahoe touches Kammanah and Little Akara in the south, and Tafoe in the west. Gold is also dug here and taken to the market of Great Akara for sale.

The Territory of Kammanah touches Kuahoe in the west, in the north a different Quahoe, Aboera and Bonoe in the south, and Equea, Latabi [Labadi] and Little Akara in the east. The inhabitants live by agriculture and feed many of their neighbors.

The Territory of Bonoe touches Aboera in the west, Kammanah in the north, Great Akara in the south and Equea and Ningo in the east. The inhabitants are mainly traders and take their goods to their neighbors for sale.

The Territory of Equea touches Bonoe in the west, Kammana in the north, Ningo and Latabi in the south. The inhabitants also live by trade.

The Territory of Latabi touches Equea and Kammana in the west, Little Akara in the north and east, Ningo and Latabi in the south. There is a large market here where all kinds of goods are brought, but it is not as large as the market of Abonoe.

The Territory of Akarady touches Kammanah in the west, Quahoe in the north, Latabi and Ningo in the south. It is said that this territory possesses very much gold that is as good as that which the Akanier bring to the markets. The inhabitants take it to the market at Abonoe. These territories lying here about have not so many trees as Kormantin or other places lying above and are therefore not so fruitful.

The Territory of Insoko [Nsoko] lies, according to the Akanier four or five days journey from the sea. Between them are several other territories unknown to the Akanier. The latter very rarely go to Insoko because robbers make the road very unsafe. The inhabitants make very fine cloths with which they can make a good profit if they can get them through. They are brought for pieces of eight or other silver and also for several European cloths. The inhabitants, according to the Akanier, know no gold or copper and do not trade these items.

A New and Accurate Description of the Coast of Guinea, 1705

WILLEM BOSMAN

Willem Bosman worked on the Gold Coast as a Dutch of-
ficial and then Chief Merchant between 1688 and 1702.
His account, Nautokeurige Besdtryving van de Guinese
Goud-, Tand- en Slavekust, *was translated in 1705 into*
English under the title A New and Accurate Description
of the Coast of Guinea, divided into the Gold, the Slave,
and the Ivory Coasts. *The English translation, however,*
has a range of flaws. The following selections come from
this translation but with corrections, as provided by Al-
bert van Dantzig in a series of articles published in the
journal History in Africa *(HA): HA, vol. 2 (1975), 185-*
216; vol. 3 (1976), 91-126; vol. 4 (1977), 247-73; vol. 5
(1978), 225-56; vol. 6 (1979), 265-85; vol. 7 (1980), 281-
91; vol. 9 (1982), 285-302; and vol. 11 (1984), 307-29.
Lastly, readers should know that Bosman was fond of
using his descriptions of the coastal settlements of Axim
and Elmina for the entire Gold Coast littoral.

[*Language on the Gold Coast*]

I usually write what first occurs to my memory. . . . Though the
Gold Coast is not extended above sixty miles in length, yet we find
there seven or eight several languages, so different that three or four
of them are interchangeably unintelligible to any but the respective
Natives: Those of Junmore, ten miles above Axim, manage to make
themselves understood to those of Egira, Abocroe, Ancober and
Axim, but there is a great difference in their speech; the Axim language being quite unlovely, nay beastly ugly, that of Ante very different from it, though not much more beautiful. But more shocking
is that of Acra, not having the least similitude with any of the rest.
The other coastal Negroes, those of Aquamboe only [the]

except[ion], generally understand one another: But the language of
In-land Negroes is by much the pleasant and most agreeable, I mean
those of Dinkira, Akim, Acanny and after those that of the Adoms;
this difference is easily discernable to a person but the least acquainted with their languages. . . . And the Negroes, which we daily
converse with, who live about our Forts, expressed themselves as
agreeably as the others, 'twould no difficult matter to learn their
language two or three Years, which we find at present we can scarce
do in ten, at least not any sort of perfection. Some of us, amongst
which I dare reckon myself, have made such a progress, that we understand the greatest part of it, though we can hardly get the Pronunciation. The Sound of some words is so strange, that though we
have often endeavored to express them with our European Letters,
yet we have never been able to do it; and as the Negroes are not
able to read or to write, and consequently they do not have a Literature; it is not very well possible for us to find out where their Faults
are. Olfert Dapper, who was never there, incorporated into his "Description of Africa" several different ways of giving names to things
and ways of counting of the Negroes; which, though I may pretend
to some Knowledge of their Languages, dare not attempt, being assured I shall not succeed much better than he.

Could the Negroes, as I have said, either read or write, we should
be able to learn their tongues speedily by observing the Letters
which were used by them to express one thing or another; but having no other assistance than the bare sound, I think it is folly to attempt farther. . . .

[*Social Hierarchy and Nobility*]

I have observed five Degrees of men amongst the Negroes; the first
of which is their Kings or Captains, for the word is here synonymous. The second, their Cabocero's or Chief Men which reducing
to our manner of expression we should be apt to call them Civil Fathers [i.e., town council officials] whose Province is only to take
care of the welfare of the City or Village, and to settle disputes
which may arise. The third rank are those who have acquired a great

Reputation by their Riches, either devolved on them by Inheritance
or gotten by Trade. And these are the Persons whom said author regarded as noblemen; but whether he is right or not, shall hereafter
plainly appear. The fourth rank is formed by common people such
as wine-tappers, fishermen, farmers &c. The fifth and last are the
Slaves, either sold by their Relations, taken in War, or became so
by Poverty.

These five being the only Degrees which are to be found amongst
the negroes. . . . First, The Dignity of King or Captain in almost all
the Negro Countries, descends hereditarily from Father to Son, and
the latter lacking, to the next Male heir. Sometimes, too, the Ability
of such an heir is taken into consideration, as well as his wealth in
Slaves and Money, so that he who is plentifully stored with these,
is often preferred to the Right Heir. Nothing much special occurs at
the Election or Confirmation of a new King; for Coronations and
Coronation Oaths being here any unknown, the new King is shown
to the People, and sometimes carried through Territories; after
which the matter is terminated with a merry Day: But in case of dis-
cord, and if two pretend to that Dignity at the same time, for confirmation of the loyalty of their Followers, [the] Pretender obliges
his Respective Party an Oath of Allegiance; otherwise, as I have
said, everything is done in a very easy-going manner, and only a
few sacrifices are made, which is done at all important Transactions.
The Principal Men commonly are limited in number, but the places
of the Deceased are not so quickly filled again; but if they become
too weak, they assemble and choose out of the commonalty Persons
well advanced in Years to complete their number (for young Men
are seldom, admitted into this Honourable Assembly) who are
obliged to express their Gratitude to their Electing Brethren by a
Present of a Cow and some Drink; after which they are lawfully admitted and confirmed. At Axim it happens as follows: the one whom
the Principal Men desire to become a Caboceer must be a Native
of that Country living at Axim at least keeping a House there, inhabited by one of his Wives, or some of his Family and sometimes
residing there himself, which is somewhat like our being obliged
to keep Fire and Light to preserve our Right of citizens in Holland.

If there be one alone, or several, he or they are all brought to the Fort and presented to our Factor, with a request that they may be admitted into society, who, if he hath nothing to object against him, administers an Oath to him [using] the Bible, obliging him to be and remain true to the Netherlanders, and to aid them to the utmost of his Power against their Enemies whatsoever, whether European or Negroes, and deport himself on all occasions as a Loyal Subject. The same loyalty he swears also to show to his own Nation and People. The Oath having been taken, having confirmed each clause with the Words "That God will strike him dead if he swore contrary to his intentions, or doth not keep his Oath"; in another Confirmation of which the Bible is held on his Breast and laid on his Head, which are the Ceremonies used to render the Oath obligatory. This done, the Factor having registered his name, acknowledges him a member of their Assembly, and admits him to all the Rights, Privileges and Advantages appendant thereto; and having made the due Presents to his Brethren, he is a Caboceer during his Life. In other places on the coast the manner in which the Caboceer is confirmed is somewhat different; but it being so well regulated at Axim, I shall content myself with describing that only.

The third rank among the Negroes are those enriched either by Inheritance or Trade; who, to acquire a Reputation and great Name amongst their Fellow-Citizens, buy about seven small Elephants Teeth, which they make into Blowing-Horns; upon which they cause their people to learn, in the manner of the land, to play, or blow, all sort of tunes: Which when they have learned, they inform all their Relations and Acquaintance that they intend to show their Blowing-Horns publicly, that they may come and make merry with them for several days together; whilst they, their Wives and slaves appear with as much Pomp and Splendor as is possible, borrowing Gold and Coral of their Friends to make the greater Show, and distributing Presents amongst them; so that this extravagant Ceremony becomes very expensive. This Initiatory Festival being over they are for the rest of their life free to have these Horns blown at their pleasure at any time; which nobody who has not been ordained to it in the above mentioned manner is allowed to do. But if someone else feels inclined to have a merry Day, he is obliged, if he wants to have Horns, to beg for them on loan. How contradictory is the Course of Things in this world! In some places Men are obliged to beg hard and make interest for Horns, whilst they come home to the Houses of others as unexpected as undesired.

A Negro having advanced himself in the mentioned manner, in order to achieve still greater Honor and Esteem, then has first one, later two Shields made for himself: Of which he makes a show as public and pompous as that of the Horns and is obliged to lye the first night with all his people in Battle Array in the Air, intimating that he will not be afraid of any Danger or Hardship in defense of his People. After which he passes the next and the remaining Days of the feast, which are generally about eight, in Shooting and martial exercises, as well as Dancing and all sorts of mirth; himself, his wives and family being as richly dressed as they possibly can, and all that he hath in this world exposed to public view, and removed from place to place. But this Festival is not so expensive as the former; so instead of making presents, as usual in that, he here on the contrary receives presents, among which are some of no mean value, and when he designs to divert himself, or go to the war, he is permitted to have two Shields carried for him: A favor not allowed to any who hath not thus qualified himself.

These are now those who are supposed to be the Noblemen here on this Coast, but that in reality they are not so is plain, because no person can ennoble himself, but must be so by birth, or by creation of another: In both which some are deficient, for by birth they are only slaves and consequently widely distant from nobles, and they owe their advance only to themselves and their Money; their sort of Honor here being always open to him who is rich enough to bear the expense. Besides, in other Places Nobility engages those honored with it firmly in the public Service of their King or Country; which these are not the least concerned for, applying themselves to nothing but their Trade: But if any are fond of having them gentlemen and noblemen, I shall let them remain so. And it will not a little redound to my honor that I have for several years successively been awaited on by one of these noblemen in the capacity of a footman, without having the least respect to his nobility.

The fourth and fifth rank need no other account to be given of them, than that they are common people and slaves. . . .

[*Spiritual Culture*]

Almost all the Coast Negroes believe in one God, to whom they attribute the Creation of the Heaven, Earth, Sea and all that is thereon and therein, though in a crude indigested Manner, they not being able to form a just idea of a deity. Similarly, they do not believe in the daily maintenance and governance of all that was created. They are not obliged themselves nor the Tradition of their ancestors for their opinion, rude as it is, but to their daily conversation with the Europeans, who from time to time have continually endeavored to implant this notion in them. There are two Reasons which confirm me in this Sentiment: First, that they never make any offerings to God, nor call upon him in time or need; but in all their difficulties, they apply themselves to their *Fetishe* (of which more hereafter) and pray to him for success in their undertakings: The Second is, the different opinions which some of them have kept concerning the Creation; for up to this day quite a few among them believe that Man was created by the Anansie, a great Spider, which belief they strongly defend. The rest attribute the creation of man to God. . . . I promised just now to explain the word *Fetiche*, which is used in various senses. *Fetishe* or *Bossum* [ɔbosom] in the Negro Language derives itself from their false God, which they call *Bossum*.

Records from the (Second) Dutch West India Company Archives

In 1978, Albert van Dantzig published his collection of Dutch sources for the Gold Coast/Ghana. This hard-to-find collection entitled The Dutch on the Guinea Coast,

1674-1742: A Collection of Documents from the General State Archive at The Hague *remains a classic reference for students and scholars of Ghana. The following selections were drawn from this goldmine of a compilation, appearing in English translation and covering from Dutch perspectives the seventeenth- and eighteenth-century history and politics of the Gold Coast.*

Heerman Abramsz to Assembly of Ten, 23 November 1689

Behind Atty [Etsi] lies the great country of Accanien [Akani], which is partitioned in three main parts: to the North of or in the interior of Elmina the Akkanists are called Crysakeese, in the interior North of Cormantyn are the Cocoriteese and behind Craa [Accra] are the Akims Akkanists. On the side of (?) Accanien follow the gold-rich countries of Adancee [Adanse], Tafoe and St. Zocco [Nsoko], which is rich with mines. Adancee trades mostly with the Cororiteese Accanists, as it is situated bring their wares to Adancee, and consequently the Cororiteesde Accaniste bring most gold. Tafoo trades with Adancee, of which they are a little afraid. St. Socco, which is richer with mines, sticks to a fixed rule that forbids other nations to trade into their territory in order to spy on it or to make war on it. They do their trade outside, in a forest which is made into a market, where those of Adancee, Tafoo and other trading places render themselves and put down their gold with the weight or the price thereupon. . . .

The Accanists, who are real traders, used to trade in all these areas, and they alone controlled all trade, traveling with large numbers of slaves to carry their goods through all those places. But as a result of the wars which the blacks so often start for trifling reasons, this trade is suddenly stopped . . . the passages are closed . . . and especially since muskets and gunpowder have been introduced, things have become much worse, the natives having become much more war-like. . . . Consequently, the whole Coast has come into a kind of state of war. This started in the year 1658, and gradually this has gone so far that none of the passages could anymore be used, and none of the traders could come through. This caused considerable damage to the last Company, the more as its liabilities did not diminish, and would have destroyed it long ago if the slave trade had not kept it going. Slaves were very easy to get on the Gold Coast, because of war . . .

West Indian Company (WIC) 124: Resolution Director-General (D-G) and Council, Elmina, 24 November 1693

The D-G demonstrated that some [differences] has arisen between the Quifferse [Twifo] and the Commanise [Komenda], because the King of Commany has ordered his people to arrest some traders from Quiffer with merchandise to a value of 10:2:8 marks which they had bought from the English at Cabo Cors [Cape Coast], on account of their having slept in his village. These traders are also said to have promised to trade with the Dutch and not with the English, which promise they have not kept. Because of this quarrel the Quifferse have declared war upon the Commanise, and in response the King of Commany has distributed the confiscated goods among neighboring states, in order that they may support him in case of war. Such a war would be to the great disadvantage of the trade, and if the passages were closed to the traders from Dinquira [Denkyira] and Quiffer, we wouldn't make any money and we would find ourselves here in the same state as the factories at Cormantyn and Mouree, where, may God help us, only 3 or 4 marks of gold have been received. The question was therefore put forward whether we should lend to the King of Commany the mentioned 10 marks, 2 oz. and 8 Angels claimed by the Quiffer traders, in order to avoid the war or not. Considering that the Company may suffer at least ten times as much damage on merchandise which may spoil, and that the loan at a later date may be claimed back . . . resolved to supply the said 10:2:8 Mk. worth of merchandise in order to settle the [differences].

Van Sevenhuysen to Assembly of Ten, Elmina,
15 April 1700–16 November 1701

The English Premier Agent Buckeridge, who by his murdering the King of Commany is the cause of the earlier mentioned war, went subsequently to Annemaboe [Anomabu] in order to move the Fantynse [Fante] to help him against the Commanise. But although this request was accompanied by a promise of 300 bendas of gold, they declined. On his way back, he visited Chief Merchant [Willem] Bosman at Moure, where he complained about it, and made it known that he wished that I would co-operate with him, in particular in order to bear the war-expenses. . . . Later he expressed again his desire that we should co-operate with him through the Negroes, in particular Tekki Ankan. . . .

Because of the conflict between Assjantee [Asante] and Dinkira [Denkyira], in which Akim [Akyem] got also involved, the three most powerful countries, which are also the richest in gold, are now involved in heavy warfare. The Dinkirase have for long been very bellicose and proud of their victories, and so they have become insufferable to their neighbors. They have ruined the Akkanistse, the Tjufferse, the Adomse, the Wassase and the Awinse, but soon it will be their turn to take revenge on the Dinkirase. Most of them have decided to close (all) the passages on the beach, in order to cut off the supply of arms and ammunition to the Dinkirase, which has given a great advantage to the Assjanteese, who are much stronger in men and well provided with everything; and if they know how to make use of it, both they and we ourselves would be happy, because as soon as they attack, all the other before mentioned states will attack Dinkira too, with the result that it will be completely destroyed and that we could trade again; but on the other hand, if Assjantee, even though it is in such an advantageous position, does not dare to bite through, the others must also keep quiet, and in that case things would be even more miserable for us on this Coast. . . . At present the slave trade is in as bad a shape as the gold trade, although we thought that the present wars in the interior would rather promote the offer of slave. . . .

[A]lthough the Assjanteese . . . had a complete victory over the Dinquirase, yet we have on this very day not even 2 marks of gold in cash. This is so because the Assjanteese are so full of the rich loot of the Dinquirease, that they do not think of trading, but rather spend their days lustily in the defeated country of Dinkira. All this has mad us decide, on the advice of the principal Akkanists, on an enterprise which has so far never been undertaken, viz. to send on-dercommies David Van Nyendael (who offered his service thereto) as an ambassador to the very feared Caboceer or Chief of Assjantee [i.e., Osei Tutu] . . .

WIC 124: Minutes of Council, Elmina, 14 March 1707

[C]oncerning the sugar, cotton and indigo plantations [on the Gold Coast], that we would be quite able to continue that work, if only the required tools, slaves and other materials were sent, and especially if we were to be allowed to buy as many slaves as President Nuyts proposed in his letter of 24th April 1706. It should however be added that one difficulty in the cultivation of sugar is that much of it is stolen by the Negroes themselves, as they have a very great liking for it . . .

WIC 2: Minutes of the Assembly of Ten, 17 September 1710

Agreed, after deliberation that since the slaves being bought for the slave ships at the various factories on the Gold Coast are very costly to the Company because of the many expenses for their maintenance, their long voyage and the great mortality among them, and that they are therefore more expensive than those bought in Ardra [Allada] and Angola, to write to the D-G and Members of the Council that after receiving this letter they should desist from further purchases of slaves on the Gold Coast, and rather barter the cargoes which arrive for gold and other currently trade goods. If for some very important reason the slave trade were yet to be continued and could not be totally abolished, they should explain to us on the first occasion which presents itself the reason for it. As we presume that on receiving this letter there will be some slaves present on the Gold Coast, it will be recommended to send them to Curaçao on board of the yacht "Elmina."

WIC 126: Minutes of the Assembly of Elmina Council, 18 July 1731

[W]ith regards [to] that Christian freeman, we know very well that the Negroes have very little esteem for such Christians, because generally they have such a life-style that Blacks as well as Whites despise them, and even though they are provided with European clothes and a cane, they enjoy, it seems, not a hair's breadth higher in esteem in their own Nation . . .

Chamber Amsterdam to Overbeeke, 29 October 1734

From a letter sent from Paramaribo on 12th March 1734, we understand that the Negro Tekki, who had been accused by Abocan of wanting to bewitch him by burying a deer's skull under his house in order to make him die and who had been sent to Suriname by Mr. Pranger, has behaved very well during the riot on board on the ship "Vryheyd," and by his actions toward the slaves has saved the ship as competently as any whiteman could have done. It was therefore decided to allow him to return to Elmina . . .

NBKG 106. Journal ("Accra Correspondence"), 23 March 1742

Received from Mr. Van Kuyl a letter dated 18th March. . . . Yesterday the Assiantynen [Asante] have defeated the Akimse, which caused great confusion here and people all along the Lower Coast seek protection under the fortresses. Here the Negroes are busily repairing the Cat-yard in order to use it for their defense. They are afraid that the Assiantynen will come to make war on them too. According to rumors most of the Akimse have fled to the Lower Coast. They may also come here, in that case, the Negroes say here, they cannot give them any protection. They are seriously short of water. The Danish Governor has sent some people to Akim; these Negroes have come back and declare that the whole of Akim has been defeated, and that very many grandees have been killed. The people of Labbadde and Tessie have already fled to Bercoe. Temna fort would not be able to stand such an over might . . .

Counts of Indictment and Defense of the Negroes of Mina Contra

The deceased Director General Martinus François de Bordes heard by the Honorable Council of the North and South Coast of Africa, 17 May 1740

The following is an unpublished Dutch archival document related to the politics and polity of Elmina near the middle of the eigtheenth century. For a fuller context, see Harvey M. Feinberg, Africans and Europeans in West Africa: Elminans and Dutchmen on the Gold Coast during the Eighteenth Century *(Philadelphia: American Philosophical Society, 1989).*

Art. 1 - The Cabocier Amba and the king Annuwe, speaking for all of them, show how that, when they were tired by the fighting of the Fanti in the autumn of 1738, were ordered by de Bordes to attack great Commanise [Eguafo], and if possible defeat them.

Art. 2 - That they had been willing to do this, but had been afraid that the Fanti, who were always in alliance with the other party, would attack them from behind, unexpectedly.

Art. 3 - That they have told this Director General humbly, not meaning to go against his orders, but if only he would be so kind as to send for some people of the upper coast, who could be on the watch to block the way of the Fanti.

Art. 4 - That this had produced no result and that after a little (as there had been no hostilities on both sides) the *titjee* [*asen*, "herald"] of the Foutoese [Fetu] Homme grandes was sent this way to the Cabociers, to offer a peace on good terms.

Art. 5 - That the General, while they were busy with this important business, being told this, had sent his slaves from the quarter and had this said *titjee* (who had done no other mischief) beaten without mercy.

Art. 6 - That the next day the General had made known in the whole village, that if they Minasen [Elminans] did not obey his order to march immediately against the Aquafoese, he would have seized all the canoes, paddlers, *milhio* [millet] and what there was further as refreshment for the village.

Art. 7 - That he has really done this, for three boats loaded with corn, the sailors not knowing what the General had made known, sailed on the river against the morning, but their cargo was confiscated.

Art. 8 - That the general had let the *milhio* be brought to the hall for the present on the pretext that it would be for the Company and food for their slaves.

Art. 9 - But that false pretext was soon found to be quite the contrary, for his concubine was master of most of it, and he made his own slaves use the remainder.

Art. 10 - That they had been compelled by these absurdities to send some of their most principal Cabociers to the said General to show him submissively:

First that he had acted against all law and reason, even had violated the rights of the people (which had always been unshaken by other generals), for he had maltreated without any reason an ambassador from a foreign country sent to them.

Secondly that he, although he knew very well the scarcity of provisions in the village, had not only issued such a rigorous and unprecedented order, but also had robbed the people, not knowing the order, of their goods in an indirect way, and appropriated them for his own private use.

Thirdly that beyond all that is mentioned, it was his wish to keep the road from Commanij [Komenda] and so from the whole upper coast closed, for he did not want that the hostilities between them and the Foutoese [Fetu] would be pacified or settled by mutual agreement.

Fourthly that from all this had to follow (while the roads were closed on land as well as at sea) famine and times of dearness. And besides that they could not be capable to give something of the scanty crop to the white men, for money or for anything else.

Fifthly that they therefore, not only in the name of the other Homme grandes but also of all the lesser people of the whole village, came to implore humbly to stop his hardness in issuing such improper orders. And on the contrary to help them to redress their sad situation, that they in recompense of this benefaction always and more than ever would undertake to do everything that would be useful and advantageous for the Company as well as for him, the General.

Art. 11 - That they had expected a righteous answer; but that they have heard with surprise from the messengers the contrary.

Art. 12 - That they had received the message that the general could not be brought to reason, and even less to a good and favorable decision, saying that he knew very well that *they intended something else for him*. That, when they wanted to protest the contrary, they received an order to depart, which they did, and the gates were closed behind them and the cannon prepared for a hostile attack.

Art. 13 - That they and the homme grandes, seeing that the said General was too much prejudiced against them to get something from him with supplication of any reasons; the most principal of them, namely Amba, ordered them to prepare themselves, that if he, general, might undertake something hostile (which they did not doubt, seeing the preparations made in the fortress), they would be in a state of defense; but that they had not omitted to order the common people severely not to do anything unruly against the fortress, servants, slaves, goods, etc., of the Company.

Art. 14 - That in spite of these orders they had to confess that the orders were so far transgressed, that some of them had appeared before the fortress making unusual grimaces and caprices.

Art. 15 - But without doing the Company or its subjects any harm, for these gestures were honestly directed against the General, for whom most people had an irreconcilable hatred by his cruel government, so far that they could not be kept from these follies.

Art. 16 - That, while they consulted together in those times of distress, the crowd was shot with grape-shot with the result of two dead and 5 wounded persons.

Art. 17 - Followed by 2, 3 and more shots making a great damage in their village.

Art. 18 - The result of which was, that all the young people, with no exception, neither by severe orders of the Cabociers, nor by anything else could be kept quiet, swearing that they would kill Cocoboe (a surname given to the general by the negroes), although without doing anything against the Company, for they knew him to be a harmful person, and the ruin of white as well as of black men.

Art. 19 - That thereupon the whole crowd had approached near the fortress, with no other intention than the glory of killing a brute with a bullet, without any bad intentions for the other white men.

Art. 20 - That they would have succeeded undoubtedly, if a bullet, that went through his wig, had not warned him to be careful, and to expose himself no more.

Art. 21 - Further staying in his retreat within the walls, but to look courageous for the negroes, he had made certain dolls, that were placed on the parapet of the council chamber, showing the General, the Oppercommies Hobroek and the Commies Carstares with much likeness.

Art. 22 - That this war had gone on for 3 months together and that there had been many attacks between them, especially between them and the quarter of the General.

Art. 23 - After this some messengers from the country of the Fanti came to Elmina carrying a white flag as a sign as peace.

Art. 24 - Who, after having been kept for a while within the fortress, appeared to the most principal Cabocier Amba, saying to have come to settle the quarrel between the parties.

Art. 25 - That thereupon the other heads had been called together, to contrive all such means as were thought to be of service to settle the quarrel between both, by mutual agreement.

Art. 26 - Then at last the armistice was decided, which was confirmed by the said General with 3 shots off the fortress.

Art. 27 - That further, to avoid all suspicion as much as possible, there was sworn on the Holy Bible for all the subjects, for the white men by the Commies Carstares and for the people from the village by Amba and the king Annuwe.

Art. 28 - That after that they had lived together well-meaning and with much confidence, as if nothing ever had happened between them; that the general had sent during this time too, lots of brandy to the village recommending that they should forget the suffered hardships and fatigues of the war by being merry and gay for a while.

Art. 29 - Whereupon they started again fearless to work and build their desolate and almost completely shot down houses.

Art. 30 - That the said General had made a great distribution of brandy, during the rebuilding of the fishing village, that he had made razed to the ground during the quarrel.

Art. 31 - That the negroes had thought it their duty to make some recompense for that civility too, that would be pleasing to the General, so that they brought a well-fed cow to the gate of the castle and presented it to the General in the most civil way.

Art. 32 - But that the said Carstares had let them be given an answer in this way, *that there was still enough salted meat in the fortress to feed the white men, so that neither the General nor he needed a cow from the negroes.*

Art. 33 - That this gruff answer had caused some suspicion, but not so much, that they could have thought that the oath on the bible, which the Europeans thought and kept so holy, would be broken.

Art. 34 - But that they a short time after that had received a true message; the General together with his 2 ill-advised counsellors Hobroek and Carstares were bribing the whole country of the Fanti into coming to the village and ruin it and carry the inhabitants as slaves away.

Art. 35 - That these rumors were daily confirmed, and that the oppercommies Hobroek had gone to Cormantijn, where that harmful and deadly project was plotted, to execute everything.

Art. 36 - That the said nations, which being very eager for plunder and liking nothing more than being used for such business, had immediately started and formed in a puzzlingly short time an army of almost 40,000 men, ready to come on the first sign of the general.

Art. 37 - That it had seemed that the said General had repented inside his mad and terrible enterprise and showed no intention to call them.

Art. 38 - Which caused that it dragged on for a long time, and they Minase [Elminans] had a good occasion to strengthen their village as much as possible, constructing a wall, outside the Chapel, to prevent the enemy from approaching, at an unexpected attack.

Art. 39 - That they the day after their arrival planned to attack the village, which to prevent the Minase had appeared, but the guns of the fortresses of St. George and St. Jago saluted them in such a way, that they were compelled to retire, leaving behind many dead and wounded.

Art. 40 - Further they think it unnecessary to show, how many heavy attacks they have endured, and how they have been: compelled to fight desperately under the sharp sword of hunger and thirst, against two so mighty enemies, for this the world knows.

Art. 41 - But that it seemed that Fate ['t Geval] was tired of oppressing them any longer in these wretched and sad times and released them, for the plague of all the people (namely the General) had very unexpectedly died.

Art. 42 - Without that happy business they would have been in great danger before the end of 8 days, to have to give it up and so get in a miserable slavery.

Art. 43 - And at last that they negroes having heard of the desired death and change, had thrown down their weapons, had gone under the fortress with bawls of joy to implore the President and the further government humbly to be merciful for them poor subjects; so much that all hostilities might stop and they further might get protection against their embittered enemies, the Fanti; that this was granted them mercifully, and had the result that said birds of prey with shame had to decamp; that further they had submitted humbly after the opening of the gate, which they repeated herewith again, declaring that they certainly would do what their duty demanded as peaceful subjects, and that they would always be ready to offer their life and property and what was further dear to them for the Company. Praying further that there might be some consideration for their really deplorable situation and that they might get some relief of corn (that they nowhere could get for money) by continuation.

Pen and Contract, 11 October 1755

The following is an unpublished Dutch archival document related to the mid-eigtheenth century history of Elmina. For a fuller context, see Harvey M. Feinberg, Africans and Europeans in West Africa: Elminans and Dutchmen on the Gold Coast during the Eighteenth Century *(Philadelphia: American Philosophical Society, 1989).*

We Nicolaas Mattheus van der Noot de Gietere, Director General of the North and South coast of Africa declare herewith that before us have appeared the hommes grandes ["big men"] and Cabosiers, together with the vaandrigs of the quarters of the mancevos or the young men of the country of Elmina, who declare to maintain mutual tranquility and peace, together with the right discipline, that they had agreed among themselves to request us director general earnestly, that we might make a regulation to which anyone of them could apply and behave himself to maintain the right order: since some time ago the Mancevos or quarters had met with many disorders from the country of Mina and also against each other by arms; which has never happened here before and is not proper too, and which demand aforesaid we were willing to meet; in the future will have to be observed and obeyed between them as follows.

First! If in the future there would arise some palabbre or quarrel between the negroes from Mina, or if the one had something to assert or claim from the other, that they will bring them before the hommes grandes of the country to hear the parties and do justice after experience of the affairs; herewith are aforesaid hommes grandes seriously recommended to make use of all impartiality and to conclude all the affairs that are brought before them in right and fairness and to judge them, and in case there will be experienced that aforesaid hommes grandes were bribed by one of the parties with money or goods to conclude the case in his favor and through that frustrate perhaps another man from his legal claim, shorten it, and in such a case by those who might maintain to be wronged and might come to appeal to us Director General about the judgment of the aforesaid Grandes, and requested to inquire into his case further, and we might find that aforesaid hommes grandes had not acted faithfully as judges, that in such a case, they hommes Grandes, will be condemned to a fine of 2 Bendas Gold or 1 cow. N.B. But in case someone comes to appeal to us Director General about the judgment of aforesaid hommes grandes, might lodge frivolous complaints against aforesaid hommes grandes, in such a case will be condemned likewise to the profit of the aforesaid hommes grandes.

Secondly! The Mancevos or the young men may, when they quarrel with another, whatever the cause might be, belonging to a quarter, bring their disputes before the grandes of their own quarter, to be determined and finished by those, but none of the Mancevos may try to accuse of their own quarter people by another quarter to give dassie [dash], on the confiscation of a fine of 2 Pees gold, to be divided in that quarter, to which he belongs, and in case one of the Mancevos might happen to act against this and that in consequence there might arise some disturbances of fighting and knocking, and that quarter to which he belongs might come to blows with the other quarter, to which he might have accused his colleague or given for a dassie, that such Mancevos, who might be the immediate cause or aggressor of such a quarrel or rebellion, will be sent out of the country as a disturber of the public peace, irrespective of persons (ipso facto).

Thirdly! In case somebody might try, inside as well as outside the Crom [*kurom*, "town"] or village, to assail one of his fellow inhabitants with an axe or a knife, and to hurt, that such a person will have to be delivered to us Director General, to let him be punished after experience of the case and absolutely once for all herewith be confirmed, to prevent all disorders in the country, that such a negroe, who might dare to knock about the place and to assail his fellow inhabitant with anything sharp or a stick, be sent from this coast as a disturber of the public peace (ipso facto).

Fourthly! In case it might happen that in the quarters of Elmina there might happen to arise some differences, then they will have to bring those differences before us Director General, so that we might conciliate them among them: But if they against expectation, did not observe properly this our good intention to maintain the public peace and might neglect, but on the contrary, as for several years has been usually done with them, to want to be their own judges, and to arm against the other, that we will consider them then as rebels and disturbers of the public peace, and also letting act against them as against such people and if they will persist in their intention and within the reach of the artillery of this fortress might happen to shoot the other with sharp [weapons], that we will consider them as enemies, for there is nothing else to expect from aforesaid disorder as a ruin of the entire country of Elmina, and a complete obstruction in the trade of the honorable West India Company, that is why that has to be countered with powerful means to maintain the public peace and to let the trade thrive.

Thus done and concluded by us Director General and signed to ratify this, besides the hommes grandes, Cabosiers and the vaandrigs of the quarters of Elmina, and affirmed by them with an oath of the bible.

In the headfortress St. George d'Elmina.

Journal and Correspondences of H. W. Daendels, Governor-General of the Netherlands Settlements on the Coast of Guinea, 1815-1817

Based on John Furley's manuscript notebooks (part of a larger series entitled "Elmina Diaries and Correspondence"), Herman W. Daendels's journal and correspondences up until January 1817 were mimeographed at the Institute of African Studies, University of Ghana at Legon in 1964. The following selections use Furley's notebooks rather than Daendels's archive in the Netherlands. On the value and utility of Furley's collection, readers should consult Albert van Dantzig, "The Furley Collection. Its Value and Limitations for the Study of Ghana's History in European Sources for Sub-Saharan Africa before 1900: Use and Abuse," Paideuma 33 (1987): 423-32.

The Employment of Mulattoes

5 October 1815

J. Goldberg to Governor General

To the Governor General of the Coast of Guinea

It is not to be denied that great services have been rendered to the Motherland, especially in recent times, by the colored people or Mulattoes on the coast of Guinea; and that where it is possible, justice should be done to their position which forming the link between the Government and the natives is of the highest importance.

As this is true, and is it also true that care must be taken that this usefulness is not lost to the Motherland; and this would happen in the event of the colored people being blended with the Government, for in that way the good that they can do by giving an independent example of submission to the just orders of the Government would be entirely wanting. In addition to which the respect which the negro nations have always had for the Whites would be diminished.

Although I am quite willing to suppose that this is most fully realized by most of them, and that from love for the welfare of the land of their birth they will not choose the worthy honor of governing above the honour that consists in being of the highest importance alike to the Government and to the natives; yet it is still possible that some of them may drive their mistaken ambition so far that deaf to the interests of the motherland and of themselves, they may try to take the reins of Government into their own hands, or at least to obtain a considerable influence over it; and this my secret letter particularly serves that U.H.B.G. may be watchful as to this.

Except therefore a few unimportant offices, it appears to me that no Government posts whatever should be conferred upon the colored people or Mullatoes: for when it comes to upholding the interests of the Motherland all other considerations rest be set aside, for however useful in other respects their services may be, prudence forbids that they should ever be called to posts as a reward therefore, whereby they can in other cases be less useful.

The liberal system that has been introduced by His Majesty with regard to trade on the Coast of Guinea, will by doing much for their own sentiments, be sufficient for them to find reward for them, and if this, as I trust with the greatest tranquility, is wisely modified by U.H.EG. I am assured that seldom will anything more be insisted upon by them . . .

Report of 1st Assistant W[illem] Huydecoper, Embassy to
  "King of Ashantee"

Report to Governor General Daendels, received 23 May

Excellency, I am pleased to report to Your Excellency by this my safe crossing over the river Bossum Pra. I am now on the way to the [Asante] King. This place where I am now is an Assin Crom ["town"], inhabited by women, as the men have marched out with the Ashantees. This, and other villages passed, are suffering from severe famine, all their farms having been entirely plundered by the soldiers who have had their camps there from time to time. From

Elmina onwards I have not yet had to stop weighing out gold daily to the people for subsistence. Your Excellency can form no idea of the numberless expenses which will fall upon this expedition. The gold goes well, but drink and cloths are the expenses which especially mount up. Everywhere I rest I am almost obliged to present a piece of cloth to the owner or Caboceer of the Crom, and much drink to the followers or site of such a Caboceer. I have now but one anker of drink left. Had I not watered the ankers now and then I should already have been quite denuded of this article. . . . [I] therefore ask for more ankers and also rice to be sent him. . . . [After] the crossing of the Prah [River] by canoe . . . [we came to a place] called tjetjewerry, that is to say "Keep courage" a suitable name for our solace because we greatly need good courage. . . .

(Signed) W. Huydecoper, in the village tjetjewerry / 12 May 1816

Letter from Assistant Huydecoper, received 26 May

"This native who says he is the King's son, is going to d'Elmina for trade. Wherefore I have given him this so that he can apply to the General, immediately on his arrival for the goods which he requires for his gold.

(Signed) W. Huydecoper / 15 May 1816

P.S. I am now 2 days from the King's capital, and if no difficulties arise, I shall be there next Saturday.

Letters from Huydecoper Dated the 25th and 26th of May
from the Capital of the King

H.E.G. Sir, I have the honour to report by this that I arrived safely at the Capital last Wednesday the 22nd instant. Every honour was shown to me by His Majesty on the day of my arrival: no greater preparation could be made for a King than what was done for me. More than 100 Caboceers and quite 50 thousand men surrounded me on all aides. I was most splendidly received, music, drums, flutes: Of gold and other things there was no lack. I had to shake hands with one by one till I came to His Majesty with whom I had

the honour to shake hands three times. I was almost blinded by the
sight of so much gold of all kinds of workmanship. After having received all compliments from each one, I was shown by His Majesty
a large Place under a great tree on a hill where I also in turn must
go and sit to receive the return compliments. Being seated, I first
received from 25-30 men before His Majesty arrived, and being
about 10 paces from me His Majesty got out of his basket and came
to me on foot, and took my hand three times saying—"Welcome!
Welcome! Welcome!" and then went up the hill with all his followers: after which quite 20 other Chiefs also paid their compliments.
Everything is noted more fully in my journal. I counted 54 large
umbrellas today, besides the small ones which must have been 60
besides. This lasted from 2 o'clock to 7 o'clock in the evening, and
everything came to an end nothing was discussed this day. On the
23rd the King had me told that he was anxious to hear my message,
and was already seated with his chiefs and was waiting for me. I
went immediately and having come he shook me by the hand three
times and asked me to speak.

I spoke the following words. "Sire, the reasons for my coming
are concerned with very important submissions which it is not permitted me to state publicly. My order is that I must make this serious
message known to Your Majesty in a private Interview: therefore if
Your Majesty will fix a day that is pleasing to you it will be a great
honour for me to speak with you alone." The King was so pleased
with these words that he said to me, "It is enough (*'matie matie'*
[*mate*]), I understand you." He fetches the Governor's presents to
the King from his house, accompanied by General Pokoe and 3
other men, and presents them to the King. . . .

All compliments being ended I want to my house, but in the
evening about 7 o'clock, I was secretly summoned by the King. I
went at once, and walked through several rooms before we came to
the King, whom we found sitting in a large square in his house with
Generals Pokoe and Adum Atta and four of his Speakers. A large
Umbrella protected His Majesty's head from the night air, six soldiers were behind him, and 4 boys with lamps in their hands. He
gave me a chair, I went to sit down and got a dram of brandy from

a glass quite 4 times as large as our dram-glasses. He then asked me, "Have you got your paper with you," I said "Yes," and took my Instructions out of my pocket. He took them and having looked at them he said "Read them aloud so that I can hear." I did so but he understood them as a new-born baby. Then he said, "It is not like the papers that got from General Torane." I said "This is Dutch; the others were English." Then he said, "Tell me now all the good news that you have brought with you." I did so by telling him it article by article in his native language. He took the greatest pleasure in everything and after it was finished he said "Everything is good we will speak about it again." I thereupon departed. . . .

For my part I think I can report to Your Honour that everything will succeed except the meeting which I do not believe will take place since His Majesty is somewhat at variance with the Wassaws: otherwise everything is in our favor. . . . Nothing more of importance. . . .

(Signed) W. Huydecoper.
Capital Koemassie, 25 May 1816

Daendals's Journal of 18 June 1816

The subjoined letter I have today written to the King of Ashantee, and sent along another way than that via the Camp, so that it shall not be stopped by the Ashantee generals who know quite well that they are not obeying the King's order. I shall try, as at Java, to add a translation in the native language, written in our letters, for the Natives cannot write, they therefore have no letters. . . . [He] who has to translate my letters . . . will only have to read the translation in order to make the King understand my intention.

Letters from Huydecoper via Four "Ashantee Messengers,"
received 11 July

King's Capital, Koemassie, 7 June 1816
    On the 6th instant the news was reported to the King that Cudjoe Coema had been killed: whereupon he called me and on the glad

news drank a dram with me out of one of the cellarets brought by me. This he had not yet done since I have been here . . .

Capital Koemassie, 14 June 1816

The King asks for velvets and chintz to be got for him from Holland. I have again spoken to the King today about what I am to do with my men, but he said that he would give me a reply about everything next Monday with which our conversation ended. . . . He [the King] said to me this morning "Stay a while here with your people. If you go away when shall I get such a good friend again? It would not annoy me if you stay for some months yet with your people." To which I replied by saying that it would give me very much pleasure if I already knew the good results of the commissions entrusted to me. I could then stay with more tranquility. This I only said, laughing, to test him, but his reply was only "After this Adai [Adae: highly sacred day of (public) ritual cleaning and rites], I will speak with you about everything: everything is just as good as if I said yes." This is all the news for 4 to 5 days.

(Signed) W. Huydecoper

To Governor General H. W. Daendels:

Your Excellency: I have the honour to report to Your Excellency the very much desired good fortune, that I have now, after all possible labour, accomplished everything according to your wishes and desires. From the 18th to the 20th I took every possible trouble to persuade the King to let me have some information about my Commission, and today I have received all His Majesty's final answers.
. . .

(Signed) W. Huydecoper The King's Capital, Koemassie 22 June

Report to the Department of Trade and Colonies about the State of Our Relations with the English Government on This Coast as Well as with the King of Ashantee, Wassas, Fantees and Coast People

The trade of the English has very much diminished through the total ruin of the Fantee Nation, which has been brought to such a state of poverty and lamination that they are offering their children on the Windward Coast and here, for a nominal price so as to be able only to buy a little food for the preservation of life. Their lands for the most part still lie uncultivated, their villages have been burnt, most of their inhabitants are dead or have been carried off, and as they continually have an Ashantee army on their boundaries they have lost heart even for cultivation and trade, and unarmed Ashantee traders traverse the whole of the Fantee without any insults being offered them. The Fantee country begins not far from Elmina along the leeward coast to close to Accra.

It is my good fortune to persuade the King of Ashantee not to attack the Wassaw people, in order to prevent a still greater dearth of provisions, and so that this Nation could serve for buying the trade goods for the most part from our Factories and so carry them for sale to the Ashantees and other nations. This people extend from Fantee to the river Ancobra. They are a very bad and treacherous People, still their fear of the Ashantees and the weakness over against them, make them a very tractable and useful people for us, for the Ashantees have not yet acquired the habit of all going to the beach themselves to traffic their own against European goods. The Wasaaws have big palavers with the people of Cape Coast, and so do not go there to buy goods. They come and trade here, at Chama, Saccondee, Boutry, Dixcove, Axim and at Apolonia. We have as far as possible removed out of the way palavers with them. There is only one Caboceer among them who is entirely intractable and with whom nothing whatever is to be done, namely, Attobra Penien.

The Ashantee traders come here to trade much more than to Cape Coast: a few however go there and the most easterly provinces of that Kingdom drive their trade at Accra and Anamaboe. The trade of the interior at Elmina is already very considerable, and at Axim a strong trade is also carried on from time to time. The trade of Cape Coast, other English Factories on the leeward coast has lost a great deal through the crushing of the Fantee Nation. They carry on no trade with the Wassas, and have many less Ashantee traders than we. With the King of Ashantee we are on the best understanding. He has much respect and friendship for the Dutch: he calls himself their slave [and] acknowledges the Dutch Governor as his master. I have had not [heard] from Huydecoper for three months . . .

Report to the Department of Trade and Colonies Regarding the State of Trade on This Coast, 1816

The slave trade has caused the trafficking of goods for gold and ivory to be very greatly diminished. It has extinguished industry, and not only paused a reduction in the number of gold-diggers, but also the regular work in the mines to cease in the dry season: so that now digging for gold is practically only done by the slaves of Kings and Caboceers, who win a very small amount compared with former times. It has also so much lessened the desire for agriculture that one finds periodical famines in many places where formerly abundance prevailed, the supply of one year then being first consumed in the one following. The uncertainty of not any day being seized and sold to the ships extinguished the courage for all peaceful labor, and made the negro into an armed and restless robber who laid snares for his fellowman to catch and sell him, as he feared and expected for himself and his.

Report to the Department of Trade and Colonies on the Cultivation of Colonial Products in the Dutch Settlements on the Coast of Guinea

The slave trade, which although (it is) little one ever hears of murders and house breakings, had brought the wild-tempered negro to (such) a state that he lived in a continual quarrel with his neighbors, so that soon there existed no Krom which had no palavar, claim, or dispute with its nearest neighbor from which resulted the panyarring, capturing, and carrying off of men, women and children, who thus neglected all regular work in the field and limited it to the most necessary of foodstuffs—has not only depopulated the countries along the Coast of Guinea, but has caused such a decline in cultivation and increase in the forests that on the one hand it will cost a great deal of trouble to reclaim this country afresh, while on the other hand no doubt remains that the present circumstances inspire infinitely more security not only to the Negro, but also the European who desires to commence the cultivation of Colonial Products.

Huydecoper's Account of an Oath Swearing Ceremony
in Kumase, 9 December 1816

Whereupon the Wassa Ambassadors replied that they would first go and tell their masters: and that they were only young men. Upon this all the Generals, officers [and company] to the number of at least 200 rose up passionately, and on the order of the King [of Asante], and in honour of our General [Daendels], took up their swords, and swore to the Wassa Ambassadors, each in turn, these words:

"I swear by the great oath of Cormantyn that where the General our master have charged the King of the Ashantees to place the great road, so that he the General can honour our King to come and see him here, the same shall be Placed without alteration: and those who will not have the General's wish carried out by us, I will take up arms against, and show them that I am the slave of the King Saij [Osei Tutu Kwame; also known as Osei Bonsu]. I swear if Eltifor [Ntsiful, Wassa ruler] does not keep quiet till the matter comes, but hinders the General with deceits as all the Wassas are (sic), I will take up arms and without mercy make him Eltifor flee out of the way, and place the desired road there where the General pleases to lay it. I swear to this by the oath of Cormantyn and Saturday."

Afterwards the King gave orders that they must all, one by one, swear before me, in honour of the General. Whereupon with the greatest pleasure they drew their swords and swore with them right against my nose, saying:

"Bronie! [*boroni*, "European/white person"] I swear by the great oath of Cormantyn, I swear on 'Saturday' and by my King Saij that where your Master the General wishes to have the great road, there shall it also be laid, and if anyone will stop the General with equivocations he will see that I shall leave no roof on his house. I swear by the honour of your General that I will make those who wish to prevent us making the ordered road pay with their goods, slaves, and their own heads. I swear that the will of the General our master shall be done."

Your Excellency's very obedient servant, (Signed) W. Huydecoper

[*Postscript*: On 10 January 1817, Daendels, frustrated with Huydecoper's lack of correspondence, wrote to the "King of Ashantee" that "Huydecoper is not fit to remain any longer with you as Envoy! He would more likely to diminish than to increase our friendship. A whiteman, born in Europe, is ready to replace Huydecoper after he shall have been here 3 days. I shall require that time to collect information to enable me to draw up instructions for my new envoy [who is left unnamed]." In another (draft) letter composed that same day, Daendels wrote to Huydecoper, "I do not reply to your letters for after five months silence they signify nothing. On the contrary, you dishonor your character as a Christian by drinking fetish water instead of swearing on the bible, if swearing was applicable. You could have put better arguments before the King than the wretched drinking of oaths." Huydecoper was admonished for not telling the Asantehene he (Daendels) wanted "slave for agriculture, cattle for plough, and horses for wagons from the King as return-presents" and to leave Kumase within two days receipt of that letter. It is not immediately clear if this letter was sent or if Huydecoper received it, though we do know Huydecoper left Kumase, since his diary ends in May 1817. Dutch agent Jacob Huydecoper, a son of Willem Huydecoper, arrived in Kumase in 1837 and stayed until 1842.]

— 7 —

German and Danish Sources

Second Voyage to the Gold Coast, 1614
SAMUEL BRUN

Samuel Brun (or Braun) was a young surgeon who later served as a barber-surgeon for Fort Nassau at Mori/Mouri, the first Dutch fortress on the Gold Coast. He lived on the coast between 1617 and 1620.

On the last day of March in the aforementioned year we embarked on our ship, called the Weisse Hund, and sailed from Teasel (Texel).
. . .

Assine [Assinie] lies about 80 miles from Quaqua. There the gold trade begins. Not far from there, the Portuguese have a small fort called Asim [Axim]. We therefore trade there at great risk; for the Portuguese come with perhaps three or four galleys if they observe our ship or other Dutch ships. But they often receive a good thrashing from us. We sailed on, however, to Capo de Aves Pintes [Tres Puntas, i.e. Cape Three Points], a country which has three points, and from there to Commendo [Komenda], till we saw the Castle de Mina [São Jorge da Mina], which is Portuguese. Finally we arrived in front of More [Mori] and Fort Nassaw, where we met several Dutch ships lying below the said fort. There we fired three shots in honor of the States General's fort, as is customary. They did the same in return.

The next day, however, we sailed on to Carmandin [Kormantin], where we met a whole fleet of ships and four belonging to our company. Since our ship was well-manned and not too large, we were quickly sent off to Accara [Accra], which is the last place where one finds gold. We stayed there about six weeks to trade in several kinds of merchandize. We traded with the people on board our ships, for we cannot trade on shore on account of the great enmity between the people there and their neighbors.

The people of Accara are not large in stature, but very quick and swift in all matters. The beliefs, religion and way of living of people throughout the Gold Coast (or borders) are the same, and more will be said about them when we discuss the fort.

When they go out to sea, they have canoes: these are hollow trees, which they prepare with skill, so that about twenty or more men can sit in them. They have no clothing except a small *quaqua*, with which their loins and pubes are covered, the rest of the body being quite naked. But the Acaniah traders, who bring the best gold, about 60 or 70 pounds, all the way from Acania to there, have another cloth over the shoulders as a coat; and they move about very imposingly after their fashion, with perhaps 150 or more slaves; for the Acanists have no horses, and the goods they receive in exchange for gold, such as iron, copper, brass basins, beads, swords and other large knives, are heavy. The slaves must carry these articles home on their backs, like donkeys, and all in a single file; just as in our country the horses pull carts. If they have to stay the night in a place, they blow their horn. The gold they bring there is tied in little skins, each of which is a measure of weight. They can speak no language except Acanish and so they use people from Accara as their interpreters. They are also clever at deceiving foreigners, for they use two kinds of weight: when they buy, they use the heaviest weights, and they sell with the lighter ones. When they come aboard ships, however, they generally become sick; for they are not of a strong constitution and must therefore soon return to the land and entrust the trading to the Accara people. The latter then do as they please. Then, when they bring ashore goods which have been traded but with which the Acanists are not content, they go back to the ships and fetch a little brandy, which they are immeasurably fond of drinking. They are soon quiet and content.

When we had stayed there about three weeks, a fresh war broke out between the King of Great Accara and the King of Atty, who fought hard against each other. Since the King of Accara lost most of his power, the trade in gold was impeded. The king requested the Dutch to be so kind as to provide him with about 20 or 25 sailors (whom they call *brunny* [*boroni*]), for an attack: he would then give each of them two *bände* of gold, i.e. about 8 *loth*, making 32 ducats. On hearing this, several of the sailors were ready; and when the gold had been weighed out in front of them, they at once marched off at night with a thousand Accara people. With their muskets they instilled such terror into the enemy that the king could actually have conquered the whole country; for he obtained about 600 heads and marched home again with great joy. . . .

This country [the Gold Coast] stretches about 70 miles along the coast; it extends eastwards and about 300 miles inland towards Arabia and Great and Little Akanye. It lies 5° north of the equator. It is a hilly country, but not all that high; a fairly good country, although it produces few fruits. [The settlements are] built on the coast, for the people are mostly fishermen. The gold traders live 9 or 10 miles inland, namely in Sabou [Asebu], Fontain [Fante] and elsewhere. Since these are pleasant places, the kings have their residences there, and all kinds of plants unknown in our country are found there.

In agriculture they have a very great advantage; for they cannot cultivate the soil as is done in our countries, but instead they just cut the shrubs down and let them become dry. Then they set fire to them and thereby the whole country is cleared. It then begins to rain at a certain time, which is known to them through experience; for in their country it rains for three months a year. When the land has been made damp, it [the ash] serves in place of good manure. Then, when they want to sow, they make little holes, throw the seed into them and cover it up. When the rain falls on it, it grows a span high in three days. They then transplant it very skillfully and in three weeks it grows to a man's height, so that they often have a harvest in seven weeks. They have three kinds of crop. Our corn, however, will not grow there as theirs does. They have two harvests in four months. The [remaining] eight months of the year it is so hot in their country that everything dries up on account of the great heat, just as in our country everything freezes in winter on account of the great cold.

They have no mills: instead the women grind the corn on stones, as in our country people grind or whet iron on stones. It becomes very pure. When they want to bake it, they cook it in water (for they have no ovens) and prepare a very thin dough [by mixing it] with water. When it begins to rise, they wrap it in a green leaf from a tree, tie it up, lay it in a pot of water and let the water boil down till the dough becomes dry like bread. It has no crust, but otherwise is good to eat.

When they have no fruits, they take roots and make bread out of them too, called *kancty*.

They have a kind of fruit which they lay on charcoal and roast. They call it *brody*. It is very good for [curing] diarrhoea.

Their dwellings and towns are not made of brick or stonework. Nevertheless, the Lord God and Nature have endowed them with such thick, intertwined hedges, the height of a man that one cannot shoot through them with any bow. The vegetation on them is so tough that it just cannot be hewn down. On top it looks like a small forest. Their gates are so narrow that only one man can go through them; and they are remarkably strong. Such hedges go right round their dwellings and are called *ohou* by them.

But in the open country the peasants (called *sanfou*, i.e., wine-growers) have scattered dwellings. These people come to market in groups of about 200 or more and bring nothing but fruits and wine. The wine they carry on their heads in long *matetts*, which are broad boards on which they have three or four large tubs or bowls full, containing 6 6r 8 *maass*. They sell [the wine] for gold. Their dwellings are made only of straw and brushwood.

Much sugar-cane and very strange fruit, unknown in our country, grow there.

They are simple and fearful, and even if they wanted to deceive us it would do them harm. They exchange their wine with us for a little brandy, which they call *araka* and think nothing of the trouble it gives them. They go around naked, yet cover themselves a little with a small cloth, as if with underwear. But it is almost 12 ells long, and they wrap it around themselves rather like what is seen on a crucifix. The women, however, are more covered and clothed than the men. They have peculiar hats, made from goatskin, which they stretch over a mould while it is wet: when it dries, it is a hat.

Above I have discussed their dwellings in general. But I cannot omit to say what their shape is and what they are made of; for they are made very strangely and cleverly. The walls are interlaced like a wattle and daubed with earth. The roof is made of palm fronds. They have no windows, but when they want to have air or light, they open the roof with a stick, for it is very light. Inside, the walls are coated with red earth; the floor too is red, like red ochre. Each person makes as many houses as he keeps wives; for each wife has her particular house, so that they do not annoy one another. The husband makes a fence around them, and his house is in the middle. Their parlours are separate houses, as are the bedrooms and kitchens or cooking houses. Each wife keeps her children with her. But when the boys grow up, the father takes them. These wretched people worship the Devil and yet keep some things in good order. Tuesday is their sabbath and on this day they do not go out to sea; for their god Fytysi [ɔbosom] has forbidden them to do so. If they fall ill, they promise him that they will eat no meat or drink no wine.

Fetu, 1662-1669

WILHELM JOHANN MÜLLER

Ordained as a Lutheran pastor, Wilhelm Müller reached the Danish African Company's Fort Frederiksborg in Fetu, near Cape Coast, on 13 December 1662. He arrived on the Gold Coast at the height of the European contest for this region and may have seen Fetu at the peak of its power. A century later, Fetu was absorbed by

*the Fante. The excerpts below focus on life in Fetu be-
tween 1662 and 1669.*

[*Spiritual Culture of the "Fetu People"*]

Although these blind people can adequately perceive, from the right
of nature and (as Holy Scripture attests) from God's work (namely
the mighty work of Creation) that there exists a God, the Creator of
Heaven and Earth, yet they do not fear, love, honor and have faith
in the Almighty Creator; but on the contrary, they serve the Devil,
in order that no harm may be done to them by this corrupter.

None of them will readily admit—indeed, most do not even understand—that they serve the Devil; yet the imaginary worship they
have chosen themselves is nothing other than devil-worship and can
only be termed such. Their idolatrous, superstitious belief rests on
two principles.

Firstly, they believe that there exists something from which all
evil originates; secondly, that there exists something from which all
good comes.

The first they call *samma*, and to it they ascribe all the misfortune
with which they are afflicted, such as damage, loss, poverty, illness,
early death etc.

The second is called by them *o-bossum* [ɔbosom], or *summan*
[*asuman*]. The difference between these two names is that they consider the former to be a general idol of the country, but the latter to
be a special domestic idol. When the Blacks talk to us Whites, they
call their idol-worship "fitisiken."

It is not actually known whence this name is borrowed. My opinion is that because the Portuguese call magic "fitiso" in their language and the Blacks are accustomed to pronounce words unknown
to them as if they were all diminutives, it has come about that instead of the word "fitiso" they use the diminutive "fitisiken."

In discussing the idol-worship of these blinded heathen, five aspects are to be noted.

None of the Blacks is able to say what *o-bossum*, *summan* or *fitiso* actually is, since they are led [in such a way] that they them-

selves do not know how they are led. Thus when one of them is asked what *o-bossum, summan* or *fitiso* is, he must bluntly admit that he does not know.

As far as I could learn from my experience of them, the words *o-bossum*, summon and *fitiso* are used partly in a general sense and partly in a particular sense.

In a general sense they are used to cover everything they consider sacred; for they hold sacred:- 1. The Devil himself, from whom, when in need, they seek advice, comfort and help. For example, their most distinguished *fitiso*, called *Cucu* said by the heathen priests to appear in the form of a tall, abominable, black Moor, bringing with him a hunting spear, bow, quiver and a large black dog.

The description of this *Cucu* indicates clearly that the hellish hunter must be the Devil, since the latter is expressly called a hunter in Holy Scripture. Nevertheless they regard this *Cucu* as a patron and patron saint of the whole country. For this reason he is called by them *obossum*, i.e. a saint.

In the same way the natives of the Accara [Accra] country regard the Devil as a powerful saint and pay him divine honour. It is unanimously reported by them that this *fitiso* or false god appears among them in the form of a tall, ugly Moor, talks to them and in time of need gives them advice and help. None of them likes to be alone at night at the time when they sleep, for although they consider the Devil, as I have said, to be a powerful guardian angel of the whole country, they are still very afraid of him. This supposed patron saint is called Sakun by the Accara people.

Besides the Devil incarnate, the natives of the Fetu country hold sacred:- 2. All kinds of lifeless creatures—the moon in the firmament of heaven, certain rocks and crags, trees and dumb, crawling animals.

As soon as the new moon is sighted, they jump in the air three times, clapping their hands, thanking this work of creation for the benefits they have received in the past month and asking it to continue such benefits in the coming month.

On the seashore below Friederichs-Berg has a large rock which is regarded as highly sacred by them. Indeed, this rock, called Acquitti, is held in such honor that they may well hesitate ten times before swearing by Acquitti.

The aforementioned rock near the castle at Cabo Corso [Cape Coast] is likewise held to be very sacred. No one will venture to set foot on it, if he intends to remain unpunished and unbeaten. This rock is named after false heathen god, Tabri.

The whole country is full of such *fitiso*-rocks and stones. Once, at Cabo Corso, when I sat down on a big stone to rest, a large number of black women ran up to me and shouted that I should watch out that no harm were done to me, [for] the stone on which I was sitting was dedicated to their *fitiso*. To this I answered that I, as a Christian and servant of God, the Creator of Heaven and Earth, had nothing to fear from their *fitiso*.

The whole country is full of trees which the Fetu people hold sacred. One such tree stands below Friederichs-Berg, not far from the harbour; others, as mentioned above, in the market-places at Fetu and Cabo Corso, and likewise one at the cistern behind Cabo Corso. At Fetu I have seen a tree which was wonderfully contorted and plaited. It is considered especially sacred.

Among the worms and crawling animals, lizards and snakes are held sacred. Although lizards often run around the houses of the Blacks, none of the Blacks has the heart to kill or injure them.

At the bottom of Friederichs-Berg, not far from the quarters of the black Danish soldiers, lived a big, monstrous snake, to which people sacrificed daily, because it was regarded as a *fitiso*. Various Whites had intended to kill it when an opportunity arose, but out of fear of the Blacks they were not able to put this into practice.

The Blacks in the Fetu country hold everything sacred that they do, swear or consecrate in the name of their *fitiso* or false god, or wear oft their body in its honor.

If someone expects something bad from another person, he buries some iron or wood in the earth, uttering special incantations in the name of his *fitiso*. He considers it capable not only of protecting him powerfully, but also of suddenly killing the person who bears malice towards him, as soon as he walks over the buried iron or wood.

It is very common throughout the country to see placed in the ground in front of all houses, dwellings and compounds little sticks with a barb on top and painted with red earth. In many houses one finds several hundred sticks, indeed a thousand in one bundle. In such bundles one finds another stick which is large and long, and on which hang all kinds of rubbish, bark of trees, chicken-bones, sheeps' and goats' heads colored with blood, eggshells and even old swaddling clothes.

These red-colored sticks are seen by these winded people as highly sacred, for they obstinately and firmly imagine that they serve to avert evil and attract what is good. Thus if someone goes off on a journey, the barbs are pointed towards the place [to which he is traveling], but when he is expected to return home, they are turned round again.

Some consecrate their newly built homes with water, in the hope that through this all good luck and prosperity will come to the people in the house. . . .

The word *summan* or *fitiso* is applied in a particular sense to the one which the head of a household holds very sacred for himself and his heirs, and from which he believes every good thing that happens to him and his people originates.

What this actually is, as I have said, none of the Blacks can say. Nevertheless, since it is passed on by the parents and grandparents to the children, it is regarded as extremely sacred and is loved, honored and feared as if it were God in Heaven. (Each family or clan has its *summan* hereditary *fitiso* or household *fitiso*, known by a special name, such as Quassi, Tuttu, Abboa, Affuffu, Effrimmum, Serraquu, Emmoni etc. . . .

Just as the heathen in the Fetu country distinguish between the supposed land, sea, hereditary and household idol, so they distinguish between the priests who are used in the service of such false gods.

One they call *o-bossum-fu* [ɔbosomfoɔ], another *summan-fu* [sumanfoɔ], and *com-fu* [ɔkɔmfoɔ] or *sophu* [ɔsofoɔ].

O-bossum-fu is a heathen priest who alone waits on the *o-bossums*, the supposed patron saints of the whole Fetu country.

None of the priests but he may undertake to question an *o-bossum* and receive an answer from it.

Such an *o-bossum-fu* is held in great esteem and honor among them. When one of these Blacks has committed a misdeed and merited death but flees to the residence of an *o-bossum-fu*, he is declared free.

In 1668, when such an *o-bossum-fu* died in Fetu, certain days of mourning and lamentation were appointed for the whole country.

Summan-fu is a priest who is used in the service of the *summan* in slaughtering, sacrificing, cleansing and similar work. He too is highly honored, but not as highly as *o-bossum-fu*.

Com-fu or *sophu* is simply a sorcerer who keeps a *fitiso* of his own at the great expense of other people. By means of this *fitiso* he claims to predict the future. . . .

In 1665, when the English at Cabo Corso [Cape Coast] were desperately waiting for ships from England, a *comfu* from Carmentin [Kormantin] (the old English fort, which was conquered in 1665 by the Dutch Admiral de Reuter) came to Cabo Corso. He offered to tell the English truthfully, if they gave him a good present, at what time ships from England would come to the Cabo Corso roadstead, by means of the *fitiso* he had.

When promised a present, he said ships would certainly come within thirty days. When all but three days of the time given had elapsed, an English ship arrived at Cabo Corso, but was immediately driven away by the Dutch. In this way the Carmentin *comfu* rose so high in the esteem of the English that not only was he given large presents, but the English afterwards wanted to know more from him than either he or the Devil himself could know or say.

. . .

If one tells them of the wonders which God performed long ago in the Old Testament, they immediately ask how many years ago it was that such wonders occurred—as if to say, if such a long time has passed, how can one actually know such things? Others can tell of wonders which the Devil, their supposed *obossum* and patron saint, has performed, since they have not only heard such wonders narrated by their father, but have in part (so they claim) witnessed them. If one speaks to them of God, of the Godhead, in particular of Christ . . . then one hears the blind people say all kinds of insulting and mocking things.

Sometimes it is asked: as Jan Comme or Jan Compo is such a great Lord and so without doubt has a large number of wives, did he not have more than just one son? This impertinent question arises from the fact that these blind people seek their grandeur and high status in polygamy and that they do not understand what it means to be God's Son from everlasting to everlasting.

Concerning the conception and birth of our Savior, Jesus Christ, they have their carnal ideas in the same way as the Turks, since they consider it impossible that a woman can become pregnant without the action of a man and give birth without losing her virginity. According to the Annunciation of the Angel Gabriel, with God nothing is impossible; yet these blinded people are not prepared to understand or learn this.

If one tells them of Christ's suffering and death, they ask: "What evil had he done? He must have sinned, or else his father, Jan Comme, would not have let people deal so cruelly with his son."

This question was put to me by the *day* of Fetu through an interpreter, when he saw a crucifix hanging on Friederichs-Berg. I answered: "God's Son had done nothing wrong, but his Father, in letting him be martyred so cruelly and actually killed, had done so purely out of love, not only for us Whites, but also for them, the Blacks, so that we might not lie forever in the fire of Hell."

At this the pagan man was silent and shook his head. What his thoughts may have been, one can imagine from this. Of all the articles of belief which we Christians acknowledge with heart and mouth, the article of Christ's resurrection seems to these blind people particularly absurd and ridiculous.

If one talks to them of Christ's resurrection, namely that on the third day he rose again from the dead, some of them consider it an impossibility and laugh at it. Others say it is nothing new, as there have been plenty of examples among them, the heathen, of people who had been killed and had come back alive again from the dead. One of the most distinguished merchants in the Fetu country to do business with the Danish company said to me, when I told him something about Christ's resurrection, that it was not surprising that Jan Comme's son had risen from the dead on the third day.

One of their people in Fetu, he said, had been decapitated five separate times, yet every time the same man had reappeared alive.
. . .

[Authority and Society]

Although the Fetu people have a king, whom they call *ohin*, the form of government is rather an aristocracy; for the king is not allowed to lay down or regulate anything as a sovereign or absolute monarch in general matters of the courtry, unless senior personages of the kingdom and the most important [elders] of the people approve it and consent to it. . . .

Marriage, Weddings, and the Rearing of Children

When someone comes of age and is driven by lust to take a wife, he indicates this to his father and asks him to try to obtain for him a certain man's daughter who pleases his eyes more than all others, as a wife. If the youth's father thinks this is good and advisable, he seeks an opportunity to talk to the girl and her father. If the proposal pleases them, the agreement is confirmed by shaking hands.

Often, if someone has a nubile daughter, he takes her to a good friend without once asking if he wants to have her as a wife or not, and says: "I have brought up this daughter of mine. I want to give you her as a wife, since you are a good friend and acquaintance. I have not the slightest doubt that you will be pleased." Hereupon the other man thanks him for the honor and kindness, promising to take her and keep her as his wife.

They do not give their children large dowries. The most distinguished people in the country give their daughters only a *benda* of gold as a dowry. The bride usually obtains a slave from her father. The more gold and possessions the bridegroom has acquired in his spare time, the more he can enjoy them, and no one should imagine that he can obtain a rich bride. As soon as the wedding day arrives, the bride goes out with her playmates to bathe and anoint herself. She adorns herself as splendidly and elegantly as she is able to do and can afford, with clothes, golden necklaces and bracelets, rings, beads, *agri* [*akori* beads or stones] etc., and then goes back and forth in her finery to display herself at public dances. The instrument most commonly used on this occasion may be merely a basin beaten with a stick, or a drum.

Towards noon she goes with her companions into the compound or house in which the bridegroom and the friends he has invited are gathered. Then something to eat is brought, or the bridegroom just treats people to palm wine and perhaps spirits. They enjoy themselves, dancing, singing and capering till late in the night. When the time comes to go to bed, the bride goes with some of her friends to a bedroom in which the wedding bed is prepared, but they bar the bedroom door. A short while afterwards the bridegroom comes and knocks on the barred door; but it is not opened for him unless he has previously promised to treat people again the following day. Then he is permitted free entry and all the wedding guests go away. No one remains in the bedroom except the bridegroom and his bride, together with a young girl aged seven or eight, who must sleep in between them and watch out that they do not touch each other for seven days. It is hard to believe, however, that this really happens. At daybreak a group of old women relatives of the bridegroom and of the bride come in and bring the young people warm water to wash in. If the bridegroom then treats these old women to plenty of spirits, or some gold for palm wine, they call out that he is a handsome, generous man; but if he shows himself miserly, they spread the word in the open market and street that he is a *quiteriqui*, a stingy niggard, who does no one any good.

The aforementioned wedding festivities are only held when someone marries his first wife, whom he wishes to regard as the principal wife among all the others. . . .

The Relations between the Akan States and the Danish Trading Companies, 1657-1754

OLE JUSTESEN

In this original essay, Ole Justesen has selected a repre-
sentative set of Danish sources that reveal the different
forms—over the course of a century—of Akan relations
with the Danish trading companies. After a concise in-
troduction to the Danish trading companies, the records
they produced, and the Akan polities with which Danish
representatives interacted, Justesen focuses on the rela-
tions between those companies and four Akan polities:
"Accannisten" (Akani) and Fetu's relationship with the
Danes at Frederiksborg; and the relationship between
Akwamu, Akyem and Asante with the Danes at Chris-
tiansborg.

For almost 200 years—from 1657 until 1850—there were representatives of trading companies domiciled in the Dano-Norwegian
kingdom, or of the Danish Government in Copenhagen, in parts of
the Gold Coast, first and foremost in forts and trading lodges along
the coast. The Akan states in the Gold Coast established relations
with these organisations and officials, who sent back reports and
other written material containing information about their own activities, but also about the Gold Coast societies and their interrela-
tions. Most of the Danish material sent back is to be found in
Rigsarkivet (the Danish National Archives) in Copenhagen, to
which it was submitted by the relevant public institutions. As the
material produced by the Danish administration was written with
the intention of letting their superiors in Denmark monitor the local
activity, these documents should as other historical sources, written
or oral, be analysed with historical criticism.

The relations between the Akan states and the Danish Trading
Companies 1657–1754 was founded on agreements or treaties en-

tered into by Akan state representatives and the local representatives of the Danish trading companies.

The Kingdom of Fetu had in 1658 assisted the first Danish representative, Heinrich Carloff, with soldiers to conquer the main Swedish fort Carolusborg at Cape Coast. Fetu was the first Akan state to enter into a contract in a treaty in 1659 with the new representatives sent out by the Danish Africa Company. In this, against payment, the Company was permitted among other things to build a new fort, Frederiksborg, in the Fetu territories (I.4). Thereby Fetu secured the establishment of a new European trading company as competitor to whoever occupied the fort in Cape Coast.

Besides the payment to the Fetu leaders mentioned in the document, the senior officials, who probably considered the oral agreement together with the religious ceremonies mentioned in the document, as the legal basis of the relationship, also expected "costume" or "duties" paid monthly by the Danish authorities. The capability to fullfil these obligations depended on regular supplies of goods with Danish Company ships, because the goods that the Danes bought from interloper ships at "ships price" or "interloper price" could not generate sufficiant profit in the gold trade (I.17).

The monthly costume paid to the King of Fetu consisted of goods assessed to the value of 1 benda or 2 ounces of gold. Apart from these payments, the Fetu leaders expected to receive gifts at several other occasions, for example, when company ships arrived from Europe. The relative importance, the Danes attached to the various persons residing in Fetu can be seen from the values in a list of gifts, drawn up in 1680 in Copenhagen in connection with the equipment of a ship bound for the Coast (I.24). The list includes, besides the officers in Fetu, the leader of the important group of *Akanist* merchants, who brought the gold from the inland. The prices here are given in "prime costs," so that in order to compare with the local "trade value," the amounts should be increased by 100 [percent], as stated in square brackets. From a Danish report (II.17) it is evident that for long periods in the 1670's Fetu officials had a strong influence on the appointment to the positions of power within the Danish administration at the Coast.

The King of Great Accra—assisted by the Day of Fetu—entered into a similar agreement with the Danish Trading Company in 1661 concerning the building of a fortress in Osu, later named Christiansborg, which from 1685 became the new Danish headquarters on the Gold Coast. After the defeat of Great Accra the King of Akwamu received the monthly costume for this fort, and the local Danish authorities again experienced attempts, now associated with Akwamu, to interfere in the Danish administrative organisation and eventually to occupy the fort. A central figure in this was the well-known Asameni, earlier employed by the Danish administration. Several times he cooperated with and was inspired by Akwamu to seek to establish outlets for Akwamu trade with interlopers in order to compete with the established trade forts of the European trading companies (II.17, II.27, III.21, IV.10).

Later on the King of Akwamu appointed a prominent Cabuceer in Akwamu, Kwaku Kansiang, responsible for the political and commersial relations between Akwamu and the Danish authorities at Christiansborg, where the export of slaves now occupied a steadily increasing position (VIII.3, VIII.23). In 1722 Kwaku Kansiang was appointed protector of Osu town and was allocated a monthly costume from the Danish Governor and Council for services rendered to the Danish Company in its relationship with the King of Akwamu. In this way the Danish authorities were closely incorporated into the political administrative system in Akwamu (VII.32).

Among these services was the organisation of the King's trade with Christiansborg. Traditionally the king, cabuceers and great traders had credit at the fort and consequently debts, often against pawns, to the Danish Company, and this could at times be a source of less amicable relations between the two parties (VIII.38). This situation was however put to an end, when the Danes reported that Akwamu had entered into what the Danes called a treaty of "friendship," in which Akwamu promised to bring trade to the fort (VIII.41). In 1730 the relations resulted in a close cooperation where the Danes supported the Akwamus in their fighting against the Accras and other rebels (IX.14).

This close cooperation with Akwamu proved to be a political strain when the relations between Akyem, after their victory over Akwamu in 1730, and the Danish authorities were to be established. This and the Akyem division into three states or groups defered for some time the establishment of a final solution of their relationship (IX.17, IX.19), especially as the Danes as the condition for the payment of the monthly costume put forward a demand of "a continued Akyem trade" at Christiansborg (IX.35). But they did at last reach an understanding in 1733 (IX.43). Three years later in 1736 the relations between Akyem and the Danes were extended, when Akyem—against payment—invited the Danes to build a fortress at Ningo, much to the anger of the Dutch (X.4, X.6, X.11).

With their defeat of Akyem in 1742, the reception of the monthly costume for Christiansborg was taken over by the Asantes, who also during their invasion in the eastern part of the Gold Coast had demanded large direct payments from all groups, including the Danes (XI.3, XI.17, XI.42). Although Akyem had been defeated they could still exert pressure on the Danes to pay them gifts, at the same time as the Danish government were met with requirements from the King of Asante to reduce the assessment of the value of the goods included in the costume paid for Christiansborg to the same level as it was at other places along the Coast (XI.40). The geographical distance and the relatively isolation of the Akyems meant that they could succeed in exerting pressure on the Danish authorities to continue to pay them the costume for the fort Fredensborg at Ningo (XI.50), while the geographical distance to Asante also caused the need for changes in the manner of the payment of costume to the broker/Mankralo in Osu town (XI.60). But for the Danish authorities the relations and future trade with the Asantes were from now on so important that the Danes used the costume as an instrument to maintain the Asante trade to Christiansborg (XII.22, XII.26). The relation reached its climax in the period 1807 to 1823, when the Danish authorities had to submit to the demands of Asante resident commissioners and army generals.

Although the relations between the Akan states and the representatives of the Danish trading companies and the Danish Government in Copenhagen throughout the whole period up to the 1820s were regulated by treaties and agreements with a rather consistent number of elements, there was over time room for these relations to reflect the changing balances of power between the parties as well as their changing views and interpretation of the relative weight of the various elements in the relations. The Danish trading companies were representing only a small nation among the many European companies and nations trading on the Gold coast in the 17th and 18th centuries. Though much research has been carried out and published on this subject, future closer and more comprehensive analysis of all types of relations between all the different Akan states and all the different European trading companies and interlopers might contribute new insights in the changing patterns of the economic, political, social and cultural relationships.

Fetu

(I.4)   20th December 1659: Treaty between the Kingdom of Fetu, the King of Denmark and the Danish Africa Company
V.-g.K.; 77 (Letters out - October 1680, No. 48-1)
Language: German

We, *Adu Afu, Ree*; *Adiu Macu, Fetero*; *Acroissen, Tay*; *Aheno, Braffo*; and *Cobre*, Captain, do rule over the Kingdom of Fetu and its lands and coasts.

We hereby confirm for ourselves, our heirs and successors in government, and proclaim by these presents that we have entered into a treaty with the honourable Joost Crahmer, Governor in the name and on behalf of Your Royal Majesty of Denmark and your Noble Chartered Danish Africa Company, with respect to the following articles, which we and our successors shall observe and fulfil in perpetuity, which we have also confirmed in our own manner by swearing an oath and eating fetish.

1. First, we have, for the sum of 50 *benda* of gold, perpetually sold and transferred to the said Cramer, on behalf of his principals and their successors, the hill of *Amanfro* (which the Germans call Friedrichsburg) with its coasts and harbours, so that this shall hence-

forth belong to the Chartered Danish Africa Company as free property; and we the above-mentioned and undersigned have received full payment from Joost Cramer, each his part in our own hands, and are thus satisfied.

2. Secondly, we do grant the said Danish Africa Company a free lodge at *Cabo Cors* with our consent that a stone house may be built there at any time, for better protection against fire and other mishaps. . . .

In order that each and every thing thus agreed shall be observed loyally and inviolately by us and our successors in perpetuity with respect to the said praiseworthy Danish Africa Company and its officers, and shall be fulfilled in all respects, we have eaten the fetish called *Coassy* to this effect, and have confirmed the three [copies] of this contract with our own marks and signatures, such that one copy shall be sent to the Noble Company in Denmark, the second [shall remain] in the keeping of Governor Cramer, and the third shall be given into the hand of our *Tay*, *Acroissen*, called *Jan Claessen*.

Given in *Fetu* in this Year of Our Lord 1659, the 20th of December, old style.

L[ocus] S[igilli] *Aduaffu A, Ree*
 Adiu Macu, Fetero
 Acroissen, Tay
 Aheno, Braffo

(I.17) 29th May 1679: Governor Witt, Frederiksborg,
to Johan O. Bremer, Glückstadt
V.-g.K.; 77 (Letters out - October 1680, No. 46 A)
Language: German

It is no longer possible for us to hold these possessions, since there are neither more goods nor more gold, and the little that is left is taken from us by the Dutch when we peacefully try to send supplies from the fort of Frederiksborg to the fort of Christiansborg, which lie thirty miles apart. As we will get no ship from the Company between the 14th of March and the end of July, the Negroes will murder us, because we can no longer pay their monthly *costuym* [i.e., dues, duties] for they approach us every day with threats and claim to be able to get enough for this from the English and Dutch. And they then asked us, when this ship had come, whether a Company ship could be expected any longer. So I have comforted them by saying that one is on the way, and that they must wait from five to six months. Then they were somewhat placated; but if it does not come, I must find out what to do about their *cos.*, as I have held them off for a long time with fair words, saying that a Danish ship will come, from which I can pay them their *cos.* Well, much ado about nothing, and I owe them more than eighty *bendas* of gold....

(I.24)   Undated [July 1680]: Officers of the Company,
         Copenhagen, to the Directors of The West
         India and Guinea Company, Copenhagen
         V.-g.K.; 77 (Letters in - July 1680, No. 29)
         Language: Danish

Gifts to the inhabitants of the country of *Fetu*, where Frederiksborg lies.

To the king:

7 ells of scarlet cloth @ 3 rdl.	*sldl.* 31:2
10 ells of taffeta, violet-coloured @ 1 rdl.	15
Gold lace worth	30
Embroidery of the King's [Christian V's] name and crown	10
1 staff mounted with silver and gilded with the King's [Christian V's] name	20
1 length of Leiden say, azure @ 12 rdl.	18
4 lengths of long white calico @ 6 rdl.	36
2 ditto striped @ 4 rdl.	12
1 cask of French brandy	8

2 fifty-pound kegs of powder	21:3
6 muskets, blued with inlaid stocks @ 5 rdl.	45
	dl. 247:1
	[ounces 20]

The *day*:

7 ells of scarlet cloth @ 3 rdl.	31:2
10 ells of taffeta, green, @ 1 rdl.	15
Gold lace worth	30
Embroidery of the King's [Christian V's] name and crown	10
1 grey hat with a broad gold galloon attached with mountings gilded with "C5" [Christian V], lined within with a sweatband and crown sewn in, the hatband of broad coloured ribbon, gold wrought in	15
1 partizan with HM's crown and arms, gilded and with some colourful silk ribbons	12
1 staff mounted with silver and gilded with HRM's name	20
50 lbs of powder in a keg	10:3:8
1 cask of French brandy	7:2
6 inlaid muskets	45
	dl. 196:3:8
	[ounces 16]
	dl. 444:-:8

The *fetero* or chancellor:

2 lengths of Leiden say @ 12 rdl.	*dl.* 36
4 lengths of white calico @ 6 rdl.	36
2 lengths of coloured ditto @ 4 rdl.	12
2 casks of French brandy @ 5 rdl.	15
2 casks of corn ditto @ 4 rdl.	12
	dl. 111
	[ounces 9]

The caboceers or elders of the council:

2 casks of French brandy @ 5 rdl.	*dl.* 15
	[ounces 1,2]

The captain of the *Accanists* or chief-merchant:

1 cask of French brandy @ 5 rdl.	*dl.* 7:2
25 lbs of powder in 1 keg	5:2
½ a length of say	9
	dl. 22
	[ounces 1,8]

The captain at *Cabo Cors*:

½ a cask of French brandy	*dl.* 3:3
½ a cask of corn ditto	3
1 twelve-pound keg of powder	2:3
	dl. 9:2
	[ounces o,8]

The caboceers at *Cabo Cors*:

1 cask of French brandy @ 5 rdl.	*dl.* 7:2
1 cask of corn ditto	6
6 iron bars	9
	dl. 22:2
	[ounces 1,8]
	dl. 624:-:8

The *mansebos* or young men at *Cabo Cors*:

1 cask of corn brandy	*dl.* 6
3 iron bars	4:2
	dl. 10:2
	[ounces 0,8]
	dl. 634:2:8
	[ounces 52,8]

(II.7)   Undated 1681: Andreas Jacobsen, Frederiksborg, to the Directors of The West India and Guinea Company, Copenhagen
V.-g.K.; 78 (Letters in - September 1681, No. 38)
Language: German

I, Andreas Jacobsohn of Norway, have served the Noble Danish Africa Company for eight years. When I first came to the hill of Frederiksborg, Mr. Crijel [Crull] was General on the hill. I served him for five years. When he died, Pitter Wette then became general. I served him for two whole years. When he died, Mathias Hanssen became general. He came to this through the *deije* [*Day*] and the *braffo* and the *fetero* and all the other Blacks, as he gave the Negroes many gifts so they would make him general, which indeed happened. I thus served him for five weeks. Now, after that time Pitter Valck had got the Blacks on his side and had promised them many gifts so they would help him to become general. Some gifts he gave them at once—what he was allowed to by *Effijbaa*. And when he became general, Pitter Valcken was to give them back their pawned goods. Thus Pitter Valck had all the Blacks who were in the fort and outside the fort on his side, for they had known him well for a long time. . . . Now, one night at about twelve o'clock there came a *Hader* [Allada] to General Matthias Hanssen for the key to the gate. The *Harder* said that a canoe had come from *Accraa* with a letter. The general was so foolish as to give the Negroes the key to the gate. And there were only three of us Whites in the fort besides the rogue Pitter Valck, who had played this villainous trick on us to panyar us. And so it happened that the gate was opened without any White being present or knowing anything of it. But the rogue Pitter Valck knew it well.

So when the gate was opened there came about 100 Negroes into the fort and overwhelmed the fort with their muskets, powder and shot in their bandoliers. Then they went with Pitter Valck into General Mattias Hanssen's quarters. Pitter Valck ordered the Negroes to take Matthias by the head and drag him out of his quarters. When the Blacks had done this, they then took him and shoved him from one to the other and beat him until he bled, and he screamed and shouted for help. . . .

Now we Whites . . . we had announced to the King of *Fetu* that we could no longer bear to watch the bestial life that was led here; he squanders the money and gold, and God knows how it will go with the fort in the end. So the king had well understood everything from us. He departed the next day. So one day the king sent his people to our fort, and they seized Pitter Valck and led him out of the gate and then to the king, and there Pitter Valck had to till like a slave. Then we other Whites looked to see what monies there were. When we searched, we found in all 10 *engels* in gold and a few pawns belonging to the Negroes. There were still some goods in the warehouse. We had to give these to the "young-men" as board money, because they complained that they had not received board money for two months and said they would run away as we gave them so little board money. Thus we were forced to give them their due. And Pitter Valck governed for four months on the hill. So suddenly there were only three of us Whites. And among us was an old man, about fifty years old. We made him our general. When he had governed for five weeks, he died. So after this we were only two Whites. Then the king came into the fort and asked if I now wished to be general; otherwise he would appoint his son. I thought to myself, I have served for seven years. . . . Thus I preserved the fort with the slaves as long as I governed, which would be about two months. Then the Royal ship *Havmanden* came, bringing a General, who was Magnus Prang. As soon as he came into the fort, I surrendered all that was in and outside the fort . . . and then he died, which was a great grief to me and all the Whites.

Akwamu

(II.17)   23rd June 1688 - 7th April 1689: Daybook kept by
          Governor Fensman, Christiansborg
          V.-g.K.; 120 (Diary 23.6.1688 - 7.4.1689)
          Language: Dutch

Monday the 13th ditto [August 1688]:

Today the son of the King of *Qvamboe, Bobbie,* left for *Qvamboe.*

Monday the 27th ditto [August 1688]:

Bobbie Piconino has just come to greet us, and I have paid him three months' *costume* in says, up to the 30th of June.

Friday the 21st September 1688:

Yesterday evening after the closing of the gate, our Gunner, Thomas Bentzen, came to ask us to spend one white say, 1 *slaplagen*, 1 tablecloth, 3 fathoms of gingham or Turkish stuff and one anker of brandy, as he intended to *caasaere* Mr. Hans Lücke's Negress, called *Jamenie.* . . . . Yet considering our weak garrison, I must often turn a blind eye to what he does. For he is such a wretch that he is usually drunk on brandy before seven o'clock in the morning, which is why he has stirred things up among the Noble Company, myself and the Negroes here that he never dares answer for nor defend. It is worth noting that a year ago last evening, as soon as the Noble Hans Lücke was dead, he had a cow (for which he was going to give one *bende* in gold) brought into the fort without my knowledge to slaughter and regale the Whites who were to attend the funeral of Mr. Hans Lücke. Since I did not allow him to do so, he later promised 6 *bende* in gold to *Asmonie* [Asameni], our Company slave (who already had it in his hand, and who to this very hour has not given it back), if he could arrange with the King of *Quamboe* that he, Thomas Bentsen, could take command. And indeed this went so far that on the 18th of December 1687 the Negroes from *Quamboe* and *Asimonie* ate sacred fetish with some *Orsoese* caboceers to take me prisoner on the 19th ditto, to take the fort by surprise and lay it waste. So in my opinion he is the instigator of all the trouble there has been between me and the King of *Quamboe* and the Negroes here all along. Had I not been warned by someone so that the whole of the above explanation was revealed to me, this might well have become a great inconvenience to the Noble Royal Company. However, when I consequently brought him to book for this, and he did not deny it, I had to let it pass. . . .

(II.27)   Undated [1698]: H. Meyer, Copenhagen: An account of
          Fort Christiansborg 1659 - 1698
          V.-g.K.; 187
          Language: Danish

In June 1693 this fort of Christiansborg, because of the Governor
Harding Pettersen's poor supervision and precautions, was overrun
and taken by some *Quambuish* natives from the capital of this kingdom, with the approval of the king. The Christians were ill-treated,
imprisoned and killed. Among these was the merchant, whom they
barbarously carved up, so to speak, joint by joint. The governor was
also very seriously wounded, as he was stabbed four or five times
in the throat and all the tendons of his knees were almost severed,
so he would be unable to escape from them. He was later cast into
the dungeon, but he escaped from there again. He had himself
dropped from the wall by night, [and] then he travelled for two days
to reach safety in the Dutch fort, situated about 1/4 of a mile from
the Danish fort. In this surprise attack on the fort . . . Councillor of
Trade Nicolay Jansen Arff lost 71,315 rdl. according to the cost
price account in the books, and Nicolay Fensman lost the value of
4,000 rdl. [in goods], as well as 4,164 rdl. in gold cash, which all in
all amounts to 79,479 rdl.

In December the same year two frigates sailed from Glückstadt,
called *Christiansborg* and *Gyldenløves Våben*, unaware of the fate
of the fort. They were immediately informed of this on their arrival
at the Coast, and went with all possible haste to the place, where
instead of a Danish Royal flag they found a blue flag waving with
a blackamoor with a dagger in his hand. They anchored in the Dutch
roads, and the two Chief-Factors on the ships—Hartwig Meyer as
Factor on the *Christiansborg* and Johan Thrane as Factor on
Gyldenløves Våben—decided that on behalf of their principals they
must get the fort again through the King of *Quambue*. Hartwig
Meyer was sent there to negotiate this, and indeed he succeeded so
well that the fort was surrendered to them again against payment in
goods worth 3,000 rdl. After this Thomas Jacobsen was appointed
governor and was given about thirty seamen volunteers by both
ships.

(III.21) 23rd December 1698 - 1st September 1703:
Journal kept at Christiansborg
V.-g.K.; 884 (Journal kept at Fort Christiansborg
in Guinea from 1699(98) until 1st September 1703)
Language: Danish

December 30 [1699]

The governor learned that the well-known Negro *Assemonj*, who had previously overrun the fort with his gang, was now once more on the shore, a long cannon shot from our fort—that is, in *Labordé*. There, with an extremely large canoe belonging to him, he wanted to establish a proper trading station for interlopers, which could not be done without endangering the fort and spoiling its trade. The governor therefore let him know that he neither could nor would permit him to do any such thing, but that the said *Assemonj* must be prepared to depart from the shore and the site of the fort immediately with his soldiers. To this he sent the reply that he would remain in *Labordé* and engage in his trading with the interlopers unless the governor could drive him from there by force. Then the governor sent down some White soldiers, and the caboceers of this town and their people, with guns to destroy the canoe; but as his gang was large and numerous, our Negroes grew afraid and came back without accomplishing anything.

December 31 [1699]

The said Negro, *Assemonj*, in order to work even more mischief, had a number of the governor's cabrits (which were kept in the field not far from the fort) shot dead by his soldiers, taking some of them and leaving others lying in the field; where upon some live cannon shot was fired at the Negroes.

A messenger has come to the fort here from the King of *Aquambu* with an apology. He was loath to learn that *Assemonj* had dared to resist the fort and us Whites. Would soon make this good and have *Assemonj* punished. He had also sent his messenger to him about this.

It was then immediately resolved to send one of the Royal Company's officers to King *Addo* of *Aquambu* to complain of the said *Assemonie's* deeds and to demand adequate satisfaction on his account. To that end the Merchant, Mons. Hans Pedersen, has today been sent on a journey to *Aquambu*. . . .

January 2 [1700]

The Merchant, Hans Pedersen, has come back from *Aquambu* with assurances from the king that he would immediately have the well-known *Assemonj* brought to him and would ensure that he would at no time hereafter come with his canoe to the shore, or resist the fort and us Danes in the slightest way. . . .

January 26

The Negro *Assemonj* has removed his canoe from *Laborde* and taken it to the Slave Coast to a place called *Nungo* [=Ningo], about seven miles from the fort. . . .

February 3

The well-known Negro *Assemoj* has gone away from *Laborde* to *Aquambu*. This has happened because of several harsh messages sent to him by the king. . . .

(IV.10) Journal kept at Fort Christiansborg from the
12th September 1703 until the 25th May 1705
V.-g.K.; 884 (Copy of Journal kept at Fort Christiansborg
12th September 1703 until 25th May 1705)
Language: Danish

21st [Oct. 1703] The King of *Aquambue* sent word to me that he will come to the fort tomorrow. A rumour arose that *Asmuny* [Asameni], the Negro who overran the fort in Councillor of Commerce Nic. Jansen's day, had shot an *Aquambuish* caboceer a few days ago, and that in revenge he had been ambushed yesterday evening by the same caboceer's friends [i.e., relatives] and shot dead, beheaded, and his right arm and left thigh had been cut off. . . . [We had] a little trade. . . .

(VIII.3) 10th February 1722: Governor Herrn, Christiansborg,
    to the Directors of The West India and Guinea Company,
    Copenhagen. General Letter
    V.-g.K.; 121 (General Letter from Guinea, 10.2.1722,
    with enclosures)
    Language: Danish

The present received for King *Aqvando* of *Aquambue* has immediately been sent to him. He desires the Esteemed Directors to be
thanked for it, but has informed me that he had expected a *pankies*
[= pantje], just as well as he gets each year for the Dutch and English forts, which send him a properly embroidered *pankies*. Similarly one of his most prominent Caboceers, named *Qvacu*, who is
now here and who, when he has been here, has always slept in the
fort and in addition eaten at the governor's table, and who is always
good Danish and always helps for the benefit of the Company when
there is a palaver with the king, as can often happen, would remind
of a beautiful *pankies* for him. . . .

(VIII.23) 10th April 1725: Governor von Suhm, Christiansborg,
    to the Directors of The West India and Guinea Company,
    Copenhagen
    V.-g.K.; 122
    Language: Danish

At New Year the king's most prominent and favourite caboceer
[Kwaku Kansiang] came down here with the greeting that since the
king had promised me to pay his debt, he had now been sent down
here with orders to stay, and the king would gradually send slaves
down, and would settle accounts with us.

Your Lordships can well imagine that this man was welcome to
us, and I made him so. Some fourteen days later the king's people
came down and had 14 slaves with them. We took six of them and
gave the rest back. But as soon as the king's people had departed,
claiming to be fetching even more, up to 70 including these, the

caboceer asked that they might stay at the fort in the meantime; and so they did, but the six who had been taken on account were immediately sold to one of Mister Mouritz' ships [*Maria*], which lay in the roads and still had an account outstanding with us from last year. A few days later, after the ship had sailed up the coast, the king sent us a message asking why I had sold the slaves. They were free Negroes whom he had only sent down to be hidden, and I must make sure I got them back. I sent the messenger on to the caboceer who had sold them to us, and told him that if he would send us other good slaves instead of them, I would release them when the ship came down again from the [Upper] Coast. A month passed, and although I kept their ship for six days in the hope of good trade and announced the same appointed time to the king, the slaves came, but not until two days after the ship had sailed from the coast. The king therefore had to deem himself or his people guilty, and he sent me a fat whether as thanks for having done my best in this matter.

However, the Dutch did not refrain from alleging to the king that if it had been they, they would not thus have sold his free Negroes and so on.

The friends [i.e., relatives] of the free Negroes came, as well as others, who told the king that his people would think he had done it deliberately, and that he would sell his subjects to pay his debt and save his own slaves, etc.

At that the king closed all the roads, so that no supplies came down. However, as he was ashamed to send his own messenger down, he told me through an *Accraisk* Negro that he knew well that I had not come to do harm, since I had taken my family with me, and that I also knew well that he was a good man; but if I was his friend, I should get those people back.

Now since I was in the right, and was well supplied with *millie*, and since the trade did not suffer from this either, I acted as if it did not affect us at all, wanting him to send a messenger first. But since this closing of the roads was more of a burden on the Dutch and English than on us, and they therefore cried to high heaven, and this agitated the *Qvambuiske* people even more, and since I was well enough aware that the king was not his own man in this matter, I sent a Mulatto up with a small gift of brandy and told him that since the towns lying here by the sea were his people as well as those in *Qvambue*, I asked that he would not let them starve, but open the roads. True, I had heard that it had been done because of us, but I could not believe it, for since the king had once been satisfied with me, he must not demand impossibilities. The answer I received was that his caboceer and his people were up in arms, and that he must have something to satisfy them with, and since the Dutch and English had already given 5 ounces to have the road opened, then we, who were the main cause of this, must give 8 ounces in goods which he could distribute to the people who were posted at the roads, and then the whole matter would be settled. . . .

(VIII.32) 1st January 1727: *Sekret* Council resolution re
     Kwaku Kansiang
     V.-g.K.; 880 (Copy of *Sekret* Council minutes
     30.9.1726 - 9.9.1727)
     Language: Danish

Inasmuch as the Caboceer *Qvacu Kansiang* has always been very obliging towards the fort and now for the future promises to be faithful and helpful to the Company, both in his own person and with his people, whether in palavers or other services which he can perform and do, and inasmuch as the King of *Aqvambue, Ensanqvau*, has ceded this town *Orsue* to him and granted [him] it as protector, it is hereby resolved to accept the said Caboceer *Qvacu Kansiang* as a protector for the town and as one who ought to and shall be loyal to the Company and serviceable in palavers or with other service, and accordingly allocated him . . . 8 rdl. a month in *costume* from this day on and to continue as long as he behaves faithfully and honestly and obligingly as a servant of the Company in the Company's affairs and thus keeps the promises he has made.

Christiansborg, 1st January 1727
H. v. Suhm   F. Pahl   A. Wellemsen   R.N. Kamp

(VIII.38)11th-23rd August 1727: *Sekret* Council resolution re
the forfeiture of the gold pawned by King Akonno
V.-g.K.; 880 (Copy of *Sekret* Council minutes
30.9.1726 - 9.9.1727)
Language: Danish

Since the King of *Aqvambue* sent word yesterday to the governor
and announced that as he has heard that the gold pawned by the former king, *Aqvando*, has been forfeited, he claims that either the governor should now deliver the gold back to him or all the debt that
the Company has outstanding with *Aqvando* or with others in *Aqvambue* must be cancelled. In addition he should be given 30 *benda*
for the injury that has thus been done to him. He also sent word that
if these demands of his were not acknowledged and met voluntarily
by the governor, he would seek and demand them by other means.

It is thus evident from this that a palaver from his side is to be
feared, for which reason it has immediately been decided today to
send word to the Assistant Kamp at *Ponny* [Kpone] to close the
lodge at that place and take the goods which are there up here to
the fort, since we cannot be sure that the king and his people will
not suddenly attack and destroy the lodge. . . .

Christiansborg, 11th August 1727
F. Pahl   A. Willemsen   C. Hougaard   O.L. Grue

In the year 1727 on 20th August after the above resolution the
Bookkeeper Andreas Wellemsen and the Assistant R.N. Kamp have
been in the King of *Aquambue's* house, lodging with the Caboceer
Amo in the Dutch town, and have held a palaver with the said King
of *Aquambue*, called *Ansangqvau*, over the demands which he is
making on the fort for some gold that was pawned during the time
of the former King, *Aqvando*, and which in the time of the former
Governor Suhm, on 8th October 1725, was forfeited. Then the
palaver was concluded, and it was agreed with the King, *Ansanqvau*
. . . that the debt of the former King, *Aquando*, which remained and
amounted to 67 *bender* and 13 rdl., should be forgiven the King,

Ansanqvau. In addition he is to be paid a settlement of 46 *bender* and 1 *bende* is to be paid to Caboceer *Amo*, which altogether amounts

(each *bende* at 32 rdl.) to . . .	47 *bende*
Of this, paid to him to date	
in various goods . . .	29 *bende*
Outstanding in the king's favour . . .	18 *bende*

(eighteen *bender*) which will gradually be paid to him in goods, each *bende* counting as 32 rdl. . . .

F. Pahl   A. Wellemsen   C. Hougaard   O.L. Grue
Christiansborg, 23rd August 1727

(VIII.41) 21st October 1727: *Sekret* Council resolution
re treaty with Akwamu
V.-g.K.; 880 (Copy of *Sekret* Council minutes
6.3.1727 - 16.5.1729)
Language: Danish

Now that the King of *Aquambue*, Caboceer *Qvaku Kansiang* and Prince *Ensanku* have been here in the fort and have taken their leave before going up to *Aqvambue*, [and] irrespective of the fact that each, earlier on the death of the late Pahl and on the instatement of the present governor, was given rather good and costly gifts on behalf of the Company, as can be seen from the Trade Journal, page 173, they have nevertheless not wished to be content with this, but since the king in particular demanded a good gift when he was here to take his leave, then in view of the fact that he still was not quite satisfied and made it clear that he was still complaining about the gold that has been forfeited, we have been obliged to have him as well as the other two and several more of the king's caboceers very lavishly and magnificently regaled by the governor at the governor's own expense . . . to keep all their friendship and favour for the benefit of the trade. After this the king as well as *Qvacu Kansiang* and Prince *Ensanku* have sworn an oath to be the Company's, the fort's and the governor's friends and to bring trade to the fort and in all cases to be of service to the fort and not to start any palaver or anything else against the fort. The king was given a note and written agreement to this effect with the Noble Company's seal and the governor's signature dated 4th October 1727, in return for which each, as reported above, was given a gift. Thus resolved and proclaimed for the benefit of the Noble Company and the progress of the trade.

Witnessed at the fort of Christiansborg, 21st October 1727
A. Wellemsen   R.N. Kamp   C. Hougaard   O.L. Grue

(IX.14) 30th August 1730: Governor Wærøe, Christiansborg,
           to the Directors of The West India and Guinea Company,
           Copenhagen
           V.-g.K.; 122 (Enclosure to General Letter from Guinea,
           28.12.1730)
           Language: Danish

The reason and origins of why we are so hindered in the trade here at *Accra*. It was well known to Your Lordships the Directors before my departure from Copenhagen, from the letter that came from Guinea, that the Dutch at *Accra* had one of the King of *Aqvambue's* kinsmen in their keeping, who was killed by a slave in the Dutch fort, Creveceur, at *Accra*. The king now made a claim on them for this murdered kinsman for a few thousand *bender*, each *bende* at 32 rdl. . . . .

But now this above-mentioned *Amoe*, who was the Dutch Caboceer in the Dutch town under the Dutch fort, colluded with the Dutch factor and the factor deceitfully with him as to how they could think up [a way] of harming the King of *Aquambue*, indeed also how they could wholly ruin the King of *Aquambue*. . . .

They called the whole army of all the *Accra*s, hill and *Berkuser* Negroes gathered on the hill *Acue Apim*, which means the thousand companies. While this was going on, they closed off the road down here to *Accra* against *Qvambue*, so that no trade came from *Qvambue*, nor did any *Quambu*s dare to come down here out of fear of being sold as slaves or killed. For that reason the trade stopped for me here. . . .

These *Accraiske* Negroes as well as their allies wanted to wait to ruin the *Quambu*s until the 7th and 8th of September. At that very time the *Aquambuiske* came and attacked the *Accraiske*, so that the latter had to flee in the greatest shame and mockery. . . .

On the 12th of September the King of *Aquambue* sent me a boy and a *teetye*, that is the same as a messenger or a herald in our wars in Europe, as I have reported before. These two had with them ten *Berkuske* Negroes of those who had been beaten in the hills, and who had before sided with the *Accra*s, but who at this time had subjected themselves to the King of *Aquambue* again. They came first to our Caboceer *Tette* in the Danish town. . . .

In the meantime our Caboceer *Tette* sent word to the Dutch town and told them that these had come and whether they would come and take them here; they were in his house. Then they came immediately (while the boy and the *teetye* were still standing and telling me their business) and took flintlocks and cartridge bags and all that they had with them that was in Caboceer *Tette*'s house—including seven of the ten Negroes whom the boy and the *teetye* had with them, and immediately chopped off the heads of the two who would not go with them willingly. Then all the Negroes, as well as the Negresses, who were in our town fled to the Dutch town, as well as that rascal the caboceer. . . .

They entered into an agreement that no one under the threat of great punishment would in any way let *millie* or bread come to the Danish fort. . . .

On the 28th of December, the day after the Christmas holidays, God fortunately sent us the *Håbet Galley* to anchor here towards noon, which made our secret enemies rather frightened about their own intentions.

On New Year's Eve I sent *Christian de Widt* and the Company's messenger, *Accra*, up to the king with an anker of brandy, and had written orders given to him about what he should say to the king. . . . The Negroes who saw with their own eyes that we had enough powder asked who was to be first to have some of that powder . . .

they or the *Quambu*s. To this I replied that whoever came with gold and slaves could get some. Then they continued to come here and leave again as friends until the 8th of January. . . .

On the stroke of 3 o'clock [8 January 1630] in the afternoon the Dutch Negroes came here and before we knew it and before the carpenters had come home they had taken many of the Company's cabrits away from the bush, as well as a calf and a boy who tended the cow beasts, and at the same time they lured away most of our Company slaves, 14 men slaves and two women slaves with one boy, so the slaves had to go with them, some of them willingly, and some against their will. . . .

In the morning when the gate was opened, I immediately had the canoes inspected, and we found them badly mauled, both sawed and cut through, for canoe wood is very loose, light wood. Later in the forenoon ten Black lads came here with guns from the Dutch to see whether there was any more here to steal, whereupon I greeted them with a six-pound shot on the road, so that they had to withdraw. About an hour later salutes were fired at the English fort for the commandant who was being buried. . . . Just as I was standing above the fort observing the salutes that were fired over the deceased, musket balls came flying around my ears as if it was hail— they were being shot from our abandoned town, where the Dutch Negroes were staying hidden among the houses to attack us. Then I had to go to the batteries as quickly as I could and gave them the treatment they deserved. . . .

On the 10th . . . I sent a small to Great Ningo, to Prince *Amega*, who I had been told was there with a large force of *Quambu*s (this Great Ningo belongs to that prince) and asked him whether he would come up here to keep the *Accra*s from the fortress. . . .

On Monday morning, the 23rd [of January], at dawn, we saw the Danish silk flag with the Noble Company's arms in it, which I had given to the king on behalf of the Company, when I was up with him in *Qvambue*. They came straight to the town, and as soon as they [the Accras] discovered this, they fled along the beach to the Dutch as fast as they could. And the *Quambu*s did not fail to search the town to see if there were any *Accra*s, but they had already gone.

Before all the *Quambu*s had come into the town, the *Accra*s were already advancing, marching on the *Quambu*s who had come down here—that is five caboceers with their people. These immediately offered the *Accra*s battle and fought with them until towards noon, when they rested on both sides because of the heat of the sun. In the meantime the *Quambu*s got better powder, for the powder they had was no good. As 3 o'clock approached, they began again and went at each other rather hard after the custom of this country. Towards evening the *Quambu*s drove the *Accra*s almost home, and then they came back again to our town. Throughout the night they had outposts around the town, so now we could rest easier, and could also go outside the fortress without fear.

Christian Petersen [*Witt*], who had been sent up to the king and had now come with these, greeted me from the king and said that I should let these have what they needed for the defence; he would pay me back for it in slaves. They were to stay here with me until grand *bon die* ["auspicious days"] then he would himself come down to pay them for their work. . . .

On the 26th these *Accra*s stayed quiet. In the evening a great Caboceer called *Qvassie Bibrie* [Kwasi Biri or Bibiri] came down here with his people from *Quambue*. He was the king's brother-in-law, so there were now enough people here in the town to fight with, over 2,000 men. . . .

On the afternoon of the 14th of February the King of *Aqvambue* came with a large force to the Dutch town, where the *Accra*s would have liked to meet him in the bush. But the king's people simply marched in on the *Accra*s and tried to take them with their hands, so that it was hard for the *Accra*s to try to get back to the fortresses, the Dutch and the English. As soon as the forts were able to fire at the *Qvambu*s, they shot as much as they could with heavy artillery. The *Qvambu*s took no notice of this but pursued them almost all the way in under the fortresses. The English fort also showed that it could shoot. It too fired with a will at the *Quambu*s with heavy artillery. As soon as the sun had gone down both the towns were on fire, the English and Dutch. The *Qvambu*s attacked the fortresses all night, and the fortresses replied with heavy artillery and hand-guns. . . .

Akyem

(IX.17) 18th November 1730: Governor Wærøe et al.,
         Christiansborg, to the Ship's Council on the *Håbet Galley*
         V.-g.K.; 880 (Copy of *Sekret* Council minutes . . .
         28.5.1729 - 23.12.1730)
         Language: Danish

For the situation is such that the *Akenist*s have overcome and ruined the *Aqvambu*s, since we got the above-mentioned ten men from
you for the defence of the fort. What a change there has been since
then! Are there now any more *Aqvambu*s? Do not the *Akenist*s rule
now, to whom the Dutch *Accra*s have with daily cunning traduced
us as much as possible with all the lies they could pile on, and have
thus ruined and oppressed us Danes?

We have indeed lived in greater doubt since that time than before.
For as long as the *Aqvambu*s were there, it was our hope to get assistance from them - but from whom now? You would probably answer by saying of the *Akenist*s that we are not sure of them yet. For
they have only sent us messages about this through some lads [i.e.,
servants], but none of the leading figures has been here yet, such as
Frempung [Frimpon/Frempong Manso, ruler of Akyem Kotoko],
Bang Qvantin or *Abroqva*. We are still none the wiser as to how
they want to deal with us, either peacefully or as enemies, so from
this it can be seen clearly enough that we have had plenty of reason
since the 21st of August to keep the ship here, since those who were
our refuge here before, the *Qvambu*s, are now utterly ruined.

(IX.19) 24th December 1730: Governor Wærøe, Christiansborg,
         to the Directors of The West India and Guinea Company,
         Copenhagen
         V.-g.K.; 122 (Letters from Guinea . . .
         17.5.1730 - 2.10.1731)
         Language: Danish

But since it has happened in the meantime that the *Accanist*s have totally beaten the *Aquambu*s (of which news came on the 17th of September), we had every possible reason to keep back the ship for a time. For no sooner had the Dutch or their Blacks heard of this than they immediately sent their messenger to *Aquambue* with gifts for the greatest caboceers of *Accanie*, and also filled them with lies saying that the Danes were rogues. On this account the most prominent *Accanie* caboceers were minded to seek the destruction and ruin of the Danish fort (as the daily intelligence that came to us told us). So in order to pre-empt their plans, I as well as the Dutch sent a gift to the three leading caboceers of *Accanie*, who were staying in *Aquambue* after their victory. The Dutch wanted to forbid me this, but irrespective of that I quickly sent my messenger on the 18th of September (and also took care to find out whether the Dutch Blacks intended to arrest my said messenger, which did not happen however). The messenger came back on the 20th ditto and told me several things that the Dutch Blacks had shamefully told lies about with regard to us Danes here. For this reason we could . . . not let the ship leave here before we were sure whether the *Accanist*s would behave towards us as friends or enemies. . . .

But God provided far better for us, since on the afternoon of the 25th of September there came here to the town a lieutenant of one of the three greatest caboceers, called *Frempung Menson*, from the *Accanist*s, with a large number of people. After he had arrived in the town, I sent a messenger to him with a request that he would come into the fort. And he did indeed accompany this messenger, and on his arrival some salutes were fired from this fort. Then I gave him several gifts, since he was the first *Accanist* to enter the Royal Danish fortress. He revealed to us, perhaps because he wished to return the courtesy we had shown him, that the Dutch Blacks who had been with his master had not only told him that we had done both this and that against them (that is the Dutch Negroes) but even added that there were a large number of escaped *Aquambu*s in the Royal Danish fort. In order to scotch this last untruth foisted upon us, I let the said lieutenant make an inspection anywhere he wished in the fort. Since he now found no *Aquambu*s (and in all truth there was not a single one in the fort), he said quite openly that the statements of the Dutch Blacks were based on sheer lies and untruthfulness. For that reason he decided to stay here in the town with the people he had under him.

Now when the Dutch Blacks learned that he was settling down here, they sent three or four messages here to the said lieutenant that he should move away from us to the Dutch town. To this he replied: "No, I will stay at this place to see how long the honesty of the Danes lasts in future." On the very same day as these messages came to him, there came a large number of *Abude*s (who had been allied with the *Accra*s against the *Aquambu*s). The said lieutenant, on behalf of his master, took these as captives or slaves. . . .

[O]n the morning at 7 o'clock a large number of Blacks came from the Dutch town, and went down to the *Abude*s who were on the beach (among them was a mob of the Dutch Blacks, who were there more to steal from these *Abude*s than to help them). Now that I realized that it would come to an engagement, I sent a messenger to the *Accanie* lieutenant and assured him that I would help him and support him—he should simply do his best. These newly arrived then began to attack the *Accanist*s. I could not tolerate this, mostly because it happened below the fort entrusted to me, but immediately fired some live shots from the fort at these lads. When the *Accanist*s now saw the assistance they got from me, they thrashed the Dutch Negroes with a will and drove them to flight. Yet he could not prevent them dragging some of the arrested *Abude*s along with them; but he chased the rest of the said *Abude*s, and got them all, along with women and children, as captives and booty.

Once the battle was over and he had preserved his spoils, he came into the fort here and thanked me for the help I had given him, also saying: "Now I can see that the Danes are honest people, but the others are rogues; this I will explain to my master when I arrive home." He said this because Mr. La Planqve here at the fort had tried to involve himself with something that was no affair of his, while I on the other hand sided with them, since I had better reason to seek my interest in this than Mr. La Planqve, who had yesterday made an effort to get this fine loot into his bag. I gave the lieutenant a chest of *millie* for the sustenance of his people, until on the 28th of September he went up to *Accanie* to his master with all the slaves he had acquired. He then came down here on the 6th of October with a greeting to me from his master and his thanks for the service I had done his people. Then he told me that he [Frimpon/Frempong Manso], as the *Aquambu*s had formerly done, would hereafter receive monthly dues from the Royal Danish fort, and in return would defend it when necessary. Then I sent several gifts up to him. . . .

(IX.35) 26th May 1732: Governor Wærøe et al., Christiansborg,
      to the Directors of The West India and Guinea Company,
      Copenhagen
      V.-g.K.; 123 (General Letter from Guinea,
      30.3.1732, with enclosures)
      Language: Danish

The *Achenist*s came down here in April, but not with any trade, only to have their monthly *costyme* from the three forts here for the time after the *Aquambu*s were defeated. The governor has already, almost two years ago, paid three months' *costyme* to one of the great Caboceers, by name *Frempung Mansong*, but since then has seen nothing of his people. Those who now come here are from a Caboceer named *Bang Qvantin*, and demand monthly payment from the time the *Aquambu*s were beaten until today. The governor will not grant that, but is as soon as possible sending both the Company's messengers up to *Acanie* with a present for the said caboceer, and further sends word that when he sends trade that continues, [and] then he will immediately receive monthly *costyme*. To pay monthly *costyme* and not have any trade from them, such a thing we cannot justify to our Noble Principals. About whatever may come out of this, we will write to Your Lordships the Directors as soon as possible. . . .

(IX.43) 30th March 1734: Governor Wærøe et al., Christiansborg,
         to the Directors of The West India and Guinea Company,
         Copenhagen. General Letter
         V.-g.K.; 123 (General Letter from Guinea,
         30.3.1734, with enclosures)
         Language: Danish

The *Aqvambu*s have been quite defeated and driven out, and there
is no hope that they will ever come to possess their country again.
The small trade, we now have (and we could have had more if we
had been supplied with the goods they demand) is brought by the
*Akenist*s, to whom we and the other two forts must pay monthly
coustyme. *Bang Qvantyn* has received 22 months' *coustyme*, that is
from the beginning of January 1732 to the end of October 1733, besides the three months' *coustyme* paid to Caboceer *Frempung Man-
gron* [sic], so in all we have paid 25 months' *coustyme* to the
*Akenist*s. The two caboceers themselves agreed with one another
on this. Some time ago Caboceer *Frempung* sent his Lieutenant,
that is *Naqviba*, down here with both gold and slaves, but we got
very little of this because we did not have Danish flintlocks. At the
same time the affair was settled so that his master, *Frempung*, transferred his monthly *coustyme* to *Bang Qvantyn*. Both the Dutch and
English forts have paid the said monthly *coustyme*, and furthermore,
when we complained about paying monthly *coustyme* before we
saw any trade, Eleth offered to pay for us, against us renouncing
any claim to the trade that comes down here. We thus have to do
the same as the other forts in this matter. . . .

(X.4)   4th December 1735: P.N. Jørgensen, Ada, to Governor
         Schielderup, Christiansborg
         V.-g.K.; 887 (Copy Letter Book . . . 12.8.1735 - 4.4.1738)
         Language: Danish

Likewise there has come to me on the 13th of November in this
casse, with the brother of the caboceer, one of *Ursue's* [Owusu, ruler
of Akyem] men by name *Addade*, who had been at *Quitta* [Keta]

about palavers for *Ursue*. I received this man very kindly and treated him to brandy and then drank a toast to *Ursue*, and he in turn drank a toast to the governor, whom he praised highly and bowed and scraped for. Two days later [he] asked me to come into his *casse* and regaled me there and told me that *Ursue* had said that he wanted a Danish White to be at *Ningo*, and this man said that I should write to the governor and greet him from the said *Addade*, saying that he would tell *Ursue* that the Danes should have the place *Ningo*; and when he heard that there was a Danish flag at *Ningo*, the said *Addade* would himself come down there and would obtain good trade. We became very great friends, and [he] then said to *Soja* that the [Danish] White was not like the Dutch. . . .

(X.6)　21st March 1736: Recommendation and resolution of the *Sekret* Council re the establishment of a fort at Ningo V.-g.K.; 881 (*Sekret* Council minutes . . . 1736) Language: Danish

Since I have long considered in what way the Noble Company could take possession of Great *Ningo*, and that it could be maintained sensibly and remain the perpetual property of the Noble Company, I have not earlier expressed my thoughts out of a fear that it would come to the ears of our neighbours, which with all my power I would attempt to prevent, for which reason I had my Servant *Ferdinand* go up to *Orsue* [Owusu] in *Akenie* at that time under the pretence of settling the palaver between Caboceer *Dacon* and our town. I took the oath from my said servant that he would not give any indication that he had orders to negotiate with *Orsue* about *Ningo*, which was his most important charge. This matter has now finally been decided by *Orsue*, and his demands are so much moderated that he asks 20 *bendos* for *Ningo*, and wishes us to pay for each slave that belongs to himself, that is for a fine man slave 7 ounces, and a woman 4 ounces. In return he will permit the Danes to build a fort as solid as they desire, and he will be responsible not only for every single stone that is stolen from *Ningo*, but even for the slaves who might find the opportunity to run away from there.

Now it is well known to everyone that *Ningo* is a profitable trading place, for example also convenient for trading with the Portuguese, which out of fear of the Dutch they do not dare here at *Accra*. In addition it is well enough known that *Orsue* does not sell many of his own slaves, but prefers to chop off their heads, and so that we should not fear that others, secretly and in his name, might demand the same for their slaves, he has eaten fetish to this effect, and permitted that when his messengers come with slaves, they are to be obliged to eat fetish to the effect that the slaves belong to *Orsue*, if we so demand. Since he sent a caboceer down with my servant to settle the palaver, I am thus asking for the consideration of each [of you].

Christiansborg, 21 March 1736
S. Schielderup

Resolution.
Inasmuch as Great *Ningo* is a good and convenient place both for trade with the Portuguese, who do not dare to trade here at *Accra* for fear of the Dutch, and the said place is [in] the midmost part of *Crepe*, where good trade can be expected to take place, a contract has been entered into with Caboceer *Orsue* in *Akenie* as regards our taking possession of the said place. [He] demands for the same 20 *bendos* or 640 rdl. In return [he] guarantees not only that we may make the said place *Ningo* as useful to us as we know how and can, but even that he will assume responsibility for anything that might be lost from there, and to procure it for us again, and in all conceivable ways to protect us. In addition, that we shall have the full disposition of all places on the Lower Coast counted from *Temma* to *Agona* [Anlo], which is a distance of 24 to 26 miles, and our lodge at *Ada* is in the same district. Likewise the said Caboceer *Ossue* demands for any slaves who belong to himself 7 ounces per man and 4 ounces per woman, since it is known that *Ossue* sells few slaves, but would rather massacre them; then it is unanimously resolved by us that the said 640 rdl. are to be paid to Caboceer *Ossue* on the above-mentioned conditions, such too that he is conceded the

proposition concerning his own slaves in consideration of the fact that the said *Ningo* can in future be of great benefit and interest to the Noble Company. . . .

Christiansborg, 21st March 1736
S. Schielderup   E.N. Boris   N.S. Schmidt
P.N. Jørgensen   T. Wendelboe.

(X.11) 9th November 1736: Governor Boris, Christiansborg,
to the Directors of The West India and Guinea Company,
Copenhagen
V.-g.K.; 887 (Copy Letter Book 12.8.1735 - 4.4.1738)
Language: Danish

[Reference to letter of 26th July 1736]

This is further to inform Your Lordships that at present there are here in the fort, reserved for The Noble Company, 11,300 rdl. in gold, of which I have collected 1,000 rdl., although all saleable goods except flintlocks were sold before the death of Counsellor Schielderup. So what I have had to trade with is goods I have bought from foreigners.

As regards the trade, the *Akenist*s have not been down here for two months because of the heavy rain that has fallen, which has made the road so difficult that they cannot walk on it, and also [because] they want to go to war with the *Assiante*s, as it is rumoured here. But they are now expected to come down any day, both *Frempung's* people, who are the true traders, and also *Bang's* people. Then good trade will come. . . .

In our General Letter with the frigate *Jomfruen* we have reported to Your Lordships the Directors that we have entered into an agreement with Caboceer *Orsue* in *Akanie* for Great *Ningo*, and that we intended to build a small fort or a defensive lodge, and that in order to initiate this I was to go down immediately after the departure of the ship. This has now been accomplished. A small fort has been built down there, called Fredensborg, with two bastions, in a triangle of 60 feet, on which there are 10 cannons, 1-, 2- and 3-pounders, and it can be maintained and defended by 3-4 men. Its completion and erection will, along with the 20 *Bendos* paid to *Orsue*, come to cost the Noble Company 1,2-1,300 rdl. in coast prices. . . .

The Dutch have created several obstacles to get us away from there with rewards to the *Akenist*s and the *Accra*s, but could not achieve what they wanted.

Our own town here below the fort is now being finely built up and expanded, since they have been allowed to build on their old sites, where their dead lie buried. . . .

Christiansborg, 9th November 1736
[E.N. Boris]

Asante

(XI.3) [11th] July 1743: Governor Glob Dorph et al.,
         Christiansborg, to the Directors of The West India and
         Guinea Company, Copenhagen
         V.-g.K.; 123 (Letter from the Government in Guinea of
         11.7.1743, with copy and enclosures)
         Language: Danish

At the first opportunity that arose in our time, we have not wished to neglect to inform Your Lordships of the sad state of things here at the fort. The negligence and poor conditions of the last government meant that they did not, in accordance with their duty and obligation, long ago report the misfortunes we have had to the Noble Directors.

We hope that the frigate *Grevinden af Laurwigen*, under the protection of the Almighty, has arrived safely in Copenhagen. Shortly after the departure of the said frigate the Akenists were completely defeated, whereupon a number of *Assiantes* came down to the coast in May 1742 and attacked first the *Ningo* town, and then surrounded the fort, but did not attempt direct hostilities. However they made great claims on the place, saying that it belonged to them, which the commandant [there], the present governor, was obliged to accept, because of the scarcity of *millie*. Then they went up to *Accra* and on the way plundered the English fort *Prampram*, and the Dutch one at *Temma*.

All the Negroes, both our own and those of *Labode* and *Tessing* [Teshi] as well as a number of Dutch and *Temma* Negroes with women and children, had sought refuge here in the fort. Your Lordships may easily infer that our fort was so filled up with so many Negroes that they would have been a great impediment to us in defending ourselves against any hostile attack.

Furthermore the fort had not been supplied with *millie* by the former governor, so that in the few days the *Assiantes* were here, the Negroes in the fort already began to suffer great need. Thus we had to pay them 110 *bendos* or 3,520 rdl. and also had to lend to our and the other above-mentioned Negroes in the town 30 *bendos*, which is 960 rdl., in the best sorts of goods that we had in the fort. The Dutch fort was still more unfortunate than we, and although the chief-merchant and general bookkeeper from *D'Elmine* had been sent down to settle this palaver, they still had to pay 200 *bendos* gold in cash, and surrender all their Caboceer *Dacon's* slaves and all his friends [i.e., relatives], who were at that time here at *Accra*, to the *Assiantes*. The reason for this was that the Dutch had allowed the same caboceer to go up with his people to *Akim*, where he fought with the *Akenists* against the *Assiantes*. . . .

We see neither *Assiantes* nor *Akenists* down here, and we do not know what we should do if *Oppoccu* [Opoku Ware, Asantehene, c. 1720-1750] were to send [a messenger] down to have his *coustyme* fetched before the arrival of a Danish ship. For it is now over a year since we have paid our *coustyme*. There are otherwise rumours that *Oppoccu*, the King of *Assiantee*, wants to fight with the *Fantes*; if this happened, and we then had goods in the fort and ships to trade with, then it could be fortunate for us, since we could earn for the Noble Company what it has lost in these times. . . .

(XI.17) 8th May 1744: Sekret Council Minutes, Christiansborg,
        re presents to the King of Asante
        V.-g.K.; 882 (Sekret Council minutes . . .
        3.2 - 19.10.1744)
        Language: Danish

Oppocu, the King in *Assianté*, has on the 2nd [sic] inst. sent his
messenger along with the *Aqvambuiske* Caboceer *Aqvando Chuma*
[Akonno Kuma, Akwamuhene, c. 1730-1744] to us to collect our
two years of outstanding monthly *coustyme* for the fort of Christiansborg, and promised us before long to open the roads from *Assiante* to *Accra*, and that we must necessarily send a messenger up
to him (this is to be understood as the Blacks' way of saying that he
must have a present from us), and since we have nothing in the
warehouse that is out of the ordinary, the Honourable Governor
Billsen has handed over one graditour [?], 36 ells long, worth 96
rdl. slave price, which is to be deducted from his salary account,
and which is being sent up to the said *Oppocu* along with some flintlocks and powder, as is customary.

Christiansborg, 8th May 1744
L.F. Römer Joost Platfues

(XI.40) 3rd February 1744 - 31st December 1745: Diary kept at
        Christiansborg
        V.-g.K.; 885 (Diary kept in Guinea from
        3rd Febr. 1744 to 31st December 1745)
        Language: Danish

14th April [1745]:
    The two *Akimske* lieutenants who had gone on the 10th inst. to
the Dutch fort came to visit the governor, and greeted the governor
from *Pobye* [Pobi (Pobbj) Asomani, ruler of Akyem Abuakwa until
1765], who is in *Ursue's* place, *Achraduva* [Asare Akraduwa], who
is in *Bang Qvantyn's* place, and *Brunny* [*boroni*], who is in *Frem-*

pung's or *Apau's* place, and said that we had still not, since they had been defeated, sent up [a messenger] to them to offer our condolences to them; that they had therefore gone to the Dutch, although they knew that we had better goods. Thereupon the governor excused himself by saying that the roads had been closed, that the other nations had sent their messengers through *Fante*, which we have no opportunity to do, but that he would now send up his greatest messenger to the said three caboceers with a gift (which was meant to make their hearts good again). These two lieutenants were content with this. . . .

[July] 22nd:

The *Aquambueshe* Caboceer, *Aqvando Chuma*, came here and said that in the name of the King of *Asianté* he was to ask that the price for the goods sent up as monthly *coutyme* might be changed [to] ship's price, such as they are up the coast, that is Danish gingham 4 rdl., calawapores 5 rdl., English romals ditto, and so on.

24th:

Since the *Asiantes* would not stay any longer, their palaver has been settled such that since we do not sell our goods to anyone otherwise than as they are taken to him, *Opocu*, then another price cannot be put on them, and so some have been returned. On the other hand they have said that all palaver about monthly *coustyme* would cease if they might have Danish flintlocks, which, because of their peacefulness, have been given to them.

NB: One sees from this that monthly *coustyme* is never delivered properly, for nowhere near all has come back that was sent up, so along the way the best disappears, or else necessary expenses have prevented *Opocu* from sending more back. It would appear that this king might become difficult, since he knows that he is mighty. So it will be necessary to deal carefully with him.

He also appears to understand that when he sends traders down, then the prices of all goods must be marked down substantially, and he states that the *Fantes* come up to the markets in the country and sell French ginghams at 4 rdl. a piece, perpetuanas for 2 rdl., English flintlocks for 2 rdl., allejars for 4 rdl. and so on. . . .

(XI.42) 4th May 1745: C. Glob Dorph, Copenhagen, to the Direc-
tors of The West India and Guinea Company, Copenhagen
V.-g.K.; 188 (. . . documents re Interim-Governor in
Guinea Christian Clob Dorph 1744-47)
Language: Danish

Your Excellency and all the Noble Directors. Anno 1742 on the
25th of April I was besieged at the fort of Fredensborg by 8,000 *Assiante* Negroes. In March these Negroes had driven out and completely defeated the *Akenist*s, and then I sent word to them that if
they did not stay away from the fort entrusted to me, I would soon
see them off with the cannons. Then they answered that they would
make sure they moved so far from the fort that I could not shoot at
them, but they also knew that I did not have supplies of *millie* for
more than a few days, and then they would see what I would do. I
was thus obliged (considering that there were in the fort 150 or so
Blacks, both the Company's slaves and other free people) to be rid
as well as possible of such a large number of obvious enemies. I
therefore gave the *Assianteische* caboceers large gifts, amounting
to at least 1,800 rdl. . . .

(XI.50) 20th August and 9th September 1746: Governor Platfues
et al., Christiansborg, to the Directors of The West India
and Guinea Company, Copenhagen. General Letter
V.-g.K.; 124 (Letters and documents from Guinea, 20.8.in)

Here, yet another claim has arisen which we have necessarily had
to meet, to wit [from] the successor, *Pobby*, to the protector of the
fort of Fredensborg in *Akim*, *Ursue*, who fell in the recent war. He
[Poby] has reminded us a few times in Mons. Hackenborg's time
of the monthly *coustyme* due for Fredensborg. He [Hackenborg]
was unable to accept this partly because of the scarcity in the warehouse, partly also because of the unreasonableness of the claim, but
has fobbed off his messenger with fair promises and a few small
gifts. But he [Poby] has been unwilling to be satisfied with this. He
has sent a lieutenant down with a moderate force of Negroes to be

told plainly whether he might expect anything or nothing. Although we have tried first with fair words and then with harsh to reject this claim, we have had to learn that our objections were in vain. Nevertheless we could not consider it useful to dismiss him completely in anger, not because of the harm they could do to the fort of Fredensborg, which is already capable of good defence, but because the poor town might [have] been destroyed, which would then have been to the detriment of the fort. But since it is an adopted convention here at the Coast that all forts must pay *coustyme* to certain great Negroes, and this was the rightful heir to this claim, and since in addition no *coustyme* had been paid since the recent war, we have with great effort talked him round. In this, his share of the gifts sent out by the Noble Directors has helped a good deal, since instead of the 52 ounces for 4 years nd 4 months he first claimed, he has accepted 20 ounces, which is the least he would agree to as payment for the above-mentioned period, against the promise that hereafter as before he is to have his usual *coustyme*, which is 16 rdl. a month.
. . .

(XI.60) 5th June 1747: *Sekret* Council resolution re separate
      account for Broker Adoui
      V.-g.K; 883 (Sekret Council minutes . . .
      22.6.1746 - 22.9.1748, p. 30)
      Language: Danish

Our Broker *Adoui* here at *Accra* has several times asked at this time of scarcity to receive his usual 4 rdl. a month, which he has always had from Christiansborg's monthly *coustyme*, since he cannot wait until matters are settled between the *Akenist*s and the *Assiante*s (and consequently) [to see] which of them becomes the master, and thus should have our monthly *coustyme*. It has thus been resolved to favour this Broker of ours, *Adoui,* in this, and that hereafter we shall keep a separate account of this in the General Trade Ledger.
. . .

Christiansborg, 5th June 1747

(XII.22) 10th April 1753: Sekret Council resolution re payment
of outstanding monthly *costume* to the King of Asante
V.-g.K.; 883 (Continuation of Sekret Council minutes
1753, 8.1. - 31.12., p. 295)
Language: Danish

Inasmuch as the *Assianteiske* King *Qussij* has asked to have his
outstanding monthly salary paid out, which is a substantial sum,
which at this juncture is being demanded at an inopportune time,
considering that these goods could be used in the trade for the dispatch of the ship; and although we have in all possible ways tried
to persuade him to be content with half or two thirds; [but inasmuch
as] this has borne no fruit; thus, considering that the trade from the
Assiantes is at present of very great importance, and also in order
to encourage the said *Qussij* and his traders to favour the Danish
nation with their trade; we have therefore resolved, as we hereby
resolve, to pay the said King *Qussij* his whole outstanding monthly
pay, all the more so as the arrival of the Danish ship is imminent,
for which a number of slaves are necessary, to which only the *Assiante's* trade can contribute, so that if we were to deny them their
request, the trade would thereby be weakened.

Thus resolved for the benefit of the Noble Company.

The fort of Christiansborg, 10th April 1753
C. Engman   C.M.L. Schmith   C. Jessen

(XII.26) 30th July 1753: Governor Engman et al., Christiansborg,
to the Directors of The West India and Guinea Com-
pany, Copenhagen. General Letter
V.-g.K.; 125 (General Letter and enclosures from
Guinea of 30th July 1753)
Language: Danish

It appears that there is certainty about the treaty the *Akanist*s have
made with the *Assiante*s to pay a certain sum and then move back
to their own country. However, this will not happen so quickly, but
if it happens then there will also be good traders here at the Lower

Coast, whereas the *Assiantes* will withdraw with their trade to the Upper Coast. We would not like to see this, because the *Assianteiske* King, *Qussy*, has sent a lieutenant with a few hundred men and a little trade so that at all three forts here he can collect his outstanding monthly *coutyme*, which amounted to 1,548 rdl., -, -, from the fort. We have not been able to resolve on any other course than to pay him this, and also to send him a gift with a request that, when the *Akenists* come to their country, he will favour the Danish nation with some *Assiantee* trade, since one party of traders could go upwards and the other party could come down here to the coast. The messengers have not yet brought back a reply to this message, since they have not returned at all yet, but we flatter ourselves with the hope that the *Assianteiske* trade will not wholly cease with respect to the Danish flintlocks and powder kegs with good hoops and also the beads, which are much in demand, and which at present give preference to the Danish trade here at the Lower Coast for that reason . . .

A Short and Simple Account of the Country Guinea and Its Nature, 1697

ERICK TILLEMAN

Erick Tilleman was an agent of the Danish West India-Guinea Company based in Copenhagen. The Company was chartered in 1697, the year this former army officer published his account. Once Tilleman got the Christiansborg fort in order, the fort was handed over to the Company in December 1698.

[*The Gold Coast and Its Gold*]

The Gold Coast is considered [to extend] from Assené [Assinie] to Nungo [or Ningo], which, in a straight line, is a distance of 100 and ten [*sic*] miles, where one receives mostly gold for the wares brought from Europe. Yet, that gold is not found everywhere on this coast, even though it is called Gold Coast, but it comes from a good thirty miles inland from the shore, and mostly from the kingdom of Acania [Akani], which is held to be the largest kingdom in Guinea, stretching in length east-northeast to south-southwest a distance of ninety miles.

This gold is not brought by the Acanies directly to the Christians but to the *Natureller* in the neighboring kingdoms of Acara [Nkran/Accra], Fantyn [Fante], Sabu [Asebu], Fetu, Adumb [Adom], and other small provinces at the coast, and that gold is clean and pure without any adulteration at all. . . . The Acanies, with permission of the Christians, have their own merchants living at the main castles *St. George d'el Mina* [Elmina], *Cabo Corsso* [Oguaa/Cape Coast], and *Friderichsberg*, who understand the *Acania* language and can trade on their behalf, but not in the kingdom of *Acara*: Since whatever they want to get from the Christians they must buy through the *Qvambus* [Akwamu] who do not permit any *Acanies* to go through the kingdom of *Acara* to the coast in order to negotiate personally. . . .

[*Spiritual Culture*]

Throughout the entire country there are some Negroes who, in Portuguese are called *Fitisseiro*, and in the language of the country *Comfu* [ɔkɔmfoɔ], who are clearly wizards so that with Satan's help they can predict the future, which later proves to be true, although it does often prove wrong.

These people are used by the *Natureller* for all manner of things, so that nothing of importance is undertaken or carried out before they give their consent, which however, does not happen before he [ɔkɔmfoɔ] upon payment from the petitioner, has made various sacrifices in the bush, at crossroads, and on the shore and other places, when he finally announces his opinion of what seems best for them to do or refrain from doing, which the *Natureller*, thereupon, must accept precisely as the proven and true faith. In the event that that advice proves to have a fortunate outcome, as predicted, be it in war or business, marriage, or anything else, it is considered to be the *Fetisseiro* alone, with his sacrificing and sanctity, who has made it happen. If, however, the outcome is not as predicted, which often happen, and they complain about it to that *Fitisseiro*, and demand that he be brought to trial before the chief Fitisseiros, then he knows exactly how to excuse himself in every way, such as that the sacrifice was too poor, that the place where the sacrifice was made was unclean, or with other excuses, which the *Natureller* believe and dare not contradict; but they must often, on the contrary, provide another sacrifice which is better and finer, at their own greatest expense and to the profit of the *Fitisseiro* who enjoys the best of it. . . .

Furthermore, that same *Fitisseiro* ordains for each person on which days he shall sacrifice and which days he shall keep holy, which among these people is Tuesday, just as ours is Sunday; and again, he tells them which days will be the best for work, so that their work will be successful and make good progress. . . . The *Fitisseiros* apparently can perform a number of tricks (much like conjuring) and other witchcraft with snakes, lions, tigers, and other animals, with Satan's help. Many such acts have been described, and I, myself, have seen a great number which would be considered unbelievable.

Finally there is this to note, that all the inhabitants in the Kingdom of *Acara* (apart from the *Qvambus*) have their children circumcised when they are more than seven years old, like the Jews; which, however, is not done anywhere else on the entire Coast. But in all other things, their belief in the *Fitisseiros'* magic in everything is found throughout the land.

A Reliable Account of the Coast of Guinea, 1760
LUDEWIG F. RØMER

Ludewig Ferdinand Rømer was an assistant clerk who
was eventually promoted to Chief Merchant in the service
of the Danish establishments on the Gold Coast. He also
procured and sold enslaved Africans to the "West Indies"
(i.e., the Americas).

[*Religion and the Fante ɔbosom Nananom Mpow*]

Inasmuch as a people's nature and customs usually flow from their
religion, I shall begin with that first, although it is difficult to write
about the religion of a people which for them is not a precise system. For most of them never bother to think about such things, and
the elderly among them who are meditative in most cases have opinions as distinct from one another as east is from west.

What I write here is according to the statements of a chief priest,
namely our Caboceer [headman], Putti [Okpoti] of Labode [Labadi,
a Gã town east of Nkran/Accra]. Not only is Putti the greatest and
most famous priest (fetish-maker) on [the] Gold Coast, but the important oracle (fetish) on the Gold Coast is also to be found in Labode. I am careful to say that it is the most important, but it is not
the most powerful, this being the one in Fante—as explained later.
. . .

As mentioned above, the Fante fetish [*ɔbosom*] is the most powerful one. Above Annamaboe [Anomabu], two miles from the shore,
several hills of considerable height and overgrown with thick brush
and tall trees form a semi-circle. Between these hills the ground is
quite flat. (I am writing here of a place which I have never seen, but
I record it according to the testimony of many). The hills are considered to be so sacred that not even the priests dare approach them
but must keep a certain distance. This fetish [Nananom Mpow] appears three times a year. At other times, if someone wishes to ask
about something, he answers through the mouth of one of his priests

or priestesses, just as the other fetishes do, and mostly in the same way as it is done in other places. This fetish is not as clear [in his pronouncements] as the one in Labode, and is very bloodthirsty. At [the beginning of] every month the Negroes must sacrifice a human being, and after he has accepted the human being, as an extra gift they sacrifice to him a pair of oxen. The sacrifice must be performed in the following way. When he himself is to be present, on one of the three times in the year, he is accompanied by an earthquake, and all the tall trees bend to greet the fetish. Then a whirlwind blows up, and all the Blacks, forming a semicircle with the hills (thus making a complete circle) fall on their faces, just as at Labode, and the fetish makes an oration. It is to be noted that he speaks like a man quivering and trembling, [almost] hiccuping hoarsely, and stammering. I cannot claim to know all that the Blacks say about his voice, [but] am relating this according to the description of Corrantrin's son Bassi, who, as I mentioned before, was in France for several years. I and several other [Whites] have often been entertained by Bassi imitating the voice of the fetish, and delivering speeches to us in the language employed by the fetish. He himself had visited the fetish on only one occasion, when he arrived home from France and Corrantrin, his father, obliged him to accompany him, in order to observe the sacrifice he had offered the fetish in gratitude for his son's safe return. But Bassi, who was angry with his thievish father, told me that he had only offered a goat, [despite the need for gratitude] for the beautiful goods which his father, at that time, had already intended to steal from the poor French.

We come, then to Bassi's description of how the fetish receives his offering. The person or animal which is to be sacrificed is brought forward by about fifty priests and priestesses, who advance singing—and the song is just as melancholy as the one sung in Labode. The Negroes, sitting ten, and at times twenty, men deep, open their circle on one of the sides between the hills and themselves. The sacrifice is dragged three times around the circle, and all the Negroes sing the same song. Finally they stand up, and the priests and priestesses form a smaller circle around the sacrifice, not far from the [sacred] grove from which there comes a whirlwind which lifts the sacrifice up into the air. As long as they can see it they hear it screaming and roaring, but [after that] it is never seen again. Bassi and the others have assured me that as soon as the sacrifice leaves the earth, it is both twisted around and turned over, in the same way as an Easterly known as a "twister" (*Trompe de Mer*) draws water up out of the sea. The revolving is less noticeable and slower when the sacrifice is not far from the earth, but the higher into the air it goes, the more twisting and the more circles it makes.

The Negroes do not feel this [whirl]wind, but they remain very quiet. Just as the symbols (*signa*) of the Labode fetish are some old drums, so fire is the symbol of the Fante fetish. It is kept permanently [burning] at a certain place night and day, year in and year out, at which place the priests sing an ancient song, and dance, every morning and evening. And since no one in that country can dance without a drum, they also have several players or drumbeaters. But these drums are not sacred.

According to what the Negroes claim, the Fante fetish, in one of his regular orations, delivered the following parable. A player or drummer lived in a place where there were many lovely fruit trees. When he had an appetite for eating, the drummer played some lively music under the tree, and the snake which lived in the tree threw down to him as many of all the varieties of fruit as he wished. Thus he lived, satisfied, for several years, and became comfortable and fat. But it happened that he fell ill. He could not then play the music for the snake as usual, and from his house he could barely walk to his position under the tree, where he asked the snake for a couple of . . . fruit[s] resembling our plums but very mealy and healthy to eat. Although the sick man promised to repay him after he recovered, the snake showed no goodwill to our drummer by throwing fruit down to him. The sick drummer had to be grateful for the unripe fruit growing low down on the tree, and he finally recovered. As was his due, he wanted to take revenge on the merciless snake. With his drum, he placed himself under the tree where the snake lived and called up to her. As usual, she needed to stick her head down out of the tree, in order to hear the music better. Being pleased that her drummer was well again, she did so, as requested. But, instead of drumsticks the drummer carried two chopping knives, and he swiftly cut off the snake's head. By telling this story the fetish intended to warn his listeners not to be lukewarm in their worship, or what the drummer [had done] to the snake he would do to them.

According to Bassi, the first words of the Fante fetish when he arrives at his grove are, "I greet you all!"—this being a translation of Bassi's "*Je salue vous Autres!*" He speaks these words clearly, but then he begins to tremble and quake. Another time the Fante fetish said, "If you do not love Good and follow it, and if you do not hate Evil and shun it, I shall in person support your enemies, and I shall murder you, also all the relatives close to you. It is only for the sake of your pious forefathers that I have spared you until now." So much for the reports of Bassi and others about the Fante fetish.

History of the Caribbean Islands, 1777
CHRISTIAN G. OLDENDORP

Christian George Andreas Oldendorp was a Moravian clergyman who visited the Danish colonies of St. Croix and St. John in the late eighteenth century. Oldendorp's account is significant because he interviewed a number of predominantly Akan peoples originally from the Gold Coast but enslaved in the colonies. Most of Oldendorp's informants understood Twi (Akan), Gã, and Ewe. An annotated German language edition of his complete manuscript from the Archive of the Evangelical Brothers was published under the title Historie der Caribischen Inseln Sanct Thomas, Sanct Crux und Sanct Jan.

Book 3, Sec. II. About the various nations of the blacks, their fatherland Guinea, their religion and other customs there as well as their languages

The greatest number of slaves brought to the West Indies, are from the Gold Coast and its region. They consist of many nations. The most noble, belligerent nation, which also most often practices the capture of persons, even among itself, is the nation Amina. I have talked to five respectable and intelligent blacks of this nation. One was a noble and rich merchant and slave capturer, who had also been traveling far and near, another the king's brother, another a cousin of a "sub-king," who had had a large army of blacks 3,000 men of it had been under his command. They had on each side of their heads three incisions, one beneath the other, from the ear to the eye. They said that they had these because they considered it beautiful and also to distinguish themselves from other nations. These had already been made when they were children, by their mothers. The skin is cut with a knife and palm oil mixed with coal is rubbed into it, so that it cannot grow shut again, and several times more palm oil is brushed over it.

One had lived a day's journey, another [individual] a fourteen days' journey away from the ocean, one a day's journey from a British fort.

They have a belligerent spirit and great courage and there are brave people among them. They do not like to work in Guinea but rob, if they are can, the neighboring nations and capture people from them, sometimes also among their own countrymen. They have only one king and "sub-kings," or governors in every district. In these lands such blacks are called Caboseer ["headman"]. They are feared by their neighbors because of their power and cruelty. They (the people telling the stories) named many nations with which they are at war: the Fante, Akkim [Akyem], Akkran [Nkran/Gã], Bemang [Abrem], Asseni [Assin/Asen], Kifferu [Twifo], Atti [Etsi], Okkau, Adansi [Adanse]; this nation—and also the Bibi—they called cannibals, who ate people of their own and other nations.

They named as cause of these wars, that thereby they were able to capture people and sell them. They have firearms, which they obtain from Europeans; their enemies, for the most part, have only bows and arrows. The occasions for internal wars are often given by the many heirs of the king and the sub-kings, who also would like to become persons of importance and are trying to oust others or start a fight for succession among themselves.

Their land is very large and full of villages, of which some could be called cities because of their size. They have plenty of gold, but no iron. The former merchant had traded in the country with gold, which he had obtained from the whites (as payment) for slaves and he got for a piece that was about as big as half a hand, 10 pieces of *Achten*, if one counts it in the currency of the West Indies. For a knife, such as is used to cut sugar cane, they would, he said, give about 10 pieces and for an axe 20. There they pay in gold, partly in grains (of gold), partly in whole pieces, or with shells or slaves, whatever they have and are able to do it with. Five shells, which are called *bujis* or cowries amount to approximately one West Indian Stueber or half a penny. He also traded with gold, ivory and slaves. One Amina nation, which he called Quahu [Kwawu], kills many elephants.

From these he bought a tooth for about 4 pieces of West Indian money and sold it again to another nation for 10 pieces, and took those elephant teeth also often to British or Dutch manufacturers. If a nation owed him something, he gave them three month to pay. If they did not pay, he waited another month. If after that nothing was done, he sent people out to way-lay them and capture whoever they could. He let them prey especially on the children of his debtors and he sold whoever he got, to the whites as slave. He said that life in Guinea was good; one did not have to work as hard as in the West Indies, but one's plight there was insecurity, because people tried to catch and sell one another.

He told about the elephants, that two strong blacks are unable to lift one of their teeth. By pushing their large ears together, the elephants make a sound that can be heard an hour away. Their tail is given to the governor as a fly swatter. He told of the big snakes in his country, which according to his descriptions are two cubits wide and several hundred cubits long. If one of those snakes sees a cattle from a distance it pulls itself closer and closer and throws, when it is close enough, the back its body over the cattle, wraps itself around it and crushes its ribs and legs. Then the snake searches the area two miles in diameter and looks for the type of ants, which are able to kill such a horrendous snake. If it finds those, it leaves its prey lying there and retreats. If it does not find any, it pulls the ox or the cow further and further into its mouth and remains lying there until the animal has become entirely digested in its body. The snake is so helpless during this time that it cannot move on. If somebody there encounters a big snake, which can especially happen to a hunter while he is hunting, then—when he is close to it—there is no way to think of escaping. He surrenders to it, because otherwise it would attack him and crush him. He lies down in front of it and lets it swallow one of his feet. The foot will not be hurt by this, for generally snakes do not crush what they swallow; if it is not too thick, but they pull it gently and neatly into their body. He spreads the other foot so the snake cannot take it in. When the leg has been pulled in up to the hip, he takes the big knife that he carries and forcefully slits open the throat of the snake on the inner side. That way he can extract himself from it again. Thus the snake is numbed and cannot do anything to him. He leaves it lying there and runs away quickly. It is a desperate, but the only method to save oneself from death. Another one told that at the time he was there, a tired hunter in Amina land was lying down to sleep in the bush. His gun was lying next to him and he held his big knife in his hand, which he rested on his chest. While he slept, a big snake came and started to pull him in, headfirst. He awoke while his head and half of his body were already in its gullet. He recognized immediately where he was, he knew those snakes, cut it open on the side with his knife, crawled out and escaped.

It is known that there are enormously big snakes in Guinea and other countries. One also knows that people, who are acquainted with such horrifying animals and accustomed to them, have unbelievable audacity when confronted with them. There are people who ride on crocodiles. There are Indians in South America who sit down on big snakes and kill them. There are Indian boys in North America, who in winter crawl into the den of a bear, and have to yank him and taunt him until he gets out and can be shot dead; and more of the same. The general name of the god of the Amina, who they evoke in Guinea, is Jankombum [Onyankopɔn]. He is also the sky. But some say that god in the sky, who made the world and their nation, is called Borriborri. This one has a wife Jankomaago and a son Jankombum, who is the intercessor at the great god and to whom they pray in all their concerns. Another one also told me that they have three gods, but that in his region the father is called Quereampum [Twedeampɔn], the mother Kieampum and the son Jankombum. They are close to the son and call him also father. During war they sing in the midst of shooting to Jankombum: He should help us, he is the father, [and] we are his children and cannot help ourselves. Every morning after they have washed themselves they call to him that he should protect them, give them good nourishment and let them be happy. Many blacks, especially on the Gold Coast, have learned from the whites the division of time into weeks. The Amina celebrate every week the day on which they are born, for instance Monday. On that day in the morning before washing themselves, they grind up Portulak—Aggra in their language—or another weed which they call Sombee, in water and take a mouthful of the water three times and every time they spit out the water they pray to Jankombum. They do not know why they are doing this or where they acquired this custom. They simply do it as an old habit. Someone who owes another person something also pleads with Jankombum to pay for him. They especially call to him or one of the other gods in time of disease for recovery.

Journey to Guinea and the Caribbean Islands in Columbia, 1788

PAUL ERDMANN ISERT

Paul Erdmann Isert was chief surgeon to the Danish headquarters at Christiansborg and a merchant. He published his Reise nach Guinea und den Caribäischen Inseln in Columbia *(Journey to Guinea and the Caribbean*

Islands in Columbia [*i.e., the Caribbean*]) *in 1788. Excerpts appear below.*

[*The Akuapem*]

The Aquapims [Akuapem], or Mountain Blacks, in some respects differ in their customs from the Coastal Blacks. Their language is very different from Akra [Nkran/Accra], so much so that unless an Aquapim has learned the language of the Akra, he cannot make himself understood at all. The Aquapim language has a great similarity to the Assianthee [Asante] language, from which it differs only in dialect. The Aquapims are of only medium stature but very well-built. Their skin is usually blacker than that of the Coastal Blacks. They wear a beard more commonly than those on the coast are in the habit of doing. The Aquapims are very dextrous, quick on their feet, and in general they have keen minds. They are expert in the handling of firearms, and the majority of them know how to hunt, a necessity for them because of the lack of fish, other than the dried fish they obtain by trade with the Coastal Blacks. Their clothing is not different from that of their neighbours.

Indeed the Aquapim lives almost as if in the first innocence of Paradise, with but few differences. Everything he plants he harvests more than a hundredfold. As a result, a Black works three or four weeks at the most throughout the entire year. He spends the rest of the time in purely enjoyable pursuits and in practising his customs. The head of a household never works himself, but has one or more slaves, or even his children, who plant the maize and yams, cultivate the plantains and bananas, cut down either the old plants or the old stems—new stems shoot spontaneously from the root—tap palmwine, go hunting, etc.

The Aquapims make very few dishes out of the maize and raise no more than they think they can eat freshly roasted. Their preferred vegetable from July to December is the yam, which is said to be far tastier here than it is in Columbia. When it is roasted they eat it as we eat bread; or they cook it in a soup containing meat and crushed palm nuts; or they make a kind of pleasant tasting dumpling of it.

They plant it in the same way as we do the potato, but the root is so large that a single one can weigh 25 pounds or more, hence they cut it into small pieces. The yam is best when it is roasted or cooked until it becomes snow-white, and it tastes much like potatoes. I once made an experiment with it to see if emmer, or starch flour, could be made out of it. The experiment fulfilled my expectations when, from an eight-pound root, I actually obtained one-half pound of very good starch which had a great similarity to that obtained from the potato. By experiment I noticed also that the root is capable of a spiritous fermentation, but since I had no distilling apparatus, and could not obtain one here, I could not determine how much *spiritus* it was able to produce.

In the remaining six months of the year there are no yams avail-able, because they are harvested only once a year and cannot be stored for the rest of the year. Consequently the Aquapims use the fruits of the plantain tree instead, a tree bearing fruit the whole year and found throughout the forest. For the preparation of plantains as a vegetable they are plucked from the tree when they have become large but are not yet fully ripe. They are then cooked in water until they are very soft. The leathery skin is removed and the fruit is crushed, with a pestle of very hard wood, in a wooden mortar made out of a tree trunk, until the pulp acquires the characteristic of a very light dumpling or pudding. This is then placed in a calabash in the form of small balls, and when it has reached this stage it is called *foi foi* [*fufu*]. . . .

To be sure, they have other forms of nourishment, but these are not at all as common, although enjoyed at times as delicacies. In this category belongs the edible arum [cocoyam], or what in Co-lumbia is called *tannies*, of which they cook the leaves like a cab-bage and eat the root like yams. The leaves of this plant are much like our spinach and the root is like our chestnut. Throughout the whole year there are also great quantities of fresh fruit to eat, the major part of which grows wild. The main fruits are the banana, the pineapple and the pawpaw. Limes also grow wild here. . . .

The fetish worship that the Aquapims practise resembles that of the Coastal Blacks very closely, but the latter serve their fetish much

more poorly, in that at various points in the roads and at crossroads
the Aquapims construct a kind of altar formed from the stalks of
palm leaves. Cooked and raw yams and all the kinds of food that
they themselves use are collected at the altar, and in addition, a calabash of wine is placed there. In the ground around the altar they
fix a number of sticks each of which has been painted white and
has a kind of raffia wound around its middle. In the centre of the
road leading from Kommang to another small Black settlement I
found twelve human heads planted side by side in the ground at the
root of a tree, and beside them some pots and bottles filled with
water and half-buried in the ground. These were surrounded by a
sort of fence, although this was a very extensive area. When I inquired as to the reason for these heads having been placed so
strangely—an arrangement which I had never seen before, notwithstanding my having been in the country for nearly three years—I
could see that they did not want to reveal the true reason. Nevertheless, I was finally told that they were the heads of a particular
family. I could not conceive of their being the heads of a conquered
enemy, because had that been the case, they would not have been
shown so much honour; while members of families here would always have been buried with their heads in place. Even if these were
the ransomed heads of friends who had been conquered in war, they,
too, would have been buried in the same manner as intact bodies
are.

I stayed in Aquapim for ten days, partly in order to become better
acquainted with the lie of the land and with its boundaries, and
partly because my friend Attiambo did not want to let me go. In fact
I would always have found sufficient nourishment for my spirit had
I stayed an entire month. I made daily excursions from here to the
surrounding area and always found my efforts rewarded! The Duke,
however, did not allow me to go with my Blacks alone, but always
gave me an armed escort of his own. The concern the Blacks
showed for me was exaggerated. If a stone was lying in the road, or
a branch was hanging so low that it might hinder me, these things
had to be cleared away immediately. Such exaggerated shows of
politeness, and the extraordinary curiosity to see a White man, since

none had been here before now, resulted in people crowding around at every place in which I was seen, which hindered me somewhat in my walks. Old women could not even abandon their cupping when I went past their houses, but came running out holding to their temples the large gourd used here for a cupping-glass. They wanted to see that wonderful animal, the European, about whom they tell each other daily so many things before they have ever seen him. Indeed, if I wanted to have peace in my room I had to place a guard in front of the door to keep people from storming the house. Everything about me seemed to them a source of wonder. Once, when I was eating in front of a crowd of people, the entire crowd cried out, "Look! The White Man can eat, too!"

Aquapim is supposed originally to have been settled by people from a nation lying further inland, most probably by the Assianthees, with whom they have a great deal in common, both in custom and in language. Even their name seems to indicate that they originated from another nation, since it means "1,000 slaves," that is, *pim*, "1,000," and *aqua* or *quaqua*, "slave." According to my rough estimate Aquapim is 30 miles long and 25 miles wide. Inland, on the east it is bordered by Aquambo [Akwamu]; on the seaward side by Krobbo [Krobo]; on the south, or towards the coast, by Akra; on the west by Fanthee [Fante]; and on the north by Akim [Akyem]. The population living in this widespread district, if I reckon from the 1,200 men who can carry arms—I am told that this is the number—and if I include wives and children for each man, the highest estimate possible is a total of not more than 9,000 persons. Their numbers must have been tremendously reduced since towns are mentioned here and there which once must have been flourishing but of which nothing is known today except the name . . .

Early-Twentieth-Century Descriptions
of Kawu (Akpafu): Two Views

The first account of Kawu (Akpafu) comes from David Asante (ca. 1834-1892), and the second from Andreas Pfisterer. The first, as you will see, is the more significant of the two. David Asante's account is the earliest description of Kawu (Akpafu, which he called "Apafo") written by an African in an African language. The original was a report of a journey made in early 1887 by Asante, who was the son of a Christianized local leader in Akropong and one of the first Africans to be trained in Basel. Together with a few unnamed European missionaries, Asante traveled throughout what is today the central Volta region of Ghana, visiting Nkonya, Boem, Akpafu, and Santrokofi, amongst other places. He wrote down his experiences in Twi (Akan) and sent the report to Basel Mission headquarters in Basel, Switzerland, where it was subsequently translated into German by J. G. Christaller. Andreas Pfisterer's report entitled "Akpafu" appeared in two issues of Monatsblatt der Norddeutschen Missionsgesellschaft *in 1904.*

David Asante's Apafo (Akpafu), 25 January 1887

When we departed in the morning [January 25], the chieftain of the town gave us a guide until Apafo. From Teteman we should have actually traveled by way of Beyika to Lolobi, but we heard here that this path had been closed off and could not be walked on anymore, but the way across Apafo would be good and short, also that this bad disease had not been in Apafo itself, but had been in Adome, and was already extinguished for a long time.

We were very happy to arrive in Apafo, which is renowned for its iron smelting and forging. On the entire path, which we walked, we saw the coals with which they smelt the iron. They chop green wood, dig a hole into the ground, stack up the wood in it, cover it well with leaves and earth and leave only one hole open through which they ignite the wood; only eight days later they extinguish the fire and take out the coals. When we had ascended the mountain to its plateau, we soon saw the place where they smelt the iron, a small distance from the village. They built their oven like a rice pillar [in which rice is stored], but they make the walls much heavier than for the rice, about 5 feet high and open on top, below is a hole through which they insert the coals, then the entire excavated iron ore is poured onto the coals, and once these are ignited, the hole is closed with soil except for a small opening through which air can enter; also 5 or 6 small holes are made into the oven so the fire has air and does not go out. If everything goes alright in the blaze, one sees the molten slag flow out slowly from a small hole, which was made below, but the good iron remains behind in the oven; one takes it out only at 24 hours after the igniting of the oven. But the heat remains in such an empty oven for a long time, thus any food which one puts into it can be cooked in it until done. Next to one of the smelting ovens is a deep somewhat steep abyss; if one lets a stone roll off there one can hear it roll for 5 to 7 minutes and then it still has not arrived below. Children, who busy themselves around here, have fun with this.

We arrived in Apafo at about 9 o'clock. The town is large, the main street is wide; when we arrived the entire population of the town flocked together to see us, even the blacksmiths stopped their forging and came too, because no European had ever arrived here. If it had been up to them, we would have had to spend several days here. They led us to a farmstead, where we could put our luggage down; and from there we went to greet the king, a strong old man. They took us to their smithies and showed us everything they make there. Their anvil is not made of iron, but a big rock of quartz, which is affixed to the floor and its upper surface has been polished. When they are forging they do not remain standing in one place, but are moving around the anvil. They themselves produce also their own tools, such as hammer, tongs, chisel etc.; their hammers are not as those of the Europeans, but the handle is also like the part with

which one beats made of iron, short and polished throughout; some
are big some are small. Their bellows are like those of olden times,
one grabs them with both hands and works them like a drum; therefore this is done not by only one man, but 3-5 persons are taking
turns doing it.

All tools, which they are forging, are made in the same way; a
long curved iron becomes a cutlass, a hoe or a puncturing tool. . . .
Their hoes are different from ours, they are round; others are like
the ones we use here, [flat with 2 edges] only the cutting edge is
rounded off. Afterwards they also showed us where they mine the
iron; it is on the same mountain on which their town lies. The iron
mines resemble the goldmines in Akem [Akyem]. They dig into the
depth and make lateral corridors below so that one is able to get
from one pit to the other. A few people here understand Twi, we had
one of them, who earlier had been in Cape Coast, translate our ser-
mon. Their king, as tall as a giant, was very generous towards us
and wished that we should remain for several more days, but our
schedule did not allow that. We talked with him about the word of
God and he said he would like very much if we could appoint somebody to his city.

The people here at Boem are the brightest. That the children go
naked did become the custom, also here. Because of their ironwork
they live in proper circumstances, because one comes here from
everywhere to purchase iron tools. Here, not all houses are not covered with grass, but have flat loam roofs. They do not call them
adán (ordinary houses of the blacks), but abán (houses such as forts
and houses made of stone). The Boems live in such houses in the
following villages: Borada, Apafo (Akpafo), Teteman, Beyika,
Lobobi, and Santrokofi. The towns in which one works with iron
are: Apafo, Santrokofi and Lolobi. There are two Apafo-towns:
Apafogã (the big one), which lies on the mountain, and Apafo-
Dome which lies in the plain. Lolobi consists of two towns,
Santrokofi has 3 towns, [and] each is in less than five minutes distance from the other.

Because of the ironwork, which takes place here, there are many
blacksmith shops in the town. One is awestruck when seeing their

diligence in forging and smelting of iron. One of the blacksmiths showed us a magic trick: after he had rubbed his hand in the dust on the floor of his shop, he took a fiery piece of iron from the fire and stroked his hands across it, so that sparks were flying, but it did not hurt his hands. The diligence of the people, their hospitality and their calm behavior pleased us so much that we became very fond of them. If we would not have been short of time, we would have loved to stay a day longer according to their wish. When we said goodbye, the king said we should return soon and bring them guns that they could purchase, because all their guns were damaged. We told him that we were preachers of the gospels and did not engage in such business. He gave us a guide who brought us to Santrokofi on the evening of the same day.

Andreas Pfisterer, "Akpafu," 1904

One of the strangest landscapes of the Togo-region is the little country of Boem, located about 6-7 day-trips to the north of the coast. It almost seems as if a Babylonian confusion of languages had taken place here; because on a distance of only twelve hours on the road one travels through no less than six different language areas, not only different dialects, but really different languages, of which some are spoken by less than 1,000 people. The two most Northern languages Tapa and Worawora were almost entirely replaced here by the Tschi-(Asante-) language in the course of time. For this reason did the Basel Mission begin its work here in the Tschi [Twi] language in the hope, that also the remaining tribes Borada, Boviri, Akpafu and Santrokofi would adopt this language, but one could never agree upon where the main station was to be built. In the meantime it had, however, become obvious that it was more in the interest of the Boem-people, to learn the Ewe-language and not the Tschi-language; therefore the entire region was finally given to the North German Mission, which worked in the Ewe-Region. Therewith the question of the appropriate location for the main station is apparently definitely settled. Akpafu, the second largest city in Boem, beautiful, open and healthy and yet not situated too high up, is ideally suited for this and presents the very handy advantage, that a spring, very close to the city, supplied good drinking water throughout the entire year.

The city of Akpafu numbered nearly 1,000 inhabitants and comprises together with the two locations Lolobi (700 inhabitants) and Odome (250 inhabitants) the Kefu or Siu language-tribe. These are therefore not two different languages, but only different names for the same language and despite the fact that the people of Akpafu themselves call their language "Siu," the neighboring tribes, however, call it "Kefu." The way the name of the city is written is a similar matter. The Tschi-people write and pronounce "Apafo," the Ewe-people however "Akpafu," while the Akpafu-people themselves call their town "Mawu." Moreover, the Europeans fused the two previous names to Akpafo. So, who is now correct? We, as representatives of the Ewe, are writing Akpafu. As yet it could not be determined where the people had their original home. According to the information of some, they are said to have lived previously in the Anum-region, according to others in the Amedzowe-region. In Akpafu itself they are living apparently only since about 150 years. Before that time they lived in the Nkunya mountain range which is still today haunted by one of their main fetishes, Togbaiko.

According to the descriptions of a few old people the entire tribe must have numbered 8[,000] -10,000 heads. Through wars with the neighboring tribes, mainly through the invasions by the Asantes, who exterminated entire villages, as well as through diseases, mainly smallpox, the number decreased so much that they number no more than 2,000 souls today. . . .

The ban of slavery was a bitter command for them. However, slavery still exists not only here, but also among the remaining tribes, but the relationship between slave and master hardly deserves this name anymore. The children are often looked upon like one's own and are usually betrothed in one's own family. It is even considered as a severe wrongdoing when a "free man" reprimands a child, thus bought, a slave. Also the adults, who almost all are married, enjoy a rather good treatment, so that most of them do not even care to get their freedom. Maltreatment or physical castigation because of unsatisfactory work performance does not occur. Every slave knows very well, that he can find in such a case strong protection through the government and his master knows this just as well. So one can hope with certainty that this evil will die out entirely by itself, if the government would only reinforce that slave trade is no longer allowed to take place. Even if this is attempted now and then, it only seldom succeeds. Two years ago a woman was supposed to be sold to Akposo. She had come to Akpafu as a very small child about 30 years ago, was then given in marriage in her master's family, and then was passed on after the death of her husband to his heir and after his death to the next heir. Now she was supposed to go to a region, the language of which she was not able to understand, leaving her five children behind. Her pleas, that one should leave her with her children, were in vain; she had to go with the two men, who where supposed to bring her to her new master. But before they arrived there she was able to escape.

She returned to Akpafu and pleaded for protection at the missionary station. It sufficed that the missionary handed her over for protection to the chieftain reminding him, that he was responsible for the enforcement of the ban of slavery. Since then the woman enjoys her freedom; unfortunately, however, she does not know how to use it, that is to say she is just too free. . . .

Very unclear and confused are the religious concepts of the people. They believe, as all their neighboring tribes, in a higher being called "Ea," who created the world and the people and lives with his wife in the "City of God." But there he seems to be so busy that he cannot take care of the world, because he is rarely or never is suspected to intervene in the fate of a human being. Only when an old person dies a natural death, one says, Ea has called him

In his place innumerable deities greatly varying in power and rank rule the earth, the so-called fetishes. Some of the most important among them are: Orentabora, Togbaiko, Koko, Gayapanã. Each of these fetishes has his protector and his servant. The latter has to bring him his previously agreed upon sacrificial meal at a certain time. If such a protector or servant dies, the fetish himself appoints a successor, who is most often still a boy. But these are no fetish priests. The communications between the humans being and the fetish is mediated only by fetish priestesses of who there are seven or eight. As long as everything in the city goes its normal way and the fetishes do not bother the people, one leaves them alone and just gives them "food," which constitutes the entire service. Everyone, including Ea, gets yearly a portion of rice at harvest time. In addition to this, Ea gets also a white ram. Togbaiko, who always changes his location when his servant dies, and then makes his living quarters now in Akpafu, then in Odome, gets a billy-goat in addition to his rice and of several types of antelopes the first animal, which is shot after this meal of rice. Besides this one has to bring him an antelope every five years to the Nkunya-mountains, where he has his true home. The little fetishes are most often satisfied with a rooster. But if a misfortune or a disease befalls a house or the entire city, or if it does not rain for a long time, or if it rains too much during harvest time, the priestesses have to ask the fetishes, which one of them is angry and with what special sacrifices he can be appeased again. However, as far as rain is concerned, a certain rainmaker named Kwadzo has still greater power over it than the fetishes. When Kwadzo has "tied up" the rain, one implores the gods in vain. . . .

Four Years in Ashantee, 1875

FRIEDRICH RAMSEYER AND JOHANNES KÜHNE

Friedrich Ramseyer was founder of the Basel (Prebyster-ian) Church in the Asante capital of Kumase. He and Johannes Kühne were held captive and prisoners in Kumase between 1869 and 1874, eventually prompting a British expedition to Asante in 1873-1874. The following comes from the book coauthored by Ramseyer and Kühne, drawing on their stay in Kumase.

The Government of Ashantee

As it has been easy to perceive by the reading of these pages, that the reins of the Ashantee [Asante] government are not exclusively in the hands of the king, nor does he possess unlimited power, but shares it with a council which includes, besides his majesty, his mother, the three first chiefs of the kingdom, and a few nobles of Kumasi (Coomassie). This council is called "Asante Kotoko," or the Ashantee porcupine, which means that like the animal of that name, nobody dare touch them. The principal drum in Coomassie has as its peculiar strain or motto, *Asante Kotoko, wokum apem, apem reba*, which means "if thousands are killed, thousands are coming up again."

It is this Kotoko council which rules the entire kingdom, and deals with the people, who must obey, whatever their own wishes or inclinations may be, in the most despotic way. In case of war the people have no voice, and to enforce obedience they must be ever under the consciousness that the king and his council are the arbitrators of their life or death. In important matters all the other chiefs of the kingdom are called together to discuss the case, but they are sure to vote in accordance with the view of the council, for who would dare to oppose the Kotoko?

At the Yam festival, usually held in October, all the chiefs of the kingdom meet at Coomassie, and have to report the events of the year in the parts under their jurisdiction. The chiefs belonging to the household of his majesty have in important matters no voice in courts but they have nevertheless great influence, and lose no opportunity of advising the king privately.

In court and in ordinary meetings the king takes his place in his skillfully carved and gold ornamented chair on a kind of platform at the bottom of the court, and over him is held his state umbrella (now in South Kensington Museum), while around him stand some of his sword-bearers and other satellites. On his right and left side are the two state swords, and suspended from each is a large gold nugget. One of these is the war sword. If the king has taken it in his hand, the war is decided.

On the platform near his majesty are seated his mother and the nobles of Coomassie. A little lower down the court, on his right, we find the linguists and some other chiefs, surrounded by under chiefs and servants. On the left are the chiefs belonging to the royal household. In front of his majesty, placed so as to allow a free though narrow passage, are the court criers in great numbers, and lastly the executioners, whose business it is to praise his majesty, "to give him names," as they say, i.e., to cry out his titles, as for instance, *ode tuo tia gyina mpreno ano*—"with a little gun he is standing at the mouth of the canons." *Pambo*—"he sews stones together; he tears and binds together again." *Bore* (the name of a venomous serpent)—"you are most beautiful but your bite is deadly."

According to court etiquette, the speaker has to address himself to the linguists, who place the case before the king in more eloquent language.

If an accused person is brought before the court the linguists have to discuss the case, to find him guilty, and to pronounce the sentence, which, alas! is too often a sentence of death. The king can ratify the judgment or mitigate it, by changing it into a fine, or to the mutilation of any prominent part of the face, but in some cases the king is obliged to give way to the will of his chiefs.

The rank of the chiefs can be seen by the different insignia or emblems of their dignity, which always follow them. The three first dukes of the kingdom have large silk umbrellas topped with gold, a large band of elephant tusk blowers, and several drums. They are also allowed to have sandals ornamented with silver and gold, like those of the king. The duke or king of Dwaben has his own kete-band.

Chiefs of the second rank have silk umbrellas topped with carved wood, and a very nicely carved arm-chair, ornamented on each side with brass nails. They are preceded by a party of about twelve boys, each of whom carries an elephant's tail; they have also horn-blowers and drummers.

The dukes of the third rank have a carved arm-chair, and servants who carry elephants' tails, but their umbrellas are made of cotton. The chiefs of the fourth rank have the same, but in place of elephants' tails their boys carry horse tails.

Those of the fifth rank have a large portly umbrella, but their arm-chair is common and less ornamented. All the principal captains have their special strains or mottoes for their horns and drums. For instance, Amankwatia's drums say, *piridu, piridu*—"go on, push forward." Boakje Tenteng's drums say, *donkofo didi in atom ene sen*, or the *donkos* (negresses from the interior), insult me for what? Bobie's horn has for a motto, *Bobie annae o five agyaman agyaman ne nsam ade wo*—"Bobie keeps watch for the king, there is something in the king's hand . . ."

English Sources

First and Second Voyage, 1555-1556
WILLIAM TOWERSON

*William Towerson was an English merchant and naviga-
tor who made three voyages to the West African coast in
1555, 1556, and 1577, respectively. The excerpts that follow focus on his first and second voyages, wherein he
traded on the Gold Coast and then escaped death during
a Portuguese assault near São Jorge da Mina (Elmina)
in January 1556. His account provides one of the earliest
English descriptions of the Twi (Akan) language.*

While they were at the shoare, there came a young fellow which
could speake a little Portuguise, with three more with him, and to
him I solde 39 basons and two small white sawcers, for three
ounces, &c. which was the best reckoning that we did make of any
basons: and in the forenoone when I was at the shoare, the Master
solde five basons unto the same fellow, for halfe an ounce of golde.

This fellow, as farre as we could perceive, had bene taken into
the [São Jorge da Mina/Elmina] Castle by the Portugales, and was
gotten away from them, for he tolde us that the Portugales were bad
men, and that they made them slaves if they could take them, and
would put yrons upon their legges, and besides he told us, that as
many Frenchmen or English men, as they could take (for he could
name these two very well) they would hang them: he told us furthers
that there were 60 men in the castle, and that every yeere in the cas-

tle of there came thither two shippes, one great, and one small carvell, and further, that Don John had warres with the Portugals, which gave mee the better courage to goe to his towne, which lieth but foure leagues from the Castle, wherehence our men were beaten the last yeere.

This fellowe came aboord our shippe without feare, and as soone as he came, he demaunded, why we had not. The English brought againe their men, which the last yeere we tooke in anno 1554 away, and could tell us that there were five [Africans] taken away by Englishmen: we made him answere, that they were in England well used, and were there kept till they could speake the language, and then they should be brought againe to be a helpe to Englishmen in this Countrey: and then he spoke no more of that matter.

Our boates being come aboord, we wayed and set sayle and a litle after spied a great fire upon the shoare, and by the light of the fire we might discerne a white thing, which they tooke to be the Castle, and for feare of overshooting the towne of Don John we there ankered two leagues off the shoare, for it is hard to fetch up a towne here, if a ship overshoot it. This day we tooke seven pound, and five ounces of golde.

This towne lieth in a great Bay, which is very deepe. The people in this place desired most to have basons and cloth. They would buy some of them also many trifles, as knives, horsetailes, hornes: and some of our men going a shoare, sold a cap, a dagger, a hat, &c.

They shewed us a certain course cloth, which I thinke to be made in France, for it was course wooll, and a small threed, and as thicke as wosted, and striped with stripes of greene, white, yellow &c. Divers of the people did weare about their neckes great beades of glasse of diverse colours. Here also I learned some of their language, as followeth:

Mattea, mattea, [*mate,*	
"I have heard/understood"]	*Is their salutation.*
Dassee, dassee, [*da ase,* "to thank"]	*Thanke you.*
Sheke,[*sika,* "gold, currency"]	*Golde.*
Cowrte,	*Cut.*
Cracca, [?*krakra,* "bar, bolt"]	*Knives.*
Bassina,	*Basons.*
Foco, foco,	*Cloth.*
Molta,	*Much, or great store.*

The eight day in the morning we had sight of the Castle, but by reason of a miste that then fell we could not have the perfect sight of it, till we were almost at the towne of Don John, and then it cleared up, and we saw it and a white house, as it were a Chappell, upon the hill about it: then we hailed into the shoare, within two English miles of Don Johns towne. . . . The towne of Don John is but litle, of about twentie houses, and the most part of the towne is described walled in with a wall of a man's height, made with reede or sedge, or some such thing. . . .

The sixteenth day I went along the shore with two pinnasses of the Frenchmen, and found a Baie [bay] and a fresh river, and after that went to a towne called Hanta, twelve leagues beyond the Cape. At this towne our Negros were well knowen, and the men of the towne wept for joy when they saw them, and demanded of them where Anthonie and Binne had bene; and they told them that they had bene at London in England, and should bee brought home the next voyage. So after this, our Negros came aboord with other Negros which brought a weight with them, which was so small that wee could not give them the halfe of that which they demaunded for it.

The Negros here told us that there were five Portugall shippes at the Castle and one pinnasse, and that the Portugals did much harme to their Countrey, and that they lived in feare of them, and we told them againe, that we would defend them from the Portugals whereof they were very glad. . . . Then wee departed and went to Shamma [Shama], and went into the river with five boates well appointed with men and ordinance, and with our noises of trumpets and drummes, for we thought here to have found some Portugals but there were none: so wee sent our Negros on shore, and after them went divers of us. . . .

The 23 our men came from the king Abaan, and told us, that he had received them very friendly, but he had litle gold, but promised, if we would tary, to send into all his countrey for gold for us, and he willed our men at their comming home to speake to our king to send men and provision into his countrey, to build a castle, and to bring Tailors with them, to make them apparel, and good wares, and they should be sure to sell them: but for that present the Frenchmen had filled them full of cloth. . . .

The Voyage of William Rutter, 1562
WILLIAM RUTTER

William Rutter, another English merchant, made a voyage to the Gold Coast (then also called the "Guinea coast") in 1562. His account, like William Towerson's, was published in Richard Hakluyt's The Principal Navigations, Voyages, Traffiques and Discoveries of the English Nation.

In the afternoone we set saile & came to the town of Don Juan called Equi, where the 22 [of April 1562] in the morning we went a shore to traffike, but the Negros would not untill they had newes from Don Luis, for at that time Don Juan was dead, and the 23 came Don Luis his sonne and Pacheco minding to traffike with us, at which said day came two galies rowing along the shore from the castle, minding to keepe us from our traffike. The 24 we set saile and chased the galies to the castle againe. The Negros being glad of that required us to goe to

Mowre. Mowre [Mori], which is some 3 leagues behind, and

thither would they come for that they stood in feare of the Portugals, and there we remained for the marchants that came out of the countrey which were [to] come with their gold, but Anthonio don Luis his sonne, and Pacheco were aboord the Minion. And the 25 in the morning came the two galies from the castle againe unto us, the weather being very calme, they shot at us and hit us 3 times, and shortly after the wind came from the shore, at which instant we descried the ship, & the caravell comming towards us, then we weighed and set saile, and bare as neere unto them as we could: but it was night or ever wee met with them, and the night being very darke we lost them. The next day plying to the shore, at night we agreed to go with Cormantin [Kormantin], but the next morning being the 28 we were but a litle distant from the great ship and the 2 galies, having no wind at all, and the caravell hard aboord the shore. Then being calme, came the 2 galies rowing to the sterne of the Minion, and fought with her the most part of the forenoone . . .

A Voyage to Guinea, 1735

JOHN ATKINS

John Atkins was an English naval surgeon who, in 1735, published an account of his voyages to West Africa under the title A Voyage to Guinea, Brasil, and the West-Indies. *His account of the Gold Coast describes the nature of transatlantic slaving and several key slaving ports in the region. In the following selection, the original text has been reproduced, except that the character resembling [f] has been replaced by [s] for readability.*

The Gold Coast is the middle and smallest part of the Division, stretching from *Axiem* [Axim] a *Dutch* Settlement, to near the River Volta, an extent of 70 or 80 Leagues [approximately 210 to 240 nautical miles], but of more consequence than the others, in respect to our's and the *Dutch* Company's Forts, who together command the greatest part of it. There is one Danish Fort at *Accra* indeed, (the Leewardmost of our Settlements) but in a decaying State, and will probably (as that of the *Brandenburghers* at *Cape Tres Puntas* [Cape Three Points]) be relinquished in a little time.

Our Company's principal Fort is at Cape Corso [Cape Coast]. That of the *Dutch*, two or three Leagues above, called *Des Minas* or *St. George de Elmina*; each has other little ones up and down this Coast, to gather in the Trade that centers for the respective Companies, at one or other of the aforesaid larger Forts. The *African* Company was erected under the Duke of York in K[ing] Charles II's Time, and therefore Royal; the Epithet being still retained, tho' that Prince's Superstition, and Third after Power, have long since justly banish'd him the Realm.

In it's first flourishing Condition, it was allowed by authentick Accounts to have gained annually to England 900,000£ whereof in Teeth, Camwood, Wax and Gold, was only 100,000 £ and the rest in Slaves; which in the Infancy of their Trade were in very great demand over all the American Plantations to supply their own wants, and carry on a clandestine Commerce with the *Spanish* West-Indies. On Computation, *Barbados* wanted annually 4,000 *Negroes*, Jamaica 10,000, Leeward lslands 6,000; and because the Company ('twas complained by such as wished them ill Success) could not supply this Number, having only imported 46,396 Slaves between the years 1680 and 1688; Interlopers crept in, and contended for a Share; which the *Company* represented as contrary to the Privileges of their Patent, and withal, that the Accusation was groundless and unjust, because they did supply enough for demand, and maintained Forts and Garisons at a great Charge, for a wing and subjecting the Natives to trade, and maintaining an Industry equal to the *Dutch*, without which it was plain to all impartial Considerers, it would be but very difficultly carried on. However, their Adversaries, after some years of grumbling, obtained an Act of Parliament 1697, whereby private Traders for making good this deficiency of Slaves, should have Liberty of Trade, allowing the Company 10 percent, towards defraying their extraordinary Expence. From this time the

Company more visibly decayed, insomuch that in eight following years they only imported to the West-Indies 17,760 Slaves, and the separate Traders in that time 71,268. Their 10 percent, in the first ten years amounted to 87,465 £ and therefore finding their Trade under great disadvantages . . .

Eighteenth-Century Royal African Company Records: Selected Excerpts

The Royal African Company (RAC) of London succeeded the Royal Adventurers, and when its commercial monopoly ended in 1689, English merchants obtained licenses from the company and paid taxes to company officials. In the eighteenth century, at the height of transatlantic slaving, England was the leading slaving nation, and thus the records of the RAC, especially those related to the company's operations out of its major bases on the Gold Coast, are of great value. The following excerpts come from records located in the National Archives of the United Kingdom at Kew.

The Memorandum Book Kept at Cape Coast Castle from 13 January 1703 to 2 January 1704

4 Feb. 1703

A Complaint was brought before the Generall that quashoo a black Carpenter one of ye Company's Slaves had sold his Wife's Son named Braboo on board a 10 P C Ship. The fact was prov[e]d against quashoo & against a woman in the Towne who being sent for declared that Braboo's mother (lately dead) was her Slave & Consequently Braboo & 3 Children more whom she had by Quashoo to whome She was [conceived] by her Mistress, after ye

Death of Braboos father. But some brought a testimony that Braboo himselfe was given for Slave to Quashoo when he [conceived] the mother.

The Generall sent a Letter to ye Comelet of ye Dolphin & a Slave desireing him to Exchange Braboo, who had been sold ye morning after some nicetyes he Consented to ye Exchange & Braboo was brought to ye Generall—upon Inquiry it Appear[e]d that Braboo was sent to Peter Quashooe house the Linguester [ɔkyeame] by the Black Carpenter & the other woman Peter gave him his Cane for a passport & pr[e]tended to send him to a Consort of his who lives at Compoint in the way 4 of Peeters men & some others met Braboo, bound him carr[i]ed him to Compoint & from thence before day light to ye 10 Ct Ship ye Dolphin Capt Besswarver Comdr at an Anchor in this Roade where he was sold for three ounces two Akys in gold. The Generall ordered that Peter Quasho who had received that mon[e]y should bring it to him & a man Slave besides. Such one as was given in Exchange for Braboo and that Peeter Quashoo should bring before him those four men of his who had bound & sold Braboo.

It was ordered further that Braboo who belonging to a Compa[ny] Slave had furthermore been redeemed on this Occasion should remaine one of ye Companys Slaves & that Quashoo ye Carpenter and two daughters of his who were detected should be Confind in the Castle amongst the Slaves. Upon 'eh Quashoo begged pardon, brought his two Daughters to the Generall and one son & desired that they should be received in the number of ye Company's Slaves acknowledging himself and his Children to belong Lawfully to the Company he declared that he had one little Son more, who was at pawn for some money he owed that he would bring him Alsoe— Braboo own[e]d himselfe likewise Willingly & w[i]th returne of thanks to ye Generall to belong to the Compa[ny] to who he own[e]d this present released & desired that he might have ye Entertainment & prerogative of ye Compa[ny] Slaves at Cape Coast.

Jan. 29 [1704]

The C[h]ief Cabbash of Cap[e] Coast w[i]th ye other Cabbashrs
of the towne agreed w[i]th Sr Dalby Thomas Generall: That any
fre[ed]man whom soe ever that shall Consaw (it is their terme for
marrying) any of ye Companys Slaves or Cohabitt wth her shall
thereby become Slave to the Comp[any] he & his Chilldren & likewise if any free woman doth Consaw w[i]th one of the Companys
Slaves she & her Chilldren shall be Slaves to the Company.

Feb. 12

An explanation offered to the Generall that 2 slaves were seized
by a mistake and Sent word ye a Cabbashr of ye mine did owe a
debt to 37. Dey of feetoo [Fetu] Brother whoe Sent his people to
paniard those Slaves thinking they did belong to Some of ye Inhabitants of ye Mine town [of Edina/Elmina] (a Custom they have of
Seizing on Some of ye Same Towne or for ye Debts of any one of
the same place & the freinds of ye person Seized for the Other to
give Sattisfaction & soe are released)

Sept. 1

Ware Sent by the Braffo Fanteen [Fante] two blacks To be [k]ept
heare in Irons for Hindring Traders In the way from Comeing
heather.

Sept. 4

Came two Blacks Sent by John Cobus in Irons to be sent to Bar-
badoes for bringing Disturbance against our Settlement at Suc-
cundee [Sekondi].

Sept. 6

Quow [Kwao the] Canoeman was pawned The 3: of Ins[tance]
By Acrong whose Slave he is to redeem a woman at 6 p Aky and 3
p pts more given him in all 10 ps 3: till that sum be paid in arkany
[Akani] goald he is to work for the Company. . . .

Sept. 9

Abboo Canoeman pawned himself to the Company for two Ounces and 8 Ackys that ware paid to him in purpets.

Sept. 20

The Queen of Fetoo Came & Stayed 8 or 9 Dayes. . . .

Abstract of Letters Received by the Royal African Company of England from the Coast of Africa
Cape Coast Castle, 26th October 1716
Messrs. Gore, Phipps, Blane

Hear the Ackims [Akyeam] have Intercepted the Ashantee [Asante] Traders on a report of their King's Death, w[hi]ch will put a Stop to Trade.

Cape Coast Castle, 30 June 1729
Messrs. Brathwaite & Cruikshakk write

The County of Cuifferoe [Twifo] which is the Key of Ashantee, and the Path by which their Trade is brought to the Waterside, being now in the Hands of Intuifferoe [Twifo], who is under great Obligations to Your Hon[o]rs for the Protection given him in Your Fort, at Succondee [Sekondi], some Years Ago, when he was expelled his Country, by the Ashantee in Acknowledgment whereof, he sent to us one of his Principal Officers with the Jaw Bone of one of his Enemies (according to the Custom of this Country) to Notif[y] his Victory, and Assure us of the Continuance of his Friendship, in Token whereof he sent us down about 60 of his Captives Signifying at the Same Time that he had ordered his Subjects to bring their Trade to us, and had prohibited all Commerce with the Dutch, against whome he is very much incensed. . . .

Commenda [*Komenda*] *Fort Diary, 5 April 1715*

In time of the Cuifferoe wars Bumbo Cudgeo [Kwadwo] a Cuif-feroe man Pawnd his Wife at Elmina & went himself to Akim [Akyem] [when] after the Warr Returning & wanting money to Re-deem her Askd Apeo Cousine to Jn° Cabess [John Kabes] to Lend him some But he not being Able To Advance so much money at that time and Yet willing to Oblige him, Took a Boy formerly given him to keep By a Cuifferoe man at the Beginning of the said Warr, and pawnd him for six pees to a man of Cape Coast called Cansue & therewith Redeem[e]d the said Woman at Elmina. Sometime af-terw[ar]ds Fanee—Sister to Stoockomee being at Cape Coast Saw the Boy & knowing him Gave him to Mr. Phipp to keep in the Cas-tle Lest he might be again Stole or Sold by his Master & being then Sure to Receive him after the pallavers were over—When, the Cuif-feroes Comeing to demand the People as Women & Children &c [when] they had given the Gent[leman] to protect in time of the wars—also demanded this Boy [when] Mr. Phipp in Respect the Boy was a pawn deny'd to Deliver till the money was paid. But the Cuifferoes being very uneasy and Importunate the Gent[leman] Sent to Cabess their Own Boy Intim & Bawffoe a Cuifferoe man Desire-ing his Cusine Appeo to Redeem the Boy [when] he had unjustly pawn'd. But J[oh]n [Kabes] wowd hearken to Nothing and beat them Both out of his Town with contempt [where]upon they Re-turn'd & Told the Gent how he had Treated them & Represented how much all the Cufferoes were affected with the Boys Reined in Iron To q^c the Gent[leman] Answerd they Might Take what Satis-faction of J[oh]n [Kabes]. they Cowld qt was the occasion of the first Difference—After qt Jn. Redeemed & Return'd the Boy but Not till His Mother had Stab[be]d herself for want of her Sone qt is also a pallaver on J[oh]n [Kabes] and the Occasion of the Continu-ance of this. However they have Ended all pallavers and in consid-deration of the Wrong done by J[oh]n [Kabes] he has paid them 4 Bendys qre of part is to be sent to y[e] King of Ashantee for his Trouble therein.

I have seen them take fetish & show Each other all marks of

Friendship and Heard them Renounce all pallavers and Demands on Each other. . . . Note Jn. Cabess at the makeing of this pallaver abundantly show'd by his Equivocations and false pal-lavers, His Unwillingness to compose the Difference & Bent Inclin[ed] to Turbulence & I cou[l]d heartily wish the Cuifferoes were either altogether Rowted or Enjoy'd the peaceable possession of their Countrey for they are at present onely a Scatterd Nation harrassing their Neighbours [when]ever they have opportunity onely Liveing by plunder & Roguery qt will never Do Right where they at present are the Trade of this place being oblig[e]d to pass that way which is scarce ever free of pallavers between that proud Turbulent Nation & J[oh]n Cabess's stiff necked people.

Richard Graves to [Council at Cape Coast],
James Fort Accra, 3 April 1742

It seems Apocho [Opoku] among the rest of the pretences for this Warr with the Ackims [Akyem] says it was to serve the Quomboos [Akwamu] who were drove out of their Country by the Ackims; and he says he will now do all he can to serve the Danes because they Assisted the Quomboos, and now he says that he knows the Dutch were principally concerned in hireing that Warr upon the Quomboos, and that the English were Neuter in it. If these are his Sentiments I don't see that if there doth come any Trade thro' him to this place but we shall have as fair or rather a better Chance than the Dutch (If the place is well supplyed.)

We are pretty sure that Apocho is at Banquendens Croom [*kurom*, "town"] where he hath been some time, and that he hath Dispersed severall parties of his people all about the Ackim, Quomboo and Aroffoo Countrys with Orders to all people that may have taken any Ackims or other people prisoners to keep them for him and that if he hears any of them do sell a Slave that they have Catched since his Defeating the Ackims he will be reimbursed by them, he sent the same Message to Ningo and Tuberkoo two days ago: It is likewise Reported that he will be in the Quomboo Country sometime within the Compass of the next Boon Day which begins to-Morrow.

I am also very well Informed that Darracoon is Dead. I acquainted you in my Letter of the 20th March that he was left by his people with only two Boys with him (to continue it): He Immediately went into a Bush and sent the Boys away, but one of them his Fetish Boy (a Quomboo born) Betrayed him to Popisaa a Quomboo Cabboceer; Popissaa went directly to him and told him he would now make him pay for what his Father had done who was the Chief Instrument of killing the Quomboo Country, Darracoon offered to give him a hundred Bendies of Gold to save his Life and offered to stay with him till the Money came but that would not satisfye him he did not want Money but Revenge and that Instant Struck off his Head: he afterwards would have had the rest of the Cabbooceers to join with him in the Action and I hear he offerred the Head to Cuntoo the King of Acroan but the Cabboceers and Cuntoo refused to have anything to doe with it, as there was not any Money with it their Reasons are that Apocho will require the Head when he hears who hath it and if he finds there is not Money with it he may take it in his head to make the Man in whose possession it is Shorter by the Head.

The Council's Answer to the Return of the Lords of Trade

As to the Chiefs keeping the Paths shut so as to confine the trade, within the Extent of their own Monopoly, it is out of their power to do it even were they ever so inclined which however cannot be Supposed to be the Case, as it is obvious the more Slaves they buy the more Profit they have to refute this Charge we beg Leave to make the following Remarks—It often happens that the Cap[tai]n of a Ship on his Arrival at Annamoboe [Anomabu] barters for One Half or a third of his Cargo to the Chiefs at the different Forts and purchases the Remainder from the Natives; this last part of the Cargo is very often disposed of before the Chiefs have collected a sufficient Number of Slaves to pay for their part, and in such Case they are put to the disagreeable Necessity of borrowing a Number from some other Ship, or what is still more so to the Chiefs when no Slaves are to be borrowed detaining the Ship; some few Instances have been known of this kind, which God knows if only for 2 days causes murmuring enough Now if the Chiefs had it in their Power to shut and open the paths at pleasure, there wou[l]d be no necessity for us to be put to either of those Inconveniences.

Every judicious Master of a Ship or other Persons experienced in this trade, must well know that all the Presents, Messages and intreaties in the World will never prevail on the Fantees [Fante] to let the Shantees [Asante] come down thro' their Country; this has been the sole Bone of Contention, between those 2 Nations for many years past, and from the opinion of many able Men, it appears that should the King of Shantee once find his way to the Waterside, he would make a Conquest of the Fantees and thereby become sole Master of the Whole Country called the Gold Coast, that is to say from Cape Appolonia to the River Volta, a measure that would not only change the Situation of Affairs, but probably be attended with the total Loss of the British Interest in this Country. The mode of carrying on trade between the Fantees and 'Shantees is by establishing Markets at different places, near the Boundaries of their respective territories; here the Several Traders meet, where the 'Shantees exchange their Slaves and other Commodities for European Goods, carried up by the Fantees, and these latter bring them down to the Waterside; while it is the Interest as well as Duty of the Committee's Officers to maintain & encourage an intercourse of this kind, the Publick cannot doubt of its being done; in Justice to the Committee's Servants however we beg Leave to Observe that if any further restrictions are laid on their trade, many Occasional Presents which are now made by themselves must be paid by the Public. . . . Coast money, being unknown among the Blacks, of course they were obliged to be paid in Trade which is the common Currency of the Country.

[J.] Roberts to John Vaughan Esq., Cape Coast Castle,
15 May 1750

[O]n my Arrival there 6th I Conv[e]ned the principal Cabbaceers i.e. the Heads of tow[n]s and the people and found on Examination they were so far Engaged with the Dutch and the Rebellious they

had Joined and had taken Fettish (i.e.) a Ceremoney have Convinc-
ing Each Party of the others friendship and Confirming their Agreements as Sacred Amongst them as the Sacrament is to a European.
. . .

[*J.*] *Roberts to Captain Hill, C.C.C.* [*Cape Coast Castle*],
23 Nov. 1750

The Ahantas are Chagrind at an Alliance Enterd into, which I
have been some time bringing to bear, with Intofferow [Twifo] the
King of Warsaw [Wassa], one of the Most powerfull Men, in Men
and Money upon this part of the Coast, it is Conclud. And his Messengers that were down here to perform Ceremonys the Natives
have when they Contract Engagements with Europeans, dispatched
yesterday, I took the Advantage of a falling out he had with the
Dutch General, who had sold some of his people of the Coast, and
have Enter'd into an Alliance Offensive & Defensive with him, As
I knew him to be an Inveterate Enemy to the Ahantas, who are In-
tirely Devoted to the Service of the Dutch. Ever since the Ahanta
War in Mr. Cope Time, by his Assistance I hope to Increase, Cultivate, Preserve, and Advance Brittish Power, and Authority, Equal,
if not Superior to that of any other Nation.

[*J.*] *Roberts to J. A Hillhouse*

Trade is very bad Owing Chiefly to the Ashantee paths being so
long shut up by the Warsaws, (the former a great and populous
Country, and the Latter a people that have Join[e]d with those of
the Water Side Against the Ashantees) whereby Gold and Teeth are
become Curiosities, and the Number of Slaves so few, buyers so
Numerous, and prices so Exorbitant, that 11 a 12 Oz. of Merchandize will Scarcely purchase a Good Man Slave.

[*J.*] *Roberts to Lord Hallifax, Cape Coast Castle, 28 Sept. 1750*

The former (Trade) was never so totally declin[e]d on the Gold

Coast, as at present, and will be irreparably lost to Windw[ar]d Soon, the first so reduced, by a National Contention between the Warsaw [Wassa] King and Apoco [Opoku] of Ashiante, the former having block[e]d up the trading Paths for near 200 leagues along the Sea Coast, these 10 Years past, whereby, there is scarce a Slave Tooth or Oz of Gold to be bought.

[J.] Roberts to the Dutch General, C. C. C. [Cape Coast Castle], 8 [October] 1750

Sometime past I troubled you with a Message by your boy, relating to a Debt, due from Coffebah a Mulatto Woman, in Elmina town, of Oz 1: 7: 6: To our Castle Bomboy, which the said Coffee-bah has frequently promis'd to Satisfye, but has not yet been so good as her word. Achaio a Negro Woman (Wench to your late Caboceer Amah) allso detains a pawn for a Man Slave, who run away from the Bearer, whom I send to Inform you of the Palavour. As the Woman will neither deliver him the pawn, nor make Satisfaction, I doubt not your doeing him, and our Bomboy (English Subjects) Justice, which will prevent my permitting them, to take such Redress as the Custom of the Coast allows, and I shall always be glad to render any of your Subjects, on the like Occasions, the same Justice.

[J.] Roberts to Dutch General, 14 Nov. [17]50

Ando an English Subject of Commenda [Komenda], who by My Order Attends you herewith, haveing desird he may be permitted to panyar upon Femere a Dutch Subject of Elmina Town, there are more Natives of that Name, but to prevent Mistake, the person Meant, Sojourns with his family at the house of Amayo, and was a Near Relation of Ama, your late linguist decease[e]d. I Refus[e]d him permission to panyere, till I had first Acquainted yr Hour with his Intention as I am Satisfyd you will Interpose with Yr Powr, and Authority to Oblidge the aforesaid Femere to Render Ando the Complainant Such Satisfaction as the justice of his Cause demands, for which End I beg to Lay before your How's the Origin of the Debt, as near Truth as I can learn. In a Certain Season of Warr, some five or six years past, Femere ow'd Oz 1 (?) to the Negro Assano (otherwise Crass) a Dutch boy now at Chama [Shama], and being press[e]d for the money, and not Able to pay it Applys to Ando, to pass his word for the Same, which the said Ando Agreed to, and in Consequence became Answerable from the Same Demand. In process of time (War being Ceasd) Assano the Creditor, Renews his Application (first by desire of Ando) to Femere for the Debt, but meeting no Relief comes on Ando, Upon the Surety ship, who gives them (Assano) otherwise Crass a Slave pawn for the value of his demand, which the said Assano sold off the Coast, whereupon Ando brings his palaver Against Femere, in hopes Yr. Hon will give him Redress, and humbly Submits the Legality of it to Yr. Determination. (Agrees to do the same for the Dutch Genl. should the occasion arise.)

Extracts of a Letter from Thomas Melvil, Chief Agent etc. at Cape Coast Castle to the Committee of the Company of Merchants Trading to Africa

Thomas Melvil to the Committee . . . , Cape Coast Castle, 11 July 1751

The Fantees [Fante] are an avaricious unruly people, live in a manner without Government, and I am afraid if we have a Fort among them we must either be their Slaves, or be eternally at War with them, but this I shall be a better judge of when I have been longer in the Country, every Messenger of John Currantees presses me to begin & build, John offers People to carry Stones & Lime. The true motive of John's Anxiety is this he has by rapen and every Indirect Method raised himself to his present Greatness. he is very old and knows very well that after his Death those who dare not Mutter against him now, will make his Family refund the money he has unjustly taken, and therefore he wants to make a merit with us in Building the Fort which he will expect we are to employ in the Protection of his Family which may be destitute as the Post of Capt.

of Annamaboe [Anomabu] is elective and in all Probability without our Assistance will go into another Family.

Same to same, Cape Coast Castle, 23 July 1751

The Hasiantees [Asante] who are the great Traders on this Coast have not been at the Water Side these 7 Years, upon Account of a Quarrel with Intuffero [Twifo] King of Warsaw, who left his country with all his People, and put himself under the Protection of the Fanteens [Fante]. Many attempts have been made by the English and Dutch to make up this Palaver (or Quarrel) but to no Purpose. In course it now falls to my Lot by the assistance of Cudjoe [Kwadwo] Cabboceer here, who is a faithful Servant, & to whom it is owing that Cape Coast is still ours. I made a beginning. I got him to Propose the thing at a Meeting of the Fantee nation and secretly to Dispatch a Messenger to the Priests of Bura Burum Weiga [Nananom Mpow], who is the God of that Country; utters Oracles and Govern's that otherways licensious People with a more than dispotick Sway. In ten days I am to have the response of the Oracle which if favourable they are to have 20 Goods slave price, by some means or other the Fanteens at Annamaboe [Anomabu] have got Notice of what Cudjo and I have been about (tho' they do not yet know all) and they are continually sending Messengers to me that they will have the Paths open[e]d, and have sent to the Dutch General to declare the same, intending to make a Merit of what, I believe, by the God's assistance we should have done without them.

Same to same. Cape Coast Castle, 14 March 1752

While our Deputies were on Shore at Annamaboe I was trying the Fanteens by another Quarter, I sent a secret Message to their Priests offering 20 to them to make their God declare in our favour. But to my great Mortification had this answer, John Currantee has offered 60 to speak for the French.

Same to same.

The affairs of this Country are at present in such a Situation That I confess I cannot see what will be the result. We are told by some

that this Year that (sic) the Ashantees & Intuffero are either to fight
or make peace. but have had that story every Year. However the
Fanteens are quite tired out & some of the most considerable Cab-
brs. in that country have dispatched secret messengers to the King
of Ashantee to let him know that if he comes to fight they will remain neuter, if so, they will have the Satisfaction to be last devoured.

re Mr. Thomas Thompson an itinerant Missionary from the Society for propagating the Gospel. He finds the Negroes Credenda
not quite so bad as he expected, their Fetich having something in it
analogous to Witchcraft.

Thomas Melvil to the Committee, Cape Coast Castle,
11 March 1753

Re[:] the treaty made with the Fantees.
The proportion of those who have sworn to observe the Law is
to Annamaboe as 20 to 1 accords to the best acc[ount] I could Procure & in the No. is their Legislature. The Braffoe & Curranteers
by & with the advice of their God, whose Oracles they receive from
the priests, are the Fantee Legislature. The Braffoe & Curranteers
never drank fettish (their manner of Swearing) before this to observe
any treaty; at first they refused it to observe the law, but by the
steadiness of Abra & the priests they were obliged to take it.

Same to same, Cape Coast Castle, 14 March 1753
The Accomfees & the Bura Bura Fantees [Borbor Fante] who
recognized our rights on the 6th ulto. were originally the same people, but now they've 2 Braffoes (or Stadt holders) & 2 Sets of Curranteers (or Senators) they are neither under the same circumstances
in point of Union as the Switzers & Grisons, nor as the united
provinces of Holland. I call their Connexion a federal Union for
want of a better expression, tis an Union founded on Manners, Customs, & religion, for they are under the same Subjection to the Father (or God) of Fantee as the Western Fantees are. . . .
The priests of Bura Bura Wergan (i.e., the Father of Fantee) have

sent [h]ere to make a Fetiche in the following manner. To write on a pg. of paper in the English Language these Words, "the practices & designs of the French & J[oh]n Currantee are bad." then the Messenger was order[e]d to carry the paper to the Water side, there to tear it & throw it into the Water. I took this for a Joke, but Cudjo (who is a firm believer in these matters, tho' he does not ch[oo]se to have it thought so) assured me it was not so meant, & therefore takes care to have it performed according to their directions.

A Description of the Castle's Forts and Settlements Belonging to the Royal African Company of England on the Gold Coast

Dixcove
   The Country that runs along the Shore on which this Castle stands is still called the Hantee [Asante] Country, and the Village under its protection is by the Blacks called Infuma, which divides itself into Two, and is distinguished by the great and little Infuma; in both which, and in the Villages dependent immediately upon them, there is Computed to be about two thousand Souls. Its Situation as to Trade was some years past reckoned very Advantageous, (the Country of Warsaw lying not above 3 or 4 days Journey behind it,) and would still have continued so, had not formerly a Quarrel between Apocho King of Asiantee, and Entufero King of Warsaw not only in some measure stop't up the Bath, but Obliged Entufero to remove his Residence to a part of his Country more to the Leeward; which naturally carried with it all the Trade that would otherwise have flowed here. . . . The Cove has heretofore too been famous for producing Lime Stone; but it has of late years been found there in such small Quantities, as would by no means answer the Expence of Procuring and conveying it. The present Chief however has lately been so fortunate as to discover a Cove between 5 and 6 Miles to Windward, which gives him more than a probable Assurance of being able to Load a ship of 200 Ton in 12 Or 14 days; allowing that he is supplied with Slaves, Canoes and other proper Helps for Collecting and Shipping it. Fish is not found here in such abundance as might be expected from so fine a Cove, which possi-

bly gives but little encouragement to the Natives to try for it, as you seldom see above 5 or 6 Canoes out in a Morning.

Commenda [Komenda]

The Situation as to Trade was heretofore, and would still have been very Advantageous, had not the Dutch built a little Fort at Chama (a Village about Ten Miles from hence bearing W. by N.) upon the very Spot where all the Paths divide themselves that communicate the Asiantee Trade to this part of the Coast, which undoubtedly offers to Sale more Slaves than any other Country known to the Europeans: Gold and Teeth: as they are the Produce of Warsaw and Dinkara [Denkyira] (Countries that lie to the Windward) have not so free a passage as to the Forts more immediately in their Way. . . .

They have had to add to the Walls of the fort That it might the better keep under or secure People grown obnoxious to their Neighbours, as well as Troublesome to the Chiefs by their Numbers: Particularly as they have by the Indolence of their Nature no other Employment to keep them from Mischief, but Fishing, which at this place abounds so plentifully, that threescore or Fourscore Canoes are generally every Morning to be seen within a small Compass of the Fort engaged wholly in it.

Tantumquerry

The Number of Inhabitants are Computed at not above 1000 Souls, but of such a turbulent and lawless Disposition as makes it very difficult for the Chiefs to keep them under any tolerable Subjection.

The Situation of this Castle as to Trade when it is not infested with Disputes between the Up-Country and See Coast Natives has always been look't upon to be as good as any of the Leeward Forts; as the Akims [Akyem] constantly bring down their Commodities of Gold and Slaves to a Weekly Market not above 33 Miles from hence, bearing N. by E called Mennan in the Country of Enquina from whence they are conveyed by the Fantyns [Fante], the general Name the Inhabitants of this part of the Coast bear to the Forts by the Waterside, of which this of Tantumquerry is not the least Considerable.

Winenbah [Winneba]

As this is the Market from whence all the Trade is brought that comes to this Fort, it would naturally give it the Advantage, did not the continual disputes of the Natives generally put a stop to it; For these late Years the Inhabitants of Simpa (for so Winne-bah is called by the Natives) have been so embroiled with their Neighbours, that they mutually fear, and of Consequence never venture to have any Intercourse with each other.

Accra

[A]nd certain it is, that when the Natives can agree among themelves, it has always been esteemed the best upon the Coast for Gold and Teeth, Slaves do not come here in such Quantities as to the Forts to Windward, but they are much better[.] The Fishery about here is generally very good, or at least would be so, were not the Inhabitants a too Lazy set of People even to get themselves Provision at the Expence of their own Labour. It is but very lately that they even attempted to plant Corn, in a Country, which undoubtedly promises as well or better than any under the Protection of the more windward Forts: it is true they heretofore employed themselves in making of Salt, for which there was formerly a great demand here, but as that decreast, they were very hardly brought to cultivate their Land for Corn to keep them from Starving, it is even now often so scarce there, that they gladly purchase it with gold, and that too at a Price four times its first Cost.

The little Shade there is in this open Country probably never Tempted any of the Chiefs to Pitch upon a Spot of Ground for a Garden, or at least gave them no Encouragement to keep it up: however there is about 4 of an Acre of Ground staked in, where the Chiefs attempt (tho' I believe in vain) to raise a few greens for their Table . . .

An Account of the Gold Coast of Africa, 1812
HENRY MEREDITH

Henry Meredith, English navigator and governor of the British fort of Winneba on the Gold Coast, died in 1812 after being wounded and killed in a local affair. In the year of his death, Meredith's An Account of the Gold Coast of Africa: With a Brief History of the African Company *was published.*

Government

The government along the coast partakes of various forms. At Apollonia it is monarchical absolute. In the Ahanta country it is a kind of aristocracy. In the Fantee country, and as far as Accra, it is composed of a strange number of forms; in some places it is vested in particular persons, and in other places lodged in the hands of the community. In the Fantee country they very often change their forms of government on certain occasions, and unite, for their general safety, under particular persons, to whom implicit obedience must be paid. When the cause of this union is annulled, they recede into their accustomed form of government.

Laws

The laws of the Gold-coast are particularly strict. At Apollonia, where the whole authority is vested in the king, there are no subordinate tribunals: his power is absolute. In other states, the laws differ according to the nature of the government. During the slave-trade, they all agreed in their ultimate tendency, that of slavery: for a trifling offence a man lost his liberty, if he were incapable of paying a sum adequate to the injury.

Customs

The customs of the Gold-coast are numerous; some of them abound with absurdity. The vile practice of *Panyaring,* a custom attended with the most pernicious consequences, but confined chiefly to the Fantee country, deserves particular notice. If a person became involved in debt, and was, either from the want of ability, or from whatever motive, dilatory in the discharge of its the creditor was at liberty to seize and confine, or, according to their phrase, "panyar," any person or persons belonging to the said family, or even to the same country, state, or town, with the debtor; and if opportunity offered, they were sold, without a delay or ceremony. This destructive practice was carried to such up extent during the slave trade, that many innocent persons were sold. For, besides, the customary mode of proceeding in such cases often offered plausibility or pretext for imaginary debts being contracted, and offences committed. No man had a lawful right to question the justice of the seizure; and every needy person, for the promise of a reward, or a portion of the spoil, might seize and sell without restraint; and very frequently the person, at whose suit panyaring commenced, would retaliate, which never fails to extend it to a ruinous issue.

A practice is rigidly observed every year, and happens in August. It has some similitude to the

custom followed up by the husbandman, when the labor of getting in the harvest is at an end. It is a season of mirth and joyous festivity; it continues for six or eight days, and a cessation from labor is observed during that period.

Antecedent to this festival, when yams are fully gown, they celebrate the occasion by feasting and rejoicing. In general, the natives are particularly, and in some places they are especially interdicted from eating yams, until they arrive at full maturity, which is a most prudent caution, for yams, before they are perfectly ripe, are unwholesome, and even dangerous to be eaten.

On the death of any person, it is an invariable custom to solemnize the event, by a conjunction of condoling and carousing. If the person be of consequence, this custom is observed very extra vag[r]antly. For, not only every branch of the family contribute, but the friends of the dead come forward with something emblematic of the regard they had for the deceased, or respect for the family. Cloth, spirits, and gunpowder are generally lavished on these occasions; and until the body is deposited in the ground, it is a continual scene of dancing, singing (or rather shouting), firing volleys of guns, and, at intervals, lamentable exclamations, that do not betoken much *real* anguish or sorrow. It is necessary to remark, that all this is a customary action that must be followed, and the actors are principally persons employed for the occasion, who have no inward feelings of grief, excepting what sympathy will create. After the interment, and when calmness, we may say, is restored, we then behold real sorrow and affliction, and the habitation of the departed may be appropriately termed the house of mourns big.

There is great attention shown in this country to the dead, and in proportion to rank, family, or the situation the person was in. The body is exposed to public view, decorated with the riches and ornaments of the country, for three or four days, and sometimes six; and when buried, gold, vain able pieces of cloth, and other articles, are put into the grave. In some places human sacrifices take place, and the victims are selected according the rank and quality of the deceased.

In the year 1800, when a king of Apollonia died, one or two human beings were sacrificed every Saturday, until the grand ceremony of making custom took place; which did not happen till six months after his decease. On that occasion, upwards of fifty persons were sacrificed; and two of his youngest wives were put in the grave. The lid of the coffin was covered with human blood, and gold-dust sprinkled upon it, and much gold and rich cloths were deposited the grave. . . .

There is a rigid observance paid to certain days of the week, as it regards a cessation from labor. Tuesdays the fishermen do not cast their nets; Friday is held sacred by some; and men in easy circumstances observe their birth-days.

Polygamy

Polygamy exists on every part of the coast; [a] man is at liberty to have as many wives as he can maintain.

Religion

When we take a view of religion in this part of Africa, we shall find it to consist of a mass of barbarous superstitions, which have been handed down among them from time immemorial; and which they continue to observe, merely on that account.

They have some idea of a Supreme Being; but it is so imperfect and confined, that nothing, pleasing or satisfactory can be extracted from it. They appear to hold the Moon in greater veneration than the Sun, for they welcome her appearance with rejoicing.

Superstition is so firmly planted in this country, and holds its sovereignty so triumphantly in some states, that all the calamities that befall them, are to be ascribed, in a great measure, to the implicit confidence and obedience paid to it. In some places, no act of any consequence will be attempted without first consulting the object of worship, through the medium of a set of cheats and impostors. Their object of worship, no matter what it is, goes by the indefinite term, *Fetish*, and those persons Fetish men or women; for women are considered as capable of concealing the mysteries of their superstition, and expounding the perfections of their Fetish, as the men. Where monarchy does not exist, and where the government is lodged in the people, those persons I assume much consequence, and sometimes arrogate much authority, and employ certain means, which generally carry destruction with them, to secure and enforce their power. If any person offend the Fetish, by either disregard, or by destroying anything appertaining to it, he is not safe, unless the injury be fully requited, or the anger of the Fetish appeased by presents or sacrifices, in proportion to the offense and the circumstances of the offender . . . .

Historical Account of Discoveries and Travels in Africa, 1817

JOHN LEYDEN

John Leyden compiled a work that would later be en-
larged and updated by Hugh Murray after Leyden's death
in 1811. That work was published in two volumes in 1817
under the title Historical Account of Discoveries and
Travels in Africa.

[*The Gold Coast*]

The district of Acra [Accra], which contains Aquapim [Akuapem],
is subject to the king of Aquamboe [Akwamu], whose maritime territory is very inconsiderable, though one of the most powerful
princes on the coast of Guinea. The Aquamboans are a bold martial
race of men, and, like the other Coromantyn [Kormantin] negroes,
as the natives of the Gold Coast are denominated, extremely ad-
dicted to war, in which, from the fluctuating nature of their government, they are continually engaged. Their chief exercises unlimited
despotism, and hence the proverbial saying on the coast, that at
Aquamboe, there are only two classes of men, the royal family and
the slaves. The Aquamboans are formidable to all their neighbours,
though frequently engaged in intestine dissensions. The Acranese
[Akani] formerly composed an independent state, but were conquered by the Aquamboans in 1680, when the greater part of the
nation, with their king, emigrated to Little Popo. . . .

   On the west of Aquamboe lies the powerful state of Akim
[Akyem], sometimes denominated Akam, Achem, and Accany
[Akani], which occupies, almost all the interior of the Gold Coast,
and is supposed by the natives of the coast to extend to Barbary.
Akim, or Accany, was formerly a monarchy, but, being involved ill
domestic factions, its power was diminished, and its government
changed to the republican form. It frequently, however, asserts its
supremacy over the kingdoms on the coast, and the king of Aquam-

boe can only avoid subjection by exciting civil dissensions among the Accanese. The Accanese are represented as carrying on an extensive commerce with the interior kingdoms of Africa, particularly Tonouwah, Gago, and *Meczara*, by which Muzzouk . . . seems to be intended. They are a bold intrepid nation, much esteemed as well as feared by their neighbours, for their honesty and fair dealing in commerce. The northern border of Akim extends to Tonouwah [located north of Asante], denominated also Inta [Gonja], Assiente [Asante], or Assentai, from the capital city of that name, which stands about eighteen days' journey from the Gold Coast. The inhabitants of this city are reported, by Mr. Norris, to have often attempted, without success, to open a communication with the coast through the territories of the Fantees and their confederates. The different nations of the Gold Coast resemble the negroes of Acra and Aquamboe in their manners, customs, and religious opinions. They all believe in one supreme God, the creator and preserver of all things. But in order to fix their ideas, they require some definite figure, and generally invest him with the human form, as the most perfect. To believe in a being devoid of form, seems to the negro a belief in nothing, for is only test of the truth of an idea, is the liveliness of his conception. To this supreme being prayers are often offered, when his worshippers turn their faces towards the sun, as the most glorious emblem of his majesty . . .

Mission from Cape Coast Castle to Ashantee, 1819
THOMAS E. BOWDICH

Thomas Edward Bowdich was born in Bristol in 1791. The son a merchant, Bowdich joined the African Company of Merchants (ACM), which replaced the Royal African Company in 1752, and headed to Cape Coast in 1814 under the auspices of his uncle, John Hope Smith, Governor-in-Chief of the settlements of the ACM. In 1817, Bowdich conducted his mission to Asante "for the

*purpose of establishing the trade with that kingdom."
Two years later, he published his* Mission from Cape
Coast Castle to Ashantee; *he and his wife then went to
Paris for three and a half years "devot[ing] himself to
study, with the view of preparing himself for another voy-
age to Africa." After publishing several pamphlets and
works on natural history, Bowdich set out for Sierra
Leone and in this pursuit he lost his life in January 1824.
Before his death, he had stopped in Lisbon to investigate
public and private archives on the early history of the
Gold Coast and had hoped to be of service to the British
governor on the Gold Coast. Bowdich's daughter, Tedlie
Hutchison Hale, whose name comes from the men who
accompanied Bowdich on his mission to Asante—Mr.
Tedlie and Mr. Hutchison—edited the 1873 edition of
Bowdich's* Mission.

[*Asante History*]

To speak of the death of a former King, the Ashantees imagine to
affect the life of the present equally with inquiring who would be
his successor; and superstition and policy strengthening this impression, it is made capital by the law to converse either of the one or
the other. The inability of the natives to compute time, and the comparatively recent establishment of the Moors, may be pleaded as
additional apologies for the imperfect history I have collected.

According to a common tradition, which I never heard contra-
dicted but once, the Ashantees emigrated from a country nearer the
water-side, and subjecting the western Intas [Gonja], and two lesser
powers, founded the present kingdom. These people being comparatively advanced in several arts, the Ashantees necessarily adopted
a portion of their language with the various novelties; which probably created the limited radical difference between their language
and that of the Fantees; for I could not find, after taking the greatest
pains, more than 200 words unknown to the latter. The weights of

the Inta country, in particular, were adopted with their names, by the conquerors, without the least alteration.

The tradition, scanty in itself, is very cautiously adverted to, the Government politically undermining every monument which perpetuates their intrusion, or records the distinct origins of their subjects: but, from the little I could collect, it appeared to have been an emigration of numerous enterprising or discontented families, to whom the parent state afterwards became subject. I am inclined to think (the account of their coming from a country nearer the sea being too general for conjecture to revolt from) that they emigrated from the eastward of south, where the territory admitted to be Ashantee Proper is remote, compared with its extent southward, or westward of south, and the former consequence of Doompassie, and the towns eastward of it, support this: yet the very few natives who pretended to any opinion on the subject, had an impression that their ancestors emigrated from the neighborhood of a small river, Asinshue, behind Winnebah: a croom ["town"] called Coomadie is to be found there, but there is nothing else to countenance the report.

The Ashantee, Fantee, Warsaw, Akim, Assin, and Aquapim languages are indisputably dialects of the same root; their identity is even more striking than that of the dialects of the ancient Greek. Now the Fantees and Warsaws both cherish a tradition, which exists also in many Ahanta families, that they were pressed from the interior to the water-side by the successful ambition of a remote power; whence it may be concluded, that the Ashantee emigration we are now considering, was posterior to a more important movement of the whole people, corresponding with that of their neighbors. I will not dilate upon this secondary subject by referring to internal evidence; there is nothing to recompense either the investigation or the perusal.

One curious evidence, however, may be added of the former identity of the Ashantee, Warsaw, Fantee, Akim, Assin, Aquamboe, and part of the Ahanta nations; which is a tradition that the whole of these people were originally comprehended in twelve tribes or families; the Aquonna [Ekoɔna,] Abrootoo [Bretuo], Abbradi [Abradie], Essonna [Asona], Annona [Anona], Yoko [Oyoko],

Intchwa [Aduana], Abadie, Appiadie, Tchweedam [Twidan], Agoona [Agona], and Doomina; in which they class themselves still, without any regard to national distinction. For instance, Ashantees, Warsaws, Akims, Ahantas, or men of any of the nations before mentioned, will severally declare that they belong to the Annona family; other individuals of the different countries, that they are of the Tchweedam family; and when this is announced on meeting, they salute each other as brothers. The King of Ashantee is of the Annona family, so was our Accra and one of the Fantee linguists; Amanquatea is of the Essonna family. The Aquonna, Essonna, Intchwa, and Tchweedam, are the four patriarchal families, and preside over the intermediate ones, which are considered as the younger branches. I have taken some pains to acquire the etymology of these words, but with imperfect success; it requires much labor and patience, both to make a native comprehend, and to be comprehended by him. Quonna is a buffalo, an animal forbade to be eaten by that family. Abrootoo signifies a corn stalk, and Abbradi a plantain. Annona is a parrot, but it is also said to be a characteristic of forbearance and patience. Esso is a bush cat, forbidden food to that family. Yoko is the red earth used to paint the lower parts of the houses in the interior. Intchwa is a dog, much relished by native epicures, and therefore a serious privation. Appiadie signifies a servant race. Etchwee is a panther, frequently eaten in the interior, and therefore not unnecessarily forbidden. Agoona signifies a place where palm oil is collected. These are all the etymologies in which the natives agree.

Regarding these families as primeval institutions, I leave the subject to the conjectures of others, merely submitting that the four patriarchal families, the buffalo, the bush cat, the panther, and the dog, appear to record the first race of men living on hunting; the dog family, probably, first training that animal to assist in the chase. The introduction of planting and agriculture seems marked in the age of their immediate descendants, the corn stalk and plantain branches. The origin and improvement of architecture in the red earth; and of commerce, probably, in the palm oil; indeed, the natives have included the Portuguese, the first foreign traders they knew in that family, alleging that their long and more intimate intercourse with the blacks has made the present race a mixture of the African and Portuguese. The servant race reminds us of the curse of Canaan. This resembles a Jewish institution, but the people of Accra alone practice circumcision, and they speak a language, as will be shown, radically distinct, yet not to be assimilated to the Inta, to which nation they are referred by the Fantees, merely because it is the nearest which practices circumcision. Accra is a European corruption of the word Inkran [Nkrãn]; which means an ant, and they say the name was either given or assumed on account of their numbers; this must have been before their wars with the Aquamboes.

When Adokoo, chief of the Braffoes, a Fantee nation, consulted the venerable fetish men of the sanctuary, near Soopreooroo, on the Ashantee war, they answered that nothing could be more offensive to the fetish than the Fantees preventing the peaceable intercourse of their inland neighbors with the water-side, because they were formerly all one family.

The conduct of the later emigration of the Ashantees is ascribed to Sai Tootoo [Osei Tutu], who, assisted by other leading men of the party, and encouraged by superstitious omens, founded Coomassie [Kumase], and was presented with the stool, or made King, from his superior qualifications. This account is supported by the mixed nature of the government, founded on equality and obligation, and the existence of a law, exempting the direct descendants of any of Sai Tootoo's peers and assistants (in whom the Aristocracy originated) from capital punishment.

The Dwabin monarchy is said to have been founded at the same time by Boitinne, who was of the same family as Sai Tootoo, being the sons of sisters. Boitinne and his party took possession of Dwabin [Dwaben], the largest of the aboriginal towns (leaving Sai Tootoo to build Coomassie), whence it seems his followers were the more powerful; indeed, I have heard it confessed by a few Ashantees, that Dwabin had formerly the pre-eminence, though they have always been firm allies in war, and equal sharers in spoil and conquest. This common interest, preserved uninterrupted more than a century by two rising powers close to each other, with the view of a more rapid

aggrandizement, and their firm discretion in making many [a] serious disagreements subservient to the policy, is one of the few circumstances worth considering in history composed of wars and
successions. I do not think there is such an instance in our heptarchy,
nor do I recollect any other in history, but that of Chalcis and Eretria
. . .

A Voyage to Africa, 1821
WILLIAMS HUTTON

*Following Thomas Bowdich's visit to the Asante capital
of Kumase in 1817, Williams Hutton accompanied
Joseph Dupuis as part of the British government's mission to Asante in 1820, though Hutton stayed in Kumase
some months after Dupuis departed. Hutton would publish his* A Voyage to Africa *in 1821. The excerpts that follow come from this account.*

[*Indigenous Spirituality and Islam in Asante*]

The natives in this part of Africa are Pagans. It is true they have
fetish men or priests [*akɔmfoɔ*], but these ignorant wretches do more
harm than good, frequently practicing the most shameful excesses
upon their still more ignorant and superstitious followers, who are
silly enough to have faith in what these priests profess. They appear,
however, to have some idea of a Supreme Being, whom they call
Yaung Coompon [Onyankopɔn]; and when they hear thunder they
will sometimes remark, that it is Yaung Coompon riding in his carriage. Their usual method of offering sacrifices is to break eggs, and
leave them on the ground, which they consecrate to the Fetish; some
tie a piece of string round a stone, and leave it on the public path;
others cut out a small wooden image and fasten it to their doors,

which they daily worship; and having, on one occasion, inadvertently kicked one of these wooden gods before me, the fetish man demanded a penalty of a bottle of rum for having done so, which he said was necessary to appease the Fetish; but, as I considered it would only encourage these Fetish-men to practice similar impositions upon others, I would not pay the demand, which appeared to give great offence. They have no regular mosques, but little places are erected, sometimes with mud, but more frequently with sticks and leaves, in the form of a small arbor, where they leave eggs, stones, and earthen pots; and in supplicating the Sooman [*asuman*, "talismans"], they make a most dismal noise, calling out upon their father (Majeh [*m'agya*, "my father"]), or their mother (Minnah [*me na*, "my mother"]). . . .

The Ashantees, like the Dahomyans, dare not speak of the death of a former king, or of the person likely to succeed to the throne, on pain of death; consequently, it is not very easy to trace their history. But according to common tradition, they emigrated from near the waterside, and subjecting the western Intas and two other powers, founded the present monarchy. The language of the Ashantees and Fantees is nearly the same, which leaves room for the hypothesis, that they were originally one and the same nation, although in one particular, they have not the most distant resemblance to each other; and that is, in warlike skill and determined courage, for which the Ashantees are remarkable; while the opposite traits are well-known characteristics of the Fantees. . . .

The Moors [Muslims] have hitherto exercised the greatest influence at Ashantee, and a few lines written by Baba, the chief of the Moors at Coomassie, is believed to possess the power of turning aside the balls of the enemy in battle, and is purchased at an enormous price; writing paper is consequently very valuable at Ashantee. Mr. Dupuis gave Baba several quires, which highly pleased him. I have said that the Moors have hitherto possessed the greatest influence; it is therefore proper I should explain why they do not still possess this influence to so great an extent as they formerly did. In the late battle between the Ashantees and Buntakoos [Bonduku], when the balls were flying about rather briskly, Baba skulked out of the battle, and was not to be found until it was over; when, it is said, the king reproached him thus: —"How can you expect that I can have faith in your fetish, if you are afraid of the balls yourself?" Since that period Baba and his companions have lost much of their influence, and it was a long time before the king would be friends with him. Indeed, during my stay at Coomassie, I could not perceive they had half the influence which I should have supposed they had, from reading Mr. Bowdich's work. Doubtless, however, they still possess influence to a certain extent; but I never observed them present at any of our meetings, except on public occasions, when they attended with the rest of the people.

Time, and a more intimate acquaintance with Europeans, will, no doubt, convince the Ashantees of their folly in believing the mystical absurdities of the Moors. Two of their inferior priests accompanied Prince Adoom on his embassy to Cape Coast, where they lived at my house for some time; and the gross falsehoods they frequently told me will appear from the following. When I asked them if the path to Coomassie was in good order, they immediately assured me it was a fine broad path well cleared! To an enquiry respecting the houses at the capital, they said I should find them much superior to that which I occupied at Cape Coast! And on asking them if I should be able to get a horse to ride at Coomassie, they replied, certainly, that their chief (Baba) would make me a present of one; when it will be seen elsewhere, that on Mr. Dupuis applying to Baba, he had not one belonging to him even to lend us! The reason for these people telling such falsehoods, it is difficult to imagine, except that they are so habituated to lying, that they seldom speak the truth. They visited us several times at Coomassie, but Mr. Dupuis generally communicated with them alone . . .

Eighteen Years on the Gold Coast of Africa, 1853
BRODIE CRUICKSHANK

Brodie Cruickshank was a member of the local Legislative Council and then lieutentant-governor on the British-controlled Gold Coast. His years spent on the coast were chronicled in this two-volume book, Eighteen Years on the Gold Coast of West Africa, *published in 1853.*

[*Spiritual Culture and Its Reach into Daily Life*]

We shall now, however, attempt to describe the nature of this superstition, which exercises such an illimitable influence over the minds of the masses of the population. An analysis of this description is beset with no ordinary difficulties. We derive little assistance in our investigations from the ideas of the idolaters themselves, which are extremely vague and indefinite, and we are still farther puzzled to discriminate between such impressions, as may be the result of an effort of their own reason, or the consequence of their fears, and such as without the knowledge of the existing generation may have been derived from a more enlightened people, and handed down to them as a portion of the creed of their forefathers. There is great room to believe that the idea of one great first cause, the Creator of all things, has prevailed among them from time immemorial; for the Fantee words Yankompon [Onyankopɔn]. . . by which they designate God, would seem to indicate that the idea of a benevolent Creator was coeval with the language; but there can also be little doubt that indefinite as this idea even now is, in their minds, it must have received its confirmation from an intercourse of more than three hundred and fifty years with Europeans, whose acknowledgment of one God must soon have become universally known. Even before their intercourse with Europeans, it is possible that this great truth might have been disseminated by the Mohammedan population of the interior. Be this as it may, the natives of the Gold Coast generally acknowledge the existence of a Supreme Being, who made and governs the world, but they cannot be said to worship him. They sometimes invoke his name, and call upon him to bless those whom they love, and much more frequently to curse those whom they hate. . . .

When oppressed with afflictions and over-whelmed by any great calamity, for a release from which they have sacrificed to their idols in vain, we find them resigning themselves submissively to their fate, with the exclamation that "they are in God's hands, and he will do whatever he thinks best." But they neither offer sacrifices to him, nor do they think of seeking by supplication to avert what (if their idols fail them) they seem inclined to regard as their inevitable destiny. To this extent, then, we may regard them as predestinations, acknowledging one Supreme Governor of the world, who has appointed all things according to his pleasure, and to whom it were in vain for man to appeal with any hope of changing his immutable decrees. They believe, however, that this Supreme Being, in compassion to the human race, has bestowed upon a variety of objects, animate and inanimate, the attributes of Deity, and that he directs every individual man in his choice of his object of worship. . . . From the moment that he has made his choice, he has recourse to this god of his in all his troubles. He makes oblations to it of rum and palm wine; he lays offerings before it of oil and corn; he sacrifices to it fowls and goats and sheep, and smears it with their blood; and, as he performs these rites, he prays it to be propitious to him, and to grant him the accomplishment of his petition. . . .

The character of the Gold Coast African, the nature of his government, his ideas of justice and its administration, his domestic and his social relations, his crimes and his virtues, are all more or less influenced by, and even formed upon their peculiar superstition. There is scarcely an occurrence of life into which this all-pervading element does not enter. It gives fruitfulness to marriage; it encircles the newly-born babe with its defensive charms; it preserves it from sickness by its votive offerings; it restores it to health by its bleeding sacrifices; it watches over its boyhood by its ceremonial rites; it gives strength and courage to its manhood by its warlike symbols; it tends its declining age with its consecrated potions; it smoothes its dying pillow by its delusive observances; and it purchases a requiem for its disembodied spirit by its copious libations. It fills the fisherman's net; it ripens the husbandman's corn; it gives success to the trader's adventure; it protects the traveler by sea and by land; it accompanies the warrior, and shields him in the battle; it stays the raging pestilence; it bends heaven to its will, and refreshes the earth with rain; it enters the heart of the liar, the thief, and the murderer, and makes the lying tongue to falter, quenches the eye of passion, withholds the covetous hand, and stays the uplifted knife, or it convicts them of their crimes, and reveals them to the world; it even casts its spells over malignant demons, and turns them for good or for ill, according to its pleasure. It might be supposed that a religion with pretensions of this nature could not stand the test of a single week, and that no ingenuity of the Fetishmen could conceal the multitude of their broken pledges, or save from exposure the hollow tricks by which they manage to prop up their tottering faith. That a race of men, who are by no means devoid of intelligence, and who upon many other subjects are perfectly open to reason and to conviction, should continue, time after time, the dupes of such a childish infatuation, can only be accounted for by man's innate consciousness of the helpless nature of his being, and his necessity for supernatural assistance; his need, in short, for some faith in things unseen, on which to rest the anxious burden of his hopes and fears. . . .

We have now taken a general view of the people and of their superstitious belief, and would desire to place before the reader some account of their ordinary habits of life; but this we find impossible, without being obliged to recur, at every step, to their Fetish practices, so much are they incorporated with the every-day occupations and pleasures of the African. It is to be lamented that the heathen should, in this respect, exhibit a more constant; steadfast and pious dependence upon his idols than the Christian does upon God, and that man, relieved from his superstitious fears, should so often subside into indifference with but few indications of a reverential and grateful heart. It is rare for them to omit, morning and evening, to make some oblation to their Fetish, or to pay their homage when they eat or drink. They undertake nothing even of ordinary importance, without raising their thoughts to an unseen intelligence, and propitiating it by some observance, while humble thank-offerings invariably attend its successful issue. If they were content to confine themselves to this humble and thankful dependence, we might regret their ignorance of the true object of worship, while we applauded the spirit which dictated it; but, un-fortunately, their belief in a multiplicity of deities leads to the idea of a variety of discordant attributes, which render necessary a multitude of observances. Their vague ideas of a future state of rewards and punishments, amounting practically to a disbelief of such a state, limit the operation of their spiritual instincts chiefly to the circumstances of their present existence; which are all more or less influenced by them.

War is never undertaken by kings or states without consulting the national deities. The Fetishmen "go up to inquire" of their idols, after sacrifice being made, and unless the response be propitious, they will not engage in it. Renewed offerings and sacrifices are made to obtain the favor and assistance of their gods, and a promise of success. This once secured, they meet their enemies with confidence, relying as much upon the protection of their gods as their own bravery. After victory, the glory of which belongs to the Fetish, they propitiate a continuance of his favor by sacrificing many of the prisoners taken in war. These are considered especially grateful to their tutelary gods [abosom]. This idea seems to arise from the belief that, in international wars, the protecting deities of one nation are contending against those of the other, and are equally interested in the result of the warfare with the mortal combatants.

Fetishmen accompany the warriors to the field, and urge them to deeds of daring and bravery by the promise of supernatural aid, and by the invocations which they never cease to make. Their captive enemies are consequently regarded as the enemies of the victor's Fetish, and no sacrifice is so acceptable as their blood. Hence those wholesale slaughters of vanquished enemies which attend the victories of the kings of Ashantee and Dahomey, proceed not so much from the blood-thirsty disposition of the African, as from a religious sense of duty to their gods. Want of success is sometimes, but not always attributed to the inferiority of the gods of the vanquished. The Fetishmen do not easily give up their defense, and frequently manage to convince the conquered that their failure is owing to their displeasure, for the omission of some observances, for national impiety, or for inattention to prescribed ceremonies. After the conquest of Fantee by Sai Tootoo Quamino [Osei Tutu Kwamena] in 1807, the faith of the Fantees was considerably shaken in the Braffo Fetish Mankassim, which, up to this time, enjoyed an extraordinary share of national favor. The Fetishmen, however, had always been averse to the war, and they now took occasion of this known aversion to excuse their defeat, and the worshippers were soon brought back to its altars. It is worthy of remark, that although the Ashantees destroyed Mankassim, they had respect to the Fetish grove [i.e., Nananom Mpow] in its immediate neighborhood . . .

Nine Years on the Gold Coast, 1898
DENNIS KEMP

Dennis Kemp was ordained in 1887 and then volunteered for missionary work on the Gold Coast. Six years later, he was appointed military chaplain to the "Ashanti Expedition." He would return to England in 1897 and publish an account of his experiences entitled Nine Years on the Gold Coast *in 1898.*

[*Language and Christian Proselyzation*]

A translation committee was formed, whose duty it was to revise the translations of the various books by ministers and laymen of the district. The publication of Genesis and the four Gospels by the British and Foreign Bible Society, whose generous aid is beyond all words, was also accomplished. In his work Mr. Cannell was aided by the suggestions and hearty cooperation of the Reverends Andrew W. Parker and Jacob B. Anaman, native ministers, whose experience was simply indispensable. It may here be mentioned that in recent years the work of revising the translations of the whole Bible has been entrusted to Mr. Parker. The whole of the New Testament has been published, and the Old Testament is rapidly approaching completion.

One feels bound to explain that the reason that so little attention had previously been paid to this all-important branch of mission work arose from the mistaken idea of earlier missionaries that the English language would supersede the vernacular. It is quite true that our language is making enormous headway, that it is, indeed, the "Court" language of the whole Coast, and the anxiety of the young people to acquire a knowledge of it can be abundantly attested but millions in the interior of the Colony will pass away without ever having uttered a word of it.

We cannot speak too highly of the forethought of the devoted, self-sacrificing German missionaries in being far ahead of us in vernacular publications. But, unfortunately, their principal work has been carried on in a neighborhood where a composite language is spoken, so that their Twi translations are about as serviceable for general circulation among the Akan speaking tribes as would a composite translation of three distinct dialects of this country be for general circulation in England. . . .

[*Views on Gold Coast Societies*]

Among our Gold Coast people there are distinctions greater than those which wealth can create. We have the unsophisticated bush man, and the coast man; the illiterate, and the scholar. The difference between the bushman and the coaster is almost as great as is the difference between our own Hodge and the town dandy. The bushman still retains "the primeval simplicity of his manners." He regards the white man as a living wonder, rivaled only by the horse, each being equally rare. He is most courtly in his welcome. His garb is simply a native cloth, like the Roman toga, thrown over the left shoulder, and hanging in folds down to his knees, or rolled round his waist.

During a heavy downpour of rain the cloth is carefully folded up, and the owner indulges in a delicious shower bath. On such occasions, our friend, not being over conventional, cares little whether the fig leaf is worn round his waist or is growing on a tree miles away. He is convinced that Nature's garb is sufficient for Nature's gentlemen.

His town brother is poles removed from him. In many instances he has, through the enterprise of the merchant, and the encouragement of the Government, adopted European dress: this touches what to some is a sore spot. For my own part I am supremely indifferent in the matter of native dress, provided that due regard is paid to decency. It is true that there is an air of stateliness in the toga of the native; but it certainly was not designed with a view to ease and comfort when performing manual labor. It is equally true that educated natives, who avoid excesses in the matter of style, find European clothing as suitable as do Europeans themselves. But there is great tendency to carry the fashion to absurd lengths the tall silk hat, high collar, patent leather shoes, must be as uncomfortable to the aristocrat, as the gorgeous Christy-minstrel attire of the humbler classes is grotesque. The coast gentleman usually requires the services of a boy to carry even the smallest parcel; a great number of retainers denotes importance.

Reference must be made to African royalty. Our ideas of English royalty account for much misconception respecting African potentates. It will prove a great shock to those who have spoken with bated breath of West African princes to be told that some of us have engaged gentlemen bearing royal titles as bricklayers' laborers at wages of nine pence a day. Much misconception concerning English royalty is also observed among our Gold Coast natives. It was once reported at Cape Coast in perfectly good faith that the Prince—when in England—was in the habit of calling every week to have a chat with Queen Victoria. But, unfortunately, the Governor of the Colony happened to tell the Queen that Prince was "no good!" So the next time that gentleman called at the Queen's house, her Majesty "shut the door in his face!"

Other distinctions are the "illiterate" and the "scholar." The former needs no explanation; but with regard to the latter it must be pointed out that our friend does not necessarily come within the category of divines and scientists of our own country. The "scholar" of the Gold Coast may have spent only sufficient time at school to enable him to write a misspelt letter, but still he is known by the title.

And yet another distinction must be named—the "lady" and the "woman." "My wife is a lady!" Oh, indeed! What is the difference between a woman and a lady? "The lady wears a European dress, the woman only wears cloth!" "Ladies," at least when in their advanced dress, do not perform all the menial duties that their less favored sisters do. But generally speaking the gentler sex are industrious. Long before daybreak they may be heard grinding corn or beating *fufu*, or sweeping the . . . yard in order to be ready to go to the farm to prepare produce, or to the market to barter it. Very frequently they may be seen with fifty or sixty pounds weight of oil or rubber on their heads, and a babe on their backs, trudging uncomplainingly to town. I have seen a woman removing sacks of palm kernels weighing one hundred and forty pounds from warehouse to sea-shore. It is needless to say the poor soul required the assistance of another woman and man to enable her to lift the load to her head.

As a rule the women are cheerful and neighborly; although often painfully shy in the company of white men, they are usually thoughtful and kind. There is a pensiveness on the face when not excited, often passing to a languor and listlessness, which might suggest oppression had we not the conviction that they are resigned to their inferior position. They are possessed of excitable dispositions, and are most demonstrative in affection and sorrow, and turbulent in dispute. Although hasty in speech and gesture, they are patient in suffering, and heroically struggle against disease. . . .

[Fante History]

As we regard it our duty to teach our people to "honor the king," I called upon his Majesty of Mankessim. From him I gathered traditiona[l] information respecting the history of his people. I think I may venture to repeat it, for it was given in the presence of the principal officers of state, and was confirmed by sundry grunts of approval on all sides. "Mankessim is the oldest Fanti kingdom. When the Fantis came from Takyiman they halted in that neighborhood preparatory to branching out in various directions and forming minor kingdoms. The great yearly council, however, was held at Mankessim, whose king naturally presided. At these gatherings matters affecting the whole Fanti community were considered. Criminals under sentence of death were taken to the old capital, and were executed by spear, or knife, or gun. Occasionally victims for sacrifice were buried alive. When the Fantis paid their visit to the place they acknowledged as their chief idol one which was known as Nanaam [Nananom Mpow]." It was interesting to note what the stately old king Kweku Mbill said concerning the superstition of his ancestors, and his thankfulness that the Gospel light was penetrating the dark places of his kingdom . . .

The Works of Robert S. Rattray:
Selected Excerpts, 1921-1927

Robert Sutherland Rattray was born in 1881. In 1906 he joined the customs service of the West African colony of the Gold Coast and between 1914 and 1929 studied anthropology and law, while serving as assistant district commissioner in Ejura, captain in the Gold Coast regiment, assistant colonial secretary and clerk to the legislative assembly, and special commissioner and the first "government anthropologist" of Asante. He retired from colonial service in 1928, a year before he published his Ashanti Law and Constitution, *which provided a blueprint for British "indirect rule" on the Gold Coast, and a decade before he died.*

Account of a Wednesday Adae, 10 May 1921

This ceremony was witnessed at Tekiman [Takyiman], a town some seven days' journey, on foot, northwest of Coomassie [Kumase] and situated in the Brong country of Northern Ashanti [Asante]. The Brong [Bono] are, in my opinion, undoubtedly a branch of the Akan stock, to which the Ashanti and the Fanti [Fante] belong. They will be proved, I believe, upon further investigation, to be either the residue of a single migration from the north-west (the remainder of whom passed on southward, becoming the Ashanti proper) or just possibly a later migration of the same people, coming from the same direction as the first, all being driven-by causes at which we can now only guess-from the open lands of the north into the dense forest region that now lies between the fringe of the Sahara and the sea.

The Fanti again, I consider, are either a much later migration of these Brong—who passed round or through the earlier migration which had remained in Ashanti proper—and settled near the coast and became Fanti; or—more likely still—they are a branch of the first migration which peopled Ashanti, passed on to the coast, and severed connexion with their kinsmen. Much later, and almost within historical times, they were joined by a second wave of their people; of this we have an authentic record both in Fanti traditions and in those of the northern Brong. The Brong were later conquered by the Ashanti and became vassals of the great Ashanti Confederacy. I have prefaced the account of the custom, now to be described, by this very brief note, because I wish to make it clear that I consider the similarity in Brong customs and language to those of Ashanti, is not due to their conquest by the latter, but rather to the fact that these peoples sprang from a common stock. If this view is correct, then Northern Ashanti, hitherto untouched by the anthropologist and hardly opened up to the European, should be the ideal ground upon which to study Akan customs and beliefs. The Wednesday Adae, called, as we have seen, Wukudae or Kupadakuo in Ashanti proper, is, though also known by these names among the Brong, generally called by them Muruwukuo. The Brong do not appear to celebrate any Sunday Adae. The day before their Wednesday Adae they call Adapa, as in Southern Ashanti.

The Muruwukuo falls upon the same Wednesday as a Wukudae falls in Ashanti proper—a particularly suggestive fact—and it falls once every forty-two days. I had often noticed this commonly recurrent cycle, or forty-two-day divisions of time. The Ashanti call this period *adaduanan*, lit. forty days. One day I overheard one of my men saying that in olden times, when the King of Ashanti was in doubt as to any date for a festival, he always referred to the Brong, who were the keepers of the king's calendar, so to speak. This led me to ask about it, when I discovered that time was reckoned in periods of forty-two-day cycles, every day of which had a particular name, each day in this period coming round again forty-two days later. The following are the names of each of these forty-two days. It will be noticed that they consist of the commonly used Ashanti names for each of the seven days of the week, with a prefix. This in each case drops back one day each week, becoming prefixed to the name of the day immediately before that day to which it applied the previous week. I have not yet been able to discover just what these prefixes mean, except in one case, the prefix *fo*, which may be translated "festival" or "holy" or "lucky."

Commencing our cycle with a *foda* (a holy day), say with a *fo*-Monday, and running through the whole cycle, we have (in each case the first syllable is the prefix, and the second the ordinary Ashanti name for that day of the week):

1. Fo-dwo = Fo-Monday.
2. Nwuna-bena = Nwuna-Tuesday.
3. Nkyi-wukuo = Nkyi-Wednesday.
4. Kuru-yao = Kuru-Thursday.
5. Kwa-fie = Kwa-Friday.

6. Mono-mene = Mono-Saturday.

7. Fo-kwesi = Fo-Sunday.

(Each of the prefixes, it will be noted, now falls back one day)

8. Nwuna-dwo = Nwuna-Monday.

9. Nkyi-bena = Nkyi- Tuesday.

10. Kuru-wukuo =Kuru-Wednesday.

11. Kwa-yao = Kwa-Thursday

12. Mono-fie = Mono-Friday.

(And again each prefix falls back one day, and the previous week's mono-Saturday now becomes)

13. Fo-mene = Fo-Saturday

The following Friday, the nineteenth day, will be Fo-fie; the Thursday following that, the twenty-fifth day, Fo-yao; the Wednesday following, the thirty-first day, Fo-wukuo; the thirty-seventh day, Fo-bena; and finally on the forty-third day, Fo-dwo, from which we started, will again have come round, and the whole cycle begin once more. This supplies the explanation—in part at least—why the Adae and many other ceremonies, in connexion with birth, death, &c., are repeated in forty-day (really forty-two-day) cycles. The ceremony witnessed on this occasion was, I was informed, an unusually quiet and inconspicuous affair, owing to the fact that almost all the able-bodied members of the community had gone to collect snails (*ko nwa*).

On the Adae morning, the old head priest of the [ɔbosom] Tano Kese and the elders left in the town went along to the omanhene's palace and I saluted the chief, after which we all paid a visit to the Pantheon where the shrines of Ta Kese and other [*abosom*] to be enumerated later were kept. We were preceded by the chief's white stool, with bells hanging from the ears. The uncovered shrines of the [*abosom*] were all ranged along the low ledge running round the sides of the room, with the shrine of Ta Kese—the head [ɔbosom]—high above the others, on the altar. I shall describe in more detail the inside of this temple when describing the Ashanti [*abosom*] in another chapter.

We all sat down inside this room. Including the omanhene and the chief priest [ɔbosomfoɔ], there were only some half-dozen persons present. No palm wine or any other offering was made. The chief said that if the people had not been away, wine would have been given, and the gods asked for life, health, children, food, good hunting for the hunters, and good profits for the traders. The remainder of the wine would have been drunk by those present, after which he, the omanhene, would have held a reception at which he would have danced. On this occasion, after sitting before the uncovered shrines for a few minutes and conversing on general topics, we all left the temple. About 5 p.m. the small drums called *borobi* (hung over the shoulder and beaten with two sticks) called us again to the chief's palace. Again only a few persons were present, the Gyase chief, the two old "linguists" [ɔkyeame], the omanhene, myself, and several of my companions, who had accompanied me from Southern Ashanti.

A small low door on the right-hand side of the chief's compound was opened, and disclosed a very small room upon floor of which, but resting upon a long board, were seven blackened stools. In front of each stool had already, been set a little pile of boiled yams, plantains, and ground nuts, and upon a very small low table was an old metal teapot, containing water, and two dishes covered over with plates, which I was told contained "food." The Gyase chief now held a calabash of palm wine, and one of the "linguists" held an empty calabash at the foot of each stool, while wine was poured into it by the Gyase chief, who said the following words:

> *"Tekyia Kwame nne Muruwukuo wo nana Yao Kramo nsa mu nsa ni, wagye anom, ma wagyina n'akyiri akyi-gyina pa, osere wo kyere, osere wo akwahosan, kuro yi nkwaso, mma ne marima nkwaso."*

"Tekyia Kwame (one of the dead Kings of Tekiman), to-day is Muruwukuo (Wednesday Adae), here is wine from the hand of Yao Kramo (the chief of Tekiman), may you accept it and drink, and may you stand behind him with a good standing. He begs you for a long reign, he begs

you for long-continued, health, life for this town, life for
the women and men."

Upon reaching the seventh and last stool the calabash was re-
plenished and the wine again poured into the second calabash, with
the words:

Ta Kora wo die ni o.
    Ta Kora (the great [*ɔbosom*] of the Ashanti), this is yours.
Ta Mensa wo die ni o.
    Ta Mensa (another name for the [*ɔbosom*] Ta Kese),
    this is yours.
Obo Kyerewa wo die ni o.
    Obo Kyerewa, this is yours.
Ati Akosua wo die ni o.
    Ati Akosua, this is yours.

We now all went out again into the court-yard and joined the
chief. It will have been noted that he took no part in the ceremony
in the stool-house, and did not even come inside. We all sat down,
and the wine, that had been poured into the large calabash and offered to the ancestral spirits and to the gods, was passed round, the
two linguists drinking first. After sitting for a little, and after some
general conversation, we all set out for the Ta Kese temple, preceded by the chief's stool-carrier carrying his white stool. Here the
old head priest awaited us and led us into the room where the
shrines of the [*abosom*] reposed. Since morning the raised altar
upon which the chief [*ɔbosom's*] (Ta Kese's) shrine rested, had been
draped over with a white cloth which completely covered the two
shrines of the [*abosom*] next in order, Ta Kobina and Ati Akosua.

The brass basin, or shrine, of Ta Kese was uncovered but tied
round with a colored silk handkerchief. Upon the smooth top of the
ingredients which formed the contents of the pan were reposing five
eggs. Against the raised altar itself were resting three elephant tails,
one *afona* (state sword), and the two rods of the linguists, which
they placed there as soon as they entered the Pantheon. The walls

of the room, like the altar, were draped with white kente cloth and
Manchester brocades. All the shrines of the lesser and lower graded
[*abosom*] stood uncovered on the low ledge running round the
room. Several blackened stools—of departed priests—were at the
end of the room opposite the altar. As each person entered he said
to the priest:

"*Obosomfo maha o.*"

"Man of god, greetings."

The omanhene now handed a pot of wine to his linguist, who in
turn handed it to the priest with the words:

"*Nne Muruwukuo, nana Yao Kramo se ne nsam nsa a ore
be fwe Tano anim ni.*"

"To-day is Muruwukuo, Grandfather Yao Kramo (the
chief) says that here is wine from his hand which (he
gives) that he may look upon the face of Tano."

The wine was then poured from the pot into a calabash, and the
priest filling his mouth with it sprayed it against the wall, saying:

"*Abanmu Ta Kese Birimpon, nne Muruwukuo, wo nana
Yao Kramo se ne'nsa mu nsa ni, osere wo nkwa, osere
wo ahooden, osere wo amanno, osere wo akwahosan;
kuro yi nye yiye, mmawofo nwo mma, mmarima nwo
mma; ye pe sika, yenya bi; wo mma a beko hahane mu
be ko fa nwa benya bi benfa mera, ma ye nya bi nni yenya
bi nton nto niama nfura.*"

"Ta Kese Birimpon (whose temple stands in the quarter
of the town known as) Aban, to-day is Muruwukuo, your
grand-child Yao Kramo says here is wine from his hand;
he begs you for life, he begs you for strength, he begs

you for love of his people, he begs you for continuing
health; may this town prosper, may the bearers of children bear children, and the males beget children; when
we seek for wealth let us get some; as for your children
who have gone to the forest in order to get snails, grant
that they get some to bring, grant that we get some to eat
and some to sell that we may buy cloths to cover ourselves."

Following this offering was one of wine, given by the "linguist"
as his own offering. This the priest again sprayed from his mouth,
saying:

"*Ta Kese Birimpon, wo nana ne Kwesi Ntwi (the 'linguist') ode nne Muruwukuo na ne' nsam nsa ni, osere wo
nkwa ope sika a, onya bi; ne nkurofo nkwaso; mma no
nya' Boroni amane; mma no mfom Yao K ramo; Oboroni
yiko wuran a, onya 'sono nkum, ma ye nya bi nni.*"

"Ta Kese Birimpon (the god), your grandchild is Kwesi
Ntwi; he says that to-day is Muruwukuo and that this is
an offering of wine from his hands; he begs you for life,
&c., &c.; when he seeks for money let him get some; life
to the people of his village; do not let him get into trouble
with the white man; do not permit him to offend (his
chief) Yao Kramo; when this white man goes to the forest, permit that he kill an elephant that we may have
something to eat."

The wine was poured out at the foot of the altar, as before. What
was left was handed round and all sipped a little. We remained
seated for a few minutes and the conversation was general, but conducted in subdued voices. The death of the poor fellow, who had
fallen upon his spear, which I shall mention later, was discussed. I
was asked about my hunting and also why I was interested in their
[*abosom*], and why I did not, like other white men, say they were

bad and foolish things to be burned and cast away. Shortly after we all dispersed. The food at the foot of the blackened stools would later, so I was informed, be given to the stool-carriers' children. Thus ended what I was told was a particularly quiet Adae. It is of course just possible that, owing to the absence of certain persons, some of the formalities and rites may have been omitted or altered.

The interesting point to notice is the mingling of the propitiation of ancestral human spirits with the worship of non human spirits— the [abosom]. This concludes the account of these Adae ceremonies . . .

The Asante Odwira, 1927

I propose now to describe, from information given me by an Ashanti eyewitness and an important actor in many such ceremonies, the proper sequence of events, the details, and the raison d'etre for this [Odwira] rite. All these are hidden or obscured from the ordinary uninitiated spectator or even casual participator in these ceremonies, by the tumult, the barbaric pomp, the splendid, sometimes ghastly scenes, the marching and counter-marching of thousands, in fact just all these sounds and sights which forcibly attract our attention. These were, however, after all, only the background and the setting for the real business on hand. As to what that business was, previous historians remained silent because they were uninformed; nor is this surprising when we realize that not one Ashanti in a hundred, even of those who took part in these rites, really understood their inner meaning. An account of this rite is not at all out of place here, as it is essentially a rite in connexion with the dead. The title "Yam Custom" by which it has hitherto been known is incorrect, at any rate as far as Ashanti is concerned. Its proper title is Odwira, concerning the derivation of which there is no possible doubt. Dwira means "to purify" or "to cleanse," and Odwira means simply "purification" or "cleansing." The account which now follows is mainly a translation of what was told to me in the Ashanti language.

The Odwira or Apafram was an annual ceremony held in September in honor and propitiation of the Ashanti kings who, had gone elsewhere, and for the cleansing of the whole nation from defilement. Such was the definition given to me by an Ashanti. He might have added—as will be clear from what follows—that it was a feast of the dead, very closely associated with the crops and the first-fruits. Indeed this has, apparently for Europeans, been the most noticeable part of these rites; hence the name "Yam Custom" by which this ceremony has hitherto been universally described. My informant might also have noted that, not only was it a cleansing of the nation, but the purification of shrines of ancestral spirits, of the [abosom], and of lesser non-human spirits. These rites are I think among some of the most interesting and instructive that have been recorded in connexion with the Ashanti. The source of my information has been checked, in its most important points, from other quarters, and is to be trusted. This custom is no longer held in Coomassie. It recalls, in some respects, such rites as the Apo and the Afahye ceremonies, which were described in [the book] Ashanti. A particular Monday immediately following a Kwesidae (a Sunday adae ceremony) was chosen for the commencement of this ceremony. On that day the reigning King of Ashanti paid a semi-state visit to the mausoleum at Bantama and "borrowed from the ghosts" gold dust to the value of £300 to £1,000. This treasure was kept in kuduo (metal vessels), or in the "brass coffers" which were set before the coffins containing the skeletons. The king presented a sheep, which was killed for a repast for the ghosts, at the same time addressing them as follows:

"*Afe ano ahyia, ye be twa odwira, omma bone biara mma, na afe foforo nto yen boko.*"

"The edges of the years have come round, we are about to celebrate the rites of the Odwira; do not permit any evil at all to come upon us and let the new year meet us peacefully."

Before sunset on the same day a meeting was held in the open space within the palace called *kyinhyia* (the whirlpool), at which the king presided, attended by all the hereditary office-holders, whose titles and precedence have already been described. The approaching ceremony was discussed and messengers were dispatched to outlying towns and villages, to warn the chiefs to assemble at Coomassie and to collect further contributions. Eleven days elapsed before the ceremony proper began. This interval was employed in making preparations. Houses were repaired, the state regalia, chairs, stools, drums, and state umbrellas were cleaned and overhauled. The eleventh day from the Monday, when the king went to Bantama, was a Thursday. Upon that day the chiefs of Kokofu and Nsuta arrived (as they might not travel on a Friday); on that day the King of Ashanti and all his councilors and ministers, preceded by the Golden Stool, paid a ceremonial visit to the houses of certain persons for the purpose of pouring out libations and making certain sacrifices.

First the king went to the door of Amo, the head of the stool-carriers of the Golden Stool, and poured out a libation at the door; next, to the house of the chief of Dominase, where a sheep was killed and its blood smeared over the stools of the ancestral ghosts; thence he proceeded to Bantama, where with bare shoulders and sandals slipped, he entered each chamber in turn and poured out a libation before each of the skeletons. From Bantama he went to the site of the present Fort, which was formerly called Anowo, where the house of Owusu Yao, the father of King Osai Yao stood; thence in turn to that part of Coomassie called Asokwa, to the house of the head linguist; at each of these places the usual libation was made; then to the house of the Queen Mother, where a sheep was sacrificed for the ancestral Queen Mothers' stools. Next a visit was paid to Nkwantanan, the four cross-roads, where Adum and Bank Street now intersect; there wine and sheep's blood were poured on the shrines (i.e. the stools) of Boakye Yao Kuma, who was the father of King Kwaku Dua I; to Akyeremade, where Efiriye, father of King Osai Kojo, lived, where similar offerings were made; to the dwelling of the chief executioner Totoe, head of the *adumfo*, and guardian of the Ahema 'gwa (the blackened stool of Nyanko Kusi Amoa), and finally to the house of Owusu Ansa, the father of King Bonsu Panyin. In each case on the libation of wine or blood being poured out, the "linguist" repeated the following words after the king:

"*Asamanfo munye nsa ne ogwan yi mma asem'one bi mma, ye be twa odwira.*"

"Spirits of the dead, receive this wine and sheep, let no bad thing come (upon us), we are about to celebrate the Odwira ceremony."

The Golden Stool, the shrine and symbol of the national soul, which has cost us so much in lives and treasure, was borne by Amo upon the nape of his neck, and sheltered from the sun by the great "umbrella, made of material called in Ashanti *nsa* (camel's hair and wool). This umbrella was known throughout Ashanti as *Katamanso* (the covering of the nation). On either side of the stool walked attendants, each supporting one of the solid gold bells which were attached by thongs to the "ears" of the stool, and formed a portion of its regalia. Two other bells of brass, also attached to the stool, hung down over Amo's chest, the thongs attaching them to the stool being grasped by his right hand, while his left held the stool in position on the nape of his neck. The remaining insignia of the Golden Stool consisted of iron and gold fetters, gold death-masks of great captains and generals, whom the Ashanti had slain in battle since the time of Osai Tutu. Among these were likenesses of Ntim Gyakari, King of Denkyira; Adinkira, King of Gyaman; Bra Kwante, King of Akyem; and Mankata.

It will be noted that this royal progress was for the express purpose of informing the ancestral ghosts of all the famous houses in Coomassie of the business on hand. When we read Bowdich, Ramseyer and Kühne, and Ellis the only impression we obtain is that this cavalcade was concerned in filling great brass pans with intoxicating liquor, from which all drank "like hogs." It is true that much wine was given to the populace, the rabble, the slaves, and the hangers-on. I have already been at some pains to point out elsewhere that we have been most unfair in judging these customs by these outward signs; yet that is what the historians have uniformly done.

The next day was Friday. It witnessed the arrival of the outlying subjects of the Coomassie Asafohene, i.e. Denyase, Manso-

Nkwanta, Berekurn, Ahafo, Kwahu, Asante-Akyern, &c., and the subjects (*nkoa*) of the great Amanhene, i.e. Bekwai, Juaben, 'Asubingya, Mampon, who halted outside the town, into which they made their official entry on the following morning. "On Friday, the 5th of September," writes Bowdich, "the number, splendour, and variety of arrivals thronging from the different paths was as astonishing as entertaining." He wrote this nearly a hundred years before the scenes witnessed and described by my informant were enacted; yet the actual day of the week (not date of course) for this and other particular days of the ceremony still hold good. "The following day was Saturday," continued my white-haired Ashanti friend, who was recounting these events, "and about two hours after midday the king received the chiefs at Apremoso," i.e. "at the place of cannons." "In the afternoon of Saturday," wrote Bowdich, "the king received all the caboceers and captains in the large arena, where the Dankira cannons are placed." At this gathering of all the heads of the great territorial divisions, the oath of allegiance was taken by anyone who had not already done so, and problems of state were discussed. In this respect the *Odwira* ceremony, combined with its purely magico-religious aspect, was of great political significance and practical utility. Among a primitive people superstition, the cult of the magical, religion—call it what you will—does as much as force and arms to keep cohesion in a far-flung rule, such as was the Ashanti confederacy; for it was at customs and rites such as these that the many loosely bound, and often hostile factions, which owned nominal allegiance to the Ashanti king, came for the time being to think themselves part of a nation rather than branches of a family or clan.

The following day was Sunday. A captive of war was executed early in the morning at the spot called *Nkra'm*, which has already been described. All the skulls of the generals or kings who had been captured or slain in the various wars were brought from Bantama on this day. They reposed, in the ordinary way, before the coffins of the particular kings who had commanded the victorious armies responsible for their capture. On this occasion the skulls were smeared with bands of red clay interspersed with white. . . . Among the skulls were those of the following persons: Ntim Gyakari;

Adinkira; Bra Nkante; Mankata (Sir Charles Macarthy); Ofusu 'hene Apenten; Frimpon Ampim; Ame Yao Kwakye; Worosa (Banna 'hene); Boadu Akafu, and many others. As the king sat among his chiefs, each skull was placed on the ground before him, and upon each in turn he placed his foot, saying as he did so, "Such-and-such of my ghost ancestors slew you."

In the afternoon of that day the *odwira suman* (the fetish called *odwira*) was carried by the chief of Asafo to Bampanase, before the king. I shall presently give such information as I have seen gorgeous robes and dressed himself in *Kyenkyen* (bark cloth), the garb of the poorest slave in the realm. On the *odwira suman* being set before him he smeared it over with *esono* (red dye, made from the roots of the *edwono* tree) and placed new yams upon it, and then poured wine upon it, with the words:

> "*Osai Tutu 'Dwira gye nsa nom, obiara a ompe se osom wo ma menya no menkum no mfa ne 'ti nto 'Dwira.*"

> "Odwira of Osai Tutu, accept this wine and drink, anyone who does not wish to serve you, let me get him, and let me kill him, and let me throw his head [on you], Odwira."

The king was also smeared all over with the red *esono*; then he took some of this and rubbed it across the forehead of certain of the chiefs, including Bantama and Asafo. Towards evening, or perhaps later, the king, seated in his hammock, was borne towards the quarter of Coomassie then called Subenso (where the old bungalow of the Chief Commissioner now stands), accompanied by a vast throng. In front marched executioners carrying new yams, smeared on one side red, on the other with black, and a bodyguard of seven *atumtufo* (gunmen). On arriving at a certain spot the king's *okyeame* (spokesman) advanced and cried out in a loud voice:

Awo e! Awo e!   Awo e! Awo! Awo! Awo! (a name).
A voice from far away replied:
Yes! Yes! Yes!   Yes ! Yes ! Yes!

The spokesman then called out:

Afe ano ahyia, ye be twa odwira
Be gye aduane di.
Obiara a ompe se osom Asanie 'Hene ma yen nsa nkum no senea
ye kum too ne wo nkurofo.

The edges of the years have met, we have come to celebrate the Odwira.
Come and receive this food and eat
Anyone at all who does not wish to serve the King of Ashanti, let our hand slay him as we slew you and your kinsfolk.

With these words the yams were cast towards "the spirit who had answered"; guns were fired; and then everyone turned round and ran homeward in complete silence. Anyone falling down was killed on the spot where he fell. . . . Bowdich writes, speaking of the events of a Sunday: "Towards evening the populace grew sober again, the strange caboceers displayed their equipages in every direction, and at five o'clock there was a procession from the palace to the south end of the town and back . . . ." The day following the events just described was a Monday. On this day a rite of paramount interest and importance in helping us to a better understanding of Ashanti religious beliefs was performed. In order to understand its full significance it will be necessary to refer again to those exogamous divisions on a patrilineal basis known as *ntoro*. It has been noted, in that chapter of *Ashanti* which deals with this subject, how each of the *ntoro* divisions had its own taboo or taboos; that the most important *ntoro*, socially so to speak, was the *Bosommuru ntoro* to which so many of the Ashanti kings belonged; that Bosommuru's day of observance was a Tuesday, and that one of its taboos (I shall not call it a "totem") was an ox or cow. By "taboo of an ntoro," I mean something (generally an animal) which was held to be "hateful" to the spirit of that particular *ntoro*, and in consequence was rigidly taboo to all its votaries. Now, without this previous knowledge the rites about to be described would not have any special significance to us, and "would appear not to record anything more than the ordinary sacrifice of an ox."

The following was the rite. An ox was dragged before the king, who, seated at the spot called *Abogyawe* in front of the palace, was again smeared with the red *esono*. The king then rose up and took the gold *afona*, state sword, known as Bosommuru—the shrine of that *ntoro*—whose taboo is an ox, and struck the ox three times with it, saying as he did so: "Wo ni o! Wo ni o! Wo ni o!" ("This is yours! This is yours! This is yours!"). The ox was immediately killed by one of the *adumfo* (executioners). The carcass was cut up, and was, I am informed, eaten by the *adumfo*. Here we have a deliberate and public violation of a taboo and pollution of the potential dwelling-place of a sacred power. Such an act would in ordinary circumstances be expressed by the phrase "*wa to n'adu*" ("They have poisoned it"). The reason for this strange conduct will be seen presently.

On this day (Monday), the great *amanhen'* (paramount chiefs) returned, each to his own country, there to continue and complete the Odwira-the "purification" which was the essential part of this rite. The following day was a Tuesday, which, as we have seen, was the one day, in the seven-day week, set aside for the propitiation of the *Bosummuru ntoro*, whose shrine and cult had the day previously been publicly and deliberately defiled. On this day the King of Ashanti made an equally public sacrifice. A sheep was brought to him, held over the golden sword—the shrine of *Bosummuru*—its throat was pricked, and the blood allowed to fall on this emblem. Roots and leaves of certain plants were also squeezed into a bowl with water from the sacred rivers, such as the Tano, Abrotia, Akoba, Apomesu, in which white clay had been mixed; with this the shrine was also sprinkled, the following words being spoken by the king:

"*Bosommuru afe ana ahyia, wo wo nam, na mede wo akyiwadie ma ka wo, nne na me bo wo asuo, ama w'ano sore bio. Me ne me 'yonko, osa 'hene biara ehyia, wo twa ne 'ti ma me, na wo gwan, me de bo wo asuo, e ni.*"

"O Bosommuru the edges of the years have met; you were sharp but I took that thing which you abhor and touched you (with it), but to-day I sprinkle you with water in order that your power may rise up again. When I and my equal, some war lord or other, meet, cut off his head and give it me; and along with the water, with which I sprinkle you, here is a sheep."

The Friday following was a Fofie, i.e. a sacred Friday which comes round once every forty-three days; this was a day of purification for all. The king and his court, dressed in their best, and preceded by the Golden Stool and the ancestral blackened stools the *odwira suman*, the *Bosommuru suman*, the shrines of the [*abosom*], together with all the paraphernalia of the household, stools, chairs, drums, horns, &c., were marched to the stream, near Akyeremade. Here the war-chair called *fwedom* ("drive back the enemy") was set up, and upon this was placed the Golden Stool. The numerous blackened stools, the shrines of ancestral spirits, were held in front of the bearers, each by its respective stool-carrier. The king held in his hand a branch of the plant called *Bosommuru adwira*; this he dipped into a large brass basin that had been filled with the sacred water, and with it sprinkled the Golden Stool, repeating as he did so the following words [in English translation]:

"Friday, Stool of Kings, I sprinkle water upon you, may your power return sharp and fierce. Grant that when I and another meet (in battle) grant it be as when I met Denkyira; you let me cut off his head. As when I met Akyem; you let me cut off his head. As when I met Domma; you let me cut off his head. As when I met Tekiman; you let me cut off his head. As when I met Gyaman; you let me cut off his head.

The edges of the years have met, I pray you for life.

May the nation prosper. May the women bear children. May the hunters kill meat.

We who dig for gold, let us get gold to dig, and grant that I get some for the upkeep of my kingship."

Then the Odwira, Bosommuru, the ancestral blackened stools, and the assembled people were likewise sprinkled, and similar prayers offered up, asking for prosperity for the nation, freedom from sickness, plentiful crops, and many children. Then everyone returned home; sheep were sacrificed to the ghosts of the kings, and wine and new yams offered to them, with these words [in English translation]:

> "The edges of the years have met, I take sheep and new yams and give you that you may eat. Life to me. Life to this my Ashanti people. Women who cultivate the farms, when they do so, grant the food comes forth in abundance. Do not allow any illness to come."

Fresh yams were also placed on the shrines of various *abosom*, on the *Odwira* and on *Bosommuru*. New yams were sent to other burial-places of the royal house, which will be noted presently. A week later the chief of Bantama gave new yams to his ancestral ghosts. Only after ghosts, [*abosom*], and other non-human spiritual powers had partaken of the new crops, might the king, his chiefs, and the nation eat of them.

I will close this account with the method of conducting the human sacrifices which were made on the occasion of the Odwira ceremony. The reigning king proceeded to the royal mausoleum at Bantama, whither the victims, generally twelve in number, were also conducted. These were generally captives or criminals already sentenced to death. With a *sepow* knife through the cheeks, and arms pinioned behind them, they were lined up before the *Aya Kese* (the great brass vessel), which has already been described. The King of Ashanti now entered the "great house" to visit each of his ancestor's skeletons in turn, and to pour out wine before them. A drummer, with his *ntumpane* drums, stood waiting for a given signal. As the king entered each chamber in succession, beginning with Osai Tutu and ending with Kwaku Dua II, "the divine drummer" sent the message of death, which was the signal for one of the waiting men to be dispatched. Just before cutting off his head the executioner would say to him: "*Ko samandow ko som Osai Tutu.*" "Off with you to the land of ghosts and serve Osai Tutu" (or whichever king he was being sent to serve). . . . We should not forget that these same men [beheaded] were capable of composing and sounding forth this stanza:

The stream crosses the path,
The path crosses the stream,
Which of them is the elder?
Did we not cut a path to meet that stream?
The stream had its origin long long ago.
The stream had its origin from the Creator.
He created things.

The bodies were then dragged into the forest behind Bantama, at the spot known simply as *bom'* (in the hollow). When I penetrated the dense undergrowth and visited this place a year ago I had only to turn over the mould with my foot to disclose bones and fragments of skulls. The Ashanti state that King Kakari (always misspelled Karikari in official and other records) made a humane rule that only twelve persons should be sacrificed on this occasion, the number previously not having been limited. The king after visiting Bantama for the purpose of these sacrifices returned to the palace, where he was entertained by the music of the *kete* drums and *kete* reed-pipes. These *kete* players, and also singers, are somewhat like the minstrels the Ashanti name Kwadwumfo. They recount in song the names and heroic deeds of the dead, "whereupon the king would weep and give orders that a captive was to be killed." These sacrifices, I believe, generally ended the ceremony. There was little real rejoicing at the coming in of the New Year. My Ashanti friend remarked, "*Eyee me de na menya me ti*" ("I was glad I still had my head") . . .

Funeral Rites for a Priest [ɔkɔmfoɔ]

The funeral of a member of the priestly class has an interesting additional ceremony as a distinguishing rite. This is rendered necessary owing to the priest's or priestess's close association with his or her particular [ɔbosom]. We have seen elsewhere how the [abosom] manifest themselves to their servants by using them as the media through which their influence acts. It is therefore perhaps feared that on the death of a priest (or priestess), the deceased may carry away forever the emanation of the particular power he has learned to control. This is one interpretation given to account for the ceremony. It seems to me, however, that the wording of the incantation or prayer, which in this case accompanies the sacrifice, points to the fact that by death the servant of the [ɔbosom] has defiled the shrine of his particular deity and so rendered it unacceptable to the spirit which is expected to enter it. This supernatural element which they fear may be lost, or taken away by the dead, is in Ashanti called *nkomoa*, a noun derived from the verb *kom*. The German missionary Christaller defined this word as "to dance wildly in a state of frenzy or ecstasy, ascribed by the negroes to the agency of a fetish; to be possessed by a fetish, to perform the action or practices of a fetish man."

It has already been mentioned how the outward and visible signs of mourning, the red ochre and the funeral clothes affected by the ordinary mourners, are taboo to a priest. He must wear white and sprinkle himself with white clay, as if as far as he is concerned death and mourning and sorrow do not exist. The corpse of a dead priest is draped in white and sprinkled with white clay, symbolizing the antithesis of ordinary funerary customs, which possibly mark out the wearers as being in a state of sorrow and defilement. The rite is as follows:

After a priest has been buried, a sheep is sacrificed over the shrine of his particular [ɔbosom] "to prevent the *saman* (ghost) taking his *nkomoa* to the spirit world." The following words are spoken:

"*Wo'komfo de akom, wo Odomankoma obo adie na obo owuo a wabefa no ko. Wagye ogwan yi na wa te efi a ka too atwene, na wa te w'ani afwe yen a ka yi so.*"

"The Creator, who created things and (also) created Death, has come and taken away your priest, who used to become possessed by you. May you receive this sheep and pluck and cast away all uncleanness that has touched you, and may you open wide your eyes and look upon us who are left behind . . ."

Komfo Anotche [Anokye]

I will give the story of Komfo Anotche's life as nearly as possible in the words of his descendant, the narrative being recounted in the vernacular, of which the following is a free translation:

Kwame Frimpon Anotche Kotowbere was the son of Amea Gyata, who had come forth from a spot in Adanse called the *Bona Bom* (the *Bona* rock). Amea Gyata died in Adanse, leaving a daughter, Nana Dufie Gyampontima, and a son, Dampte, who later became a priest. Amea Gyata belonged to the *Asenie* clan. This clan later left Adanse and went to 'Santemanso, and later again to Nkuruoso (near Bonwere). Various members of the *Asenie* clan founded Stools which afterwards became famous. Thus, Adu founded Aduaben; Akosa Yadom founded Amakum; Sa Kodie Date founded Agona Akyempim, near the present town of Agona. Anotche was born at Adanse Akrokyere, and was the second son of Dwirawiri Kwa (an *Asenie* woman) and of an Adanse man called Kyei Birie. Dwirawiri Kwa was the daughter of Nana Dufie Gyampontima. Adu Twumuwu had married a man called Twumasi Amponsem, who was a brother of Owusu Panyin, who was the husband of Manu, the mother of Osai Tutu. Anotche's elder brother was Yamoa, who also became a priest. He was killed along with Obiri Yaboa in the Domina war. Anotche was stated to have been born already holding two lumps of *dufa* (medicine made into balls or cones) and a *bodua* (cow's tail) in his hand. As a child he would disappear for days at a time; he once jumped and stood on a flower called *Fwentema*. When still a youth, he commenced to travel. (In these wanderings, legends grew up around the places he visited, these spots being "cursed" or "blessed" according to the reception given to him.)

At Effiduase lived a weaver, called Babu, whom Anotche informed that he would die three days after he had finished a cloth which he was weaving at that time. To delay the completion of his task, Babu used to pass his shuttle through the shed only once or twice each year. At Ntonso he was using the village latrine, and was abused by the villagers for fouling one of the cross-sticks. He invoked a curse upon the town and foretold that quarrels would arise whenever it became necessary to make a new latrine. The Ntonso villagers therefore invented a new kind of latrine which did not necessitate much constant renovation. At Apa the villagers laughed at him when he wished them to adopt the [ɔbosom] Aboasu as one of their deities, and he caused all the subsequent generations to be born with thin lips and protruding teeth. The blacksmiths of Fumasua, a village near Kumasi, once refused to forge him an adere (sickle), and he prophesied that the villagers would always be toilers at the forge and never grow rich. At that time when Komfo Anotche was growing to manhood, Osai Tutu was in Denkyira, where he had been sent as an elephant-tail switcher to Amponsem, the King of Denkyira. Here Osai Tutu had had an intrigue with a woman called Aka Abena, a sister of Amponsem, and wife of one of the Elders of Denkyira. The child later born to Aka Abena, of whom the father was alleged to be Osai Tutu, became the famous Ntim Gyahari. Osai Tutu, as the result of the discovery of this intrigue, had to flee for his life. He went to Akwamu, where his spiritual father resided—the [ɔbosom] Tutu—whom Manu, Osai Tutu's mother, had consulted before his birth. Meanwhile, Anotche had wandered to Akwapim, and visited Awukugua and Apiride and learned all about medicines, amulets, and charms.

Osai Tutu met Anotche in Akwamu. The latter was a prisoner, having committed some offence for which he had been fastened to a log. Osai Tutu obtained his release. At this time Obiri Yaboa was on the Oyoko Stool at Kumasi, and had gone to war with the Domina. He was killed in the fighting that ensued, as was also Anotche's brother, Yamoa. Osai Tutu was summoned from Akwamu to come to Kumasi. The Chief of Akwamu gave him thirty men from Annum to accompany him. These men were under Annum Asamoa, who became the first Adum Hene of Kumasi. After Osai Tutu had set out, the Chief of Akwamu regretted having allowed him to depart, and sent after him; the party was overtaken while crossing the Volta in a canoe. The canoe men ceased paddling, when Osai Tutu seized one of them and cut off his head, casting it into the rapids. This enabled them to escape. Osai Tutu was enstooled at Kumasi, and Komfo Anotche succeeded his brother, Yamoa. The powerful Chiefs at this time were Kyereme Sikafo—the Domina Chief who had killed Obiri Yaboa-and the head of the *Asenie*, the Amakum Chief. Nsuta, Kokofu, Juaben, and Kontenase were all ruled by Oyoko, and were thus already bound to Osai Tutu by the common tie of blood.

What Komfo Anotche now achieved was the amalgamation of the other clans-*Beretuo*, *Asona* (Offinsu and Ejisu), and *Asenie* (Amakum)-under Osai Tutu, to fight the Dominas, whose Chief was an *Aduana*. So remarkable did this achievement seem to the Ashanti, who were accustomed to the isolation and strict independence of the numerous petty Chiefs, that they ascribed the feat to Anotche's magical powers. He accomplished this unity by means of his medicines. The hitherto independent Chiefs met at Amoako, and were given palm wine to drink mixed with medicine, the mixture being afterwards known as *ngyegyesa*. Their combined forces met Kyeteme Sikafo's at Toperemanukwanta (near the site of the old W.A.F.F. officers' mess at Kumasi) and defeated them, killing the Domina Adonten Hene, Akyetekokogyan. Instead of killing the Domina Chief, as was the Ashanti custom with the defeated general of the enemies' forces, Komfo Anotche decreed that he should be appointed soul-washer to Osai Tutu, presenting him with a gold plate (*dwinie*) as his badge of office to suspend round the neck by pine-apple fibre. This victory against the Domina had been achieved in the following manner. Before the commencement of the campaign, the army leaders told Komfo Anotche that his brother had promised them the victory in the previous war, which had ended in their defeat and in the death of Obiri Yaboa, and they demanded a sign from Anotche that they would be victorious.

Komfo Anotche therefore bade Amankwatia, who had followed

Osai Tutu from Akwamu, to stand at Diakomfoase, where he told him he would meet a leopard. He ordered Amankwatia to lead the leopard by its left paw and bring it to him. Amankwatia did as he was told, met a leopard, and led it to Anotche by the left paw. Osai Tutu then cut off its head. Its skin was made into a hat for Amankwatia, and he was given the title of Ko'ntire Hene (Commander of the fighters). The skull of the leopard was buried at Toperemanukwanta. Anotche then asked Osai Tutu for one of his "sons." He was given one Saben, a son of Obiri Yaboa. A shield was made and given to him, and he was told that so long as the front of the shield was presented towards the enemy, they would retreat. Saben was also informed that the taboo of the shield was palm wine. Anotche then ordered Osai Tutu to make *afona* (swords) and hand them out to his commanders, and he decreed the form of an oath that they should take. This is how the taking of an oath before going to a war was instituted. Komfo Anotche himself took one of the swords and, standing before Osai Tutu, swore: *Me ka Osai 'se, se me boa wo ama wakyere Kyereme Sikafo, na menko me gwane . . .* (I speak the name of the father of Osai, that I will help you to catch Kyereme Sikafo, and that if do not fight but run away, then have I violated the oath). All the commanders took a similar oath.

The fighting lasted seven days, and the combatants had not anything to eat. One day, Ohene 'ba Saben saw a woman carrying a pot of palm wine. He forgot all about the taboo, and drank, and turned the face of his shield away from the enemy, who rallied and turned upon the Ashanti, who retreated to Apeboso (near the site of the present Scottish Mission Church in Kumasi). Anotche was accused of having deceived the Ashanti, but was able to show how Saben had violated the taboo. All the swords that had been made were now cast, by Anotche's orders, into the stream called Awomfana (now drained; it formerly flowed near the present W.A.F.F. lines); new swords were forged and the oaths again taken. Saben was warned that he would be killed in the fighting. This was the origin, of the horn call, "Whatever happens, Sabeu will die." The Ashanti (as related above) were now victorious. Komfo Anotche now set out to make the Golden Stool. He had found that, when united under one

Head, the Ashanti were strong. A test was made to find out who this Head should be. Komfo Anotche took three cuttings of a tree called *Kumnini* (kill the python). One he caused to be planted at Juaben, one at Kumawu, and the third at Kumasi. Those at Kumawu and Juaben died, that at Kumasi grew. Hence Kumasi I was chosen as the new Head. Anotche next buried gold, silver, brass, copper, lead, and iron bars at the spot known as Dwabirim (where the post office now stands), thus making the new power to stand firm.

Kyereme Sikafo's *obosom* (god) was Tano, and Anotche captured its spirit and put it in a brass pan and appointed one Dansu as its custodian. Anotche also buried a python under the *sumpere* (raised earthen platform) upon which Osai Tutu sat on great occasions. Osai Tutu now exercised a certain authority over other Chiefs, and compelled them to come to Kumasi if called upon. The third Domina war now arose. Kyereme Sikafo had died, and had been succeeded by his nephew, Domina Kusi. He rebelled against Osai Tutu and was defeated. He was not killed, as is so commonly stated, but was sent to Asokore Mampon, where Anotche had caused, a temple to be built, to be a priest to [Onyame] (Nyame). This temple has now fallen down. Domina Kusi had two sisters, Ofuwa and Asiedua, both of whom Komfo Anotche married. Asiedua gave birth to Agyapa, and Ofuwa to Beresiama. This was before the third Domina war. Komfo Anotche had not yet come to Agona; his village was Nkuruoso, near Asokore Mampon. At this time the Taffo were very powerful; they had not taken any part in the Domina wars; their *ntabera* horns and *fontomfrom* drums could be heard in Kumasi. Osai Tutu demanded that these instruments should be handed over, and when the Taffo refused, attacked and defeated them, capturing their Chief, Safo Akonton, who was killed. His brother, Koroboa, was put on his Stool. This is how *fontomfrom* drums and *ntabera* horns first came to Kumasi.

After the defeat of the Taffo, Osai Tutu heard of the great wealth of the Chief of Sefwi, Brumankama. He sent to Denkyira to get powder and gun from Ntim Gyakari, who was now King of Denkyira. Ntim Gyakari refused, saying that Brumankama could breathe fire from his mouth and was like a *sasabonsam*. Komfo Anotche advised Osai Tutu to go to Sefwi with his own army. This he did; Brumankama was defeated. Among the loot captured were many articles of European manufacture, the *aya kese* and *dwete kuruwa*, and the *kuruwa kese*, which were brought to Kumasi. Brumankama's successor, Akesantifo, was enstooled and "drank the gods" to serve Osai Tutu. One of the Asafo Chiefs, the Akwamu Hene, was appointed his *Adamfo*. The King of Denkyira now increased his demands for tribute. (Originally, as we have seen, the form this tribute took was the supplying of such simple articles as were in everyday use among a primitive people, i.e. firewood, red clay, *baha* fibre, and the performance of menial services. We can thus trace the progress in wealth and in civilization that had already been made in Ashanti, which resulted in these primitive levies being changed to demands more in keeping with the new era of advancement which had undoubtedly been in progress in Ashanti for possibly some hundred years before the final overthrow of Denkyira.) When the envoys from Denkyira arrived with these demands Komfo Anotche caused Osai Tutu to summon all the outlying Chiefs who had taken part in the Domina wars, to come to Kumasi. Meanwhile he procured some medicine which he mixed with palm wine. A great meeting was held.

Osai Tutu sat on the *sumpere* (raised mound) beneath which the python was buried. The messengers from Ntim Gyakari stood before them and renewed their demands. They were answered by a shout *Yentua o, pa fwi!* (We shall not pay, *pa fwi!*) The Juaben Hene, Adakwa Yiadom, picked up an *afona* called Domfonsan, and struck Berebere (or Abebrese), wounding him and cutting off one of his ears. The messengers were sent back to Denkyira. All the people now asked Komfo Anotche what they should do. He said he would help them, provided he was given one thousand of everything in the world. To this they agreed. Anotche said they must prepare for three years, and meantime not make any other wars. Guns and powder were brought from Korankye Abo (now Grand Bassam). Meanwhile Anotche went to Denkyira, where he turned into a red-skinned girl and sat in the market selling fish. Ntim Gyakari's servants saw her, and reported to their master that they had seen a beautiful fair-

skinned girl in the market selling fish. The fish Anotche was selling
he had mixed with medicine so that the heart of anyone who ate
them would become like that of a woman. Ntim Gyakari took the
fish seller as his concubine, and while he was asleep Anotche took
his heart and then escaped and returned to Kumasi. Komfo Anotche
next told Osai Tutu to find a stool carver. A man from the village of
Asekyerewa was sent for, and he was ordered to make two Stools.
A log of wood was cut into two; that part which had grown nearest
to the roots was made into a Stool for Osai Tutu, the other half into
a Stool for Komfo Anotche. Osai Tutu's Stool was called Osai Tutu
Amoampon; Komfo Anotche's, Anotche Amoampon. After the
Stools had been carved, Anotche became possessed and danced.
Something descended from the sky which Komfo Anotche caught.
This, and the heart of Ntim Gyakari, which had become ashes, were
put into the central part of the Stool, and the Chief Kuroboa of Taffo
was appointed as its carrier.

An albino was now set upon the Stool. Komfo Anotche struck
him upon the head, and he disappeared into the Stool. At the same
time Anotche made the following laws:

(a) Albinos were not to be sacrificed to the Stool.
(b) All albinos were to be sent to Kumasi to become
    Stool-carriers of the new Stool.
(c) An albino or light-skinned man was never to sit on the Stool.

Anotche ordered seven bells to be made to hang on the Stool,
three of gold, one of silver, one of copper, one of iron, and one of
brass, which he said represented seven Kings who would all be
powerful; after whose time the power of Ashanti would wane. . . .
Of the "medicine" which had been used in the making of the Stool,
he took what remained, and mixing it with copper, distributed pieces
to all Chiefs who possessed blackened stools, thus sharing with all
some of the power which lay in the Stool. Anotche also told Osai
Tutu that some one must be selected to command the army in the
coming war. Boahinanantuo, Chief of Mampon, was selected. He
had a sister (Saka?) who was barren. Anotche bade her go to the

stream called Oda and take some sand. This sand he mixed with medicine and gave to the woman bidding her sprinkle it on a mat, upon which he told her to lie face downwards for seven days, after which she would conceive. This woman eventually bore Mami-ampon, who was the child of the Oda. Anotche now asked for a volunteer who would be the first to die in the impending battle. Kodia, of Kumawu, came forward. He asked what he should receive in return, and was promised that members of his royal clan would forever be exempt from capital punishment, and he also was given the land up to the Volta.

Again, Anotche asked for a man who would allow himself to be cut into pieces, that each wound he received might save the life of an Ashanti in battle. Duku Pim, the Ejisu Hene, volunteered. He, like Kodia of Kumawu, was promised that his descendants would never be killed. Komfo Anotche also ordered Osai Tutu to give one of his own half-brothers who must die in the war. Bobie, the Chief of Bonwere, was chosen. His descendants, besides being exempt from capital punishment, were to be given the right to use *oyoko man* cloth on their umbrellas. A national army was organized with the important military posts held by the greater Chiefs. During the battle with the Denkyira army, Anotche climbed a *kyenkyen* tree along with his son, Agyapa, leaving the impress of his sandals upon the tree. Anotche looked down on Ntim Gyakari and saw him playing Wari with one of his wives: golden fetters were around his ankles. Anotche also made a silk cotton tree to expand and spread out like a fence to receive the enemies' fire. The Denkyira also had a famous priest on their side called Kyerekye, and one pitted his magic against the other. Anotche had tied a knot in an elephant's tusk and sent it to Kyerekye to untie. Ntim Gyakari was exhorted by his *kwadwumfo* (minstrels), whose noses he had cut off to enable them to sing the more sweetly, and whose flesh he had scraped from their arms that they might clash their arm bones together in time to their music, while they sang *Ako Abena Bansua oyi kwan ba Kotoko Ntim* ("Ako Abena the son of the Bansua bird who clears the path, Kotoko Ntim"). The Juaben captured Ntim Gyakari; the spot is marked to this day by a kola tree which bears white nuts (Bese

Hene), which sprang from a kola nut which Ntim was chewing when he was captured.

After Ntim Gyakari's death, his nephew, Boadu Akafu, was enstooled, after "drinking the gods" that he would serve Osai Tutu. The *Okyeame*, known as the Gyakye Hene, was appointed as his *Adamfo*. Komfo Anotche was now given one thousand of everything; all Ashanti contributed save Juaben, who claimed exemption on the plea that they killed Ntim Gyakari, until Anotche sent a cadaver ant, which entered the ear of the Chief of Juaben and whispered, "Bring the award of the priest Anotche." Kumasi at this time was very swampy. Anotche, by his magic, drained the Suben River. Its real name was Agyempansu, but Anotche changed the name to Suben, calling it after the stream which flows near 'Santemanso. Anotche now requested permission to return to his village at Agona Akyempim. Agyapa, his son, remained at Kumasi with Osai Tutu. After the battle of Feyiase, a famine in salt arose, owing to the closing of the Coast roads. Komfo Anotche said the shortage could be stopped by the sacrifice of an albino. One was accordingly killed at the spot in Kumasi known as *Aboraso*. A hut was built here, and a young girl, who had not yet had her menses, was set to live in it as a custodian and to cook food for the spirit of the albino. She had the right to exact a toll on all market produce entering Kumasi. Her face was smeared with white clay. Anotche removed to Agona Akyempim about three years after the battle of Feyiase. He became very wealthy and had always scales hanging in his *dampon*, in which he weighed out gold-dust which he lent to others free of interest.

Anotche instituted the national *Odwira* ceremony. Even after he retired to his village, Anotche used to travel. He went to Attabubu and gave them a metal drum and a metal bowl. He is also stated to have accompanied Osai Tutu to a war against Abo of Bontuku. At last Anotche informed Osai Tutu that he was about to set out in quest of a medicine against death. He asked Osai Tutu to call his nephew, Kwame Siaw, and all the Elders of Agona Akyempim to come to Kumasi. When they did so, he informed them that he would be absent seven years and seventy-seven days and nights, and that during all that time no one must weep or fire a gun, or mourn for him, although he appeared to be dead. He returned to Agona Akyempim, and entered his house, which stood on the very spot where we visited yesterday and there he "died." Before he did so he gave orders that he was not to be disturbed for seven years and seventy-seven days and nights. The town was placed in charge of his Elders. For seven years and seventy days his orders were obeyed, when his nephew at length declared that his uncle was re-ally dead, and that people should weep and that guns should be fired. The door of the room was opened; the chamber was found to be empty. On that very day, a man from Mampon was passing Agona, when at the place called *Abetene* (tall palm-tree) he was ad-dressed by a man who inquired what was happening at Agona Akyempim, as guns were being fired and people wailing. He replied that they were holding the funeral custom of Komfo Anotche. The man then said that he was Komfo Anotche, that he had obtained the medicine against death, and was returning with it, but as his kinsfolk had disobeyed his orders, he would go away forever, and the Ashanti would never find the medicine against death, whose great taboo was the holding of a funeral custom.

The foregoing account does not particularly enlarge upon the work of Komfo Anotche as a law-maker. The student of Ashanti law and custom, however, continually receives in answer to the question "why is such and such a rule observed?" the reply, "We do not know; Komfo Anotche made this a law." This applies to all such observances as clan exogamy, the keeping of Thursday as a day when no one might work in the fields, the forbidding of marriage with grandchildren, the prohibition to marry into the other half of the clan moiety. It is highly improbable that Anotche was the orig-inator of any of these rules. What he probably did was to establish, by edict, long-existing customs which were possibly already begin-ning to disappear. In any case, we may be assured, by the success which attended his efforts as a legislator, that his utterances and codes of conduct were based upon a profound knowledge of the past of the scattered tribes, whom by his genius he welded into a Nation. The last words ascribed to this remarkable man almost compel one to see in them an allegorical significance. The Ashanti would never find "the medicine against death," said he, because they had violated its great taboo, which was the holding of funeral lamentations for the dead. Death is only death because we persist in making that great change ever an occasion for mourning . . .

— 9 —

Islamic Sources

The Presence of Islam among the Akan of Ghana: A Bibliographic Essay

RAYMOND A. SILVERMAN AND DAVID OWUSU-ANSAH

Raymond A. Silverman and David Owusu-Ansah's bibliographic essay on the presence of Islam among the Akan remains a standard survey in the field. Although originally published in 1989 and a few studies on the topic have appeared since, no current and updated state of the subject exists.

The primary geographical focus for the historical study of Islam in West Africa, until recently, was the western and central Sudan. As the often-cited J. S. Trimingham wrote, "The Guinea States in the south lie outside our sphere since they were not in contact with the Sudan states and were uninfluenced by Islam." Trimingham's conclusion paralleled those of early twentieth-century French and English scholars who dealt with the issue of Islam in west Africa. Paul Marty's voluminous studies, dating from the second decade of this century, dealt with the Islamic and Muslim-influenced traditions of the various peoples of Francophone West Africa. H. R. Palmer, one of the early British writers of this century, concentrated on the northern territories of Nigeria, where Islam has enjoyed a long history.

Two factors explain the focus of these scholars on the western and central Sudan. First, the better known Islamic-influenced king-

doms of Ghana, Mali, Songhai, and Kanem-Bornu were all located
in this region. Second, the Islamic states of the western and central
Sudan, in particular, presented the greatest problem to both the
French and the British during the early periods of the colonial era.
Therefore, the focus on this area may have been motivated by the
desire of these writers to understand the Islamic factor. Whatever
the motivation of writers like Marty, Palmer, and their associates,
Trimingham was wrong to conclude that the Guinea States (i.e., the
peoples living in the coastal forest belt) were uninfluenced by Islam.
In fact, Muslims penetrated and influenced some of the coastal
states including those of the Akan. Ivor Wilks and John Hunwick
have written on the historiographical status of Islam in Ghana. Hunwick, in particular, commented extensively on studies done on the
history of Islam in that country. However, the existence of these
studies in no way makes the present survey irrelevant. In fact, we
are pleased to show that, since 1977 a number of additional contributions have been made to the study of the Islamic factor in the history of Ghana.

This paper presents an up-to-date survey of the literature pertaining to the Muslim presence among the Akan peoples of present-day
Ghana. It is divided into three sections. The first surveys the limited
but valuable Arabic literature; the second, the European primary
sources; and the final section presents the historical, archeological,
and art-historical studies that have been completed by scholars during the past thirty years.

Survey of Arabic Sources

In his *Tarikh al-Sudan*, Abd al-Rahman al-Sa'di made a definite association between the western Sudanese commercial centers of Tag-
haza and Jenne, and Bitu to the south. "Bitu," "Beetu," "Bew,"
or "Bighu" had developed as an entrepot on the northern fringes
of the Akan forest as early as the fifteenth century. Here, Malian
Wangara/Dyula Muslims did business, buying such commodities
as gold and kola nuts. The commercial situation at Bighu in the fif-

teenth century presupposes the existence in this location of both a well-structured social organization and a well-organized distributive trade. In fact, it was from Bighu that the Muslims who later settled at such places as Kong, Buna, and Bonduku in Côte d'Ivoire, and Namasa, Banda, and Mengye in Ghana, originated.

Scholarly debate regarding Bighu continues. This debate, however, has hardly diminished the importance of the relationship between Muslim Bighu and the surrounding regions, especially the Akan areas to the south. To be sure, the *ulama* of Kumase, interviewed over the years by researchers, have traced their scholarship to such locations as Buna, Bonduku, and Banda. It is not clear, however, that any Arabic documentation dating from the early period (from the fifteenth through seventeenth centuries) exists on Bighu. Nevertheless, numerous documents written in Arabic and dating from the mid-eighteenth century continue to surface, presenting valuable information for the reconstruction of the Akan past. Perhaps the best known such work is *Kitab al-Ghanja*.

Kitab al-Ghanja provides information on the history of the state of Gonja located to the north of Asante and contains short texts dealing with single themes: the founding of the dynasty, the arrival of Muslim clerics, the reign of the early kings, Gonja contacts with Asante, and the like. Some of the early *akhbar* (tales and histories) are known only from later texts into which they have been incorporated. The mid-eighteenth century *Kitab al-Ghanja* was compiled by Muhammad ibn al-Mustafa Kamaghatay and Umar Kunandi ibn Umar Kamaghatay. Sections of these manuscripts were collected first in 1930 by A. C. Duncan-Johnstone, an official in the administration of the northern territories of the Gold Coast Colony. A poorly translated Hausa version from the Duncan-Johnstone collection appears in Goody's *Ethnography of the Northern Territories* published in 1954. Between 1962 and 1966, Ivor Wilks and his research assistant, al-Hajj Uthman b. Ishaq Boyo, were able to locate fourteen manuscripts of *Kitab al-Ghanja*, which demonstrated considerable similarity to the original work. Wilks also located a number of other texts pertaining to the history of Gonja, some of nineteenth- and twentieth-century authorship, and deposited most of them at the Institute of African Studies, University of Ghana. Since *Kitab al-Ghanja* contains accounts over a three-century period, multiple authorship of the documents must be expected. A full translation and analysis of these manuscripts was completed recently by Wilks, Levtzion, and Haight. The importance of *Kitab al-Ghanja* is not limited to the subject of the introduction and growth of Islam in the northern territories of Ghana, for it also includes accounts of the early Asante expansion in the northern direction that resulted in the increase of Muslim contacts with the Akans.

Other Arabic documents have surfaced in European archives since the early 1960s. One of the most thoroughly-studied manuscript collections that date from the end of the eighteenth to the first quarter of the nineteenth century is housed in the Oriental section of the Royal Library, Copenhagen. Originally discovered in 1963 by Ray Kea, classified as Cod. Arab. CCCII, and labeled Arabic Manuscripts from the Guinea Coast, this corpus was subsequently analyzed by Levtzion and Owusu-Ansah. Cod. Arab. CCCII contains over 900 folios, over 90 percent of which are magical formulae for the making of amulets and charms. In addition there are a number of letters exchanged between the Muslims in Kumase and their brethren in the northern provinces of Gonja, Mamprugu, and Dagbon. A discussion of these Arabic letters in Wilks/Levtzion/Haight provides additional insights into the role of Muslims in nineteenth-century Kumase. A complete analysis of the documents in Cod. Arab. CCCII will surely add to our knowledge of the place of Muslims in Akan history.

Thomas Hodgkin, former Director of the Institute of African Studies at the University of Ghana, also helped to stimulate interest in the collection and study of Arabic material relevant to Ghana. His [1966] article outlined the various types of Arabic documents available to the historian. These Arabic manuscripts, systematically collected and deposited at the Institute of African Studies, provided valuable source material to such scholars as Martin, Levtzion, Wilks, and Goody, all of whom were affiliated with the Institute in the 1960s while researching Muslim-related themes.

Survey of European Primary Sources

The earliest references to Muslim contacts with the Akan are found in Portuguese sources. These documents provide information on the nature of Muslim contacts throughout the forest zone of West Africa. For example, the documents confirmed the dominance of the Islamized Mande peoples known as the Wangara or Dyula in the commerce of the region. One of many interesting insights obtained from these sources pertains to the existence of a strong Akan consumer preference for North African and western Sudanese commodities that had developed as a result of the Dyula's commercial presence on the coast. This material can be found in both the published accounts of Portuguese explorer/merchants like Duarte Pacheco Pereira and Valentim Fernandes. Moreover, information relating to the Muslim presence, dating from as early as the first decades of the sixteenth century, has recently been located in Portuguese archives by such scholars as Teixeira da Mota and McCall. Teixeira da Mota summarized his findings in a [1972] paper, "The Mande Trade in Costa da Mina According to Portuguese Documents until the Mid-Sixteenth Century." McCall contributed some interesting evidence along the same lines, in his "Who Was the Xarife on the Coasta da Mina in the 16th Century?"

It is important to note that archival sources for the reconsideration of the Muslim influences in Akan history have not been exploited thoroughly. Apart from Portuguese material, there are records preserved in metropolitan archives throughout Europe, especially in The Hague, London, and Copenhagen. The Danish and Dutch materials may provide significant information until 1850 and 1872, respectively, the years in which these two countries abandoned their possessions on the Gold Coast. The English records continue unbroken until 1902, the year in which Asante was annexed as a Crown Colony. Even though British control of the Gold Coast (now Ghana) continued until 1957, records for the years after 1902 were devoted mainly to administrative matters of the territories.

However, correspondence exchanged between British expeditionary forces in the Gold Coast and London during the second half of the nineteenth century is rich in information on the subject under discussion. Most of these materials are maintained in the Public Record Office. Between 1984 and 1985 we corresponded with Christies, London, and received a limited, but interesting, number of photographs and letters relating to Islamic material collected by British soldiers who served in the expeditionary forces that invaded Asante in 1873/74. In 1876 the Society of Antiquaries of London held an exhibition during which they displayed "various objects in bronze, and a cloth covered throughout with markings, from Coomassie" plundered from Asante. The "markings" on the cloth were *khawatim* (Islamic magical squares). Alexander G. Mackie, D. C. M., a member of another British expeditionary force into Asante in 1895/96, came across identical *khawatim* used as charms by the Asante. Both collections are similar to the contents of the previously discussed Cod. Arab. CCCII. At this moment it is not clear in what way papers in British private collections will be of utility to the subject under discussion. Nevertheless, it is probable that documents like the Christie's material will present some fresh insights.

References to the presence of Muslims within the Asante administrative system can be found in other nineteenth-century European records as well. The often-cited accounts of Thomas Bowdich, an agent of the British Company of Merchants, who visited Kumase in 1817, and Joseph Dupuis, an envoy of the British government to Kumase in 1819, are full of references to Muslims. Bowdich's *Mission from Cape Coast Castle to Ashantee* (1819) as well as Dupuis' *Journal of a Residence in Ashantee* (1824) stressed the influence of Muslims in Asante as courtiers and traders. Bowdich's observations on the Muslims in Kumase were commented upon by Biot of the French Royal Institute, Academy of Sciences. Biot's comments appeared in the *Journal des Savants*. Other nineteenth-century European accounts that deal with the position of Muslims in Asante can be found in the following sources: Jacob Simons, *Journal of Jacob Simons* (1831/32) originally deposited at the Algemeen Rijksarchief, The Hague, Archive of the Ministry of Colonies 1813-1850; T. B. Freeman, *Journal of Various Visits to the Kingdoms of Ashanti, Aku, and Dahomi in Western Africa* (1844); F. A. Ramseyer and J. Kühne, *Four Years in Ashante* (1875); and R. A. Freeman's *Travels and Life in Ashanti and Jaman* (1898).

Jacob Simons, the son of an Elmina woman and a Dutch official on the Gold Coast, was fluent in the Akan language. Working for the Dutch, Simons was sent on a special mission to Kumase in 1831/32 during which time he composed a list of the Asante authorities he saw at the ceremony held to welcome him. His list provides useful material for examining the shifting influence of Muslims in Asante, particularly during the reign of Asantehene Osei Yaw Akoto (r. 1824-33). Freeman, on the other hand, was a Wesleyan missionary. Having the opportunity to visit Kumase on two occasions, between 1839 and 1844, his accounts enable us to observe Asante attitudes towards foreign religious dogmas—material which is important in any discussion of religious conversion in centralized African states. A number of Freeman's observations can be found in documents housed in the Methodist Mission Archives in London as well as in Beecham's *Ashantee and the Gold Coast* (1841).

Ramseyer and Kühne were Presbyterian missionaries. Captured by Asante forces in the Anum expedition of 1869, the two spent four years in Kumase and had the opportunity to observe the activities of Muslims in the Asante capital. Their account, published in 1875, is a further contribution to our knowledge of the role of Muslims within the Asante government. Marie-Joseph Bonnat, a French merchant who was captured and released with Ramseyer and Kühne, returned to Kumase in 1875, a year after the Anglo-Asante war. This time, serving the Asante government while exploiting the possibilities of his own commercial interests, Bonnat had the opportunity to travel to the north and visited Salaga, an entrepôt located to the northeast of Kumase and depicted in Dupuis' 1824 publication as a booming commercial center often frequented by Hausa traders. Even though no detailed account of the status of Islam in the northern territories or its possible effect on the Akan was mentioned by Bonnat. J. Gros, in his *Voyages, aventures et captivité de J. Bonnat chez les Achantis* (1884), and subsequently in *Nos explorateurs en Afrique* (n.d.), gave detailed accounts of the declining commerce in the north—a condition that Bonnat attributed to the weakened Asante supervision of the trade routes and markets. Bonnat's observation brings to mind a theme that has been explored by scholars of Islam in Africa—the relationship between trade and politics. In the Akan milieu, Kwame Arhin's *African Trade in Ghana in the 19th and 20th Centuries* (1979) discusses aspects of this topic and is an excellent source for scholars interested in the subject.

A common feature of the nineteenth-century European accounts is their descriptive nature. This same approach is seen in the early attempts at recording the history of the Akan peoples—a good example being Reindorf's *The History of Gold Coast and Asante*, published in 1895. In this work Reindorf, a Gold Coast African, attempted for the first time a compilation of a large body of oral traditions that he had collected on the Gold Coast. There is virtually no mention of the Muslim presence in his work, except for a reference to an Arabic treaty signed between Asante and Gyaman.

Perhaps the most ambitious historical survey attempted on Asante during the first half of the twentieth century is Claridge's *A History of Gold Coast and Ashanti* (1915). This impressive two-volume work, almost exclusively based on English official documents, hardly mentions the Muslim presence. In addition, there are the works of Fuller, *A Vanished Dynasty: Ashanti* (1921), Welman, *The Native States of the Gold Coast: History and Constitution* (1925), Meyerowitz, *Akan Traditions of Origin* (1952), and Ward, *A History of Ghana* (1958); none of which contain significant discussion of Muslim interaction with the Akan. Even though the topic of Islamic influence among the Akan is not given the attention it is due in the early attempts at historical reconstruction, it does appear in the ethnographies of the early twentieth century. The well-known works of Rattray are exceptionally informative. In his *Ashanti* (1923), *Religion and Art in Ashanti* (1927), and *Ashanti Law and Constitution* (1929), there are many passages substantiating a Muslim presence and influence among the Akan. For example, in *Religion and Art in Ashanti*, Rattray comments on the use of Islamic charms among the Asante, a confirmation of the eclectic nature of Akan religious practice. The somewhat lesser, but still important, contribution of Cardinall, especially his *In Ashanti and Beyond* (1927), provides additional testimony to the Muslim factor.

Historical, Archeological,
and Art-Historical Studies since 1960

It was not until the end of the 1950s that historians began to deal with the issues surrounding the Muslim presence and influence among the Akan. In his *Ghana: A Historical Interpretation* (1959), Fage included a short passage discussing the presence of Muslim merchants in the Akan forest, and this marked the opening of a new era in Ghanaian historical studies. It was no coincidence that the new orientation began at this particular time. Africa experienced a wave of nationalist activities in the 1950s which influenced academic work as well. Thus the 1950s witnessed the birth of a new type of African history, one in which historians examined the activities of Africans rather than those of Europeans.

The watershed for the study of Islam in Asante is Ivor Wilks' *The Northern Factor in Ashanti History*. In this short monograph, Wilks examines the critical role played by Muslim Dyula merchants in the gold trade between the Akan forest and the western Sudan as well as the position held by Muslims in the nineteenth-century court of the Asantehene. Wilks' work is also the first serious examination of nineteenth-century European sources. He subsequently published a number of articles: "Islam in Ghana History: An Outline" (1962); "The Growth of Islamic Learning in Ghana" (1963); "The Position of Muslims in Metropolitan Ashanti in the Early 19th Century" (1966); "Ashanti Government" (1967); "The Transmission of Islamic Learning in the Western Sudan" (1968); "Wangara, Akan and Portuguese in the 15th and 16th Centuries: The Matter of Bitu" (1982); and "Wangara, Akan and Portuguese in the 15th and 16th Centuries: The Struggle for Trade" (1982). All these essays represent further elaborations on issues originally presented in *The Northern Factor in Ashanti History* and are the result of Wilks' digging still deeper, into the fifteenth- through nineteenth-century European and Arabic sources.

Since the 1960s a number of scholars have been working on various aspects of the Muslim presence. The majority have focused on the role of Muslims in commerce. Kwame Arhin has written several articles and edited two volumes that include information about Muslim trading activities. These include *Ashanti and the Northwest*, which he edited with Jack Goody in 1965; *Ashanti and the Northeast* (1970); "Aspects of the Ashanti Northern Trade in the Nineteenth Century" (1970); and "Atebubu Markets: ca. 1884-1930" (1971). Arhin's work deals with the volume of trade that came to the Akan markets as a result of the political hegemony exercised by Asante over the trade routes frequented by the Muslims.

Jack Goody, the well-known anthropologist of the peoples of northern Ghana, has also written extensively on the subject of Akan interactions with the North. These include "The Mande and the Akan Hinterland" (1964), "The Akan and the North" (1966), and (with T. M. Mustapha) "The Caravan Trade from Kano to Salaga" (1967). Other scholars examining the issue of Akan trade relations with Muslims are K. B. Dickson, "Trade Patterns in Ghana at the Beginning of the 18th Century" (1966), K. Y. Daaku, "Trade and Trading Patterns of the Akan in the 17th and 18th Centuries" (1971), and, once again, Ivor Wilks, "Asante Policy Towards the Hausa Trade in the 19th Century" (1971). As the titles of these papers indicate, the centralized Asante kingdom has been the focus of research, since it was this dominant Akan state which extended its hegemony into the zones already frequented by Muslim traders.

Although interest in the Muslim component in Akan trade has dominated the historical literature, other avenues of investigation have been pursued by scholars of several disciplines. One of the ongoing projects of the Institute of African Studies at the University of Ghana has been the collection of oral traditions from various regions of Ghana. For example, there is a good deal of Islamic-related material for the northwestern Akan (i.e., Bron and Abron) in the series of traditions recorded in west central Ghana by E.S.K. Owusu in 1975 and 1976.

In addition to documentary sources and oral traditions there is information about the Muslim presence to be gleaned from studying the material culture of the Akan. Archeological research has helped to improve our knowledge of the earliest period of Muslim activity among the Akan, dating from the fourteenth century and involving the Dyula. Between 1970 and 1980, Merrick Posnansky headed the West African Trade Project, a multi-disciplinary investigation focusing on the site of Bighu, the once thriving entrepôt located near the present-day village of Hani at the northern edge of the Akan forest in west central Ghana. In its heyday, from the late fourteenth to the seventeenth century, Bighu served as a major commercial center for Akan and Dyula traders. Notwithstanding the fact that the final report on the project has not yet been published, Posnansky and several of those scholars who worked on the project have published a number of articles based on their research. These include Posnansky's " Aspects of Early West African Trade" (1973) and "Archaeology and the Origins of the Akan Society in Ghana" (1977),

Leonard Corssland's "Traditional Textile Industry in Northwest Brong Ahafo, Ghana—The Archaeological and Contemporary Evidence" (1975), Timothy Garrard's "Notes on Begho" (1976), and Kropp-Dakubu's "On the Linguistic Geography of the Area of Ancient Begho" (1976). Additional evidence of early Muslim activity in the northern Akan region is presented in the recently published dissertation of the archeologist Effah-Gyamfi, *Bono Manso: An Archaeological Investigation into Early Akan Urbanism* (1985).

Other aspects of the Muslim presence have been the focus of art historians. One of the most important studies of the last twenty years is Rene Bravmann's examination of a number of masking traditions found at the northern fringes of Akan territory (in west central Ghana and east central Côte d'Ivoire), *Islam and Tribal Art in West Africa* (1974). In this seminal study he refutes the long-held notion that Islamization brought about the iconoclastic destruction of figurative imagery (including masks) used in religious contexts. This work, as well as his "Gur and Manding Masquerades in Ghana" (1979), has enhanced our understanding of the complex syncretic structures arising from the interaction of Mande-, Gur-, and Akan-speaking peoples. Garrard's analysis of Akan gold-weights, *Akan*

Weights and the Gold Trade (1980), produces evidence that the weighing system of the Akan originated in northern Africa and that it was introduced into the forest zone by Dyula traders prior to European contact. In this and other works, such as "Akan Metal Arts" (1979), Garrard convincingly argues that the introduction of the lost-wax casting technique, the technology used in the production of the well-known Akan brass goldweights, brass containers (*kuduo*), and gold regalia, was associated with an early Dyula presence among the Akan.

This same theme is picked up again in Raymond Silverman's "Akan Kuduo: Form and Function" (1983). Silverman studied a number of fourteenth- and fifteenth-century Middle Eastern brass bowls that are today revered as objects of considerable historic and religious importance in various Akan towns. His dissertation, "History, Art and Assimilation: The Impact of Islam on Akan Material Culture" (1983), considers how and why these products of the Islamic world were assimilated by their Akan owners. One aspect of their assimilation involved their use as prototypes in the evolution of the *kuduo*, a brass container used in religious and economic contexts by the Akan until the end of the nineteenth century. The theme of Islamic influence on the development of Akan material traditions is considered in the architectural setting by Labelle Prussin. In her article, "Traditional Asante Architecture" (1980), Prussin discusses the impact that Islamic design has had on the Akan-built environment. More recently Bravmann and Silverman, in "Painted Incantations: The Closeness of Allah and Kings in Nineteenth-Century Asante" (1987), have considered the perceived apotropaic powers of Arabic writing and the role of Muslim clerics (*ulama*) as producers of various magico-religious devices in nineteenth-century Asante. This same theme, the Muslim cleric as a producer of charms and amulets, has been discussed more extensively in Owusu-Ansah's 1983 and 1986 papers, in which he stresses the popularity of such Muslim amulets within the Asante army. It was, in fact, Nehemia Levtzion who first explored this issue in his *Muslims and Chiefs in West Africa* (1968), a work of prime importance to those interested in examining the interaction between Muslim clerics and

West African political leaders. Notwithstanding the many contacts between the Akan and Muslims, the former were not Islamized. Owusu-Ansah has examined the particular responses of the Asante in his "Islamization Reconsidered: Asante Responses to Muslims in the 19th Century" (1987) while in his "Power or Prestige? Muslims in 19th Century Asante" (1987), he deals with the political relations developed between the Kumase administration and Muslim residents in the capital. In a more recent paper, "The State and Islamization in 19th-Century Africa: Buganda Absolutism versus Asante Constitutionalism" (1987), Owusu-Ansah attempts a comparative study of the role of Islam in centralized states, in which he points to the nature of Asante political organization as the main obstacle to Islamization.

While a good deal of work has been done on the Islamic influence on the Akan, studies that examine the structure of the Muslim communities in this region are limited. Reference can be made to Kwame Arhin's "Strangers and Hosts: A Study in the Political Organisation and History of Atebubu" (1971) and his aforementioned 1979 publication, as well as Enid Schildkrout's "Strangers and Local Government in Kumasi" (1970). Schildkrout's further research in this area is presented in her *People of the Zongo* (1978). It is obvious that research at such centers as Wenchi, Nkenkaasu, Techiman, and Bonduku as well as Buna in Côte d'Ivoire, where Muslim communities are well-developed, will contribute further to our understanding of the organization of Muslim societies in the Akan heartland.

Research on Muslim activities among the southern Akan is even more exiguous. An article titled "Early Fante Islam" written by H. Debrunner, H.H.A. Fisher, and H. J. Fisher appeared in 1959 and 1960. This was a translation of a Basel Missionary's report of 1913, which the authors analyzed using oral data relating to the period. Since then, no serious attempt has been made to study the status of Islam among the coastal Akan. A serious study of the Ahmadiyya movement (an Islamic sect which has its base at Saltpond in the south), focusing on its roles in education and the propagation of Islam, as well as its conflicts with "orthodoxy," needs to be done.

It is clear that H. J. Fisher's four-page treatment of the subject in his *Ahmadiyya: A Study of Contemporary Islam on the West African Coast* (1963) seems inadequate.

Wilks' magnum opus, *Asante in the Nineteenth Century: The Structure and Evolution of a Political Order* (1975), stands as the most impressive attempt at reconstructing the Islamic past among the Akan. The use of archival sources and oral traditions, as well as the author's particular investigative skills, has unveiled a number of themes for further research. A topic that surely would yield exciting new insights is the history of the Asante Nkramo, a Muslim family which was granted Asante citizenship by Asantehene Kwaku Dua Panin (r. 1834-1867) in 1841 and consequently incorporated into the *nsumankwaa* (the royal physicians in Kumase). While a number of interviews have been conducted with members of this unit in Kumase, their counterparts at Nkenkaasu have received limited attention. The Cod. Arab. CCCII still requires detailed analysis. And there is undoubtedly a rich store of information to be obtained from further research in the colonial, mercantile, and religious archives of Europe. There is no doubt that much has been accomplished since Wilks and Hunwick wrote their essays identifying themes for further research. But as Wilks aptly concluded, "The . . . field offers exciting prospects for the historian, and locating, translating, editing, and publishing of such material will engage the attention of scholars for many years."

Early-Nineteenth-Century Arabic Manuscripts from Kumasi

NEHEMIA LEVTZION

The late Nehemia Levtzion was a recognized scholar of the social history of Islam in Africa and elsewhere. The following essay first appeared in the journal Transactions of the Historical Society of Ghana *in 1965, and in it*

Levtzion critically examines a set of Arabic manuscripts located at the Royal Library in Copenhagen. These manuscripts have bearing on the history of Asante and its relations with Muslims.

Introduction

Professor Ivor Wilks, of the Institute of African Studies, University of Ghana, drew my attention to a collection of Arabic manuscripts from West Africa at the Royal Library in Copenhagen. In the following communication, written in May 1964, Professor Wilks describes how he came to know about these manuscripts:

> In 1744-5 Ashanti forces invaded Dagomba, an event reported in both contemporaneous Arabic and European sources. Among the loot taken from the Dagomba towns were a number of Arabic works, and these subsequently passed into the hands of the Danes on the Guinea Coast. "We have," remarked Rømer, Danish factor at Christiansborg, "received many Arabic books at Accra, which the Ashantis had plundered" (*Tilforladelig Effterretning om Kysten Guinea*, Copenhagen, 1760). On the assumption that these manuscripts were subsequently removed to Denmark, enquiries there were started in 1961. Initially meeting with no success, in mid-1963 Miss Hertha Kirketerp-Moller of the Oriental section of the Royal Library, Copenhagen, drew our attention to three bundles of manuscripts, Code Arab CCCII, labeled on the wrappings, "Arabic manuscripts from the Guinea Coast." Since Christiansborg was the Danish headquarters on the Guinea Coast in the 18th and the first half of the 19th century, it is probable that these manuscripts arrived in Denmark from there. That they are the ones specifically referred to by Rømer seems not unlikely. Unfortunately, other than the note on the wrappings, there is apparently no further indication of provenance or donor.

Upon the advice of Professor Wilks, I visited the Royal Library at Copenhagen, on my way from Ghana to London, to examine these manuscripts. According to internal evidence, they were taken from Kumasi, and had been written, mainly, during the first two decades of the nineteenth century. They arrived in Copenhagen sometime between 1820 and 1850.

In 1817 and 1820 two British missions visited Kumasi. T. E. Bowdich and W. Hutchison of the first mission, and J. Dupuis of the second mission, paid special attention to the Muslim community in Kumasi, and were in close communication with its leaders. Both Bowdich and Dupuis obtained Arabic manuscripts from the Muslims, as well as oral information about Ashanti and the interior. Professor Ivor Wilks made use of these and other contemporary sources in analyzing the structure of Ashanti government and the position of the Muslim community in Ashanti, in the early nineteenth century. These European sources and Wilks' papers have been invaluable guides to the reading of the Copenhagen manuscripts.

Magical Formulas

The three bundles of Arabic manuscripts at the Royal Library in Copenhagen, Code Arab CCCII, hold about 900 folios. Over ninety percent of these manuscripts may be described as magical formulas, or prescriptions for preparing amulets. These Muslim amulets, and their influence on the Ashanti, were commented on by Bowdich:

> The most surprising superstition of the Ashantees, is their confidence in the fetishes or saphies they purchase so extravagantly from the Moors, believing firmly that they make them invulnerable and invincible in war, paralyse the hand of the enemy, shiver their weapons, divert the course of balls, render both sexes prolific, and avert all evils but sickness (which they can only assuage) and natural death. . . . A sheet of paper would support an inferior Moor in Coomassie for a month.

And by Dupuis:

> The talismatic charms fabricated by the Moslems, it is
> well known, are esteemed efficacious, according to the
> various powers they are supposed to possess; and here is
> a source of great emolument, as the article is in public
> demand from the palace to the slave's hut; for every man
> . . . wears them strung around the neck. . . . Some are ac-
> counted efficacious for the cure of gunshot wounds, oth-
> ers for the thrust or laceration of steel weapons, and the
> poisoned barbs of javelins, or arrows. . . . Besides this
> class of charms, they have other cabalistic scraps for
> averting the evils of natural life . . . some, for instance
> for averting nostrums in certain diseases of the human
> frame, some for their prevention, and some are calculated
> either to ward off any impending stroke of fortune, or to
> raise the proprietor to wealth, happiness and distinction.

Cabalistic formulas of all categories described above are represented in this collection of manuscripts. Most of these are written
on single slips of paper, but there are some treatises dealing at some
length with various aspects of this craft. These works might have
been copied from books brought from the interior or even from the
East, and served as sources from which the Muslims of Kumasi
used to derive their specific amulets. Among other works one can
mention: *The merits of Surat Yusuf and its advantages*, *The advantages of the month of Ramadan*, *Devices for a holy war* etc. There
are other works of astrological nature, such as *The Mansions of the
Moon*—the use of the names of the moon for magical devices, and
a list of good and bad days throughout the year.

The belief of the ("pagan") king, sub-chief, and subjects in the
power of the Muslim amulets and prayers helped the Muslims to
secure an influential position in the Ashanti court. As traders they
were encouraged to come and tolerated when they stayed, but as
believers in the "Great God," keepers of the "Strong Book," masters
of literacy and magical powers, they were much respected, revered
and regarded with awe.

Correspondence between Kumasi and the North

The Muslims in Kumasi sold amulets to anybody who paid for them, but their most important duty was to help the King. In this respect the Muslims in Kumasi did not act alone, and thus, apart from producing amulets and praying for victory, they had to be in communication with the Muslim leaders in the hinterland to get their blessings for the Ashanti King.

In this collection there are fifteen letters of correspondence between the Muslims in Kumasi and their brethren in Mamprusi, Dagomba and Gonja. These letters illustrate the relations between the Muslims in Kumasi and those in the northern states, and throw some light on the leading personalities of the Muslim community in Kumasi. This information should be compared with the records left by Bowdich and Dupuis, who had met personally some of the people mentioned in the letters.

Soon after his arrival in Kumasi, Dupuis was attended by a deputation of the Muslims. He mentions the names of nine of the principal Muslim residents: Muhammad al-Ghamba, Abur-Bakr ibn Ture, Suma, Kantoma, Abdallah ibn Ghatta, Ali ibn Muhammad, Jalal ibn Qudsi al-Bouroumy, Al-hajj Mubarak al-Salaghawi, and Ibrahim al-Yandi. Nothing more is known about the last five people, except that, for the last three, their *nisbas* denote their place of origin or previous residence. Thus, Jalal ibn Qudsi was from Bouromy, the Brong country around Atebubu, Al-hajj Mubarak was from Salaga, and Ibrahim from Yendi. These people, in all probability, were engaged in the flourishing trade between Kumasi and the interior, through their native towns in the immediate hinterland of Ashanti.

Baba of Gambaga

The most prominent Muslim personality in Kumasi was undoubtedly Muhammad al-Ghamba, more commonly known as Baba. Throughout his book, Dupuis refers to him as "Bashaw" or "Caid," as if these were his official titles. It seems that Dupuis has been deceived by his previous acquaintance with the Muslims in the Maghreb, where the titles of "Basha" and "Qa'id" are common for headmen and officials. It is possible that Dupuis replaced "Basha" for "Baba." It is important to make this point clear, for by using consistently the title "Bashaw" or "Caid," one gives him an official title which presumably did not exist.

The following letter illustrates one aspect of Baba's duties in the Ashanti court:

> From Abu Bakr, Sultan Kamsheghu to Baba, son of Imam Gambaga. Extend our greetings to the Sultan of Ashanti. Take five trees; plant one of them in the middle of the house, together with four scraps of paper in a cow's clutch. As for the other four trees, plant them in the east, west, south and north of your town. As a medicine for headache, take three small scraps of paper and hang them on your arm. Wash your body at sunset and rub it with a small quantity of powder in the morning, then at evening time wash the body in water, without medicine. Do all this everyday. Baba, tell the Sultan that I pray to Allah, but he has to give as present: a male slave, dressed in a red gown with a *mithqal* in his pocket, three guns, seven golden *riyals* and a new white gown. Let him collect all this and send it on the head of a red slave, for the health of his body. As for the good welfare of his country, and for the virgin woman, who had been the cause for the disturbances, he has to contribute seven *riyals*. Sultan Yendi Andani thanks Allah, and thanks the Sultan of Ashanti. The Sultan of Kamsheghu prays for you, Baba, that you will come back to your land in good health.

The writer of this letter, the Sultan of Kamsheghu, is Kamshe-Na, the senior Muslim elder in Dagomba. As a Muslim elder of the Ya-Na, a tributary of Ashanti, he extended his religious services to the king of Ashanti, though demanding expensive presents for these.

Bowdich has another example of similar transactions with Dagomba:

> The King [of Ashanti] gave to the King of Dagwumba, for the fetish or war coat of Apokoo, the value of thirty slaves; for Odumata's twenty; for Addoo Quamina's thirteen; for Akimpon's twelve; for Akimpontea's nine; and for those of greater captains in proportion.

As an influential person in Kumasi, and a native of Mamprusi, the sister-state of Dagomba, Baba acted as a representative of Dagomba (or the Dagomba Muslims) in Kumasi. Kamshe-Na sent his letter to the King of Ashanti through Baba. Baba himself told Dupuis that he was a member of the King's council in affairs relating to the believers of Sarem and Dagomba. This is confirmed again by Dupuis:

> The Moslems of Dagomba and Ghunja, headed by the Bashaw, Abou Beer, Cantoma, and Shoumo, came in a body to return thanks, in the name of their sovereign, the King of Yendi, (capital of Dagomba) for a present he had already despatched to that monarch.

Abu-Bakr ibn Ture was Baba's trading agent. But it seems that he acted also as his personal representative in the royal court. Baba sent Abu-Bakr to the palace to get information for Dupuis. Twice Dupuis met Abu-Bakr, together with Kantoma, sitting before the King of Ashanti. Abu-Bakr himself was probably of Hausa origin, as the *nisba* "Ture" is very common among Hausa from Katsina.

Another interesting document is a letter sent by Baba, son of Imam Gambaga, to Malik, Imam of Ghilfe (Buipe), and to the Imam of Burughu (Daboya):

> Allah brought trial and misfortune upon Ashanti, the land of the infidels. Qarantan, the Sultan, his mother Konadu, and all the elders met in council. They said, perhaps Allah

brought all this, because the Muslims' rights had been violated. They decided to set free all the Muslims—men,
women, young and old—who had been captured and enslaved, and to send them back to their countries. The
Muslims rejoiced because of that decision. But then came
forward the enemy of Allah, of the Prophet and all the
Muslims—Karamo Sali—and his son Kakura-Lima. Sali
said, "I can tell you its remedy." All the elders of Ashanti,
the Sultan and Qarantan asked, "What is it?" Sali said,
"Take a handsome slave you have captured in Gambaga,
another from Daboya (i.e. Burughu), Diber, Buipe,
Gonja-Yagbum, Yendi and Kpembi. Dress them with
Egyptian gowns and trousers, and put on some of them
golden bracelets, and on others silver bracelets. Then take
one hundred mithqals of gold and a big goat, and sacrifice all these, in the name of each town. Your affairs will
be settled. I inform you of all this. Pray that Allah will
give no blessing to Sali, the enemy of Allah, to his household and property."

Mention is made in this letter of the Ashanti Queen-Mother,
Konadu, who can be identified with Konadu, fifth Queen-Mother,
who died about 1810. The situation described in this letter may well
be related to the early phases of Muslim settlement in Kumasi. At
that time many Muslims had been war-prisoners, and their position
in Kumasi was unstable due to the rather hostile attitude of Osei
Tutu Kwame towards the Muslims at the beginning of his reign.
The council probably met not long after Baba had first settled in
Kumasi, in 1807. Baba seemed to be almost helpless, and he could
only ask the Gonja Imams to invoke God's rage over Karamo Sali.
Some years later Baba became more influential in the Ashanti court,
and the position of the Muslims improved.

According to the two letters quoted above, Baba was a son of the
Imam of Gambaga. There are, however, different versions of the
circumstances of his coming to Kumasi. We shall examine first
Baba's own accounts reported by Bowdich and Dupuis, and then

current traditions recorded from Gambaga and Walewale. Bowdich wrote:

> The invasion of the Fantee kingdom in 1807 was the first important military act of the present reign. . . . Whilst the invasion was meditating, Baba, now the Chief of the Moors, presented himself to solicit an asylum in Coomasie, having been driven from Gamba by the rapacity of the King, his near relative; and professing solely to desire the recovery of a large property withheld from him, to make the King of Ashantee the heir to it. The King promised he would oblige the King of Gamba to do him justice, on his return from the Fantee war, if Baba and his companions were fortunate in their prayers and charms for his success. The King of Gamba did not think proper to resist the demand afterwards made through the Ashantee government.

It is possible that Baba was indeed a relative of the Mamprusi King (the Na-Yiri), for the Na-Yiri gives his daughters in marriage to the Imams. Baba might therefore have been a son of a Mamprusi princess. There is also evidence to prove that there has long been tension in Mamprusi between the Na-Yiri and the Imams of Gambaga. Such could cause the dispute which led to the emigration of Baba to Kumasi.

In all probability Bowdich heard this account from Baba himself. Baba, however, had another story for Dupuis:

> When I was young man . . . I worked for the good of my body. I traded on the face of God's earth, and traveled much; as my beard grew strong I settled at Salagha, and lastly removed to this city.

This is the story of a trader; and, indeed, in Kumasi Baba continued to trade with foreign countries through the agency of his friend Abil-Bake.

The following tradition about Baba was related to me by the Imam of Gambaga, whose grandfather was Baba's grandson:

> Baba was traveling around in Mossiland. At that time Ashanti used to capture slaves in the North. When Baba came back from his travels he was told that his wife (or another woman of his family) had been taken by the Ashanti. He went to Kumasi and presented himself before the King of Ashanti Kakudia, demanding the captured woman. The King sent to bring all the captive women from the neighboring villages, among whom Baba was allowed to take out all the women he knew. The King allowed Baba to send these women to Salaga, but did not let Baba himself leave Kumasi, for he wanted him to be his malam.
>
> Baba had a son Dawuda, and Dawuda had two sons: Adam and Ramadan. After a year of residence in Kumasi Baba asked permission to send for his grandson Adam, who was more pious than Baba himself. Adam was sent to Kumasi, where he impressed the king with his piety and religious power. For three years, Adam used to spend six months in Kumasi and then six months back in Gambaga. Then Adam became Imam of Gambaga, while his brother, Ramadan, became Imam of Walwale. Adam was Imam for thirty years, and all that time the King of Ashanti used to send him annual presents.

In Gambaga, Baba is remembered mainly as the grandfather of their celebrated Imam Adam. In Walwale, the Imamship is rotated among three "gates." One of these "gates" was founded by Ramadan, brother of Adam the Imam of Gambaga, and thus son of Dawuda, son of Baba. Abdulai, the Friday Imam of Walwale, grandson of Ramadan, told me. Ramadan was appointed Imam of Walwale after he had come back from Kumasi. He went to Kumasi to visit his grandfather Yaw, who was staying there. How was it that Yaw went to stay in Kumasi? An army from Ashanti came to the North to get slaves. On their way back they came to a river, which they could not cross. They sent for Yaw, a famous Malam from Gambaga, to help them. Yaw came, and they followed him across the river, and they reached Kumasi. At that time there was a war near Kintampo, and the King of Ashanti asked Yaw to accompany him to the war and pray for his victory. The King won the war, and asked Yaw to stay with him. Yaw's family left Kumasi only before the arrival of the Europeans, when they moved to Salaga, Masaka and Yeji.

In the Copenhagen Manuscripts there is a book, *On the Advantages of the Month of Ramadan*, with a colophon: "The scribe is Ramadan ibn Dawuda Ghambagha; the owner is Karmo Tama the town—Kumasi; Saturday the 22nd. His grandfather in Kumasi. The Yaw (which is an Ashanti name)." This book was obviously copied by Ramadan during his visit. . . . [T]he Walwale tradition should be identified with the Baba of the Gambaga tradition, and both, in all probability, with the Baba of Dupuis, Bowdich and the Arabic correspondence.

Baba, according to Bowdich, was asked to pray for victory in the Fanti war, and Yaw, of the Walwale tradition, for victory in a war near Kintampo. It is suggested that the participation of Baba in the Ashanti wars, mentioned by Dupuis, was as a Malam who prays for victory, rather than as a commander of the Muslim auxiliaries.

The main theme in the Gambaga tradition, that of the ransom of the captive woman, is the subject of the following correspondence:

> From Umar Kunate to Alfa Ali Samisiku, known as Baba Samisiku, son of the late Imam Kusu. You have sent us a letter about your old woman (*kabiratuka*), asking us to tell you her price. It is impossible for us to sell her, for the sake of her father Limam Ghunu, and for your own sake. I have taken her from the infidels, in exchange for one slave. Our greetings to you, to all your neighbors, to our Imam, and to all the Muslims, men and women. Please, send me a white gown for praying.

The reply to this letter is on the back of the same folio:

> From Ali, known as Baba to Alfa Umar; I thank you for
> what you have done. You have fulfilled your promise to
> the Imam. . . . May Allah give you long life. I have heard
> all that you had done for me. I send you some oil for the
> lantern. I am tired of this world's affairs. I have with me
> all my brothers with our wives and our paternal uncle.
> Not one of them left. As for what we have talked about,
> explain it to me in a letter and send it with my sister. You
> will put her with my sons Marzuq and Yamusa until I fin-
> ish my work. Then I will certainly come. May Allah get
> us together in a blessed hour. Let me know her price in a
> letter. Greetings to you from Imam Gambaga, and from
> Mallam Sha'ban, Alfa Mahmud and all the Muslims.

Ali Baba sends greetings from the Imam of Gambaga, which suggests that he was staying at Gambaga. His *nisba* "Samisiku" resembles the *nisba* of the house of the Imam of Gambaga "Samso," or,
as it is pronounced by another branch of the same house, now at
Masaka, "Sainsheghu." Ali Baba Samisiku son of the Imam Kusu,
like Baba the Muslim leader in Kumasi, was of the house of the
Imam of Gambaga. He promised in his letter to come down to Kumasi to take the captive woman, which reminds us of the Gambaga
tradition about the arrival of Baba in Kumasi. Though Ali Baba's
letter and that of Baba to Buipe and Daboya are not in the same
hand, I would not dismiss the possibility that ᶜAli Baba Samisiku
came down from Gambaga to Kumasi, as promised in his letter, and
stayed there to become the famous Baba. Dupuis calls him Muhammad al-Ghamba, yet Hutton, a member of Dupuis' mission, refers
to him as Ali Baba.

From the early days of the Gonja state, the Muslims helped the
chiefs to gain victory in war, and to secure the welfare of the country, by praying to Allah, and by producing amulets and other medicines. After Gonja became tributary to Ashanti, the Gonja imams
extended their services to the overlord of Gonja, the king of Ashanti.
To perform these services, and to form the link between the Ashanti
king and the Gonja imams, there were two representatives of the

Gonja Muslims staying in Kumasi—Suma ibn Muhammad Bawa
and Muhammad ibn Imam Gonja. The following correspondence
between Kumasi and some of the Gonja towns, illustrates these relations.

The Gonja Muslims in Kumasi

From the Great Sultan Sai Disbi [Osei Tutu Kwame/Osei
Bonsu] to the Imam Malik and to the Imam of Ghufe
[Buipe]. I call you to pray for me; pray for the sickness
we have in our body (sickness we are aware about, and
that which we neglect, sickness of arms and legs); pray
to keep off the Devil who comes to people at night; pray
for the new house, so that plague, disease or misfortune
will never enter our house; divert an evil eye from me. I
call you to make divination for me, and do let me know
whatever you find: do not cover anything. The writer of
this letter is Muhammad ibn al-Imam. His greetings to
his beloved friend, the Imam of Ghufe and to his father,
the Imam of Gonja, and to his mother. Then, greetings
from Suma ibn Mhammad Baba to the Imam of Ghufe
and to Imam Malik.

This letter, from the King of Ashanti, is written on a paper which
has a watermark 1818 as the year of production. On the back of this
letter, Malik, Imam of Gonja, wrote his reply, which he sent also in
another copy with only slight variations:

From Malik to Muhammad ibn al-Karim and Suma ibn
al-Karim. May Allah give our Sultan, the Sultan of
Ashanti, long life that he will be very old, and in good
health. Tell the Sultan to give you a fine goat, four thousand cowries and forty kola-nuts. Then he should ask you
to read before him prayers for the Prophet, out of the
book *Dala'il al-Khayrat*. Then, he may ask Allah what-

ever he wishes for himself, for his household, for his town and country. Then he may enter the new house, and Allah will give him long life, until he will be an old man in good health. Oh, Muhammad and Suma, I ask you to send us paper, as we have not here even one leaf. May Allah give you long life. . . . May Allah save you from meeting your end in the land of infidels. May He bless your livelihood, and let Allah join us together in the land of Gonja.

There is another letter from Malik, in the same handwriting:

From Malik Imam Gonja to the Sultan of Ashanti, who subdued all countries by the help of Allah. Greetings to our son Muhammad ibn al-Imam Gonja, to [S]uma ibn al-Karim (called) Bawa, to our beloved Baba, and to all the Muslims. I pray day and night that Allah will give you long life, health, dignity and power. I pray that Allah will bless your child, your ancestors, your wives, and all your household. You have to give as present: two slaves, twelve *mithqals*, two gowns—white and red, two fowls—male and female, two goats—male and female, ten *dirhams*, two caps—white and red, two bowls—white and red, and a gun. Then take seeds and flower of guinea-corn and millet, add salt, oil, and every eatable food, and give all this as a present. Then you may ask Allah to give you long life and good health, and benefit to your country. I do not forget you even for one day; so, please, do not forget me. I rely upon you in this world, and we are happy in your land. This is why we pray to Allah to give you long life. Then, our son who came to you has some need. If Allah fulfils his need, please look at him in favour.

The following two letters were sent to the king of Ashanti by the Imam of Buipe. These not only reply to the King's letter, quoted above, but deal also with other requests of the King.

> From the Imam of Wife to the Great Sultan Osei Kwesi,
> the honest king, the savior of the Muslims, Greetings to
> you, Shaykh Suma and Muhammad ibn al-Mustafa Imam
> Gonja. Oh, Great Sultan, I pray to Allah that he may give
> you long life and good health. As for the trifle sickness
> in your body, nothing will happen, because of the new
> house and the woman Dinkara, you may marry her, but
> never come to the woman Dinkara on Wednesday and
> Saturday. If you leave her (on these two days) you will
> find good health. The present (you have to give) because
> of the woman: a black cloth, a new vessel and grains. If
> you give this you will find benefit and good health in
> your house, by Allah's will. The woman Dinkara will be
> pregnant twice. At first, her pregnancy will be spoiled,
> but later she will bring forth a healthy child. Then the
> child will be sick, on the point of dying. If he survives,
> you must bring a present of a red cow, a red cloth and
> five *mithqal*. Then you will have benefit and good health
> in your house, and victory over your enemies. When you
> enter the new house, read the Quran with *Dala'il al-
> Khayrat*.

The second letter is without the name of its sender, but since it is in the same handwriting as the last one, and in the same style, should also be attributed to the Imam of Buipe:

> Oh, great Sultan Osei Kwesi, nicknamed (*walaqabuhu*)
> Busu. Oh, sympathizer of the Muslims, who is not afraid
> of anything, but Allah. May Allah give you long life.
> What is attributed by hearsay and deceit, nothing will
> happen to you, for the sake of the Holy Qur'an. But you
> have to give in present: a woman with a child, a man, a
> horse, five *mithgal*, a new gown—all of what you like
> yourself and a white goat. If you give this, nothing will

harm you, never will the town spoil, and no bad disease
will come. As for the consequences of the *jihad*, no town
will be spoiled or put in fire. Oh, Sultan Osei Kwesi,
Dinkira was (or will be) killed one day; and all countries
were (or, will be) surprised. The present for the outcome
of the jihad against Dinkira: a black male slave, a black
gown, everything eatable, a bowl, a gun and a fowl. Oh,
Sultan of the Muslims, have pity on the Muslims; may
Allah give you long life, and bless you all your life. May
Allah give you victory, and raise you over enemies. May
Allah fulfill all your needs, and reward your goodness.

Another letter of the same nature was sent to Kumasi from Kpembi:

Muhammad ibn Abu-Bakr, Imam of Kunbi (Kpembi)
prays for the welfare of the town Kumasi, in Ashanti, so
that all its people will find benefit. Then, write four papers and bury them to the east, west, south and north.
Bury another paper in the gate of the house. Then he will
find wealth (or, power) and victory in the town, and
among all people. Then he has to read the Qur'an in four
places, so that the town Kumasi will have benefit. He has
to give presents: a (red) slave, a red bowl, gold, forty
dinar, white gown and red trousers. Then, good will
come to you. This is a letter from a brother to his brother.

It is not certain whether this letter, like the others, was sent to the
king, through one of the Muslim residents. But from the following
letter we may assume that the Kpembi Muslims also used to turn to
the representatives of Gonja in Kumasi, asking their support:

From Idris ibn al-Kunbi (Kpembi) Malam Karfa to
Muhammad ibn al-Imam Ghufe (Buipe). Imam Karfa
died; and left behind poverty, hunger and orphans. There
is no sympathizer but Allah, and your brother, the believer. I beseech you, in the name of Allah, do not leave

us calling for pity. May Allah have pity on you, and add
you benefit and long life. May He open for you all gates
of goodness and close the gates of evil.

Muhammad refers to Malik Imam Gonja as "our father," while
Malik calls Muhammad "our son Muhammad ibn Imam Gonja," or
in another letter, "Muhammad ibn al-Karim (the noble)." The Imam
of Buipe calls him "Muhammad ibn al-Mustafa Imam Gonja." From
all these references it is suggested that Muhammad was a son of
imam Malik's brother. According to local custom he is regarded as
a son of Malik, though his father's name is other than Malik. The
Iman of Gonja is senior to the Imam of Buipe, and according to custom, the Imam of Buipe is promoted to be the Imam of all Gonja.
Malik had visited Imam of Buipe, before Baba sent his letter, which
we dated as pre-1810, to "Malik in the Imamship of Ghufe," i.e.
Buipe. Idris ibn Imam Kpembi Malam Karfa addressed his letter to
"Muhammad ibn Ghufe," probably when Malik was Imam of
Buipe; Muhammad, nephew or son of Malik, was of the same gen-
eration as the Imam of Buipe who succeeded Malik. This is why
Muhammad calls him "our beloved friend," while Uthman, son of
the Imam of Buipe, being junior to Muhammad calls him "our fa-
ther Muhammad."

We can attempt to reconstruct the genealogy of Malik further. An
interesting colophon is found on one of the manuscripts:

This book was completed on Wednesday, 29th Muhar-
ram, at Salaga. The scribe is Umar Kunade ibn Umar
Laurin (al-Amin) and his mother Amila from the house
of Imam Ghunaba, Umar Kunade, father of Malik
Limam Ghufe.

Limam Umar Kunade ibn Umar is one of the two compilers of
an important Gonja chronicle completed in a.h. 1178 (a.d. 1764/65).
Hence, it is possible that Malik, Imam of Buipe, who later became
Imam of Gonja, was the son of one of the compilers of the Gonja
chronicle. A fragment of this chronicle was found in this collection

of manuscripts, and may have been in possession of Muhammad ibn Imam Gonja.

It seems that Muhammad was connected more with the Imam of Gonja, and Suma with the Imam of Buipe. Though the letter from the Ashanti king had been written by Muhammad, the reply from the Imam of Buipe was addressed mainly to Suma. Uthman ibn Imam Buipe refers to Muhammad as "our father" while he calls Suma "our slave." Presumably there was a joking relationship between Suma and the Buipe imam's son. Appendix no. 4 in Dupuis, the route from Salaga to Hausa, was written by Suma. He there calls himself, "habib Sai," i.e., "the friend of Sai," the Ashanti king. By reading these letters, one gets the impression that Baba, Suma and Muhammad were the leading Muslim personalities in Kumasi. Yet Muhammad is apparently not mentioned by Dupius. An Arabic manuscript, a route from Salaga to Mecca, printed as Appendix no. 6 of Dupuis' book, was written by "Muhammad Kama'te, known as Kantoma." The *nisba* Kama'te may be "Kamaghte," which is common *nisba* among the Gonja imams. Again, a magical formula was given by Sharif Ibrahim to "his friend Muhammad, known as Karamo Toghma." A letter was sent by four "fuqaha," addressed to "Baba, Suma and Muhammad, known as Karamo Toma." It seems obvious that Muhammad ibn Imam Gonja is in fact Muhammad Kama'te, known as Kamaro Toma, or to Dupuis, Kantoma.

Twice Dupuis met Kantoma and Abu-Bakr sitting before the king of Ashanti. As we have tried to show, Baba and Abu-Bakr acted as representatives of the Dagomba Muslims, and Kantoma (Muhammad) and Suma of the Gonja Muslims. Or, as Dupuis put it: "The Muslims of Dagomba and Ghunja, headed by the Bashaw, Abou-Becr, Cantoma, and Shoumo, came in a body to return thanks. . . ."

A Visitor to Kumasi—Sharif Ibrahim

While in Kumasi, Bowdich and Hutchison met Sharif Ibrahim, who claimed to be a descendant of the Prophet. He had been to Mecca and Medina, and came to Kumasi from Bussa, on the Niger, where

he had been an eyewitness of Mungo Park's death. "His great sanctity," noted Hutchison, "made the King of Ashantee to send for him
to pray and make sacrifice for the success of the war. The other
Moors here look on him with an evil eye, because he will not wear
fetishes as they do, and be present at human sacrifice."A dispute
between Sharif Ibrahim and Baba is recorded by Hutchison:

> Tuesday, 2 December (1817): The King today made a
> present of 10 pereguins of gold to the Moors in town for
> their services, and they were to divide to themselves. This
> created no small altercation among them; those belong-
> ing to the town wished to keep it all, and not give the
> Shereef Abraham any, who came from the banks of the
> Niger; as the King had that morning told him he wished
> him to accompany him to the war, he told them it was of
> no consequence, as he should not accompany the King
> unless he was looked on with the same degree of rank as
> Baba, as, indeed, he was superior from his knowledge,
> and belonging to Mahomet's family. On this they gave
> him three pereguins, the same that Baba had.

Wilks suggests that Sharif Ibrahim represented a trend of Puri-
tanism in Islam, by rejecting amulets and other practices influenced
by paganism. He might have been influenced by the Wahabi doc-
trine, as a result of his visit to the Hijaz, and by the Fulani *jihad* of
Uthman dan Fodio, which extended to Bussa where the Sharif had
stayed. It now seems, however, that far from revolting against the
Muslim behavior in ("pagan") states, Sharif Ibrahim himself took
advantage of this situation. He was a wandering holy-man, who
would visit chiefs to give them his blessing, and accept their generous presents. His visit to Kumasi was part of his itinerary through
royal capitals, which included later Abomey, the Dahomey capital,
and Nikki, the capital of Borgu, both ("pagan") states under some
Islamic influence. The tension between Baba and Sharif Ibrahim
was not because of a difference in their religious outlook, but rather
as a result of a clash of interests. The Sharif's visit constituted an

encroachment on Baba's sphere of influence, as is illustrated by Hutchison's account. As a visitor, Sharif Ibrahim was not obliged to be present at the royal ceremonies, which included human sacrifice. Baba and the other resident Muslims had to attend these ceremonies, though they hated the customs, were disgusted, and even contributed to its abolition by giving the example of sacrificing sheep.

Though he himself, probably, did not wear amulets, Sharif Ibrahim used to supply them. There are two magical formulas among the Copenhagen manuscripts which are said to be given by Sharif Ibrahim, (*"fi fam sharif Ibrahim"*), to his friend Muhammad Karamo Toghma, whom we have identified with Muhammad ibn Imam Gonja. In the first of these manuscripts he is called *Sharif Ibrahim Barnawi*, a *nisba* that shows that he was a native of Bornu.

The Qadinya

Wilks suggests that the influence of the Qadiriya brotherhood was extended to the Muslim community in Kumasi. There is one document in this collection which may confirm this assumption:

> This letter is from us to our friend and master, al-Alim Kunbi. If you have some need to ask for, make ablutions, put on trousers, gown and turban, and retire into solitude. Then, read *surat alfatiha*, and afterwards recite *aqasida* (poem) by the Shaykh Abd al-Qadir al-Jilani. Then step three paces, and call the name of Shaykh Abd al-Qadir al-Jilani, who will intercede for you.

Manuscripts in this collection give instructions [on] what to do and how to pray, to ask Allah for a fulfillment of some need. By initiation to the Qadiriya brotherhood one is taught how to use the Qadiri word for this purpose.

Christian Dates

Ashanti was in constant relations with the European forts on the coast. Through this contact the Muslims in Kumasi became acquainted with the Christian calendar. Dates were very important in the magical craft of the Muslims. Muslims knew bad and good days throughout the year. They had fixed suitable dates for chiefs to set out for war, or for traders to start their journeys. It seems that the Muslims in Kumasi were very excited about this novelty, and we have at least seven fragments with notes about the Christian calendar.

The earliest date, noted in these manuscripts is: "January began on Thursday, 7th Dhu al-Qa'da a.h. 1223, may Allah let us know good, and save us from evil." This date corresponds to 25th December 1808. The latest date recorded is: January began on Friday, 4th Rabi al-Awwal a.h. 1233, which corresponds to 12th January 1818. Other dates, which fall between 1808 and 1818, can be calculated from other notes: "February began on Sunday, 26th Dhu al-Hijja" (with no mention of the year). I calculate it to be 1st February 1810. May began on Sunday, 13th Jumada 11, may Allah give his blessing to this month. This date must be 29th April 1817. August began on 7th Ramadan which is 1st August 1816.

These dates agree with other dates we have suggested in this paper. The earliest letter is probably the one which mentioned the Queen-Mother Konadu, who died about 1810. On the other hand there is a letter, from the King of Ashanti, written on paper with a watermark 1818. To this letter there are replies from the imams of Gonja and Buipe. Most of the manuscripts are written on paper of European origin, produced after 1780. In general it may be assumed that these manuscripts were written during the first quarter of the nineteenth century.

The catalogue of the Arabic Manuscripts at the Royal Library in Copenhagen was prepared in 1850. At that time the Arabic manuscripts from Kumasi were already in Copenhagen. The Danes evacuated the Gold Coast in 1850. Having as yet no other clue, we must assume that these manuscripts were brought to Copenhagen sometime between 1820 and 1850.

Select Arabic/Ajami Manuscripts at the Institute of African Studies, University of Ghana at Legon

Manuscript number: Institute of African Studies (IAS) / Arabic (AR) / 4
Subject: A poem on central Sudanese history and prayer.
Name of scribe: Ali Baraw b. Muhammad Baawa.
Remark: This text contains the names of African historical cultural centers, for example: Timbuktu (Mali), Shinguiti (Mauritania), Marrakech and Fez (Morocco), Kumase (Ghana), and Sokoto (Nigeria).

Manuscript number: IAS / AR / 11/12/13
Title: Tadhkiratun lil muta-akhireen.
Subject: A text on aspects of Gonja's history, settlements, and wars.

Manuscript number: IAS / AR / 40
Subject: History of Asante kings, with lengths of reigns.
Remark: Notice board of list of Asante kings, narrated by al-Hâjj Qasim. It is extracted from a longer work by his father, Abdallâh, a former *qadi* of Gonja.

Manuscript number: IAS / AR / 41
Subject: List of twenty-three sultans of Daboya, with lengths of reigns.
Remark: The manuscript is not easily readable due to the difficulty in pronouncing the local names rendered with the Arabic script.

Manuscript number: IAS / AR / 42
Subject: History of warfare between the Gonga and Dabonga.
Name of author: Malam Maimun b. Malam Abu.
Remark: The manuscript is quite difficult to read due to the compression of the text and the instances of local names in both Dagbani and Gonja.

Manuscript number: IAS /AR / 80
Title: Tarîkh Mulûk Al-Kuffâr fî Aqâlîm Buntuq.
Subject: List of twenty-two rulers of Gyaman, ending with Yeboah.
Copy from: Dormaa Ahenkro (Malam Yusif Ibrahim Ka'agati).

Manuscript number: IAS /AR / 83
Subject: This is a poem in praise of one Alhaj Mahmoud, an indigenous scholar from Wankyi (Wenkyi).

Manuscript number: IAS /AR / 148
Subject: This is a list of Asante "chiefs" and some events surrounding them.
Remark: The manuscript is well spaced and well written and could
be read easily, except that the frequency of local names proves
wearying.

Manuscript number: IAS /AR / 254
Subject: This is a text in Hausa in which the author gives a vivid
account of the series of kings of Gonja and their warring encounters with Asante.
Remark: The writings are readable except that the local names are
not easy to pronounce.

Manuscript number: IAS /AR / 255
Subject: This is a text in Arabic which provides the names of Gonja
rulers and their warring encounters with Asante.
Remark: The manuscript is well written and well spaced, yet it is
still difficult to read due to the abundant names of local places
and personalities in the text.

Manuscript number: IAS /AR / 259
Subject: Some aspects of Gonja history and chieftaincies.
Remark: The characters are not well represented, and this, coupled
with the abundant names of local places and personalities, ren-
ders reading the manuscript difficult.

Manuscript number: IAS /AR / 260

Subject: This is a text that gives some glimpses of Gonja and Kunbi chieftaincies.

Remark: The writing is well spaced, but it is still difficult to read due to the abundance of local names and places.

Manuscript number: IAS /AR / 261

Subject: This is a comprehensive text on Gonja's history, chieftaincies, and war expeditions.

Name of author: Ma'lam Garba.

Remark: The writings are readable except that the local names are not easy to pronounce.

Manuscript number: IAS /AR / 292

Subject: A lengthy poem in Hausa in which the poets praise one of the illustrious chiefs of the Zongo community in Kumasi.

Remark: The manuscript is well written and well spaced and can be read with relative ease.

Suggestions for Further Reading

Adjaye, Joseph K. *Diplomacy and Diplomats in Nineteenth Century Asante.* New York: University Press of America, 1984.

Allman, Jean. *The Quills of the Porcupine: Asante Nationalism in an Emergent Ghana.* Madison: University of Wisconsin Press, 1993.

Allman, Jean, and Victoria B. Tashjian. *I Will Not Eat Stone: A Women's History of Colonial Asante.* Oxford: James Currey, 2000.

Anquandah, James. *Rediscovering Ghana's Past.* Accra: Sedco Publishing Limited, 1982.

Antubam, Kofi. *Ghana's Heritage and Culture.* Leipzig: Koehler and Amelnag, 1963.

Arthur, G. F. Kojo. *Cloth as Metaphor: Rereading the Adinkra Cloth Symbols of the Akan of Ghana.* Legon, Ghana: Centre for Indigenous Knowledge Systems, 2001.

Austin, Gareth. *Labour, Land and Capital in Ghana: From Slavery to Free Labour in Asante, 1807-1956.* Rochester, NY: University of Rochester Press, 2009.

Boahen, A. Adu. *The Ghanaian Sphinx: Reflections on the Contemporary History of Ghana, 1972-1987.* New York: Ghana Democratic Movement, 1989.

Boahen, A. Adu et al., eds. *The History of Ashanti Kings and the Whole Country Itself and Other Writings by Otumfuo Nana Agyeman Prempeh I.* New York: Oxford University Press for the British Academy, 2008.

Brempong, Owusu. *Akan Highlife in Ghana: Songs of Cultural Transition.* Ph.D. diss., Indiana University, Bloomington, 1986.

DeCorse, Christopher R. *An Archaeology of Elmina: Africans and Europeans on the Gold Coast.* Washington and London: Smithsonian Institution Press, 2001.

Effah Gyamfi, Kwaku. *Bono Manso: An Archaeological Investigation into Early Akan Urbanism.* Calgary: Department of Archaeology, the University of Calgary Press, 1985.

Ephirim-Donkor, Anthony. *African Spirituality: On Becoming Ancestors.* Trenton, NJ: Africa World Press, 1997.

Farrar, Tarikhu. *Building Technology and Settlement Planning in a West African Civilization: Precolonial Akan Cities and Towns.* Lewiston, NY: Edwin Mellen Press, 1996.

Garrard, Timothy. *Akan Goldweights and the Gold Trade*. London: Longman, 1980.

Gyekye, Kwame. *An Essay on African Philosophical Thought: The Akan Conceptual Scheme*. Philadelphia: Temple University Press, 1995.

Hunwick, John, and Nancy Lawler, eds. *A Cloth of Many Colored Silks: Papers on History and Society Ghanaian and Islamic in Honor of Ivor Wilks*. Evanston, IL: Northwestern University Press, 1996.

Kea, Ray A. *Settlements, Trade, and Polities in the Seventeenth Century Gold Coast*. Baltimore and London: The Johns Hopkins University Press, 1982.

Konadu, Kwasi. *The Akan Diaspora in the Americas*. New York: Oxford University Press, 2010.

Kwame, Safro, ed. *Readings in African Philosophy: An Akan Collection*. Lanham: University Press of America, 1995.

Kyei, Thomas E. *Our Days Dwindle: Memories of My Childhood Days in Asante*, ed. Jean Allman. Portsmouth, NH: Heinemann, 2001.

McCaskie, T. C. *State and Society in Precolonial Asante*. Cambridge: Cambridge University Press, 1995.

McCaskie, T. C. *Asante Identities: History and Modernity in an African village, 1850-1950*. London: Edinburgh University Press, 2000.

McLeod, M. D. *The Asante*. London: British Museum Publications, 1981.

Niangoran-Bouah, Georges. *L'univers Akan des Poids à Peser l'or [The Akan World of Gold Weights]*, vols. 1-3. Abidjan: Nouvelles Editions Africaines, 1984.

Owusu-Ansah, David. *Islamization Reconsidered: An Examination of Asante Responses to Muslim Influence in the 18th and 19th Centuries*. Washington, D.C.: African Studies Association, 1982.

Owusu-Ansah, David, and Daniel M. McFarland. *Historical Dictionary of Ghana*. Metuchen, NJ: Scarecrow Press, 1995.

Rathbone, Richard. *Nkrumah and the Chiefs*. Oxford: James Currey, 2000.

Ross, Doran. *Wrapped in Pride: Ghanaian Kente and African American Identity*. Los Angeles: UCLA Fowler Museum of Cultural History, 1998.

Ross, Doran H., and Timothy F. Garrard, eds. *Akan Transformations: Problems in Ghanaian Art History*. Los Angeles: Regents of the University of California, 1983.

Schildkrout, Enid, ed. *Golden Stool: Studies of the Asante Center and Periphery*. New York: American Museum of Natural History, 1987.

Valsecchi, Pierluigi, and Fabio Viti, eds. *Mondes Akan: Identité et Pouvoir en Afrique Occidentale [Akan Worlds: Identity and Power in West Africa]*. Paris: Harmattan, 1999.

Wilks, Ivor. *Asante in the Nineteenth Century. The Structure and Evolution of a Political Order.* Cambridge: Cambridge University Press, 1975/1989.

Wilks, Ivor. *Forests of Gold: Essays on the Akan and the Kingdom of Asante.* Athens: Ohio University Press, 1993.

Wiredu, Kwasi. *The Akan Worldview.* Washington, D.C.: Woodrow Wilson International Center for Scholars, 1985.

Yankah, Kwesi. *Speaking for the Chief: Okyeame and the Politics of Akan Royal Oratory.* Bloomington: Indiana University Press, 1995.

Yankah, Kwesi. *The Proverb in the Context of Akan Rhetoric.* New York: Diasporic Africa Press, 2012.

Yarak, Larry W. *Asante and the Dutch.* Oxford: Clarendon Press, 1990.

Acknowledgment of Copyrights

Kenya Shujaa, "Akan Cultural History: An Overview" (originally entitled "Issues in Akan Prehistory"), *Sankofa* 6, no. 1 (2005): 7-15. Reprinted with corrections by permission of the author.

Kwame Y. Daaku, "History in the Oral Traditions of the Akan," *Journal of Folklore Research* 8, nos. 2-3 (1971): 114-26. Reprinted by permission of Indiana University Press.

Carl Christian Reindorf, *History of the Gold Coast and Asante: Based on Traditions and Historical Facts Comprising a Period of More than Three Centuries from about 1500 to 1860* (Basel: author, 1895).

Kwame Y. Daaku, *Oral Traditions of Adanse* (Accra [Legon]: Institute of African Studies, University of Ghana, 1969). Reprinted by permission of the Institute of African Studies, University of Ghana at Legon [hereafter, IAS-Legon].

Kwame Arhin, "A Note on Ahafo Oral Traditions," *Research Review* 1, no. 1 (1965): 27-29. Reprinted by permission of IAS-Legon.

J. Agyeman-Duah, comp., *Asante Stool Histories*, vol. 2 (Accra: Institute of African Studies, University of Ghana, 1976). Reprinted by permission of IAS-Legon.

Adu Boahen et al., eds., *The History of Ashanti Kings and the Whole Country Itself and Other Writings by Otumfuo Nana Agyeman Prempeh I* (New York: Oxford University Press, 2003). Reprinted by permission of the British Academy.

Kwame Y. Daaku, *UNESCO Research Project on Oral Traditions: Denkyira no. 2* (Accra: Institute of African Studies, University of Ghana, 1970). Reprinted by permission of IAS-Legon.

C. E. Aidoo, comp., "History of the Denkyiras." N.p., n.d.

Kwame Y. Daaku, *Oral Traditions of Assin-Twifo* (Accra: Institute of African Studies, University of Ghana, 1969). Reprinted by permission of IAS-Legon.

Kwame Y. Daaku, *The Peopling of Assin* (Accra: Institute of African Studies, University of Ghana, 1967). Reprinted by permission of IAS-Legon.

D. M. Warren and K. O. Brempong, *Techiman Traditional State, pts. I and II, Stool and Town Histories* (Accra: Institute of African Studies, University of Ghana, 1971). Reprinted by permission of IAS-Legon.

John Kofi Fynn, *Oral Traditions of the Fante States, no. 3 Komenda* (Accra: Institute of African Studies, University of Ghana, 1974). Reprinted by permission of IAS-Legon.

John Kofi Fynn, *Oral Traditions of the Fante States, no. 7 Kwamankese* (Accra: Institute of African Studies, Univeristy of Ghana, 1976), i-iv. Reprinted by permission of IAS-Legon.

E.S.K. Owusu, *Oral Traditions of Badu, Seikwa, Nsoko, and Nkorankwaga* (Accra: Institute of African Studies, University of Ghana, 1976). Reprinted by permission of IAS-Legon.

Eustache de la Fosse, *Voyage a la Côte occidentale d'Afrique, en Portugal et en Espagne (1479-1480)*, ed. R. Foulche-Delbosc (Paris: Alfonse Picard et Fils, 1897).

Duarte Pacheco Pereira, *Esmeraldo de situ orbis* (Lisbon: Imprensa Nacional 1892).

Andrés Bernáldez, *Memorias de los Reyes Católicos* (Granada: Zamora, 1856).

A. Teixeira da Mota and P.E.H. Hair, *East of Mina: Afro-European Relations on the Gold Coast in the 1550s and 1560s* (Madison: African Studies Program, University of Wisconsin-Madison, 1988). Reprinted by permission of the University of Wisconsin-Madison.

Jean Barbot, "A Description of the Coasts of North and South-Guinea," in Awnsham Churchill, *A Collection of Voyages and Travels . . .* (London: Messrs. Churchill, 1732).

Pieter de Marees, *Description and Historical Account of the Gold Kingdom of Guinea* (1602), trans. and eds. Adam Jones and Albert van Dantzig (Oxford: Oxford University Press for the British Academy, 1987). Reprinted by permission of the British Academy.

Kwame Y. Daaku and Albert van Dantzig, "Map of the Regions of Gold Coast in Guinea," *Ghana Notes and Queries* 9 (1966): 14-15. Reprinted by permission of the Ghana Academy of Arts and Sciences.

Olfert Dapper, *Description de l'Afrique . . .* (Amsterdam: W. Waesberge, Boom et Van Someren, 1686).

Willem Bosman, *A New and Accurate Description of the Coast of Guinea, Divided into the Gold, the Slave, and the Ivory Coasts* (London: James Knapton, 1705).

Albert van Dantzig, *The Dutch on the Guinea Coast, 1674-1742: A Collection of Documents from the General State Archive at the Hague* (Accra: Ghana Academy of Arts and Sciences, 1978). Reprinted by permission of the Ghana Academy of Arts and Sciences.

Harvey Feinberg, *Africans and Europeans in West Africa: Elminans and Dutchmen on the Gold Coast during the Eighteenth Century* (Philadelphia: The American Philosophical Society, 1989). Reprinted by permission of the author and the American Philosophical Society.

Journal and Correspondences of H. W. Daendels, 1815 to 1818, mimeographed at the Institute of African Studies, University of Ghana at Legon, 1964. Reprinted by permission of IAS-Legon.

Adam Jones, ed., *German Sources for West African History, 1599-1669* (Wiesbaden: Franz Steiner Verlag, 1983). Reprinted by permission of Franz Steiner Verlag.

Erick Tilleman, *En Kort og Enfoldig Beretning om det Landskab Guinea of dets Beskaffenhed—A Short and Simple Account of the Country Guinea and Its Nature (1697)*, trans. and ed. Selena A. Winsnes (Madison: African Studies Program, University of Wisconsin-Madison, 1994). Reprinted by permission of the author and the University of Wisconsin-Madison.

Ludewig Ferdinand Rømer, *Tilforladelig Efterretning om Kysten Guinea—A Reliable Account of the Coast of Guinea* (1760), trans. and ed. Selena A. Winsnes (London: Oxford University Press for the British Academy, 2000). Reprinted by permission of the author and the British Academy.

Christian Georg Andreas Oldendorp, *Historie der Caribischen Inseln Sanct Thomas, Sanct Crux und Sanct Jan*, eds. Gudrun Meier, Stephan Palmié, Peter Stein, and Horst Ulbricht, 4 vols. (Berlin: Verlag fur Wissenschaft und Bildung, 2000-2002 [1777]).

Letters on West Africa and the Slave Trade: Paul Erdmann Isert's Journey to Guinea and the Caribbean Islands in Columbia (1788), trans. and ed. Selena Axelrod Winsnes. (London: Oxford University Press for the British Academy, 1992). Reprinted by permission of the author and the British Academy.

David Asante, "Eine Reise in den Hinterländern von Togo, beschrieben von einem christlichen Neger und aus der Asante-Sprache übersetzt von J. G. Christaller," *Geographische Gesellschaft für Thüringen zu Jena* 7-8 (1889): 106-33.

Andreas Pfisterer, "Akpafu," *Monatsblatt der Norddeutschen Missionsgesellschaft* 2 (1904): 11-13; *Monatsblatt der Norddeutschen Missionsgesellschaft* 3 (1904): 19-21.

Friedrich Ramseyer and Johannes Kühne, *Four Years in Ashantee* (London: James Nisbet & Co., 1875).

Richard Hakluyt, *The Principal Navigations Voyages Traffiques and Discoveries of the English Nation* (Glasgow: James MacLehose and Sons, 1904).

John Atkins, *A Voyage to Guinea, Brasil, and the West-Indies* (London: Caesar Ward and Richard Chandler, 1735).

Henry Meredith, *An Account of the Gold Coast of Africa* (London: Hurst, Rees, Orme, and Brown, 1812).

John Leyden, *Historical Account of Discoveries and Travels in Africa*, 2 vols. (Edinburgh: A. Constable and Company, 1817).

Thomas Edward Bowdich, *Mission from Cape Coast Castle to Ashantee, with a descriptive account of that kingdom* (London: Griffith & Farran, 1873).

Williams Hutton, *A Voyage to Africa* . . . (London: Longman, Hurst, Rees, Orme, and Brown, 1821).

Brodie Cruickshank, *Eighteen Years on the Gold Coast of Africa*, 2 vols. (London: Hurst and Blackett, 1853).

Dennis Kemp, *Nine Years on the Gold Coast* (New York: Macmillian and Co. Ltd, 1898).

Robert S. Rattray, *Ashanti* (London: Oxford University Press, 1923). Reprinted by permission of Oxford University Press.

Robert S. Rattray, *Religion and Art in Ashanti* (London: Oxford University Press, 1927). Reprinted by permission of Oxford University Press.

Robert S. Rattray, *Ashanti Law and Constitution* (London: Oxford University Press, 1929). Reprinted by permission of Oxford University Press.

Raymond A. Silverman and David Owusu-Ansah, "The Presence of Islam among the Akan of Ghana: A Bibliographic Essay," *History in Africa* 16 (1989): 325-39. Reprinted by permission of the authors and the African Studies Association.

Nehemia Levtzion, "Early Nineteenth Century Arabic Manuscripts from Kumasi," *Transactions of the Historical Society of Ghana* 8 (1965): 99-119. Reprinted by permission of the Historical Society of Ghana.